SHARON TATE AND THE MANSON MURDERS

Greg King

SHARON TATE AND THE MANSON MURDERS

Greg King

BARRICADE
BOOKS

Barricade Books•New York
www.barricadebooks.com

Published by Barricade Books Inc.
150 Fifth Avenue
Suite 700
New York, NY 10011
www.barricadebooks.com

First Printing

ISBN: 1-56980-157-6

Printed in the United States of America.

10 9 8 7 6 5 4 3 2 1

CONTENTS

DEDICATION

To Chuck and Eileen Knaus

Prologue

I T STANDS IN A FAR CORNER OF THE PARK, HIGH ON A GREEN HILLSIDE dotted with monuments. Meandering stone paths cleave past an imposing grotto, where candles burn before a statue of the Virgin. Here, the lawn levels out, reaching to an exquisitely manicured hedge; beyond, the city bustles with life, the Hollywood Hills rising sharply in the distance. In this tranquil spot, undistinguished from its neighbors, lies a small, brightly polished black marble plaque. To one side sits a stand for an American flag; in the grass before it, a vase is sunk deep in the ground. Even after thirty years, it is nearly always full of fresh flowers. Those who come to satisfy their morbid curiosity are not disappointed. Below them, embedded in the lawn, is the tombstone:

OUR LOVING DAUGHTER &
BELOVED WIFE OF ROMAN
SHARON TATE POLANSKI
1943-1969
PAUL RICHARD POLANSKI
THEIR BABY

Although only twenty-six when she died, Sharon Tate, like other stars whose lives were cut tragically short—Rudolph Valentino, James Dean, and Marilyn Monroe—stands as a twentieth century icon. On the edge of stardom, she was violently cut down, screaming, crying, pleading with her murderers, left to die in an exclusive Hollywood mansion whose front door had been smeared with an ugly epithet written in her own blood. The ultimate irony is that Sharon Tate only received that fame because of her gruesome end. Her death one hot summer night in 1969 changed America forever.

It touched a raw nerve in a country disillusioned, shocked by the assassinations of John F. Kennedy, Martin Luther King, Robert F. Kennedy and Malcolm X. The Manson Murders scared the hell out of an entire nation torn apart by war and shattered by riots. In the media frenzy which surrounded—and still envelops—the Manson murders, the victims were nearly forgotten, relegated to second place behind their notorious killers. "Murder in Hollywood," writes Mikita Brottman, "is a far more frequent, more brutal, and more talked-about event than it is anywhere else in the world. The glamour and tinsel, the beautiful people and daring love affairs have their dark side—the realm of greed, lust, jealousy and shame. As long as there is a celebrity elite living in an illusory world of sparkle and style, as long as Hollywood fuels dreams of a glamorous, sexually charged, thrill-packed universe, there will continue to be intolerable pressures, violence and catastrophe."[1]

To many, Sharon Tate remains a minor character in an American saga of mass carnage, counter-culture, and insanity, a cast member whose glittering orbit encompassed the elite of Hollywood's movie and music worlds, but whose beautiful surface cloaked a dark reality. To her family and friends, however, Sharon Tate, remains an unforgettable presence, a vibrant ghost whose beauty, gentle spirit, and love cannot be erased by the passage of time.

By the beginning of 1943, America had weathered thirteen months of involvement in the Second World War. After two years of isolationist debate mixed with patriotic fervor and European pleas for assistance, Japanese bombers at Pearl Harbor made the decision that President Franklin Roosevelt had avoided and thrust the United States into the conflict. In the Pacific, the combat made headlines: Lieutenant James Doolittle's bombing raids on Tokyo; the intense naval battles at Coral Sea and Midway Islands, and the Battles of Guadalcanal. Slowly, surely, allied forces were turning the equation against the Japanese troops. American soldiers were ferried across the Atlantic on passenger liners converted to troop ships to combat the Axis powers. Here, the land battles were drawn-out, grim. In Russia, thousands died during the prolonged battle of Stalingrad before the Soviets finally managed to surround the German Sixth Army and force a surrender. Hitler's blitz devastated London. Then the Allied forces retaliated, its bombs wreaking catastrophic destruction across Germany. For a week, Roosevelt and British Prime Minister Winston Churchill met at Casablanca, to discuss plans for the Allied land invasion of Europe, a move that would begin the following year at Normandy on June 6, that was to be known as D-Day.

Life on the American home-front was a mixture of war frenzy and fervent optimism coupled with an ominous foreboding of the unknown. Few failed to believe in an eventual Allied victory, but the deaths of husbands, brothers, sons, and fiancés brought the horrors of war into the living rooms of America. Daily life was completely subjugated to the war effort. As rationing took hold, hundreds "gardened for victory," and housewives incorporated meatless Tuesdays and Fridays into their weekly menus. Sugar, shoes, coffee, and cheese were precious commodities. When not engaged in creative household-planning, women manned the welding stations and operated heavy machinery at the industries that provided the ammunition, planes, and ships needed to win the war. At the same time, there was a giddy recklessness—a frivolity hastened by the terrible uncertainties of the conflict in Europe and the Pacific. Late into the night, young lovers jitterbugged and lindy-hopped to the music of Glenn Miller and the Andrews Sisters. A certain sentimentality crept into popular culture, where "The White Cliffs of Dover" and "I'll Be Seeing You" perfectly captured the unsettled mood of life on the edge of the abyss. It was also a time of romance. Young women, unsure whether they would see their suitors again once they went off to fight, eagerly embraced whatever fleeting moments of happiness they might find as war brides.

Paul James Tate was eager for life. A twenty-one-year-old native of Houston, Texas, he had watched the ominous rumblings from Europe with growing interest. Most healthy young men found it difficult to resist the excitement of war, and Tate, filled with patriotism, had joined the ranks of the United States Army. A dark-haired, handsome man whose short stature masked a surprising presence, he was intrigued with the burgeoning field of military intelligence. Through sheer determination and long hours of work, he would eventually rise through the ranks to that of colonel. Tate had a knack of impressing those he met with his honor, dedication, and loyalty, although he remained something of an enigma, silent and reserved, traits which worked well in his assigned career of military intelligence. But he was also a man with a sense of purpose, whose determination in pursuit of his goals proved attractive to the impressionable young women he encountered.

Undoubtedly, some of this had worked well in his quest of Doris Gwendolyn Willet, a pretty, twenty-year-old who was, like himself, a native of Houston. Although as she grew older, Doris had a tendency to stoutness, as a young woman, a friend recalls, she was "really beautiful, very, very attractive."[2] From a solidly middle-class background, Doris was raised as a southern belle, gracious and charming. Her genteel manner and soft, melodic voice were powerful tools when she chose to focus them, and her attentions were always genuine.

Paul and Doris had married on 25 January, 1942. If the complexities of the war shadowed their happiness together, such thoughts had been dispelled that summer when Doris learned that she was pregnant. It was not the most opportune time for a baby. The Tates were unsettled, with Paul's military career at its beginning stages, and the outcome of the war still uncertain. There was no promise that the situations in Europe or the Pacific might not worsen and lead to a new military assignment, leaving Doris alone to care for the baby. And yet this very uncertainty also meant that the time Paul and Doris had together was precious. With no guarantee for their future, the Tates happily anticipated the birth of their first child.

One day before the Tates's first wedding anniversary, on 24 January, 1943, Doris gave birth to a healthy daughter. They named the baby Sharon Marie. Fair-haired, with large, hazel eyes and chubby cheeks, Sharon easily captivated those around her, and her proud parents rarely missed an opportunity to show off their new daughter. And everyone who saw the infant agreed that Sharon was an unusually beautiful baby. Comments and compliments from family, friends, and strangers alike prompted Doris to make a rather unusual move: when Sharon was only six months old, her mother read about a beauty contest, the Miss Tiny Tot of Dallas Pageant. Ordinarily, both Paul and Doris Tate shunned such activities. But because of the urgings of friends, Doris entered a photograph of her daughter in the contest. "It was a whim," she later declared.[3]

When the judges examined the photograph, they saw a happy, beaming infant, her chubby head crowned with thick golden curls. Her white dress and black patent-leather shoes were impeccable. It was the rosy picture of good health and contentment the judges had been seeking.

They selected Sharon as winner, and she received the first of the many beauty titles she was to accumulate throughout her short life.

Sharon was two-years-old when the Second World War ended.

The sense of relief and exaltation was palpable, yet life remained filled with remnants of the conflict. Rationing continued, soldiers returned home maimed and unable to work, and the threat of Hitler was replaced with the growing menace of the Soviet Union. There were more personal concerns as well. The United States was in the midst of a devastating polio epidemic. With thousands of children in danger, Paul and Doris could only hope that fate would not strike down their only child.

While she managed to escape from the dreaded polio epidemic, Sharon was subject to the usual childhood bouts of chicken pox and measles. She was active, her mother recalled, with "a wilfull streak which often led to accidents."[4] Her body later bore evidence of her adventures and mishaps—scars from cuts, broken glass, and a large scar Sharon received when, at age five, she fell atop a piece of corrugated tin on which she had been playing.[5]

As parents, Paul and Doris Tate were a study in opposites. Sharon's later friends would recall Doris as warm, loving, and energetic. She doted on her daughter, and spent hours with young Sharon, teaching her to sew and embroider, dress her dolls, and help in the kitchen. The Tate family was not wealthy, but Doris was careful to ensure that Sharon's white dresses were always spotless and crisp, her hair neatly combed and tied with colorful ribbons, and her patent-leather shoes polished.

Paul Tate, on the other hand, was a quiet man, serious and, following the traditions of the day, something of an imposing presence within the Tate household. Accustomed to army discipline, Paul, in the words of a former school friend of Sharon's, "expected the same standards in his own house."[6] Because he was often away on assignment, his infrequent periods with his family assumed much significance to Sharon. Although she adored him, Sharon found her father's unbending seriousness something of a strain.

These two conflicting wills—her attentive, affectionate mother, and her quiet, sober father—pulled at Sharon throughout her childhood and youth. Doris Tate's demonstrative nature only heightened the difference between her and her husband. Indulged by one and always aware of the authority of the other, Sharon developed into an emotionally dependent, almost obsessively shy child.

The transient nature of the military also had a deep effect on Sharon. Her father's army career, with its changing assignments and frequent moves brought a sense of isolation, and much of Sharon's childhood and youth followed an unnervingly consistent pattern of new schools, new friends, and new homes. This peripatetic existence brought home the harsh realities of military life. The new house might not really be home for long. The school might be only one in a series, and the friends only temporary. By the time she was sixteen, Sharon had attended schools in Houston, Dallas and El Paso, Texas, San Francisco, and Richland, Washington.

Her mother Doris later recalled Sharon's early years as "perfectly normal and happy."[7] On the surface, she seemed not unlike other girls her age, but Sharon guarded her inner-thoughts. Although always ready to join her friends, she rarely confided her feelings to others. The itinerant nature of her life resulted in an armor of self-protection, and it took exceptional circumstances for her to break out of her self-imposed barriers.

Sharon later referred to herself as "a very quiet child...kind of introverted in a way. I was constantly looking to do things a little differently. Like, I would dress my dolls backwards, or the minute I got a new sweater, I would change all the buttons on it, or embroider something on it."[8] Such behavior suggests more than a hint of artistic repression; Sharon was intensely creative with a lively imagination, but her energies seem to have been channeled into acceptable outlets. Paul Tate, with his military precision and efficiency, was a practical man, and this taste for useful activities appears to have been copied by his daughter.

The worsening of international relations in the 1950s and the deepening of the Cold War between the United States and the Soviet Union meant that Paul Tate was increasingly involved with his duties in military intelligence. Doris remained the strongest presence in the house, even when Sharon was joined by two sisters, the dark-haired Deborah Ann, born in 1953, and blonde Patricia Gaye, who arrived in 1957. Sharon assumed the role of older sister with ease, helping her mother with their care and playing with them for hours on end. Sharon, in fact, seemed happiest when at home with her family. Although she joined friends for picnics and parties and sleep-overs, she far preferred her days spent at the side of her mother. During their afternoons together, Doris instilled a love of domesticity, teaching Sharon to cook favorite Southern recipes she in turn had learned from her mother, Ruth. Sharon became so adept, in fact, that in high school she won several baking contests, and, for a time, considered becoming a professional chef.[9]

Cooking classes were one of the few courses which Sharon pursued with vigor. She also expressed some interest in becoming a beautician following her enrollment in a high school course.[10] But Sharon's enthusiasms were fleeting. Friends remember that, although she occasionally expressed some interest in literature or art, Sharon rarely made any significant impressions in any of her classes. "She was a good student, but nothing special," her mother would recall.[11] She was certainly not bookish, at least as far as her schoolmates knew, and no one can recall any lasting aspirations on her part other than to marry and have children.

Above all, Sharon was an intensely self-controlled child. Some of this reflected the military environment in which she was raised. She adored her parents, but she also knew that the best way to win their approval was to meet expectations.

By the time she reached high school, Sharon had begun to attract the attentions of any number of potential suitors. From her birth, she had been exceptionally pretty, but, as she developed into a young woman, her great beauty became apparent. While Doris Tate indulged her daughter's love of immaculate clothes and carefully styled hair, she also warned Sharon to guard against too much pride for fear that her appearance would affect her amiable nature. "Pretty is as pretty does," she told Sharon. "And if you do nasty things, all the prettiness will go out of you."[12]

Doris Tate need not have worried. Sharon was the very model of innocence and virtue, and her rapidly maturing appearance preceded her own awareness of her physical charms. Sharon would later recall how, on one occasion, she came out of her room in a rather revealing nightgown. Doris looked her over and announced sternly, "Now, Sharon Marie, you button up that nightgown when you come out of your bedroom. Daddy's home."[13]

Paul Tate was transferred several times. For a few months, the family lived at Alameda, California, awaiting a permanent assignment. Then, in 1958, Paul Tate was posted to Camp Hanford, near the Tri-Cities in Washington State.

Sharon was fifteen when her family moved to Washington. By this time, she had blossomed into a stunning beauty, with a generous figure, large, gentle eyes, abundant golden hair and long, shapely legs. For the first time, she took an active interest in members of the opposite sex, and saw in the returned smiles and bold winks that the feelings were mutual. Schoolboy crushes, innocent and flattering, were shyly encouraged with downcast eyes and pale blushes. Yet she rarely dated, preferring to be admired from afar.

"I think," Sharon later declared, "it is a mistake for a girl to work at having sex appeal or to pay too much attention to popularity. Making friends is something that should develop naturally."[14] The friendships she did cultivate were often boisterous in nature, but shallow in content. Her high school year near Seattle was marked by a reserve which she cultivated for her own emotional protection.

Behind this reserve, however, lay a self-possession and assured certainty. Sharon did not court popularity, but seems to have had no trouble in being accepted by those she encountered. If she struck her schoolmates as reserved, it was a distance that she herself felt comfortable imposing. Sharon was content to ignore the course of popular behavior when it conflicted with her own desires. This strength of will would serve her well in the future.

With young men, her relationships were largely platonic. Paul Tate, weary of over-enthusiasm in their pursuits, often refused to allow Sharon to date the occasional friend she brought home. If a lucky young man succeeded in obtaining permission to take Sharon out, it was usually after an uncomfortable grilling at the hands of her father. His manner was firm—Sharon was not allowed out on school nights, and on weekends she had an early curfew.

Encouraged by her mother, Sharon was not above exploiting her physical charms. While her father was posted to Hanford, she entered, and won the Miss Richland, Washington, beauty pageant. Later, acting as a hostess at a local auto show, she won the title of Miss Autorama.

Sharon was only sixteen, but her succession of wins put her on the fast track to her ultimate goal—competing in the Miss Washington State pageant. These endeavors were innocent enough, but Doris later recalled that her husband "had very mixed feelings. It wasn't exactly the sort of thing he wanted to encourage."[15]

In 1959, Paul Tate was promoted to the rank of captain and appointed to the G2 Southern European Task Force stationed at Passelaqua Army Base outside of Verona, Italy. The move meant drastic changes for Sharon, both in surroundings and in the development of her personality. For most of her life, she had been reluctant to develop intimate relationships with others; her friendships were casual. Experience as an army brat had taught her that relationships were often only temporary. In Italy the obstacles would be even greater. Sharon would be not only the new girl, but a foreigner as well, thrust abruptly into unfamiliar surroundings. With some reluctance, she left America and headed into the unknown.

Chapter 1
Italy

"THE RUMOR MILL HAD BEGUN TO GRIND," REMEMBERS ART Schultz, "hinting that someone very attractive was about to start classes at our school."[1] That spring of 1960, even before the Tates arrived in Verona, a sense of anticipation hung in the air at Vincenza American High School. A month before her arrival, Sharon had appeared on the cover of the American military newspaper, *Stars and Stripes*, provocatively dressed in a bathing suit, cowboy boots and hat, sitting astride a missile. The young men whose fathers served at Aviano and Passelaqua were delighted to learn that this young beauty would soon be joining them in Verona.

Vincenza American High, catering to the children of those based at nearby United States military bases, was filled with a collection of displaced teenagers experienced in the nomadic way of life dictated by their parents' careers. Like Sharon, these young men and women were highly protective of both their feelings and friendships. As a group, however, they largely understood each other's problems—the trials of military life and the lack of stable relationships. The barriers that had perhaps separated them from others in the United States drew them together in Italy.

It was a small school. Senior classes rarely encompassed more than fifty graduates. As a result, students formed close bonds and, as one of Sharon's classmates recalls, "it was impossible for everyone not to know everyone else."[2] The students themselves were divided into two groups: those who lived with their parents in nearby Verona, and those who boarded at the institute itself. Like most pupils, Sharon lived off base with her family, and took the train each morning to Vincenza American.

"I do remember distinctly the first day Sharon started in our school," says classmate Will Melendez. "I think I was one of the first male students to see her. I remember she was checking in at the principal's office with one of her parents. I couldn't believe my eyes when I saw her! I, and every other male student in the school, went around in a daze the rest of that day. Honestly, we had never seen such a beautiful girl in our lives! I mean, the school was full of 'average-looking' and some 'good-looking' high-school girls, but this was a category way over anything we had ever seen."3 And Art Schultz, a handsome junior a few months younger than seventeen-year-old Sharon, remembers that she was "more beautiful than anything you could imagine. She was well-dressed and well-mannered, always immaculate in matching knit sweaters and skirts."4

In spite of the drastic changes, Sharon quickly adapted to her environment. Vincenza American served both middle and high school students. Officials did their best to transplant a sense of America. While small, the school managed to front basketball, football and track teams, along with a smattering of extra-curricular clubs and field trips to Venice, Rome and the Italian Alps.

For perhaps the first time in her life, Sharon allowed herself the normal friendships which most girls her age took for granted. In time, she became more boisterous, more sure of herself. On the surface, at least, Sharon had no problem fitting in with her classmates. She was, according to one, "quite a normal and charming fellow student."5 "My first impression of Sharon," remembers classmate Howard Miller, "was that she was a beautiful person, and I don't mean in the physical sense of the word beauty. She was easy to get to know and share a friendship with."6 Within her group of friends, she had something of a reputation for leading the way in practical jokes, pushing the limits of acceptable behavior. "If miniskirts had come in then, I'd have worn the shortest one," Sharon later joked.7

Perhaps surprisingly, Sharon's female classmates also welcomed this addition to their circle. The petty jealousy common among teenagers was replaced by curiosity over Sharon's accomplishments. Classmate Sheila Boyle Plank recalls the fascination with Sharon's participation in beauty pageants: "It was just incredible to us," she says. "We were like sponges, and she was very reticent to share anything that featured her or made her stand out."8

"I do remember having gym class with her," recalls Elizabeth Gedwed Stroup, who was four years younger than Sharon, "and even then, was in awe of her beauty, carriage, and confidence. She was very popular. Since most of us were under-developed physically, her perfect form was something we dreamed of being. I do remember she was nice to me which isn't always a characteristic upper classmen cultivate."[9]

Others commented on Sharon's genuine thoughtfulness. "Never did I ever sense any conceit or arrogance," recalls Sheila Boyle Plank. "In fact, she always went out of her way to make everyone feel positive and valued. She was very beautiful in the physical sense, but seemed to be more focused on being a nice person."[10]

Her popularity with her classmates was rewarded at Vincenza American. She joined the Library Club, working several hours there each day. She assisted Librarian John Demos by shelving books and helping classmates with research projects. She also joined Student Council for the fall semester, helping to plan activities and field trips.

The school's football team, the Vincenza Cougars, played area leagues. Sharon became one of five cheerleaders, following the team to Naples and nearby cities where, clad in her white skirt and gold sweater, she helped shout her classmates on to victory. "She was a great cheerleader," says Sheila Boyle Plank, "very flexible, very limber. The rest of us were all kind of cranking it up, and Sharon would get out there and just make it look like magic."[11]

At Vincenza's Homecoming Dance, on 5 November, 1960, members of the Cougars voted her queen. Sharon was genuinely surprised and took the stage attired in a pink-satin-and-chiffon gown and long white gloves, and was duly crowned with a small tiara. The following spring, she became queen of her senior prom.[12]

"There were really two Sharons," says Art Schultz, "a very public one, and a private one."[13] While she was ready and eager to join her friends, she rarely opened up, and was often happier to remain on her own. Many of her fellow students at Vicenza American saw only the cautious and withdrawn beauty. "I always experienced Sharon as being somehow in a 'different-place' than we were as seventeen or eighteen-year-old high-school kids," recalls Will Melendez. "But I think this might even have been a burden for her, that she already was somehow on a path to 'stardom' while we other 'mortals' were just walking around on the ground. The beautiful smile was maybe also a defense, and a way of hiding her own insecurities."[14]

For all of her social accomplishments, Sharon characterized herself at Vincenza as "a lone wolf, and I feel I enlarged my horizons by not being preoccupied with being part of the pack. I have always tried not to be a rubber stamp of my environment."[15]

During her time in Italy, Sharon read a great deal. Her greatest passion was psychiatry, and, for a time, she considered becoming a therapist.[16] Academic standards at Vicenza American proved something of a challenge for Sharon. "I thought Sharon was an intelligent person who knew what she wanted out of life," says Howard Miller.[17] "She was bright," agrees Art Schultz, "but not brainy, and she had a lot of trouble with her classes. She wasn't a bad student, but she didn't seem to care. She just wanted to get through her homework and have it done."[18]

Schultz often accompanied Sharon on the train back to Verona to study and have dinner at her house. Although he liked Doris Tate very much, he recalled that Sharon's father was something of an unnerving presence. "I was on the approved list," he says, "but even so, P. J. [Paul Tate] rarely said more than a word or two to me. While Doris was warm and friendly, P. J. was stern, a real loner."[19]

Sharon herself, Schultz remembers, always seemed on edge when her father was at home. "P. J. traveled a lot with his job in military intelligence," he says. "When he was away, Sharon was a different person. I used to go into her bedroom, and we would rub each other's backs, and study, and she was very relaxed. Doris trusted me completely. But when Paul was home, Sharon often met me at the door, with her purse in her hand, and suggested that we go study elsewhere. She told me she just didn't like to be home a lot when her dad was around because he was so stern, and it was all business, all study."[20]

From her very first day at Vincenza American High School, Sharon impressed her classmates with her appearance. Unfortunately, according to Jim Wilson, the Dependent Schools' Officer, this appearance was also cause for considerable worry among school officials. "She was a beautiful lady, but her penchant for wearing tight-fitting sweaters and skirts caused difficulties," he recalls. One of her teachers made unwelcome advances, and school authorities were forced to discipline him privately.[21]

The incident resulted in some whispering at the school, and there was much speculation regarding Sharon's sexual experiences. "There was quite a bit of talk as to whether or not she really was a virgin," recalls Art Schultz. "The general consensus was that she was, because she seemed so innocent."[22] Sharon was taken completely by surprise at the advances and whispers, such was her naïveté.

Sharon began an innocent, schoolgirl romance with a young

soldier who was posted to Passelaqua. Although her father disapproved at first, the Tates grew to like the young man. When his duties kept him at the base, Sharon might agree to an evening out with one of his fellow soldiers.

It was on one such date that Sharon was raped.[23] Deeply ashamed, embarrassed and hurt, she made no attempt to report the crime. Instead, she sacrificed her personal feelings for the sake of her father. "Sharon wouldn't have mentioned the rape," says Art Schultz, "because she wouldn't want to bring dishonor to her father, whose entire career was built on respectability."[24]

Sharon was traumatized by the rape, but it was a turmoil which she carefully hid from those around her. Outwardly, at least, there was little change. She was good-natured and gentle, at once approachable and distant, carefree and contemplative. But her sense of self-worth had been damaged. For Sharon the situation was hopeless. Shame prevented her from turning to her parents; even had she confided in them, she was different now. Her innocence had been stolen.

Sharon cut herself off from those around her, seeking escape from her troubled world. Although she regularly joined friends on tours of nearby Palladian villas, art museums in Venice and Roman ruins in the hills around Verona, she was preoccupied, searching for a direction which had thus eluded her.

It was during one of these trips that Sharon and her friends stumbled upon a local movie set. The American production was filming Hemingway's *Adventures of a Young Man*, starring Paul Newman, Richard Beymer and Susan Strasberg, daughter of famed acting coach Lee Strasberg. One shot called for a crowd scene, and the milling teenagers from Vincenza were asked to help fill out the frame.

During a break in shooting, the actors mingled with the teenagers, signing autographs. "Dick Beymer," recalls friend Skip Ward, "was looking at the crowd, and saw this incredibly sexy young Italian woman standing about. He went over to talk to her and found out that she was American. In a few minutes, he'd invited her to join the cast for lunch."[25] Beymer was taken with Sharon's beauty, and arranged to meet her later for a date. Quickly, the pair became inseparable. Eventually, he suggested that Sharon consider a career in the movies. Beymer gave her the name and telephone number of his agent in Hollywood. He told her that, if she was interested, she should contact him when she returned to the States.[26]

For the time being, however, the idea remained only that. Then, on a tour of Venice in the spring of 1961, Sharon and her friends happened on popular singer-actor Pat Boone, filming a special for ABC Television in America. Boone recalls: "Sharon Tate was hovering on the edge of the crowd and introduced herself. She seemed like a typical teenage girl with stars in her eyes, attractive but not breathtaking, and I just really didn't think that she would ever make it to Hollywood. Not because she didn't look good enough, I just thought a daughter of a guy in the service in Italy was a long way from Hollywood."[27]

Sharon apparently spoke with Boone's choreographer, who arranged for her to have a brief audition. In the end, she was awarded a spot as an extra, although the role was so insubstantial that Boone himself cannot remember her participation. He and his wife Shirley did speak with Sharon at some length, however, about the prospect of a career in Hollywood, and recalls that she seemed "excited."

"We were as usual cautionary," Boone says, "we didn't say to her, as I usually do to kids, particularly girls, forget it, do something else, unless you can't possibly help it, because it's rough for girls. But in this case since I didn't think she'd be in Hollywood anyway, we gave her what I thought was practical advice about staying in an all-girl dormitory type thing, getting with a good agent and being on guard against the leeches and such."[28]

Boone wasn't convinced that Sharon was serious. A thoughtful, religious man, he was cynical about the business in which he had gained fame, and worried about the effect such a career would have on others, especially an impressionable young woman. "I can count only two or three females in show business I've ever known," he says, "who had been able to combine success in a career with keeping a family together. One or the other suffers and it's usually the family and the personal esteem and the things that are really important."[29]

For Sharon, however, a career in acting seemed to provide a desperately-needed escape, a boost to her fragile self-esteem. With her pervasive shyness and quiet, soft-spoken demeanor, she did not exactly fit the traditional mold of a fame-hungry Hollywood starlet. The rape had changed her. She was injured, hurt, seeking any comfort to erase her pain. Sharon sensed that acting offered a chance to go beyond herself, to create a different environment from her everyday existence. She abandoned her fleeting plan to become a psychiatrist and threw all of her effort into becoming an actress.

To this end, she let it be known that she was always available for extra work on any production filming in the Verona area. At the time, American companies regularly did location work in the region, and sought out extras from the United States Army Base nearby to avoid the language and union problems of hiring Italian actors. Sharon clearly wanted to get more experience. While Doris Tate was enthusiastic, Sharon's father was less certain. Requests for extras were funneled through Passelaqua's Public Information Officer, a Captain De Angelo, who in turn would relay the information to the Tate household. When De Angelo rang to ask if Sharon was available for work, Doris Tate later recalled, Paul often refused to pass the messages to their daughter.[30]

In the spring of 1961, an announcement appeared in the Vincenza American High student newspaper, asking for extras to work on a production being filmed nearby. The movie was *Barrabas*, a lengthy Biblical epic starring Anthony Quinn and Jack Palance. Sharon and two other Vinceza students were given small, non-speaking roles in the motion picture. "We had a wonderful time," recalls Sheila Boyle Plank. "It was a ball. We got all dressed up like patricians, we would wait, and we'd all get called in to this part of the arena, and we'd sit there and we'd be told to stand up and do a thumbs down."[31]

Sharon was fascinated by the frenzied activity, and hovered on the fringe of the set, where she attracted the attention of Jack Palance. Although *Barrabas* was Sharon's first film, Palance recognized her potential. Like Richard Beymer, he spoke to her at length of a possible career in motion pictures. But Palance went a step further: he arranged for Sharon to travel to Rome for a screen test. Accompanied by her mother—and against the wishes of her father—she duly kept the appointment. She gained no additional work as a result, but, in the space of a few months, she had been quickly drawn to the idea of working as an actress.

Paul Tate was adamantly opposed to Sharon's involvement in this world, but Doris conspired with her daughter to further her opportunities. While she did not necessarily push Sharon against her wishes, Doris Tate had always viewed her daughter's exceptional beauty as a means to an end, whether as a beauty contestant or an actress.

Art Schultz vividly recalls just how determined Doris Tate seemed when it came to furthering Sharon's potential career. He, along with two other friends, had made arrangements to spend a Friday night in Verona with Sharon. But, when they arrived at the

Tate house, Schultz and his friends found Sharon already on the doorstep, purse in hand. She explained that Jack Palance had rung and asked if she would join him for dinner. Schultz was visibly angry at the interruption of their plans, but Doris stepped forward, saying, "Now, Art, don't be upset. This is an opportunity for Sharon."[32]

Within a few minutes, and while Schultz and the others still stood at the front door, Palance pulled up. He apologized for being late, saying that he had just had a 45 RPM record player installed in his car. "Palance was absolutely taken with Sharon," remembers Schultz, "and we couldn't help but believe that he had had this unheard-of device put in his car simply to impress her."[33]

Doris Tate seems not to have questioned the propriety of allowing her eighteen-year-old daughter to date a rather wordly actor nearly twice her age. Her encouragement seems less mercenary than innocently opportunistic. All that came of the evening was further encouragement to consider an acting career, prodding which, by now, Sharon was also receiving from her mother. The encouragement of Palance, Beymer and others was all the convincing Sharon needed.

Sharon had continued to see Beymer while production work on his film continued. Finally he returned to Hollywood, and Sharon was desperate to follow him, to both continue the relationship and to pursue an acting career. Knowing that her father was opposed to such a move, Sharon told them that she wished to return to California to investigate colleges. Reluctantly, Paul and Doris agreed, and Sharon left Italy for America.

She soon joined Beymer in Hollywood, and began to fill her letters to her parents with talk of a movie career, much to her father's despair. Doris Tate, who had focused so much of her attention on Sharon, found the separation too much to bear, and suffered a nervous breakdown. She believed that Sharon was unsafe, and urged her daughter to return to Italy. After much coercion Sharon agreed to return.

She was biding her time, knowing that sooner or later her father would be transferred back to America. After nearly two years in Italy, Paul Tate was promoted to the rank of Major and transferred again, this time to Fort McArthur, in California. "I always had Hollywood in my mind," Sharon would later say. "I was so happy when my father was transferred to San Francisco, which is within such easy distance of Hollywood."[34]

Chapter 2
California Girls

IN FEBRUARY OF 1962, THE TATE FAMILY BOOKED PASSAGE ON THE *USS Independence* and left Italy for America. Because it was winter, the ship was half-empty, and Sharon quickly befriended actress Joey Heatherton, who also was on board. The two young women spent the next twelve days turning the heads of the passengers and crew, enjoying the admiring looks cast in their direction. On landing in America, the Tate family minus Sharon went to visit relatives in Houston. Sharon headed directly to Los Angeles, where she quickly resumed her friendship with Richard Beymer.

The America to which Sharon and her family returned seemed a far different country than the one which they had left a few years earlier. The staid conservatism of the Eisenhower presidency had been replaced with the glamour and energy of the Kennedy administration. Having narrowly-avoided a nuclear confrontation during the Cuban Missile Crisis, the threat of an all-out war seemed distant, despite the increasingly bad relations between the United States and the Soviet Union. There was an optimism fueled by John Glenn's orbit round the earth and talk of a test ban treaty. It was a country whose cultural life was consumed with youth. From the glamorous Kennedys in the White House to the giddy sense of fun driving popular music and accompanying dances like the Twist and the Watusi, everything, in the words of authors Jane and Michael Stern, seemed "so modern, so capable ."[1]

California was the dream of nearly every American teenager, its sun, sand, and surf recently popularized in the lyrics of songs by the Beach Boys and Jan and Dean, and soon to be immortalized in a series of beach party movies starring Annette Funicello and Frankie Avalon. It seemed a golden land, filled with the promise of opportunity, especially to an impressionable young woman of nineteen.

Filled with aspirations, Sharon eagerly flung herself into the unknown world of Hollywood.

Sharon fit the image of the idealized, typical California girl perfectly. She was not tall, standing only five-foot-five, but her long legs and thin figure gave her the impression of added height. Her long, honey-blonde hair fell loosely about her shoulders, framing a face defined by high cheekbones and wide, hazel eyes that Sharon accentuated with dark eyeliner and thick, false lashes. It was a look very much in demand at the time in the studios scattered across the Los Angeles basin, and Sharon, aware of her power to charm and attract, determined that she would capitalize on the trend of the day and test the acting waters.

"I was very shy and bashful, because my parents were very strict with me," Sharon later recalled. "But they agreed to let me go, after all sorts of warnings. They could afford to give me only enough money to get by, and I just about made it to Hollywood. I had to hitchhike a ride in a truck."[2]

Her first move was a bold one, in view of her lack of any substantial acting experience or screen credits. On the day after she arrived in California, Sharon pulled out the card that Richard Beymer gave her a year earlier in Verona. She dialed the telephone number and made an appointment with his agent, Harold Gefsky, for the following day.

Gefsky, a quiet, thoughtful man, was vice-president of the Agency for the Performing Arts in Los Angeles. He had been an agent in L.A. for many years. Like Sharon, he was that rarity in the world of motion pictures—a member of the Hollywood establishment of whom no one ever spoke an unkind word. Actor Skip Ward, who was one of his clients, found Gefsky "the most honorable and trustworthy man in the business. He is a true gentleman, and he always looked after the true best interests of his actors."[3]

Ordinarily, Gefsky would have refused what was a fairly typical telephone call from an unknown woman seeking fame and fortune in Hollywood. But, as a favor to Beymer, he agreed to meet with this latest hopeful. Skip Ward happened to be in Gefsky's office that afternoon when the telephone call came. "Hal hung up the phone and explained that Dick Beymer had met this beautiful young woman and asked that Gefsky give her an interview. Neither of us had any idea what to expect."[4]

Given the go-ahead, Sharon quickly hopped a city bus and rode into Hollywood, walking the short distance from the stop at Doheny and Sunset to Gefsky's office. Curious, Skip Ward had lingered, and happened to be with Gefsky when Sharon walked through the door that day. "She was absolutely drop-dead gorgeous," he recalls. "She was sweet, pleasant and maybe a bit naive. But, even so, there was an extraordinary eroticism about her."[5]

Gefsky was not prone to sudden, lyrical outbursts. Nevertheless, when Sharon first walked in to his office just off the famous Sunset Strip, the agent was stunned. "She was so young and beautiful that I didn't know what to do with her," he later told an interviewer for the *Saturday Evening Post*.[6]

The agent took Sharon out to dinner where he watched in amazement as she repeatedly turned the heads of their fellow diners. To the numerous inquiries, Gefsky hastily replied that Sharon was a young Italian actress, just arrived in America, and Sharon helped maintain the charade by speaking to him only in the Italian she had learned in Verona.[7] Gefsky was struck by her innocent, almost childlike quality. It was somehow fitting that the entertainment in the restaurant that evening was a puppet show.[8]

"When she first walked into my office, I couldn't believe my eyes," Gefsky later declared. "She was almost too pretty for Hollywood. She was a wonderful person, too."[9] Gefsky's reaction proved typical. Throughout her career, Sharon was surrounded with producers, directors, agents, and fellow actors—by reputation, at least, not a very generous or thoughtful lot—who all went out of their ways to guide her and guard her against unpleasantries. Sharon's seeming vulnerability fit in perfectly with the mood of the country—a mood which Hollywood was beginning to echo—and Gefsky quickly jumped at the opportunity which had walked through his agency's door.

"Sharon was a bit naive, perhaps," Gefsky says, "but she was completely honest about her desire to succeed as an actress. She never argued, never fought with me, never protested any suggestion. It was rare to have such an agreeable client."[10]

Gefsky set up a photo shoot. He sent the resulting portfolio to casting directors and modeling agencies. Gefsky also arranged for Sharon to meet a number of motion picture studio and television representatives in an attempt to win her an audition.

At the time, although Sharon was convinced that she could make a go of things, her parents were less certain. Her mother later recalled that, as much as her father opposed Sharon's acting career, circumstances conspired to push her further and further along the road to Hollywood.[11] Sharon herself later remembered: "I used to hitchhike to Los Angeles to all the studios because I couldn't afford the cab fare. The men were so generous, especially the truckdrivers, they all gave me lifts....I convinced Daddy that I'd be safe in Hollywood."[12]

For the first few days, Sharon camped out at a friend's house in Nichols Canyon above Los Angeles.[13] She told writer John Bowers in 1967 that her father, "in Calvinistic style, had only given her a few dollars to sink or swim on."[14] Realizing that she would have to be closer to the center of activity, she returned to her parents' home, gathered up her clothes and belongings and moved into a shared apartment Gefsky had rented for her at the Hollywood Studio Club, a popular lodging place for up-and-coming actresses in central Hollywood.[15] Opened in 1926, it had served as a home to many rising actresses, including Kim Novak, Donna Reed, and Marilyn Monroe.[16]

Almost immediately, Sharon's roomate made advances. "She rang me one night," Gefsky recalls, "and told me that her roommate was trying to rub her neck and back. It made her very uncomfortable."

"Oh Hal," she asked Gefsky, "can I possibly move or get another roommate?"[17]

Gefsky attended to the matter at once, and, the following day, Sharon ended up with actress Mary Winters, in a large, double room overlooking a garden courtyard.[18] Winters later remembered Sharon as "loving, vulnerable and very disciplined when it came to her career....Sharon evoked a kind of warmth. Everybody felt very protective towards her."[19]

Gefsky landed her work in television commercials for Chevrolet automobiles and Santa Fe cigarettes. The latter proved an ordeal. "I didn't smoke or anything," Sharon recalled. "One of the other girls showed me how to do it: You take a deep puff on the cigarette, and you put a look of ecstasy on your face as you exhale. I watched her puff a couple of times, and then I went off to the audition. They gave me a cigarette. I took a deep puff, swallowed the smoke, and passed out cold on the floor. That ended my career in cigarette commercials."[20]

These television spots were sporadic at best, and, in an attempt to support herself, Sharon took a job with Lipper Productions, dressing up in Irish peasant costume and handed out Kelly-Kalani Wine to Hollywood diners at $25 a day.[21] These first few months were lean ones, but, eventually, Sharon scraped together enough money to rent a small Hollywood apartment on Fuller Street in a building managed by Richard Beymer's mother, Eunice.

Because they now shared an agent, Sharon and Richard Beymer saw quite a bit of each other in these months. In time, the pair became intimate and Sharon told Filmways' vice president of advertising Mike Mindlin that Beymer had been her first real lover.[22] The relationship was brief, lasting only a few months, but being loved and accepted proved a valuable boost to Sharon's fragile self-esteem.

This was Sharon's first independent step, and she relished the sense of freedom. With her meager savings, she furnished her apartment with thrift-store finds picked up on afternoons spent wandering along Melrose Avenue in Los Angeles. "Everywhere Sharon went," Gefsky recalls, "people seemed to bend over. backwards to do things for her, to help her out. As soon as she got her apartment, she went to a store and bought a few gallons of paint. The young men who helped her ended up coming round to her apartment that night and painted it for her."[23]

Hollywood is notoriously blasé about beauty, but Sharon proved a different story. "I'd never seen anyone like her—before or since," Gefsky later recalled. "She just took your breath away."[24] Everywhere Gefsky took Sharon—to auditions, to lunches in elite restaurants, to grocery stores to help her shop—she drew intense attention. "When Sharon went to a restaurant," he remembers, "the owner would pay for her meal. It was like that everywhere she went...It was amazing."[25]

Sharon was regularly besieged by those she met. Often they wanted something and flooded her with business cards, offering to photograph her, to obtain film roles. Every week, she handed over the cards, "dozens of them," to Gefsky to sort through.[26]

Eventually, Gefsky became dissatisfied with the work he was getting for Sharon so he called an old friend, Herbert Browar, and suggested that he might be interested in using her in one of his projects. Browar worked as an assistant for Filmways, Inc., which, at the time, was in the process of casting three unknown actresses for a forthcoming CBS-TV production tentatively called *Whistle Stop*, a spin-off of the popular television show *The Beverly Hillbillies*.[27]

"Hal," Browar recalls, "rang me one afternoon and asked if I would do him a favor and meet his new client. I nearly fell out of my chair when Sharon walked into my office. After being in the business for a few years, you get to know 'the look.' Well, she had it. She was so stunningly beautiful, poised, and elegant. She impressed me tremendously."[28]

Browar decided an audition was unnecessary. Instead, he called Martin Ransohoff, chairman of Filmways, "I have this girl in my office," he told Ransohoff, "and I think you should see her at once."[29]

Martin Ransohoff, at thirty-two, was the youngest chief executive officer of a major corporation to be listed on the American Stock Exchange.[30] One writer would refer to him as "one of the shrewdest and more successful producers in films and telelvison."[31]

Ransohoff was the product of an upper-middle class Connecticut family. After attending Colgate University, he began his career in advertising. Unsatisfied with the direction in which his life was headed, he traveled to Europe married and, in 1952, with two hundred dollars, founded Filmways, Inc., a company he developed to produce television commercials. His success was astounding. The first year of Filmways' operation, his company did $150,000 worth of business; five years later, the company's turnover topped $3 million.[32]

In Hollywood, Ransohoff quickly merged his ability to successfully create television commercials with the fertile world of television comedy. By 1963, the company was responsible for several television hits, including *Mister Ed* and *The Beverly Hillbillies.* Roman Polanski later described Ransohoff as "a smooth, persuasive talker with a slight lisp...." When he spoke, according to Polanski, he peppered his speech with the "racy language of the unorthodox, new-style Hollywood."[33]

"He looks like something out of Greek or Roman mythology," one reporter declared, "an infant bacchante. He is round and firm and fully packed, and the almost impish face is topped by a prematurely balding head across which, from some flight of fancy, he sweeps one enormously long thin lock of hair. He wears the lock like a crazy wreath, pushing it back and forth as he talks, and at the end of some particularly riveting conversation, it stands alone, like everything else about him, an exclamation point."[34]

Ransohoff was known for his somewhat abrasive personality. "He mobilizes people's anxiety about themselves," said Filmways associate John Calley. "He makes it impossible to rationalize personal failure as a product of an unbeatable, decadent system, because Marty is a constant reminder to every 'near-miss' that the system can be beaten if you've got the ability....He is the most decisive man I ever met. You get immediate decisions from him. And he's big enough to admit when they're wrong. He's absolutely fearless, laughs at catastrophe."[35]

Filmways, Inc.'s success gave Ransohoff pull in Hollywood, the power to change the course of Sharon's career. Previously, he had negotiated the rise of both Ann-Margret and Tuesday Weld. "I have this dream," he once explained to a reporter, "where I'll discover a beautiful girl who's a nobody and turn her into a star everybody wants. I'll do it like Louis B. Mayer at Metro-Goldwyn-Mayer used to, only better. But once she's successful, then I'll lose interest. That's how my dream goes."[36]

Now, he turned his attention to Sharon Tate. Even though it was late in the afternoon, Browar took her to the studio, where Ransohoff was supervising a new production. When he first saw her, Ransohoff made an immediate decision. His camera crew had not yet left, and Ransohoff asked her to do an impromptu screen test. It went well, and he asked Sharon to return the following day to view the results; he also asked her to bring her parents.[37]

As soon as Sharon left the studio, Ransohoff rang Browar.

"You're right about this girl," he told Browar.

"Marty," Browar replied, "if you handle this girl right, you know you can make a star out of her."[38]

The following day, Sharon duly appeared at the studio, accompanied by her mother, who had come from Fort McArthur. Ransohoff took them to a private screening room where the trio watched the dailies of Sharon's screen test.[39]

As soon as the lights went up, Ransohoff was all business. He began by signing Sharon to an exclusive, seven-year contract with Filmways, Inc. Mike Mindlin, Filmways' Vice President of Advertising, recalls that Sharon was one of the few such actors signed to a contract.[40] Having discovered the young woman he was certain he could mold into the next big thing, Ransohoff was determined not to let her go.

Gefsky and John Calley worked out the contractual details. According to its terms, Sharon received around $750 a month, a considerable sum for a twenty-year-old woman in 1963.[41] Sharon would later come to regret the contract, and the enthusiastic haste with which she signed it. "When I was put under contract, I thought, 'Oh, how nice, but'—I was just a piece of merchandise. No one cared about me , Sharon."[42] She seemed lost in the immense tangle of legal rights. First came parental waivers, along with lawyers awards, which officially made Sharon a ward of the courts until the age of twenty-one, thus allowing her to work unhindered in both New York and Los Angeles.

"My whole life changed from then on," Sharon went on. "I had never even driven a car, but when I signed with Marty the contract provided for one, and that was the first thing I got. That and a dog. These little things count, you know."[43]

At first, there was talk of testing Sharon with Al Simon for a role in *Whistle Stop*. Created by Paul Henning, the man responsible for *The Beverly Hillbillies*, *Whistle Stop* would tell the story of Pearl Bodine, cousin of The Hillbillies' Jed Clampett, her three daughters, and their lives in the small town of Hooterville. Henning had based the idea on a hotel run by his wife's grandparents in rural Missouri. Henning and Simon had already cast actress Bea Benaderet as Cousin Pearl, replicating her role in *The Beverly Hillbillies*. But both men wanted unknown actresses for the roles of her daughters. Sharon seemed to fit the bill and, along with Pat Woodall and series creator's daughter Linda Kaye Henning, was tentatively cast in the production.

Sharon was thrilled. Against all the odds, she had finally succeeded, landing not only her first television role, but also a major, recurring part in a weekly series. Although panned by the critics, *The Beverly Hillbillies* was a commercial success, making genuine stars of its cast, and there was every expectation that the same would prove true for those involved with *Whistle Stop*.

But, for Sharon, the series was not to be. She was extremely nervous, and could barely deliver lines on cue. Her fumbling performance, not surprising in view of her lack of experience, convinced Simon and Henning that any casting would be rushed. She was eventually pulled from the production. In the end, Jeannine Riley was cast in the role, and the show went on the air in 1963 as *Petticoat Junction*.[44]

Ransohoff had never intended to cast Sharon in the program. He did not want to launch his new protege until he had an opportunity to cultivate her acting abilities and voice projection. This was a completely new world for Sharon, and she responded with single-mindedness. Rather than give in to the pressures, she became even more determined in her pursuit. Acting had always meant an opportunity to break free of her life and of her dependency on others. Sharon never complained to Ransohoff about the path he had marked out for her; she was both too shy and too uncertain of herself to force her career. She accepted Ransohoff's pronouncements as gospel, never arguing with his cautious approach. "She wouldn't even eat a hamburger if he told her not to," one of her friends would later say.[45] All Sharon could do was wait.

Chapter 3
Forquet

IT WAS IN 1963, WHILE SHARON WAS HAVING LUNCH WITH HAL Gefsky, that Lee Wallace from Twentieth Century Fox walked up to their table, accompanied by a tall, handsome young man. He introduced him as Philippe Forquet. Forquet, twenty-three, was shooting a picture for Fox called *Take Her, She's Mine*, starring James Stewart and Sandra Dee, in which he played the romantic lead.

"We were very attracted to each other," Forquet recalls of his first meeting with Sharon. The pair spoke at length, and Sharon and Forquet agreed to a dinner date. "She was absolutely stunning, perfectly genuine," says Forquet.[1] For her part, Sharon was attracted to Forquet's maturity, charm and self-assurance. In addition, Forquet was blessed with a beauty which nearly rivaled that of Sharon. "My God, they were a beautiful couple together," says Gefsky. "They got on very well together, and both turned heads wherever they went."[2] Soon, Sharon transferred whatever feelings remained for Beymer to Forquet. "With us," Forquet remembers, "things became very intense, and very quickly."[3] They began to spend all of their time together. Sharon's days were still consumed with acting classes, photo shoots and the occasional walk-on part, while Forquet was kept at Twentieth Century Fox working on his new film. But in the evenings, the pair dined together at fashionable restaurants and danced in the nightclubs scattered along the Sunset Strip.

On weekends, the young lovers escaped the city, often visiting nearby Palm Springs. "At that time, it was impossible to get a hotel room if you weren't married," Forquet remembers. "If we wanted to share, we had to pretend to be man and wife, and we always made up false names to sign the registers."[4]

Sharon made no secret of her burgeoning relationship with Forquet, and soon, he faced the formidable ordeal of meeting her parents. "I thought her father was a very nice man. He was a sort of typical army man, rather quiet, reserved, but I think a very straight-forward kind of person who seemed to like me. I can't say that I liked her mother very much. She seemed to be more concerned about Sharon's career than Sharon herself."[5]

By this time, Sharon's parents fully supported her career. Doris Tate's early worries that Sharon would fall victim to the Hollywood system seem to have evaporated under Ransohoff's careful protection. Doris remained strict, however, and was constantly on guard. "I know I was horrible at times, I really was," she said. "I really kept a tight rein on, I had to....I felt fine about Sharon being a star, as long as I was close by."[6]

Forquet's introduction into Sharon's life seems to have greatly worried her parents. "They were very concerned about their daughter's career," Forquet recalls. "They wanted her to become a movie star, and I think there was a lot of resentment against me, and feeling that I was somehow going to stand in Sharon's way."[7]

But Sharon's career was scarcely on hold. In the fall of 1963, Ransohoff asked Al Simon to cast Sharon in a small, walk-on role on CBS-TV's *Mister Ed*. On the appointed day, Sharon duly reported for work at the General Service Studios in Hollywood, filled with excitement. Star Alan Young later recalled her great beauty, and the tragic aura which her participation lent to the show.[8]

Sharon filmed two episodes of *Mister Ed*. The first, airing on Sunday, 13 October, 1963, was a Columbus Day special titled "Ed Discovers America." In the episode, Ed, the talking horse, instructs his owner Wilbur on the true history of Columbus's voyage. The majority of the episode was a costume fantasy sequence, and Sharon, dressed in a dark wig and medieval costume, was scarcely recognizable.[9]

A few weeks later, Sharon returned to film a second episode, this one titled "Love Thy New Neighbor." Airing on 15 December, 1963, it dealt with Ed's increasing loneliness since his owner Wilbur befriended a new neighbor. Sharon played a telephone operator, called by the horse who is desperate for conversation. In the end, she hung up on him. In both episodes, Sharon was unbilled.[10]

The parts were negligible, but Ransohoff was satisfied with Sharon's performance. He agreed to give her a small role in Paul Henning's *The Beverly Hillbillies*, again insisting that she appear unbilled, and in a black wig. Her first appearance, as one of the students at a private boarding school invaded by Jed Clampett's daughter Elly May (Donna Douglas), proved something less than a success. "When we first got her she couldn't even walk through the door convincingly," said Associate Producer Joe Depew. "She was very amateurish. It was hard for her to read a line."[11]

"They got to work on me," Sharon recalled. "Make-up people, acting coaches, vocal coaches, dancing coaches, dialogue coaches, exercise coaches, riding instructors and more."[12] This was scarcely the glamorous life she had envisioned. Each morning, she attended a speech class in Hollywood, before heading to Pasadena for singing lessons. This was followed by exercise and body-building at a Beverly Hills gym, and dance instruction at a private studio in Los Angeles. Afternoons were given over to acting classes. Five days a week, for ten hours a day, she submitted to this regime. At night, she read plays, learned her lines for the following day's drama class, or studied scripts.[13] Over the course of three years, Ransohoff was believed to have invested over $100,000 in lessons, photo shoots and publicity to promote Sharon as the next big Hollywood star.[14]

One of her acting teachers, Charles Conrad, later said, "Such a beautiful girl, you would have thought she would have all the confidence in the world. But she had none."[15] It was a belief Sharon had long struggled against. "People," she said, "expect so much of an attractive person. I mean people are very critical of me. It makes me tense."[16]

Another drama coach, Jeff Corey, called her "an incredibly beautiful girl, but a fragmented personality." He remembered spending long hours trying to break through Sharon's seemingly impenetrable reserve. Once, he handed her a stick and bellowed, "Hit me! Do something! Show emotion!...If you can't tap into who you are, you can never act!"[17]

Sharon, however, was not lacking in confidence so much as experience. She clearly recognized the need for the latter, and made determined efforts to improve her abilities. A drive to act had not brought her to Hollywood; it had been her stunning looks, and desire to create a new reality, which drove her pursuit. Her astute realization that beauty was not enough to propel her career only made Sharon throw herself deeper into training and lessons.

"It was hard work," Sharon later declared, "and I can't say that I didn't get discouraged at times. Often I'd work for long periods thinking I wasn't getting anywhere, then all of a sudden I'd feel that

I had made a tremendous advance. So, it was more of a series of big jumps than a collection of small steps."[18]

It was an intense time for Sharon, but she seemed to relish the experience, and remain good-natured throughout. Mike Mindlin remembers that she was "very, very friendly, very outgoing, and very playful. A lot of actresses aren't, but she was, and she seemed bubbly and full of life. We used to joke a lot round the studio. Sharon was smart, reasonably sophisticated, and had a great sense of humor, which made her very fun to be around."[19] And Herb Browar says: "Sharon was a very sincere, nice person, genuine and very pleasant to be around. She always had a smile for everyone, but I think she was basically a rather serious person, and she treated her career that way. She always did what we asked of her, and was always on time to shoots. She seemed to have complete control of herself, but she was flexible enough to take things as they came. She had a good sense of humor, but she wasn't a giddy young woman. Her maturity and self-control definitely distinguished her from the starlets we always saw in Hollywood."[20]

The lessons began to pay off. Sharon grew in confidence, and, when she returned to the set of *The Beverly Hillbillies*, Joe Depew noted that "She learned a lot. She was a very pleasant girl and extremely beautiful."[21] Her hard work was rewarded when she was cast as Janet Trego, a member of the secretarial pool working at the series' fictional Beverly Hills Bank of Commerce. Although she was still forced to wear a dark wig, for the first time, she was listed in the credits as "Sharon Tate." Altogether, she appeared as Janet Trego in thirteen episodes, spread over the telelvision show's 1963-1965 seasons. She also had two smaller roles, including one as a guest at a party given by the Clampetts in their mansion.

The Beverly Hillbillies gave Sharon valuable experience. Shooting took place at the General Service Studios in Hollywood, where she had filmed her episodes of *Mister Ed*. Although she shared a few scenes with stars Buddy Ebsen, Irene Ryan, Max Baer and Donna Douglas, most of Sharon's work called for her to act with either Raymond Bailey, who played banker Milton Drysdale, or Nancy Kulp, who had the role of Drysdale's secretary Jane Hathaway. On set and off, Bailey was apparently very much like his difficult character, and Sharon had to learn how to avoid his angry outbursts. "He wasn't happy anywhere he was," recalled Paul Henning. "He complained a lot, but he played the part perfectly."[22]

"Sharon was a lovely young woman," recalled Nancy Kulp. "She always seemed a bit cautious when she was on set, as if she was still getting her footing. She was very sweet, and seemed eager to learn, though I think she was perhaps a bit intimidated as well. I can't say that she mixed with the rest of the cast. I do remember her laughter, though, which rang across the studio."[23]

Ransohoff was careful to control her exposure, waiting for what he felt was just the right moment to launch her upon the public. "One of the rules Marty laid down when he signed me was no publicity and no professional acting until I was ready," she later said. "So in order to give me some experience before the cameras, he put a black wig on me so no one would recognize me and I played a stupid secretary in another of his television series, *The Beverly Hillbillies*. That was a great thing for me because I could see myself changing for the better week by week."[24]

At the same time, however, the relationship with Forquet was growing increasingly troubled. "It started as a beautiful affair," says Forquet, "with tenderness and romance. After a while, though, I began to understand lots of things people were doing. Sharon had a lot of people round her, exploiting her, trying to achieve their own ends through her. We had lots of big rows about it, and things became tense. I wanted to pull away, but she kept after me, and she always managed to get me back."[25]

In the fall of 1963, Ransohoff arranged for Sharon to take lessons under Lee Strasberg at the Actors' Studio in New York. Forquet accompanied her, and the pair took an apartment together on Lexington and 78th Street. Sharon was so intimidated at the school, however, and so overwhelmed by the expected level of intensity, that she stayed for only a few weeks before bolting under the pressure. Even so, she made a lasting impression on the famous Mr. Strasberg. "She was only with me a few weeks," he later said, "but I remember her. She was a beautiful girl."[26]

Sharon continued to join Forquet on his walks to Carnegie Hall each day, where he continued to take classes. She spent her afternoons visiting museums or shopping. Inevitably, the boredom of her situation began to overwhelm her, and she was desperate for a change.

It came one night, while she and Forquet were having dinner. "I asked Sharon to marry me," he remembers, "and she said yes. She seemed very happy, and very in love." Indeed, for a time, all was well. But after a few weeks, Sharon and Forquet returned to Los Angeles, where they broke the news to both Sharon's parents and to Ransohoff. Neither the Tates nor the head of Filmways, Inc., however, seemed to be very happy about this latest development. "Ransohoff," remembers Forquet, "came in and told Sharon that he was opposed to her marriage and wanted her to stop seeing me. He threatened to drop her contract if she didn't break things off. And her parents got involved, too. They were worried that I was standing in the way of Sharon becoming a big star. I remember her mother talked about money, money, money—all the money Sharon would lose if she quit acting."27

Sharon was caught in the middle. While she pondered what to do, word of the engagement leaked to the press. On 27 May, 1964, Harrison Carroll reported in the *Los Angeles Herald-Examiner.* "Just before he took off for New York, young French actor Philippe Forquet became engaged to Sharon Tate, who at the time was expected to marry Dick Beymer. Philippe has made a number of French pictures and played the romantic lead opposite Sandra Dee in *Take Her, She's Mine.* He promised Sharon that he will be back with the ring in a couple of weeks. They expect to set the marriage date at that time. Sharon, a spectacular beauty under contract to Marty Ransohoff at MGM, is the daughter of Captain Paul James Tate."28

The pressures on the relationship began to take their toll. Sharon grew nervous, uncertain, while Forquet was increasingly frustrated. "I became very unhappy," he says, "and I flew off the handle at times." The volatile nature of their relationship erupted into shouting matches which frequently turned into violent confrontations. Both Sharon and Forquet struck out at each other, not just with words, but with fists, shoes, plates and glasses as well. "It was very traumatic," Forquet admits. "The whole time is a very bad memory for me. Once, Sharon cut me on the chest with a broken wine bottle. Another time, she stabbed me in the leg with a pair of toenail clippers."29

Inevitably, Forquet, larger and stronger, came out of these confrontations less battered than did Sharon. Forquet had a temper, and in the heat of their arguments, his frustrations got the better of him. Once, he allegedly struck and kicked her so severely that Sharon had to be rushed to the UCLA Medical Center, where she was admitted for emergency treatment.30

It says volumes about her lack of self-esteem and need to be accepted that, even after being released from the hospital, Sharon returned to her fiance. As determined and strong-willed as she might have been when it came to her career, Sharon was often ruled by her good-natured outlook and positive approach to life. Her response to trouble, whether in her career or with Forquet, was never to walk away, but to try to work through the situation and repair whatever damage had been done.

Sharon's parents attempted to intervene in the situation, counseling their daughter to abandon the relationship. But Sharon could not, or would not, break free of Forquet. "Our relationship agonized for almost a year," Forquet recalls. "It was like I was hypnotized. I couldn't move or react." After several uncomfortable confrontations with Sharon's parents, Forquet fled to New York and, finally, back to France.[31]

Sharon was traumatized by the situation. In later years, she would mention the romance in interviews, but never disclosed the abuse which had characterized it.[32] For his part, Forquet was equally shattered. "It took me ten years to recover from being with Sharon," he says. "I wouldn't allow myself to fall in love again."[33]

Alone in Hollywood, Sharon soon met and befriended another of Harold Gefsky's clients, actress Sheilah Wells, who was under contract to Universal Studios. "Both Sharon and Sheilah were living on their own at the time," Gefsky recalls, "and both were paying separate rents when neither one had much money. I introduced them to each other and, after they became friendly, suggested that, for financial reasons, they move in together."[34] Sharon, accompanied by her white poodle, Love, duly moved in with her new friend at the latter's small apartment.[35]

For Sharon, life settled into a quiet routine. In the weeks she worked on *The Beverly Hillbillies*, she was up early, off to the studio by seven in the morning, and rarely returned home before six at night. Hers was not the life of a typical Hollywood starlet: Sharon far preferred quiet evenings at home, curled up on the couch in a pair of sweatpants and comfortable shirt, watching television, reading or playing with her dog, to the fashionable nightclubs and parties sought out by many. On weekends, she visited her parents and sisters, or joined friends to ski at Lake Arrowhead.

Sharon was good-natured about her lack of success; her optimism astonished many of her friends, but she never seemed bitter. "I'm sure the three years I spent in training to be an actress will pay off," she confidently declared.[36] She seemed to take immense joy in the simple aspects of her life: cooking, shopping, visiting friends or walking on the beach at nearby Santa Monica. While she had never been an intellectual, Sharon took great pains to fill in the gaps in her education through reading. Her continued quest for self-improvement, development and reaching her goals became increasingly obvious to those around her.

In 1964, Sharon had her first motion picture screen test. Director Sam Peckinpah had signed on with Ransohoff to do a new film about a group of professional gamblers meeting for a big game in New Orleans. One of the roles called for a young, beautiful female to serve as the love interest in a series of romantic interludes. Titled *The Cincinnati Kid*, the film had already cast Steve McQueen, Ann-Margret and Edward G. Robinson. Ransohoff discussed the possibility of casting Sharon with Peckinpah, and the director agreed to test her. Sharon tested for Peckinpah with McQueen; but, after viewing the test, Peckinpah argued with Ransohoff against casting Sharon Tate—still an unknown quality in Hollywood—in the film, especially in such a high profile role. He felt that her timidity and lack of experience would show on film. In the end, Peckinpah won, and Ransohoff agreed to cast Tuesday Weld.

In August, 1964, while Ransohoff was producing *The Sandpiper* with Elizabeth Taylor and Richard Burton at Big Sur, he arranged a photo shoot for Sharon along a secluded stretch of sandy beach. The shoot went over-schedule, night fell and, with it, a heavy fog rolled in from the Pacific. Driving back to Los Angeles, Sharon had an automobile accident. Her new Triumph sports car flew off the winding road, rolling four times before coming to a stop at the bottom of a hillside. Miraculously, she escaped unharmed, with only two small scars near her left eye to remind her of the wreck.[37] The Triumph, though, was totaled. Sharon's first thought, or so she later told an interviewer, was that Ransohoff would be angry with her over the incident, and she was beside herself with worry over how best to break the news to him.[38]

The accident again triggered Sharon's doubts. While she tried to accept the slow course her career seemed to be taking, she found Ransohoff's caution frustrating. The lack of success, and relationship with Forquet had severely battered her self-confidence. Although she joked to friends about "sexy little me," Sharon remained unful-filled and impatient.[39] It was at this point, when she was at her most vulnerable, that, on Thanksgiving Day, 1964, Sharon first met Jay Sebring.

Chapter 4
Jay

Like Sharon, Jay Sebring, had come to Hollywood in search fame. Twenty-nine years old, with dark brown hair and eyes, Sebring was attractive and stylish. With Jay, image was everything. He was born Thomas John Kummer on 10 October, 1933, fourth child and second son of accountant Bernard Kummer and his wife, Margarette. Throughout his early life in Detroit, Michigan, Jay suffered from personal insecurity, both about his middle-class background and about his height: at five-feet six inches tall, he constantly felt overshadowed by others. To compensate for his short stature, he indulged in a flashy and extravagant lifestyle: driving expensive, trendy cars; attending important parties; and moving in elite Hollywood circles. The move did not sit well with his parents, and they virtually cut off all communication after his success in California.

By profession, Jay was a hairstylist, a trade he had learnt during a four-year stint in the United States Navy during the Korean War. Coming to Los Angeles, he had quickly made a name for himself by procuring a position at a top salon and attracting an impressive list of clients. By the early 1960s, the success of Vidal Sassoon had revolutionized the profession, lending a glamour and prestige previously unknown, and Jay took advantage of the dozens of men and women eager for his services. He changed his surname from Kummer to Sebring, in an effort to both distance himself from his middle-class background and to surround himself with the glamorous associations of the exciting Florida car race of the same name. "Jay," says friend Skip Ward, "had the good fortune of arriving in Hollywood at exactly the right time. Young actors in that day thought nothing of spending fifty or a hundred dollars on a haircut. These guys realized that they were in a town where they lived and made their money by their look, and Jay was smart enough to cultivate the inherent narcisism."[1]

His big break came when actor Kirk Douglas asked Jay to develop a distinctive haircut for the actors appearing as slaves in his new film *Spartacus.*[2] Sebring's work attracted further attention; soon, with the investments of several of his regular and wealthy clients, he managed to open his own salon, Sebring International, and most of the Hollywood set followed him. He counted not only Kirk Douglas but also Warren Beatty, Steve McQueen, Paul Newman and George Peppard as regular customers, and studios contacted him frequently to do hair for their films. His was not a beauty-parlor world of middle-class housewives, but a sophisticated shop filled with modern chrome and lavish mirrors, and peopled with enviably-dressed employees who epitomized current trends.

In October, 1960, Jay had married a model named Cami. The union soon fell apart, however, and, in August of 1963, they had separated. Free of the constraints of marriage, Sebring threw himself headlong into the glittering world of Hollywood. In time, Sebring became something of a celebrity himself, and the character of George in the 1975 motion picture *Shampoo* was based largely on Sebring and starred one of his former clients, Warren Beatty, in the main role.

For all of his preoccupation with the perfect Hollywood image, Jay was thoughtful, intelligent and confident—all qualities which appealed greatly to Sharon. "Jay was a real sweetheart," recalls friend Michelle Phillips, "funny, very adorable, and very gentle."[3] And Kirk Douglas remembered: "Jay was a charismatic, tiny little fellow. Good-looking. Well built. Quite a ladies' man."[4] He was the epitome of the fashionable sixties male: a man who cared about his appearance and clothes, enjoyed fine food and wine, moved in the right circles, and enjoyed life to the fullest.

"I met Jay when I went in to his salon on Fairfax to get my hair cut," recalls Skip Ward. "I was a young actor, had a hot Mustang, and Jay was fascinated by the car. He loved that car. We hit it off at once, and began to hang out, talking about cars and girls. Eventually Jay bought a Cobra, which he used to race all over town. He was a truly great driver, but there was always a sort of reckless energy that seemed to propel him, both behind the wheel and in his life. Jay was a great guy, you knew he was your friend, but at the same time, there was a hint of mysticism about him, a darker side that you could never quite put your finger on."[5]

"Jay was a hell of a nice guy," recalls his neighbor Ib Zacko. "He had a big white German Shepherd which ran up and down the road, playing with my dog, and Jay used to end up chasing it all over. I did a lot of cabinetry at the time in a shop in my garage, and he would pop in to say hello and watch me at work. He said he was all thumbs, and wished he had the patience to work with his hands, which was quite funny, given that he was a hair stylist."[6]

Sharon first met Sebring on Thanksgiving evening, 1964, at a party given by Elmer Valentine, owner of the famous Whiskey A-Go-Go on Sunset Strip, and later The Roxy. They began to dine out in Hollywood's most exclusive restaurants, ending their evenings in smoke-filled jazz clubs over martinis. His confidence inspired Sharon. "I need a strong, secure man...someone who leads, but doesn't dominate," she admitted in an interview. "And at the same time, he's got to be sensitive and adventurous—someone who likes to do different things all the time. A man is sexiest to me when he's vital and creative; what he looks like in the mirror is strictly secondary."[7]

Sebring made a favorable impression on Sharon's parents. He was thoughtful, well-spoken, educated and handsome. His career, while perhaps a bit unconventional, had resulted in financial rewards. To Doris Tate, he was charming and sociable, even teaching her how he cut hair; Sharon's father respected his business sense and military past. "He treated Sharon very well," remembered Doris Tate. "He was gentle, but I know that Sharon also appreciated his ability to take charge."[8]

Sharon began spending most of her free time at Jay's new home. Just north of Hollywood and Bel Air, above the Los Angeles basin, Benedict Canyon stretches through the hills, providing a rustic, rural setting just minutes away from the city. Sebring had discovered a house here which suited him perfectly. Hidden on a steep hillside near the end of a cul-de-sac just off Benedict Canyon Road, the mock-Tudor mansion at 9860 Easton Drive had once belonged to actress Jean Harlow and her husband, MGM producer Paul Bern. The picturesque house was rich with reminders of Hollywood history, including gutters whose tops were capped with carved wooden replicas of the heads of Rudolph Valentino, Douglas Fairbanks, Sr. and Mary Pickford.[9]

The house also had a dark history. Here, in Harlow's bedroom, on Labor Day, 1932, Bern had committed suicide just two months after their marriage.[10] Another guest at the house committed suicide, and a third man apparently drown in the swimming pool. Several years later, a maid working for the new owners is said to have hung herself in the house.[11] According to his friends, it was this tragic past which first attracted Sebring to the house.[12]

The house, not surprisingly, was popularly believed to be haunted. Sharon certainly thought so. One night in 1965, she was staying at the Easton Drive house alone. She later explained that she had felt something was wrong, and left the lights on in the bedroom while she tried to sleep; she awoke to see the figure of "a creepy little man" in shadow standing by the bed; terrified, she ran screaming out of the room and down the main staircase, only to find another horrible vision, this one of a body with its throat slashed and tied to the newel post at the foot of the stairs. When she blinked her eyes, the image was gone. Unnerved, Sharon made herself a drink, wondering if she had imagined the entire episode. But, next morning, she felt certain that she had actually seen the ghost of Paul Bern.[13]

Like his house, Jay Sebring, too, had a darker side. At the time of his meeting with Sharon, he had begun to experiment heavily with drugs. According to his friends, Jay regularly used marijuana, amphetamines, cocaine, mescaline and LSD. Under his influence, Sharon gradually was introduced to these drugs as well. "It opened the world to me," Sharon later said. "I was like a very tight knot, too embarrassed to dance, to speak even."[14] Both she and Jay moved in Hollywood circles where drugs were common. Doors opened for them up and down the canyons above Hollywood, as Jay quickly became known as a contact for many of the rich and famous who bought drugs.

Sebring's other, peculiar, passion, was sado-masochism. He liked to tie up women with a silk cord and then whip them with a small sash, often taking photographs. However, he was never violent, and any such activity was always consensual. Yet it is again revealing that Sharon continued to stay with Jay in spite of his drug use and sexual peculiarities. She would later comment to Roman Polanski that Jay approached these encounters in a gentle, "rather disarming way." Although she went along with his requests, she found Jay's fetish "funny, but sad."[15]

Although Sharon seems to have craved affection, and fell into relationships with men of doubtful character, she was not, according to Hollywood gossip—which is notorious about keeping track of such things—promiscuous. More than anything else, Sharon was the product of the changing age. She came of age at a time when the advent of the birth control pill made sex an option for women outside of marriage, without fear of unwanted pregnancy. Her attitude toward sex reflected her time in Italy and the newly-found feminine freedom, as well as the changing morals of the day. Even so, Sharon scarcely fit the definition of a modern, liberated woman: she took her relationships seriously, with an intensity which spoke of her need for acceptance and search for security.

This modest attitude impressed many of those who Sharon encountered. Because of its close proximity to the Hollywood studios, Sharon regularly had potential scripts delivered to Jay's house. One day, a production assistant happened to arrive when no one was at home, and instead left an envelope for Sharon with Paula Zacko, one of Jay's neighbors on Easton Drive. A few hours later, Sharon arrived, in the midst of a rainstorm, to pick up the script. She accepted Zacko's invitation for a cup of coffee, but refused to remove her long raincoat, which was drenched. After some prodding, Sharon finally opened the coat to reveal that she had on nothing but a silk teddy. She explained that she was on her way to a photo shoot, and the clothes she was to wear had not been ready. Before the shoot, she had met a producer and worn the only thing she had in the house, but kept her raincoat firmly buttoned. Any other ambitious starlet might have been tempted to let the coat slip open during her interview with the producer, but Sharon was too cautious to engage in such questionable behavior.[16]

Sharon was soon absorbed into Jay's charmed circle, and became close to Steve McQueen and his wife Neile. "Jay admired Steve's recklessness," says Skip Ward. "There was a rebellion in him that I think Jay wished he could emulate. They both loved fast cars, and spent a lot of time talking about racing."[17]

Sharon and Jay regularly joined the McQueens for dinner at their Brentwood mansion, a rambling stone house dubbed The Castle, perched on a bluff high above Hollywood. "I found Sharon to be nice and totally guileless," recalled Neile McQueen Toffel. "She seemed willing to do anything Jay asked her to. I don't think Marty Ransohoff approved of their relationship or of Jay's influence on Sharon, whom Marty seemed to be grooming into a Marilyn Monroe-like star. But I doubt he ever said anything to her. The one and only time I tried LSD took place at our house one night with Jay and Sharon, and of course Steve."[18]

In March, 1965, Jay was finally divorced from his wife Cami. The decree marked a turning point in the relationship between Sharon and Jay. Suddenly, he became more intense and serious, and began to talk about marriage. "Jay made no secret of the fact that he was really in love with her," remembers friend Skip Ward. "I think he would have been perfectly happy to settle down with her and have lots of kids."[19]

While Sharon later admitted that she had been in love with Jay, she was both too uncertain of her own future and too focused on her career to make such a commitment. Sharon was only twenty-two, poised on the verge of exciting possibilities; while the security marriage brought with it was certainly appealing, she was less enamored with the idea of settling down and abandoning whatever experiences life still held.

Jay spirited Sharon off to Hawaii with Steve and Neile McQueen for a week-long vacation, in an attempt to win her over to his point of view. They returned to Los Angeles still devoted to each other, but no closer to a serious commitment that they had been before. Sharon cared deeply about Jay, but she thought that she was still too young to marry. She made one concession to Jay: as a promise to him, she gave him her high school class ring, which he continued to wear until his death.

Her relationship with Jay helped occupy much of Sharon's time, but she was still anxious about her career. She constantly besieged Ransohoff's offices with letters and telephone calls, begging for any work. In late 1964, Sy Weintraub asked Ransohoff to loan Sharon to star in his new production *Tarzan and the Valley of Gold*, starring former Los Angeles Rams linebacker Mike Henry. It was hardly the kind of role which Ransohoff envisioned, and he advised Sharon that he had turned down the request.

She was stunned. Both Jay and Steve McQueen pressured her to change agents. Her contract with Filmways, Inc. was unfortunately unavoidable. With some reluctance, Sharon agreed. In the middle of 1965, she signed with McQueen's agent, Stan Kamen, of the famous William Morris Talent Agency on Wilshire Boulevard in Los Angeles.[20]

"Stan called one day," Hal Gefsky recalls, "and said that both McQueen and Sebring had managed to convince Sharon to change agents. They wanted her to be a big wheel, like everyone else, and they fixed it up for Stan to meet her. But Sharon was loyal, and told him that she would only switch if I approved and was involved in the process."[21]

Together, Gefsky and Kamen worked out what surely must have been one of the oddest of Hollywood contracts. Sharon was adamant that Gefsky should continue to benefit from her career; Kamen would pay Gefsky ten percent of Sharon's income, while he himself also took a regular commission. The deal meant that Sharon was, in effect, paying double agents' commissions to two different men, one of whom was no longer actively representing her. But she refused to abandon Gefsky. "It was one of the most selfless and loyal things anyone's ever done for me in this business," Gefsky recalls.[22]

In February of 1965, Ransohoff agreed to loan Sharon to NBC-TV for a small supporting role in an episode of their series *The Man From U.N.C.L.E.,* an espionage spoof starring Robert Vaughn and David McCallum. In *The Girls of Nazarone Affair,*" Sharon portrayed a member of an evil group led by Lucia Nazarone, determined to steal a serum which restored life to the dead. Clad in black leather, she joined the other girls in acrobatic displays during carefully-staged fight scenes.[23]

Ransohoff's hold on Sharon was powerful. He felt that she was still too inexperienced to handle a major role. However, he could not put off her requests forever. In the summer of 1965, Ransohoff signed to produce a new horror film with MGM. There was a role for a pretty young actress, and Ransohoff agreed to cast Sharon. In the fall of 1965, Sharon flew off to London to begin *Eye of the Devil.*

Chapter 5
Eye of the Devil

S HARON ARRIVED IN LONDON ACCOMPANIED BY JAY SEBRING. FOR the next few months, she commuted between the MGM Studios at Borehamwood outside London and the medieval Chateau d'Hautefort at Brives les Gaillards in the Perigord in France, where location filming took place. "The area was kind of mythical, kind of foggy and smoky, and it put me in a great mood for my part," Sharon later recalled.[1] *Eye of the Devil*, although completed by the middle of 1966, was not released until 1967, ironically after another of Sharon's films.

Eye of the Devil, or *Thirteen* as it was also referred to in its British release, was based upon a novel by Philip Loraine, *Day of the Arrow*, and adapted for the screen by Robin Estridge and Dennis Murphy. It was a strange, low-key thriller concerning a rural pagan cult. Philippe de Montfaucon, Marquis de Bellac—the film's principal character—is the victim of the cult's practice of sacrificing a human life to ensure a successful grape harvest. As the film opens, Philippe, who lives in Paris with his wife Catherine and children Jacques and Antoinette, is approached by a representative of his native village of Bellenac and informed of another impending poor harvest—the third in a row. He dutifully returns to the family chateau, soon followed by his wife and children, who have come against his wishes. There, Catherine witnesses a number of bizarre scenes: hooded figures wander through shadowy rooms, animals are sacrificed, and a threatening brother and sister, Christian and Odile d'Carey, hover ominously around the chateau. Gradually, Catherine learns of the existence of the cult, which believes it must sacrifice her husband, as lord of the manor, to guarantee the harvest. Throughout the film, the Marquis de Bellac is aware of the ultimate fate awaiting him, but, convinced by the village priest—himself a member of the cult—that he is powerless to avoid his destiny, he does nothing to prevent the impending tragedy. When he joins the twelve members of the cult in the woods below the chateau, the evil circle is complete, and the Marquis is killed by an arrow shot by Christian d'Carey. As the film ends, and his grieving family leaves the chateau, Philippe's young son Jacques has already been initiated into the cult and to his own eventual fate as lord of Bellenac.

Ransohoff produced the film, along with John Calley, and J. Lee Thompson directed. David Niven starred as the Marquis de Bellac, with Deborah Kerr as Catherine and Donald Pleasance as the village priest, Father Dominick. Originally, Kim Novak had taken the role of Catherine, but, well into filming, she injured her back and was replaced with Kerr. A third of the film had already been shot.

"Calley and I urged Marty to take the insurance money and run after Novak's accident," recalls Mike Mindlin. "But he decided to stick it out."[2] Sharon played Odile d'Carey, while her brother Christian was played by British actor David Hemmings, soon to be cast in Michaelangelo Antonioni's successful *Blow Up*. Robert Duncan and Suky Appleby were cast in the roles of the two de Montfaucon children, Jacques and Antoinette. Sharon's character, Odile, is a witch. Her principal role was to look beautiful and mesmerizing, which she did, thanks in large part to the atmospheric black and white cinematography of Erwin Hallier. Dressed throughout in black, blonde hair exquisitely framing high cheekbones and heavily-shadowed and underlined eyes, Sharon managed to be stunning and malevolent at the same time. Although she only appeared in a dozen scenes, she was listed seventh in the opening credits, and her screen presence was considerable.

Following two silent appearances, Sharon's first lines came in a scene filmed with the two de Montfaucon children, Jacques and Antoinette. Playing in the Chateau garden, they cautiously approach the mysterious Odile, whom they find sitting at the edge of a reflecting pool. Fingering an amulet which glimmers against the black background of her top, Odile, in a clipped, rather impressive British accent, asks, "Do you believe in magic? Do you Jacques?" She shines the light from the amulet in the young boy's eyes, and directs his attention to a toad perched on a lily pad. "Well, shall we turn that toad into a dove?" In an instant, the toad has transformed. At that moment, the children's mother Catherine arrives and hurries Jacques and Antoinette back to the Chateau.

Her longest sequence was shot on the roof of the Chateau. Catherine, who has been visiting the town of Bellenac spread below the ramparts, swings her car up the drive only to see her two children, watched over by Odile, playing atop the steep roof and along the cornices. She runs up the stairs, sends her children below, and confronts Odile.

"How could you let Jacques do that?" she demands. "How could you? He might have been killed! You know as well as they do that they are not allowed to play up here."

"Christian and I were playing on the roof together here when we were far younger than they are," Odile answers coldly.

"I don't want you seeing my children any more," Catherine tells her. She demands to know if her husband has not spoken with Odile and warned both her and her brother to keep their distance.

"Did he say he would," Odile asks, "did he lie to you? Oh, but you must be used to that by now. Men always lie. Personally, I have no use for them, except for Christian."

While speaking, she deliberately twists the amulet round her neck, causing the reflected sunlight to shine in Catherine's eyes. As she speaks to Catherine, her voice is flat, hypnotic.

"Catherine, what's the matter? Is the sun bothering you? Are you alright? Would you like to go in? You're getting very tired....Would you like to go in?...You're eyes are heavy...very heavy...you must go to sleep...you must go to sleep Catherine...sleep. Careful, Catherine, you might fall....Take my hand."

Catherine is mesmerized, blinded by the light from the amulet, following Odile's voice as the young woman directs her to the edge of the roof. "Odile, help me!" she pleads.

"I am helping you, Catherine," Odile says softly, "I am helping you....Just a few more steps, then you can rest, then you can hold my hand. Take it, Catherine, take it!" As she approaches the edge of the roof, Catherine reaches for the hand, which Odile has held out before the void. On the cornice, Catherine's shoe falls from her foot, spiraling to the courtyard below. Just at that moment, Odile's brother Christian, poised atop a neighboring turret, blows a hunting horn, and the loud noise pierces the spell, saving Catherine from a fall to her death.

After this incident, Odile is confronted by Philippe de Montfaucon, who beats her viciously with a whip. But she ends the scene with a strangely satisfied look on her face, uttering, "You're mad, quite, quite mad," as David Niven retreats.

J. Lee Thompson recalled that Sharon remained the question mark: "She was faced with doing a very big and important part. Could she do it? That was in all our minds. We even agreed that if after the first two weeks Sharon was not quite making it, that we would put her back in cold storage. We started work. Very soon, we all realized that here was a girl who is tremendously exciting. She has that thing that you can't really explain—star projection."[3]

Sharon found the experience a daunting one. "You would think that in three years of studying you would know it all," Sharon told an interviewer, "but the first thing you find out is that you don't. It's almost like going back to school again except that I have the groundwork so when I'm told something now I know how to apply it. And the rest of the cast have been marvelous and helpful."[4]

She was in awe of her co-stars. "Deborah Kerr," Sharon said, "is my idea of an actress, and a woman, and a person, and I learned so much from her...just little things. You know, it takes a long time, and plus, a lot of her things in acting, if you watch, are so smooth, so professional, it's fantastic, really fantastic."[5] Kerr herself declared that, "given the right breaks, and a reasonable amount of luck," she thought Sharon would be a great success.[6]

Niven helped ease her nerves on the set. "When I was younger," Sharon recalled, "I thought, This is the man that I am going to marry, so when he came up, I told him, Well, you know, I had plans on marrying you for many years. He's so suave, and so elegant, and so handsome and witty, and the funny thing about it is I did my first film with him."[7]

For his part, Niven was equally impressed. "Sharon," he declared, "is a great discovery. First of all, she's a fabulously good-looking bird. And she's got all the fun and spark and go. She's a marvelous girl. She's up on cloud nine, Sharon is, and I think she's a very, very good actress, and I think she's obviously going to make a big hit in this picture."[8]

Despite her lack of experience, according to Thompson, she took direction "beautifully. Very soon, she began to realize that the camera was her friend."[9] She seemed at ease, and worked well with the cast. Between takes, she disappeared for promotional photo shoots, or quietly slipped behind the cameras to sneak a cigarette and cup of coffee.

To give the film an authentic feel, the producers hired a rather curious man named Alex Saunders, who dubbed himself "King of the Witches." He was said to be a leading authority on witchcraft and the occult, and advised Calley on several scenes. Later, he would claim that he had initiated Sharon herself as a witch, and that he possessed photographs of her, taken in London at the time, dressed in ritual robes and with occult paraphenalia.[10] However, it seems likely that any such pictures were actually publicity stills from the film. Sharon is not known to have ever evinced more than a passing interest in the occult, in spite of later rumors to the contrary.

After location filming in France was completed, Sharon had to remain in London for post-production work at MGM Studios. "The moment that Sharon appeared on screen in her first rushes," said J. Lee Thompson, "we knew that this wonderful personality was going to make out. I think that this girl is going to be a big, big star."[11]

Filmways had rented a flat in fashionable Eaton Place for Sharon, and she shared it with her female voice coach and a small Yorkshire puppy called Guinness.[12] She spent her days working out at a local gym, or lying under an artificial sun-lamp, tanning herself.[13] In between studio work, she would often disappear to Hyde Park, to watch cricket matches, visit museums or feed the pigeons in Trafalgar Square.

Jay Sebring was forced to return to Los Angeles to take care of business concerns. Before he left London, he asked one of his friends, Victor Lownes, to look after Sharon. Lownes, a tall, handsome and charming man in his early thirties, was the head of Playboy Enterprises in the United Kingdom, and had founded the Playboy Club on London's Park Lane after working closely with Hugh Hefner in the United States.

Roman Polanski later described Victor Lownes as "tough, fast-talking, energetic, self-assertive, outspoken, and—by European standards—brash....Victor gloried in his affluence and connections; to him, entertaining and having fun were all part of the job. He courted celebrities, less for snobbish reasons than because—as he used to say—they had to be more interesting than nonentities or they wouldn't have gotten where they were."[14]

"I vividly remember the first time I met Sharon," Lownes recalls. "She was simply stunning. I saw her, and did an immediate double-take. I've been around a lot of beautiful women before and since, but nobody ever impacted people the way Sharon did. She was completely natural, not caught up on herself, and very smart, which wasn't something you might have expected if you just judged her by her looks. She had the best sense of humor, too, which I think surprised a lot of people. She was sharp, and always got the joke."15

Lownes launched Sharon into the swinging world of 1960s London. Although Sharon was no wide-eyed tourist, she found the atmosphere in London stimulating. Unlike the United States, the British capital seemed poised on the edge of a revolution in music and fashion. The Beatles and the Rolling Stones were fresh, and pirate radio stations perched just outside the territorial limits broadcast new and exciting music to counter the staid conservatism of the BBC. Sharon eagerly threw herself into life here, shopping along King's Road, hunting through used clothing stores in Chelsea and investigating the latest fashions of Mary Quant and other trendy designers who lined both sides of Carnaby Street.

Sharon quickly absorbed London style, dressing herself in leather biker jackets and mini skirts worn with sheer tights and tall go-go boots. She continued to dress for comfort in her private hours, preferring oversized sweaters and sweatshirts worn with sweatpants, but, accompanying Lownes to his stylish parties and the city's fashionable nightclubs, she dressed to make an impact, and those who came into contact with her rarely forget their impressions.

Actress Leslie Caron met Sharon during this time, and quickly befriended her. "I was really very fond of her," she recalls. "She used to come to my house when my children started going to boarding school. She was such a dear, very lovely girl, modest, sincere, with a profound warmth." Caron was struck not only by Sharon's "blinding beauty, and irresistible charm," but also by her reserve and thoughtful nature. "She was very sharp, not a fool, and had a lot of insight into what had happened to her," she says. "But Sharon suffered from mistreatment. On one occasion, she told me that she suffered so much from being pretty. She received a lot of unsympathetic treatment from both women and men. Women would try to steal her men, and despised her beauty, while men were often afraid and ignored her because they feared that they couldn't get her. Sharon wasn't very happy at it."16

Production work on *Eye of the Devil* finally wrapped in early 1965. Rather than immediately returning to America, Sharon asked her friend Wende Wagner to join her in London. For a week, Victor Lownes had charge of the pair, escorting them to parties and to exclusive clubs in Knightsbridge and Soho. "They were having a lot of fun," he remembers, "enjoying the shopping during the day and the party scene at night."17

One day, Lownes arranged to host a small luncheon for the two women, and invited a dozen of his friends, including Polish film director Roman Polanski. Skip Ward, one of Sharon's friends from Hollywood, happened to be in England on a break from shooting his latest film, *Is Paris Burning?*. "I was delayed, and I didn't arrive at Victor's until nearly three that afternoon. By then, the party was almost over. When I walked in, I said hello to Wende, and then noticed that Sharon was sitting next to Polanski. They were deep in conversation. I watched them for quite a while, as they talked and laughed. At the time, I made a mental note that Jay wasn't going to like this."[18]

Chapter 6
Roman

ROMAN POLANSKI WAS BORN ON AUGUST 18, 1933, IN PARIS. As much turmoil and intransigence as Sharon had experienced growing up as an army brat, it was nothing compared to the real life-and-death struggle which young Roman Polanski had been forced to wage.

Roman's father Riczard Polanski worked briefly for a recording studio and then in a factory. He had married a Russian divorcee, Bula Katz, and the pair lived in a shabby apartment in the XIth arrondisement in Paris. In 1936, when the elder Polanski lost his job, he took his wife and three-year old son back to his native Poland, settling in Cracow. It was to prove a fatal mistake.[1]

On September 1, 1939, Hitler's armies invaded Poland. Within a week, they had occupied Cracow. As Jews, the Polanskis were quickly confined to a Nazi-patrolled ghetto. Young Roman was often sent away to hunt through the streets and cellars of the ghetto for food. During one of these trips, the Nazis began to round up members of the ghetto community. Roman returned just in time to see his mother being forcibly dragged away in a flatbed truck crammed with dozens of their friends and neighbors. Bula Polanski motioned for her young son to keep quiet as she disappeared into the grim cortege; a few months later, she was dead, a victim of one of Hitler's concentration camps.

Bula Polanski was rounded up in 1941; soon after, Riczard made arrangements for some Catholic friends to look after Roman if the situation seemed ready to erupt. A place with a safe family in the countryside was assured. As the pace of the Nazi liquidation of Cracow's Jews intensified, Riczard Polanski decided that it was time. He took young Roman to the edge of the ghetto, snipped the barbed wire fence with an old pair of pliers, hugged his son and pushed him through the small hole, toward freedom.[2] He was just in time; a few hours later, the Polanski apartment was one of many raided, and Riczard was rounded up and sent to Mauthausen Concentration Camp.

Roman spent several years living undisturbed in the Polish countryside under the protection of a Catholic family. He had no news of his father or mother. After the liberation of Poland, he ran away from his host family, trying to make his way back to Cracow. Like many other displaced refugees, Roman survived only through the kindness of the Soviet soldiers, who regularly shared their war rations with the starving Poles. At the end of the war, he was finally reunited with his father, who had amazingly survived his internment at Mauthausen. It was only then that he learned his mother had perished. Distraught, father and son took a small apartment together, trying to recover from the shock of the war and to understand what the other had been through. Riczard Polanski eventually remarried, this time to a Catholic named Wanda Zajaczkowska. The remarriage strained the relationship between father and son, and the younger Polanski made several attempts to escape from under his father's roof. In 1953 he graduated from school and decided to enroll in the State Film School in Lodz. Roman had always been interested in motion pictures, their imagery and the ability to escape into an artificial, unreal world. In post-war Poland, with Soviet occupation and little hope for the future, a career in film seemed as good as any other to Roman. He experimented with several student films before finally deciding to focus his attention on directing.

It was at Lodz that Roman made many of the friends who would later follow him to the west and occupy important places in his life and career. This group included Krzystof Komeda, a talented jazz musician and the man who later composed the scores for several of Roman's films; Jerzy Kosinksi, the writer; and Voytek Frykowski, fated to be one of the victims at the Cielo Drive murders in 1969.

Voytek and Roman seemingly had little in common. Voytek's father was reportedly the largest black marketeer in all of Poland, a successful business in post-war Poland which provided his family with all allowable comforts under Soviet rule, and many illegal pleasures to boot.[3] Voytek was not a film student, but rather attended the neighboring polytechnic, where he studied chemistry.[4] Yet he fancied himself as a great artist and far preferred the company of the film school students to the crowd at the academy he himself attended.

Roman was drawn to Voytek's absurd sense of humor and considerable finances. Frykowski, according to his friend, "was good-natured, softhearted to the point of sentimentality, and utterly loyal."[5]

Polanski later referred to his friend as a man of "small talent but immense charm," and Frykowski certainly enjoyed a reputation as a ladies' man.[6] Handsome, tall and something of a trouble-maker at the polytechnic, Voytek was one of the few students who actually owned a car. He graduated with a degree in chemical engineering, but, after meeting Roman, he began to dabble in the arts. Roman welcomed him and his money—which made it possible for him to experiment with his own independent filmmaking—into his intimate circle.[7]

In 1955 Polanski began his first short film, *The Bicycle*. In the end, he abandoned it in favour of a two minute short called *The Crime*, a bizarre and violent view of an apparently unmotivated murder in which one man stabs a sleeping man and then disappears. It was a short glimpse of what was to come—what critic Barbara Leaming has called "key Polanskian obsessions: voyeurism and violence."[8] It is arguable that Polanski's taste for the violent stemmed from his own childhood experiences, where he, as helpless voyeur, was forced to watch the destruction of his family. His mother had been "weak," failing to survive the concentration camp, and Polanski seems to have transferred this perceived frailty to all women he thereafter encountered, often treating them contemptuously as little more than objects. Thereafter, too, Polanski would endlessly repeat romantic triangles in his films, a re-play of his relationship with his mother and father, and of the troubled re-marriage of his father, from which Roman sensed himself excluded.

A number of other films followed *The Crime*, including an evocative short entitled *When Angels Fall*. Polanski began to work under the authority of KAMERA, the state film production company in Warsaw. Working at KAMERA, Polanski met the beautiful Barbara Kwiatkowska, a rising young actress. Basia, as she was called, was soon to become famous in France as Barbara Lass. In 1959, Roman and Basia were married.[9]

Polanski continued to experiment with films, releasing *Two Men and a Wardrobe*, a short concerning the adventures of a pair of men and their struggles to move a heavy armoire. The film was shown in the west and won Polanski some notice, taking third place in the

Brussels Film Festival. His next film, *Mammals*, starred Voytek Frykowski and dealt with two men fighting over possession of a sled. After much pleading, Polanski was finally given permission to undertake his first feature film, *Knife in the Water*, a motion picture which was to enhance his already growing reputation in the west.

Knife in the Water was a careful, menacing film of rising tension between a trio played out upon a sailboat. A husband and wife pick up a passing young man in their boat and a dangerous game of psychological cat and mouse, controlled by the wife and pitting one man against the other, begins. During an argument, the husband pushes the young man—who has insisted all along that he cannot swim—overboard; when he fails to surface, the husband dives into the water to search for him but to no avail. When he returns to the boat, the wife accuses him of deliberately murdering the boy, and tells him to swim ashore to notify the police that an accident has occurred. As soon as the husband disappears, however, the young man now suddenly reappears; he has been hiding behind a nearby buoy, having lied about his swimming ability. He boards the boat and makes love to the wife; when the husband returns to the boat, the young man has again disappeared, but his wife, clearly enjoying her husband's uncomfortable position, gleefully informs him of what has just happened aboard the vessel. The husband is thus offered a choice: either he believes that he himself is a murderer, and lives with the guilt of that act for the rest of his life; or that his wife is a willing adulteress. The film ends with a shot of the husband and wife sitting in a car at a crossroads, unable to decide which way to go.[10]

The film was widely praised and received much international attention. It showed at the New York Film Festival in 1963, after having won the Critics' Prize at the Venice Film Festival earlier that year.[11] It was also nominated for an Academy Award for best foreign film, and Polanski was invited to attend the ceremony in Los Angeles.[12]

Within a few years, Roman had achieved fame, money and a job as a director. At the same time, his private life left something to be desired. His marriage to Basia had fallen apart within a year (she was having an affair with actor Karl Heinz Boehm), and the pair were divorced before Roman achieved his fame in the west. Polanski realized that there was little opportunity in Poland for him, and the country began to represent oppression and the nightmares of his past. With his new wealth and growing reputation, Polanski fled to Paris.

In Paris Polanski developed close professional ties with several other artists involved in the motion picture industry. One friend was Gerard Brach, a screenwriter with whom he eventually scripted both *Repulsion* and *Cul-de-Sac*. Another ex-patriate who moved in Polanski's orbit was Gene Gutowski, a Polish-American producer who had several important contacts in the business.

Gutowski was ten years older than Polanski, a handsome, well-dressed and soft-spoken man who enjoyed sculpting in his spare time.[13] In the mid-1950s, he had come to London to work as an independent film producer.[14] After a failed first marriage, he met and married American model Judy Wilson in 1963, and the pair settled into a comfortable house near Montpellier Square. Gutowski was important to Roman, both for his business ability and also for his fluency in English, a language with which Polanski was still struggling. Together, Polanski and Gutowski formed Cadre Films, a small production company which they hoped would attract big name backers on the basis of Roman's success with *Knife in the Water*.

Eventually, Polanski and Gutowski, through Cadre Films, signed a deal with The Compton Group, a large production company based in England. The Compton Group was eager to finance a horror movie, and Polanski and Gerard Brach completed a script in just over two weeks.[15] The film was *Repulsion*.

If *Knife in the Water* shot Polanski to fame, *Repulsion* cemented his place as a director of international repute. The central character, Carole, was based on a young woman Polanski and Brach had known in Paris, who seemed to be both fascinated and repulsed with any sexual contact.[16] In the film, Carole was played by beautiful French actress Catherine Deneuve. Carole was a beautiful but lonely manicurist living in a London flat with her sister. When her sister brings home a married lover, the sounds of the pair's lovemaking set off within Carole a violent reaction. Her sister and her lover go away on holiday, leaving Carole alone in the flat, as she is gradually overcome with paranoia and hallucinations. During one such attack, she kills a visiting beau by beating him over the head with a candlestick and then dumping his body into the bathtub. She further attacks and kills the landlord after he makes sexual advances toward her. When Carole's sister and her lover return, they find the apartment in complete shambles, two bodies in the bathtub, and Carole laying comatose beneath her sister's bed, hopelessly insane. *Repulsion* opened in London in 1965, having been given a dreaded

X-rating due to the sexual content and the explicit violence.[17] Nevertheless, the film proved to be both a financial and a critical success. At the Berlin Film Festival, it was the Second Place Award winner. The success allowed Polanski to swing directly into his next project with The Compton Group, *Cul-de-Sac*.

Like *Knife in the Water*, *Cul-de-Sac* is a tale of claustrophobic sexual tensions, this time between an older man and his much younger wife who live in an isolated castle. Into their sheltered existence come two wounded criminals, one of whom dies shortly after arriving at the castle. The other criminal, played by Lionel Standers, sets the husband and wife against each other, playing psychological games to amuse himself while waiting to be rescued by the boss of his gang. In the end, the husband, played by Donald Pleasance, is driven to his breaking point and shoots the gangster, just as his wife tries to escape from the island and her husband. And, like *Repulsion*, *Cul-de-Sac* served to enhance Polanski's already considerable reputation as a director of intelligent, bizarre films whose style was matched with substance.

Polanski's reputation soared following the release of *Repulsion*, and he eagerly indulged in the pleasures which his success brought him. Settling in London, he was taken under the wing of Victor Lownes, and could often be found at the Playboy Club, surrounded by a bevy of attractive models. Polanski learned to enjoy the finer things of life: cuisine, vintage wines, fast cars and fashionable clothes.

After so many years of deprivation and struggle, he could finally enjoy the fruits of his hard labors. "At that time," Roman later declared, "I was really swinging. All I wanted to do was fuck a girl and move on....I just liked fucking around."[18] His air of self-assurance irritated many he encountered; one acquaintance described him as "the original five-foot Pole you wouldn't touch anyone with."[19]

"Roman," says a friend, "was very successful with his conquests, and he certainly didn't lack for female company. But I later spoke with several of his girlfriends who told me that sex with Roman wasn't as satisfying as they might have imagined. He wasn't very well-endowed, and I think that surprised a lot of girls, because he came on so strong."[20]

Just after the release of *Repulsion*, but before the final editing process of *Cul-de-Sac*, Polanski met Martin Ransohoff and his partner John Calley at the Dorchester Hotel in London. Ransohoff was impressed with *Repulsion* and asked to view a rough cut of Polanski's still unfinished *Cul-de-Sac*. He liked it so much that he purchased the film for American distribution. Polanski later called Ransohoff, a "terrible Hollywood producer...a creep who makes badly done things...all kinds of shit." Although he later claimed that Ransohoff "seduced me with his artist-like attitude," he was genuinely impressed with both the producer and with Filmways.[21] Ransohoff's track record alone demonstrated his success and, unlike The Compton Group, Filmways had enough financial clout to pull all of the right strings in Hollywood.

After the deal for *Cul-de-Sac* was signed, Gene Gutowski approached one of Ransohoff's associates in London and asked about the possibility of picking up some funding for Polanski's next project. Polanski himself told Ransohoff about a vampire film he had been working on in collaboration with Gerard Brach. Ransohoff was interested and spent several further meetings discussing the idea with the Polish director. Finally, Polanski signed a contract with Filmways to arrange financing of the film through MGM Studios.[22] Polanski, in his enthusiasm at having finally attracted the attention of a major Hollywood producer, allowed Ransohoff to dictate the terms, which included final American cut on the upcoming project. It was a move he would later regret.[23]

Polanski had already decided whom he wished to cast in his new film. Indeed, several of the roles had been specifically written with certain actors in mind. For the main role of Professor Abronsius, the director wanted to cast Jack MacGowan, who had been featured in *Cul-de-Sac*. Polanski himself would play Alfred, the Professor's young assistant. For the role of the innkeeper's daughter and the film's eventual romantic interest Sarah, Polanski wished to cast American actress Jill St. John, with whom he had been briefly linked in the press.[24]

Ransohoff, however, had other ideas. He wanted Sharon Tate cast in the role of Sarah. Polanski knew little of Sharon except for their shared luncheon hosted by Victor Lownes. "I thought she was quite pretty," he later recalled, "but I was not at that time very impressed."[25] After several discussions with Ransohoff, who was adamant on casting Sharon in some role in the project, Polanski finally agreed to meet her again to discuss the film and her acting experience.

Sharon and Roman met over dinner in a quiet restaurant. The evening went badly. Throughout the meal, Sharon, clearly nervous, tried to make polite conversation and impress the director, but Roman remained largely silent, nodding his head and answering her questions with a begrudging "Yes" or "No." At Ransohoff's insistence, she made a second dinner appointment, which went no better. By the end of the evening, she was convinced Polanski was a "weirdo." Walking through Eaton Square afterward, Polanski suddenly turned to Sharon and tried to hug her; instead, both lost their balance and ended up falling into the street. Without a word, Sharon got up and quickly fled to her own flat. "That's the craziest nut I ever saw!" she told Ransohoff. "I'll never work for him!"[26]

But Ransohoff insisted and, with great reluctance, Sharon once again joined Polanski for dinner. This time, however, he warmed to her. If on the previous occasions he had silently scrutinized her appearance and projection, Polanski now was full of questions. In spite of his initially unfavorable first impression, Polanski decided that he had been wrong to dismiss Sharon as just another brainless Hollywood starlet. She answered all of Roman's queries, telling him of her life up to the filming of *Eye of the Devil*; of her acting aspirations; and of her frustration over her parents' fears for her safety.[27]

The conversation eventually turned, through small talk, to the Hollywood drug scene. Sharon admitted that she enjoyed smoking pot when the atmosphere was right, and that Jay had introduced her to LSD, which was at the time still legal in England. "She said she liked it, and that it helped her a lot," Roman recalled.[28] Polanski, in turn, described his three LSD experiences, which had ended disastrously when he crumbled in fits of paranoia. Sharon convinced Roman that he should try another LSD trip that same evening; on their way back to his flat at 95 Eaton Place Mews, Polanski stopped by a friend, actor Iain Quarrier's, house and picked up a cube of sugar laced with acid, for him and Sharon to split between them.[29]

Polanski was in the process of moving in, and his flat was sparsely furnished. As the electricity had not yet been connected, Roman lit a few candles. Sharon and him took the LSD and began to talk. She told Roman of her relationship with Jay and admitted that she felt guilty being at Polanski's flat at all.[30] All the while, she nervously chewed on the tips of her nails. He later recalled: "We spent all night talking, and it was very pleasant."[31]

Roman briefly disappeared; wearing a Frankenstein mask, he crept up behind her and shouted. Sharon was so unnerved at this scare that she sobbed for nearly an hour.[32] "I told you I couldn't take it," Sharon yelled, "and this is the end!" According to Roman, she was "flipping out and screaming, and I was scared to death." She ran out of Polanski's flat and made a dash for her own, just around the corner.[33]

Sharon's reaction may have been both a combination of her hysteria at the childish prank as well as a result of the LSD. Fifteen years later, however, Polanski told a different story. In his memoirs, he declared that, instead of Sharon freaking out on acid and leaving, the pair decided to make love.[34] In 1969, under police questioning, Polanski had said that he and Sharon had not become intimately involved with each other until several months after their first meeting. He even volunteered that they had spent a night together in the same bed. "I knew there was no question of making love with her. That's the type of girl she was."[35]

And, indeed, given Sharon's cautious nature where intimacy was concerned, it seems most unlikely that she would have gone to bed with Polanski on this occasion. What feelings Sharon had for the director were still professional and ambivalent. Perhaps more importantly, it is difficult to imagine her casually disregarding her feelings for Jay Sebring, with whom she was still romantically involved. Her lack of sexual promiscuity, coupled with her own inner strength, reserve and affection for Jay, mitigate against Polanski's later version of events.

That Sharon left Polanski's flat under less-than-ideal circumstances seems to be supported by her subsequent actions where the director was concerned. Sharon broke a date she had made with Polanski for the following day. Polanski rang and made a second date, which she also broke. She clearly seemed angry at the director, and unwilling to see him again.

Polanski was not accustomed to this sort of brush-off. Finally, he again rang, and asked Sharon to dine with him that evening. Sharon again refused, saying that she had to stay in to keep her voice coach happy.[36] "Listen, fuck you!" he told her and hung up. He was clearly irritated, and believed she was playing games with him.[37]

The relationship between Sharon and Roman, not surprisingly, "reverted to a more formal" nature.[38] They saw each other socially, mainly through the parties and orbit of those around Victor Lownes. But Sharon seems to have had little interest in pursuing any relationship with the director, and Polanski was still reluctant to cast her in his film.

Polanski continued to press for Jill St. John, but Ransohoff was becoming increasingly stubborn; after all, he held the purse strings for the project. Finally, according to Mike Mindlin, Ransohoff gave Polanski an ultimatum: "Either you use Sharon, or you don't make the picture for me."[39]

Polanski finally agreed to test Sharon for the new film. She reluctantly came to the studio and Polanski had her fitted with a long red wig to conceal her blonde hair, which did much in the way of convincing him that she could in fact pull off the part.[40] After viewing the test, Polanski rang Ransohoff and agreed to his request to cast Sharon in his film. She was to play Sarah, the innkeeper's daughter and the object of desire for both the film's vampires, led by actor Ferdy Mayne as Count von Krolock, and of Alfred, the young assistant to the famous professor, a role which Polanski had reserved for himself. When the actual production commenced on the film, the on-screen romance of Sarah and Alfred was echoed off-screen by the growing relationship between Sharon and Roman.

Chapter 7
Fearless Vampire Killers

*T*HE *FEARLESS VAMPIRE KILLERS* (ALSO REFERRED TO BRIEFLY AS *Dance of the Vampires* and *Pardon Me, But Your Teeth Are In My Neck*) was intended as a spoof of the vampire horror genre, then very popular at England's Hammer Studios with their various Dracula films starring Christopher Lee. Polanski wrote the screenplay with Gerard Brach. Professor Abronsius, a world famous vampire killer (played by Jack MacGowan) and his assistant Alfred journey to a remote mountain village in search of a vampire cult. At the inn, Alfred first encounters Sarah, the beautiful daughter of the owner (Alfie Bass). She is consumed with a desire to continually bathe, a habit, she says, she picked up at boarding school. He spies on her through a keyhole as she takes a bubble bath in the room next to his, and continues to watch as her father bursts into the room through another door and pulls his daughter from the tub, chastising her for her incessant bathing, and spanking her. Alfred is immediately attracted to her and, the following day, while making a snowman, he looks up to see Sarah watching him from a window in the inn.

Later that night, while the Professor sleeps, Alfred is startled by a knock on his bedroom door. It is Sarah, wearing a white nightgown whose low bodice reveals her generous cleavage.

"I'm not disturbing you, am I?" she asks.

"Not at all, not at all," Alfred mumbles.

"I, I just don't know what to do with myself," Sarah proclaims. "I get so bored. You can't imagine how bored I get. I don't know, I'm just not used to being locked up the whole time."

"You mean you're always locked up?" Alfred asks incredulously.

She nods. "At school—we had fun there. We used to skip over the wall. We did all kinds of things. You know what I mean. Then

Papa, I don't know what happened to Papa. My room...my room is full of garlic. He says it looks pretty."

After shyly flirting with the young assistant, Sarah asks permission to use his bath. "I got into the habit of it at school," she explains. "He's funny, Papa. You just can't change your habits in a couple of months, can you? Besides, its good for your hair. Once a day is the very least, don't you agree?"

Alfred fills the tub for Sarah, who then disappears into the suds. Again, Alfred spies on her through the keyhole. Suddenly, Sarah notices snow falling into her bath and looks up to see the leader of the vampire cult, Count von Krolock, slowly descending from a skylight. He attacks her in her bath, while Alfred, stunned into inaction, continues to watch.

Professor Abronsius and Alfred track von Krolock to his castle high in the mountains, where he has taken Sarah as his captive. After some difficulty, they gain entrance, only to be confronted first by the vampires' hunch-backed servant Kukol (Terry Downes) and then by von Krolock himself and his effeminate son Herbert (Iain Quarrier). The Count bids the pair to stay as his guests, the bumbling professor happily chatting all the while he is plotting their deaths. That evening, Alfred hears Sarah singing in the distance and discovers her in a remote wing of the castle, taking one of her frequent baths. He is forced to leave her for the time being; later, when he again hears her singing and tries to track her down, he returns to the same room, only to find the count's son Herbert, standing in a nightshirt at the side of a bathtub which he is filling with water.

Herbert is clearly interested in young Alfred, Polanski having made the homoerotic theme often found in vampire literature and films blatantly apparent here. Alfred, distraught at being alone with him, tries to flee, but Herbert, the more powerful of the two, makes him sit down beside him on the bed. Alfred has been carrying a small book taken from the castle library, a guide to ways of declaring one's love, in the hopes of meeting Sarah. Herbert takes it from him and begins to read from an entry, placing his arm around Alfred's shoulders as the guide instructs, and brushing his hair with his fingers. Alfred looks up, to see a large pier glass just opposite the bed, but his is the only reflection. He quickly jumps up and thrusts the book into the vampire's open mouth just as Herbert is preparing to attack, and flees through the long castle corridors to find the professor.

After escaping from the vampire's clutches, Alfred tells the professor that a ball is to take place that evening in the castle, a gathering of vampires at which Sarah is to be initiated into the cult. Alfred and the professor disguise themselves as guests and join in the festivities, gradually leading Sarah down the length of the ballroom toward the exit, when they suddenly find themselves before a large mirror. The dance ceases when the vampires notice that these three guests are the only ones in the ballroom to cast reflections. The professor grabs two swords, forming a cross on the floor to guard against a chase, and he, Alfred and Sarah attempt to flee from the castle. A group of vampires escape and pursue the trio, who jump into a waiting carriage and speed down the hill away from the castle, chased by Kukol in an empty coffin he is using as a sled. When Kukol flies off an embankment, it seems that they have escaped. But, in the final scene, with Abronsius driving and Sarah and Alfred in the rear seat, she turns to the young assistant and bites him on the neck, turning him into a vampire, and thus carrying on the cult.

There were numerous difficulties with the pre-production and actual filming of *The Fearless Vampire Killers*. For a British production, it was customary to hire British actors for all parts. Sharon, as an American, had to gain approval of the British Actors' Union before her contract could be formalized. After some lengthy discussions, Equity finally agreed that, as the movie was being financed by an American production company, Sharon could star in the film.[1]

A far bigger problem was the location shooting. Polanski had originally wished to shoot on location at a castle in Austria; a sudden change in the weather melted the required snow, and meant that a new location had to be found. Finally, Polanski settled on Valgardena, a location in the Dolomites, near the Italian ski resort of Ortisei. There was no castle, however, so one had to be constructed on the back lot at the MGM Studios at Borehamwood for later scenes.[2]

Sharon arrived in Italy in the midst of a snow storm. Filming took place at the height of Ortisei's ski season, so the cast and crew took rooms where they could, dispersed between a number of hotels and chalets. There was much outdoor filming, when the weather allowed, and when not, actors huddled in their hotels. During location filming, Sharon's fluency in Italian made her invaluable as a translator.

The invasion of cast and crew thoroughly disrupted the relaxed pace of life at Ortisei. Polanski had ordered dozens of coffins made by local craftsmen. Tourists, unaware that a vampire movie was being filmed, were shocked to discover that, instead of hand-carved clocks and other souvenirs, the wood shops were filled with caskets. No one knew if an epidemic had erupted, or a landslide swept away a neighboring village, but the resulting flight of dozens of tourists inspired local hotels to post messages explaining the filming and assuring customers that no danger threatened.[3]

Sharon found Polanski a demanding director. *In Eye of the Devil,* she had easily managed to accomplish what she had been given to do. But her role as Sarah in *The Fearless Vampire Killers,* apparently just as uncomplicated, was made more difficult by Roman's quest for perfection. No matter how hard she tried, no matter how many takes she underwent, she quickly found that it was never enough. Polanski constantly picked her scenes apart, forcing her to do shoot after shoot: he later recalled that in one scene he had done over seventy takes before being satisfied with Sharon's performance.[4]

Although she would later come to accept this sort of behavior as typical of the demanding Polanski, Sharon was deeply hurt and humiliated. Mike Mindlin, Filmways' Vice President of Advertising, happened to be in Ortisei during the filming, and recalls: "Sharon used to come to my hotel room at night, and cry on my shoulder because of the way Roman had treated her. She was so sweet, and it was very hard for her to take."[5]

After several weeks, Sharon learned how to accept Polanski's criticism, and how to best respond to his direction. As her self-confidence returned, Roman found himself increasingly drawn to her. At the end of each day's shoot, they began to spend more and more time together. This led to problems on the set. Although there was never any expressed anger, certain elements among the cast and crew were jealous of the time and attention, not to mention the favor, which Sharon received. She, in turn, was acutely aware that eyes were focused on her, and strove to prove herself worthy.

In time, the relationship between Sharon and Roman intensified. They had seen each other off and on during the pre-production work in London, but, in Italy, things eventually became serious.[6] Her feelings for Jay, whom she had not seen for almost six months, had faded, replaced at first with curiosity of, and then attraction to, Roman himself. Unlike Jay, Roman had no thoughts of marrying or settling down: his style of life was exciting, filled with opportunities for exploration and peopled with a charismatic, cosmopolitan mixture of actors, artists and celebrities who eagerly sought his favor.

Her decision, when it came, was quick. One night, Roman knocked
on Sharon's hotel room door and asked shyly, "Would you like to
make love with me?" and she replied "Yes," leading him inside to
her bed.[7] From that moment, the pair were inseparable, director and
actors on screen, lovers at night.

Chapter 8
The Beautiful People

AFTER FILMING IN ITALY, THE CAST AND CREW OF *THE FEARLESS Vampire Killers* returned to the MGM Studios at Borehamwood to finish post-production work. But prolonged shooting in Italy meant that the production was over-schedule, and they had to move first to Elstree Studios, then to Pinewood Studios, in order to complete most of the interior work.[1]

In London, the relationship between Sharon and Roman grew more serious, much to the surprise of their mutual friends. Judy Gutowski, wife of Roman Polanski's business partner Gene, was on friendly terms with both Roman and Sharon, eventually becoming one of the latter's confidantes. When she first met Sharon, Judy Gutowski recalls that she expected her to "be nothing more than just another beautiful and not-too-bright American girl. But she surprised me—she turned out to be rather remarkable. In a way, she was naive. But she also had this tremendous unaffectedness and sense of decency and loyalty that really impressed people. She never bad-mouthed anyone and was completely free of the neurotic ambitions one usually associates with actresses."[2]

As impressed as she was with Sharon's character, however, Judy Gutowski sensed an inner turmoil, a need to be both accepted and dominated by men, a frailty she ascribed to Sharon's insecurity.

Polanski was not a very likely candidate as Sharon's ideal mate: scarcely conventionally handsome, only five-feet-five inches tall, Polanski seemed even shorter at the side of Sharon. His frequent bursts of temper did little to endear him to those unaccustomed to dealing with his difficult and demanding manner. But part of the allure Polanski held for Sharon, at least in the beginning of their relationship, was his powerful aura. Not only in business but in his personal life as well, Polanski had demonstrated a determined persistence to accomplish whatever he set out to do. In this, he mirrored Sharon's own determination to succeed despite overwhelming obstacles, and this shared strength drew the pair together.

"It's very difficult to describe Roman," Sharon once declared. "He's...well, the first thing you notice about him, is HIM. No bits or pieces; he just comes at you in one dynamic blast. If I had to break it down, he's very sympathetic, very sensitive, very intelligent, very understanding, and a combination of explosives. He's a very strong man. I mean, mentally. Because physical looks and that stuff don't mean that much to me. I would say that Roman is interesting-looking...and you don't dwell any further on that because of the kind of person he is."[3]

Polanski, of course, was also surrounded by a sense of worldliness which many women found intensely attractive. He possessed a certain boyish charm, which often helped him out of uncomfortable situations. But he was also abrasive, always on guard against any drop in his carefully contrived image. Worse still, he had the reputation of being a relentless womanizer, of using and then casting aside countless conquests. Polanski seemed to regard most women as little more than inferior objects, provided for his sexual pleasure. "I have a very firm theory about male and female intelligence," Roman declared in 1971. "It causes an absolute outrage if you say that women on the average are less intelligent than men, but it happens to be true....I must admit that I rarely find an intelligent female companion with whom I can get along....I do dominate them. And they like it!"[4]

Not surprisingly, Sharon found this intimidating. According to John Bowers, who interviewed her in 1967 for *The Saturday Evening Post*, she "wondered if tonight she would be thrown with people who would overwhelm her with their wit, their awesome knowledge, their self-confidence. When she was out in public with Roman, she never felt adequate enough to open her mouth."[5]

Sharon, Polanski would later declare, "was an extremely bright person. But she would never be pushy about her intelligence in order to show people how clever she was. She knew it's feminine to not try to compete with men and seem dominating."[6]

Eager to please, Sharon quickly learned the rules of a relationship with Polanski. "She was so sweet and so beautiful," he later said, "that I didn't believe it....I'd had bad experiences and I didn't believe that people like that existed, and I was waiting a long time for her to show her color....But she was beautiful, without this phoniness. She was fantastic. She loved me. She was a fucking angel....I was living in a different house. I didn't want her to come to my house. And she would say, 'I don't want to smother you. I only want to be with you.'...And I said, 'You know how I am; I screw around.' And she said, 'I don't want to change you.' She was ready to do everything, just to be with me."[7]

Gradually, Sharon's clothes, books, and personal belongings ended up in Roman's flat around the corner from her own apartment. Roman was uneasy about the growing depth of the relationship. It all spoke loudly of commitment, something he had strenuously tried to avoid since the break-up of his marriage to Basia in 1962. Yet Sharon managed to convince him that she could accept his style of life. When she suggested that they make the move toward a stronger bond, he eventually agreed.[8] In April, 1967, Sharon moved the last of her belongings to his house at No. 95 Eaton Place Mews. Ironically, the house was located just doors away from No. 46 Lower Belgrave Street, where, in 1974, John Bingham, Lord Lucan, is thought to have murdered his children's nanny, mistaking her for his wife Veronica.

Roman had originally asked Krzystof Komeda's wife Zofia to help him decorate the house. "But it turned out our tastes were not the same," she remembered. "I wanted to make it macho: leather and fur covers, mirrors everywhere. So he did it himself, with crystal handles, and the bath was black, sunk into the floor—it was the first time I had seen anything like it in my life."[9] In the drawing room, a couch and chairs competed for floor space with unpacked boxes of books and clothing. A large, expensive stereo sat in one corner, surrounded by stacks of records—everything from Bach to The Beatles and The Rolling Stones. Two busts stood side by side, one of Polanski, the other of Napoleon. There were no pictures or paintings, only a framed citation for Polanski's film *Knife in the Water*. Upstairs, in the large bedroom reached by a spiral staircase, stood an enormous bed Polanski had purchased with the help of Judy Gutowski.[10] The whole place, according to one visitor, had a "transient look, as if the tenants would only be there for a short time."[11]

Polanski was a demanding paramour, but Sharon seemed more than eager to please. An interviewer from *The Saturday Evening Post* later described how, after a day out, Roman came home, walked into the kitchen and went for a drink, only to find the refrigerator filled with beer and vodka. "Sharon! Sharon!" he called out in his somewhat stilted English. "There's no liquor here! Always see to it that we have enough whiskey! Can't you do that?" A few minutes later, he went upstairs to take a bath. Soon, he began to cry again, "Sharon! Sharon!" This time he wanted her to bring him some tea. Surprisingly, Sharon didn't seem to mind his demanding treatment, relishing the role of housewife.[12]

"Of course Roman and I live together!" she once said. "Well, how else is a person going to get to know a person? Now, you answer that? How else? Modern has nothing to do with it. I think it's only realistic....I'm not ashamed for anyone to know what I do—my parents or anybody else."[13]

Sharon was genuinely happy in London, living with Roman and enjoying the life which went with his stardom. She cooked for him, hosted parties for his friends, and managed to keep him satisfied.[14] "We used to wander round the city," recalls one of Sharon's friends, "shopping for clothes at Granny Takes a Trip or Indica, and lunching at Alvaro's. She seemed content, really at peace, and very much in love. All day long, she would talk about what Roman had done, who he was seeing, what they were planning for that evening. I've never seen someone so completely absorbed with another person."[15]

"There are so many talented young people with fantastic original ideas here," Sharon declared of London. "The Mod Look, the long, straight hair for girls and long hair for boys, mini-skirts...it all started here and eventually got to America. Americans are too inhibited but they are slowly coming around to realizing what a swinging world we live in."[16]

For a time, life in London was an enchanted, psychedelic dream, and Sharon and Roman stood at its very apex. They were always in demand at parties and premiers, she attired in fashionable miniskirts and boots while he sported Regency finery. They moved in the "rich hippy" circles that included members of The Beatles, The Who, The Rolling Stones and London film society. Hashish, LSD and pot flowed freely through this privileged world of Nehru jackets and love beads, spurring innovative music and a rush of creativity. "The bright young generation in London," Sharon declared, "are a bunch of free-thinkers who are feeling their way through life and leaving an impression on the times."[17]

Sharon shone brightly in this world. "Wearing an abbreviated miniskirt," declared one reporter, "she seems to enjoy the commotion she causes wherever she goes. Sharon also affects thick, black, false eyelashes, brown eye shadow around her lips, and long ash-blonde hair that falls freely about her shoulders. Her presence in a crowd is as insignificant as a floodlight in a blackout."[18]

With such intense publicity, Sharon worried that word of her affair with Roman would leak back to Jay. Eventually, she made up her mind and told Sebring that their relationship had come to an end. "Before Roman I guess I was in love with Jay," she told a friend. "It was a fine relationship but the truth is I was no good for Jay. I'm not organized. I'm too flighty. Jay needs a wife and, at twenty-three, I'm not ready for wife-hood. I still have to live, and Roman is trying to show me how."[19]

To her friend Sheilah Wells back in Hollywood, Sharon declared in a letter: "I was very sad about breaking up with Jay but it just wasn't fair to him, plus I knew it wasn't the right romance. I didn't want to hurt him and I tried to keep it going. I just couldn't fool myself, so I thought it wiser to tell him."[20]

On hearing the news, Jay flew to London, hoping to talk Sharon out of her decision. He again asked her to marry him, but Sharon gently refused, telling him that she loved Roman, and that their previous relationship was over. Jay quizzed her at some length, as if to ensure himself that she was truly happy. "He wasn't entirely convinced," recalls a friend, "and so Sharon arranged for Jay to meet Roman, against the latter's wishes."[21]

The following night, dining with Sharon at Alvaro's, Roman was startled to see her waving across the room to her former lover, who had been sitting at a table in the shadows. At Sharon's signal, Jay joined them, kissing her and shaking Roman's hand.

"I just wanted to meet you," Jay told the director. Roman was distinctly uncomfortable, as Jay began to question him about his past, his feelings for Sharon and their future together.[22] Finally, Sebring seemed satisfied, telling Roman, "I dig you, man, I dig you."[23]

From that moment on, although their former romance came to an end, Jay became an important part of Sharon and Roman's intimate circle of friends. He took his replacement by Roman graciously, but many of his friends knew that he was still in love with Sharon. When he died, he was still wearing her high school ring.[24]

Chapter 9
Don t Make Waves

A
FTER WORK WAS COMPLETED ON *THE FEARLESS VAMPIRE KILLERS*, Martin Ransohoff contacted director Alexander Mackendrick, who was busy in Hollywood working on a new comedy, a spoof of the Southern California beach movies which had been all the rage for the last several years. The film, *Don't Make Waves*, had a secondary part for a female skydiver called Malibu. Originally, Julie Newmar was cast in the role, but canceled after she found the physical requirements too demanding. Ransohoff instead decided to cast Sharon.

Don't Make Waves starred Tony Curtis, and was based on the Ira Wallach novel *Muscle Beach*. Curtis played tourist Carlo Cofield who, while visiting Malibu, unwittingly became embroiled with a stunning former actress named Laura (Claudia Cardinale) whose last movie, having been filmed in Aroma-Rama, had led to the end of her career. A series of romantic triangles ensued, between Curtis, Cardinale and Robert Webber, who played her boyfriend; between Cardinale, Webber and Joanna Barnes, who played Webber's wife; and between Curtis, Sharon and David Draper, the former Mr. Universe who was cast in the role of Malibu's body-builder boyfriend Harry.

For most of the film, Sharon appeared in a bikini, and her physical attributes were certainly exploited to their fullest. Although she seemed not to mind, she did dislike the degree of intimacy the script required between her character Malibu and David Draper. One scene called for her to rub oil all over his back. "Treat him like a horse!" director Mackendrick told her. "Pat him just as you would an animal." Sharon complied, but, when Mackendrick yelled "Cut!" she dropped the bottle of oil and muttered a very audible "Ugh!" in front of the crew.[1]

Don't Make Waves was also the most physically demanding role Sharon had yet played. In one scene, Curtis arranges for Malibu, who is also a skydiver, to make a jump into the swimming pool of a beach house as part of a publicity stunt. Although Sharon was doubled for the stunt, Mackendrick arranged for both her and Curtis, under the supervision of Leigh Hunt (the sky-diving expert), to don the appropriate gear and hang on the skids of the plane, high above the ground, while cameras rolled to capture the moment before the dive. For Sharon, who hated to fly and was scared of heights, this was an ordeal.

She suffered further still from the film's final scene. Mackendrick had rented the house of TV producer Eliott Lewis, perched high on a cliff overlooking the beach at Malibu. In the film's climactic scene, a mudslide sweeps through the house, knocking it first on its side, then upside down, before finally cascading down the hill and into the ocean. Two interiors were constructed on an MGM soundstage: one mounted on rockers, to allow for the action of the slide; and the other built upside-down. In the mudslide scene, Sharon, Curtis, Cardinale and Draper all suffered severe bruising as they were thrown back and forth against the walls and furniture of the moving set.[2]

"Sharon was such a beautiful young woman," recalled Curtis. At the time, Curtis was lonely and depressed, in the midst of a divorce, and Sharon tried to be supportive throughout the filming process. "She reached out to me," he remembered, "but she was not a verbal person and neither was I."[3]

Her status had improved somewhat since her first major role in Ransohoff's production *Eye of the Devil.* Sharon now had her own trailer on the film set, and her name was used along with those of her two co-stars to promote the film on billboards and posters. Her role, too, had more screen time than any of her previous work. She was a natural on the California beach, in her element, beautiful in a polka-dot blouse, unbuttoned low throughout the film to reveal her generous cleavage. For her work on *Don't Make Waves,* Sharon was paid a very respectable $750 a week.[4]

She missed Roman terribly. In letter after letter to her lover in London, Sharon described the progress on her new film; her longing for Roman; and the smallest details of her daily life without him, including the proud boast that she had stopped biting her fingernails.[5] She proudly told a reporter that she never socialized with men when away from Roman; when she went out to dinner, or to go see a film, it was always with a group of girlfriends, or with her maid. She spent most of her evenings quietly, walking along the Santa Monica beach at sunset, doing needlework, or reading *The History of Philosophy* by Will Durant.[6]

The only bonus to being in California again, as far as Sharon was concerned, was being close to her family. Her father, having been stationed in Korea doing Army Intelligence work for the Vietnam War prosecution, had been reassigned to Fort Barry near San Francisco. Sharon was able to visit her parents and her two younger sisters, Debbie and Patti, who provided a relative balance to the stresses of her career.

Although she had been a formidable influence in helping Sharon pursue her career, Doris Tate constantly worried about her daughter. On one trip home, she greeted Sharon with, "Have you had your blood count recently, honey? You look so pale to me...." Nevertheless—and in spite of her fears for Sharon's well-being in Hollywood—Doris, when asked about the films and her daughter's relationship with Roman Polanski, declared, "You know, I don't care—just as long as she's happy."[7]

Director Alfred Hitchcock had turned down the opportunity to film Ira Levin's novel *Rosemary's Baby* just before its publication early in 1967. Instead, William Castle quickly purchased the rights for a meager $150,000.[8] Castle, a producer and director responsible for gimmicky, low-budget thrillers like *Homicidal, Macabre* and *The Tingler*, at first secured Paramount Picture's agreement to both produce and direct. But Robert Evans, Paramount's Vice-President in Charge of Production, realized that, for all of Castle's success, *Rosemary's Baby* would almost certainly fall into the same B-grade category as his other films simply by nature of Castle's involvement if he went ahead with the existing deal. Castle himself could not be displaced; but, rather than producing and directing, Evans asked Castle to let him hire a new director. Roman Polanski was his choice.

In the end, it was Castle's decision. At first, he was reluctant to accept the off-beat Polish director as a replacement. But, eventually—and after several weeks of discussion—Castle agreed to Polanski as director. Roman telephoned Sharon's agent at William Morris to negotiate the contract between Paramount Studios and Cadre Films. In addition to *Rosemary's Baby*, Polanski agreed to direct at least two further films for Paramount. At the time, no one guessed how successful *Rosemary's Baby* would become, and Polanski was given a flat fee of $150,000 to write and direct, with no residual payments on further profits.[9]

The multi-picture deal meant that Sharon and Roman needed to have a permanent residence in Los Angeles. While Roman remained in London packing their things, Castle helped Sharon with the search. He thought he knew the perfect house. Located along Ocean Front Highway, at 1038 Palisades Beach Road, it had been built by architect Paul Crawley for silent screen star Norma Talmadge in the 1920s; later, it was occupied by actors Cary Grant and Randolph Scott during their romantic liaison; by Howard Hughes; Irving Berlin; and by Princess Grace of Monaco during her visits to Hollywood after her marriage.[10] A large, Norman-style mansion, with its own walled garden and swimming pool, corner tower and steeply-sloped roof, the house overlooked the length of Santa Monica Beach and the Pacific Ocean beyond. A large spiral staircase swept up to the second floor, where the sloped-and-beamed-ceiling master bedroom—"the size of a small ballroom," in the words of writer Roland Flamini—opened to a bathroom tiled in lotus flower Malibu Pottery tiles.[11] When Grant had married heiress Barbara Hutton, she had installed a replica of the dining room at Maxim's in Paris, complete with mirrored walls and leather banquettes.[12] The atmosphere was, as Roman recalled, "Hollywood film set of the thirties."[13]

"Sharon," Castle recalled, "loved the house and felt that it would be just right. Later that afternoon, Sharon Tate, barefoot, stood on the beach, gazing at the ocean. Sunlight filtering through her honey-blonde hair; her eyes danced with excitement. "It's perfect...Roman and I will be so happy here."[14] She managed to convince Roman—who at first thought the place was too extravagant—to sign a lease with the owner, actor Brian Aherne.

Having settled in, Roman soon faced an unavoidable obstacle: one day, Sharon's parents—her father home from Korea—arrived at the Palisades Beach Road property unannounced to meet him. Polanski was beside himself with nerves, but both Paul and Doris Tate seemed to accept their daughter's relationship with the famous Polish director and soon Roman was at ease, chatting happily in his broken English with Paul Tate. With them, they had brought a housewarming gift: a Yorkshire terrier puppy, to replace the one Sharon had had in London. Roman decided to name the new dog

Dr. Saperstein, one of the principal characters in *Rosemary's Baby*.[15]

Polanski later described Sharon's parents as "cordial, but rather boring. Her father I liked very, very much. Her mother was very warm toward me, and very sympathetic, but she was too much for Sharon and for me in a way, kind of peddling mysticism....Her father was a lovely man. I think they loved me."[16]

Roman's father and stepmother Wanda also came to visit the new house in Santa Monica. Roman was even more uncomfortable with this visit than he had been with Sharon's parents. The Polish couple criticized the weather, the food and the luxurious lifestyle in which Roman seemed to have been caught up. Sharon, however, managed to save the day by hauling out a couple of marijuana joints and getting Polanski's stepmother Wanda stoned.[17]

Polanski spent several months writing the screenplay for the new film. He was so impressed by Levin's novel that he stayed rather faithfully to the written text. Then, with the script completed, he turned his attentions to casting the picture.

At first, Roman considered casting Sharon as Rosemary. But, after some thought, he felt it would be wrong of him, as director, to suggest his live-in girlfriend to Paramount; instead, he hoped that someone at Paramount would raise the possibility. Sharon fit Levin's description of Rosemary well, and, among themselves, she and Roman went so far as to discuss how the role might be played. But no one at Paramount ever suggested Sharon Tate as the star of the film.[18]

Instead, Sharon suggested her friend Tuesday Weld, best known at the time for her roles as Thalia on television's *Dobie Gillis*, for *Cincinnati Kid*, *Pretty Poison*, and *Lord Love A Duck*. But Castle and Paramount began to actively promote young actress Mia Farrow, daughter of actress Maureen O'Sullivan and recent star of television's popular soap opera "Peyton Place". All Polanski knew of her was that she had recently married Frank Sinatra, a relationship which had been the subject of innumerable gossip headlines due to the differences in their ages. When Polanski met Mia, he was taken with her quiet vulnerability, and agreed to cast her at once.[19]

Any number of actors—Laurence Harvey, Warren Beatty, Jack Nicholson and Robert Redford—were considered for the part of Rosemary's husband Guy.[20] Eventually, and somewhat reluctantly,

Polanski cast John Cassavetes. Neither Polanski nor Cassavetes had much liking or respect for the other, however, and frequent shouting matches between the temperamental pair erupted on the set of the film. "You just try to keep alive with Roman," Cassavetes told Hollywood correspondent Jack Hamilton in an interview on the set, "or you go under. Ask him why he's so obsessed by the bloody and the gruesome, behaving like some kid in a candystore."[21] Ruth Gordon and Sidney Blackmer were cast as the wickedly dark-humored neighbors who are actually the leaders of the Satanic coven.

Sharon and Roman spent much time discussing elements of the script, including the famous dream sequence during which Rosemary is raped by Satan. The scene was developed from bits and pieces of their own dreams, together with experiences they had had while under the influence of LSD.[22] The end result was one of the film's most chilling moments.

This dream sequence caused numerous problems on the set, most notably with Mia Farrow. When Frank Sinatra heard about the nudity involved, he firmly refused to let her do it. The conflict was but one example of the increasingly tense marriage between the older Sinatra and the younger Farrow. Sharon and Roman joined the Sinatras at their Beverly Hills house for dinner on several occasions, and also accompanied them to Sinatra's Palm Springs compound, where they spent the weekends discussing the film. It was obvious from these brief domestic glimpses that all was not well. Sinatra only seemed happy when he was alone with Roman, discussing women and his love life over a cocktail.[23]

Rosemary's Baby was, at the time, receiving a great deal of advance publicity, and Sinatra seemed jealous of the attention directed toward his young wife. He was waiting for Mia to finish shooting *Rosemary's Baby* before beginning his own film, *The Detective.* When shooting on *Rosemary's Baby* went over schedule, Sinatra demanded that Farrow simply walk off the set to join him. She refused during a screaming match on the set—one of the many battles waged by the couple before those on the Paramount sound-stages.[24]

When Farrow, anticipating her character Rosemary, had her hair cut short by Vidal Sassoon—surrounded by hoards of newspaper and television reporters eager for the publicity—Sinatra was furious, exploding in anger just as her on-screen husband Guy had been scripted to do when he saw his wife's new hairstyle. Things finally reached bottom when, as Mia was preparing to shoot a party scene for the latter half of the film, Sinatra's lawyers arrived at her trailer on the sound stage and delivered papers announcing that Sinatra had begun divorce proceedings against her.[25]

Farrow was shattered; from that moment, both Sharon and Roman took the fragile, depressed Mia under their collective wings, and she quickly became one of their closest friends. "Like the princess in a fairy tale, Sharon was as sweet and good as she was beautiful," Farrow recalled. "Generously they invited me into their lives, and since I now had none of my own, I gratefully spent my weekends with them."[26] She later called Sharon "as pure and sweet a human being as I have ever known."[27]

Roman was interviewed by *Look* magazine prior to the film's American release. When asked about the violence in his previous films, he replied caustically, "It excites me to shock. I like to shock bourgeois audiences who cannot accept that other people may be different from them."[28] While Polanski admitted to a certain eccentricity in his favorite subject matter, he believed that it was all only a part of the creative process. "I'm nuts," he declared. "And Mia, too. There are 127 varieties of nuts. She's 116 of them. That may be the reason she's so charming; I never have trouble with her....Only nuts are the interesting people. There's nothing more boring than normal men. Fortunately, show business is full of nut cases. Maybe there is the reason I so much enjoy working in the film industry."[29]

During one break in filming Mia heard Roman and John Cassavetes having a rather curious discussion. "Roman was discoursing about the impossibility of long-term monogamy given the brevity of a man's sexual attraction for any one woman. An impassioned John Cassavetes responded that Roman knew nothing about women, or relationships, and that he, John, was more attracted than ever to his wife, Gena Rowlands. Roman stared at him and blinked a few times, and for once had no reply."[30]

There was to be one lingering consequence of the film. For the role of Satan, Roman had cast Anton LaVey, High Priest of the San Francisco-based Church of Satan. LaVey, seen briefly in the dream sequence, was a peculiar, rather intimidating man who carefully cultivated an aura of evil. His role in the film brought both him and his Church a great deal of publicity, drawing followers and the curious alike. Ironically, one of those who flocked to his San Francisco Church was a young woman named Susan Atkins; in just two years, she would help stab Sharon to death.

Chapter 10
Valley of the Dolls

I N 1966, AUTHOR JACQUELINE SUSANN HAD PUBLISHED A NOVEL called *Valley of the Dolls*. It chronicled the lives of three career women trying to achieve fame and fortune in the entertainment industry, and the sordid world into which they fell as their careers advanced or declined. The central character, Anne Welles, comes to New York City, where she lands a job with a theatrical agent. When she takes some papers to a theatre for an aging Broadway star, Helen Lawson, to sign, she meets Neely O'Hara, a talented young singer working with Lawson on a show, and Jennifer North, a buxom showgirl, whose career is controlled by her physical attributes. The lives and careers of these three women—Anne, Neely and Jennifer—with their successes, failures, drug addiction, illnesses, suicides and romances, are thereafter linked. Anne, based roughly on Jacqueline Susann herself, suffers through the trauma of several unhappy, thwarted relationships with various men while achieving fame as a model. Neely, a character modeled on the career of Judy Garland, gains great fame but falls victim to drug and alcohol dependency, alienating all of those around her with her tantrums and breakdowns. And Jennifer, having only her beauty to forward her career, suffers a series of terrible disasters before taking her own life. It was all high, soap-opera-style melodrama, considered laughably and unbelievably bad even by the most generous of the critics in the mid 1960s. Nevertheless, the book was a hit, and there was every expectation that it would transfer to screen as a blockbuster of major proportions.[1]

Twentieth Century Fox Studios bought the rights to the novel in 1966 and immediately set about scripting the film version. Because the book had been completed—that, to ensure the quality of the production, no one would be cast unless they first auditioned and

undertook a screen test. This was unheard of behavior on the part
of a major studio in Hollywood, and it sent shockwaves through the
acting community, with both actors and actresses declaring that it
was beneath their dignity to audition for any screen role.[3] But the
studio was adamant, and it is some testament to her presence and
talent that Sharon, auditioned and tested, won the part of Jennifer
over several other better-known actresses.

Sharon wanted the part badly. Ransohoff, who still held her
under contract to Filmways, willingly lent her to Twentieth Century
Fox for the duration of the filming. She had few illusions about the
quality of either the book or the production, and complained that it
was really an "exploitation" picture. But she hoped that the film,
with a major studio pushing it and the attendant publicity, would
establish her as a serious actress and enhance her visibility and name
recognition in Hollywood.

"Since the book was a runaway bestseller," Sharon said, "I was
sure the leading roles would go to big name stars. You know, like
Natalie Wood, or somebody like that. But I was just thrilled to get
the role, I liked Jennifer as I read the book. I think she is the most
sympathetic girl in the group. She's sweet, unspoiled and unselfish.
She doesn't mean anyone any harm, and yet terrible things keep
happening to her."[4]

The character of Jennifer North could almost have been written
with Sharon Tate in author Jacqueline Susann's mind: "The girl was
undeniably beautiful. She was tall, with a spectacular figure. Her
white dress, shimmering with crystal beads, was cut low enough to
prove the authenticity of her remarkable cleavage. Her long hair was
almost white in its blondeness. But it was her face that held Anne's
attention, a face so naturally beautiful that it came as a startling contrast to the theatrical beauty of her hair and figure. It was a perfect
face with a fine square jaw, high cheekbones and intelligent brow.
The eyes seemed warm and friendly, and the short, straight nose
belonged to a beautiful child as did the even white teeth and little-
girl dimples. It was an innocent face, a face that looked at everything
with breathless excitement and trusting enthusiasm, seemingly
unaware of the commotion the body was causing. A face that
glowed with genuine interest in each person who demanded attention, rewarding each with a warm smile."[5]

Costume designer Travilla, who had dressed Marilyn Monroe
and Elizabeth Taylor, later remembered that his fittings with Sharon

had left an indelible impression. "Sharon Tate is divine, a real find," he said. "Just wait and see what happens when the critics and pubic see her in *Valley of the Dolls*. Sharon has everything Marilyn Monroe had—and more! She has this fascinating, yet wholly feminine strength of a Dietrich or a Garbo...a classically beautiful face, an exciting figure, the kind of sex appeal and personality appeal to become as glittering a star as Bette Davis, Joan Crawford, Rita Hayworth, Lana Turner, Elizabeth Taylor...."[6]

Shooting *Valley of the Dolls* proved to be an ordeal. The director, Mark Robson, had at first attempted to sign Candice Bergen, Raquel Welch and Ann-Margret in the three principal roles, but none of these actresses were interested in the venture. Judy Garland was hired for the part of Helen Lawson, a peripheral character, but, three days into the actual shooting, Garland was fired, apparently because she was secretly drinking and taking pills in her trailer before each scene.[7] The character of Neely O'Hara had been based on Garland's up-and-down career, and Garland herself would soon be dead from a drug overdose. Instead, Susan Hayward was signed to take on the role, and production, stalled for a few days, proceeded.

Barbara Parkins was cast in the principal role of Anne Welles, with Patty Duke—fresh from her lengthy stint as the star of television's *The Patty Duke Show*—cast as Neely O'Hara. Like their on-screen counterparts, these two women formed a close friendship with the third, Sharon. The friendships were important, for they helped the women to survive the turbulent days on the set of the film.

During the filming, Hollywood gossips filled their magazines with stories of on-set fights, jealousy and revenge. Sharon unwittingly seemed to be at the center of most. One reporter described the filming of a love scene between Barbara Parkins and Paul Burke: "The people in the background were hushed. Just then Sharon, who happened to be among the bystanders, began to move by shifting her weight from leg to leg. Just that. But the men noticed, and the attention was taken away from Barbara. One of the people present that day chuckled as he recalled: 'The idea that Miss Tate, with clothes on, was getting more attention than Miss Parkins, writhing nude in bed under hot lights, must have made every smile a tough job of acting for Barbara.'"[8]

The chief problem on the set was the director himself. Mark Robson, wrote Patty Duke, "was someone who used humiliation for effect, who could be insulting about your physical appearance and who wouldn't hesitate to bite your head off in front of everyone."[9] While Robson directed some of this hostility toward Duke and Parkins, he apparently saved the lion's share for Sharon Tate, who, being the quietest and most inexperienced of the three, was the least likely to stand up to him.

"She was a gentle, gentle creature—you could be mean to her and she would never retaliate," Patty Duke later recalled. "I was crazy about her and I didn't know anyone but our director who wasn't. What's to dislike? She was an exquisitely beautiful girl who was so comfortable with her beauty that you weren't intimidated by it. Robson, however, continually treated her like a imbecile, which she definitely was not, and she was very attuned and sensitive to this treatment."[10]

Some of Robson's instructions to Sharon were truly humiliating. In one scene, for example, he demanded that Sharon enter on her right foot and say "Hi," before moving to her left foot to say the next line and back and forth, foot to line. "It was truly demeaning," Patty Duke recalled, "like the old, 'Can she walk and chew gum at the same time?' line." In another scene, Robson continually badgered Sharon about the way she walked and sat; after several hours of this, Sharon finally broke down and fled the set in tears. Only Duke and Parkins were able to calm her down enough to finish the scene in the way Robson demanded.[11]

Although the role of Jennifer relied more on Sharon's beauty than her ability as an actress, she was determined to wrest something from the part. In an interview during the film's production, Sharon went to great lengths to dismiss the idea that Jennifer was simply a sex symbol. "I don't go into the person as thinking of her as just sexy," she explained. "I would stop and I would think, well, how is she mentally, and what moves this into that, and therefore I don't really think...of the character as being a sex symbol or a sex goddess or whatever you'd like to call it."

"I learned a great deal about acting in this film," Sharon told one interviewer, "particularly in my scenes with Lee Grant....She knows what acting is all about and everything she does, from little mannerisms to delivering her lines, is pure professionalism."[12]

The part of Jennifer, even more than the roles of Anne Welles and Neely O'Hara, was clearly conceived to provide a tragic element in the storyline. At the beginning of the film, she is a mere chorus girl in a stage production with Helen Lawson. Her first screen appearance was clearly designed to showcase her physical attributes: Sharon, clad in a tight black body leotard, models a ten pound jeweled and feathered headdress. This sets the tone for many of her subsequent scenes.

During a telephone conversation with her difficult mother, Jennifer agrees to pawn a fur coat and send the money home. "I know I don't have any talent," she says with resignation, "and all I have is a body."

During a night out at a club, Jennifer meets Tony Polar (Tony Scotti), a famous singer, and quickly, the pair fall in love. When they finally marry, it is done secretly, without the knowledge of Polar's controlling sister Miriam (Lee Grant), who, on learning of the union, treats Jennifer as an unwelcome interloper. When Tony collapses on an evening out with Jennifer, a doctor diagnoses a terminal, degenerative disease which Miriam had suspected, and Jennifer is forced to confine her dying husband in a private asylum. She aborts the child she is carrying, fearing that it, too, might be affected. To pay for her husband's hospital bills, she goes to France and makes softcore pornographic films. When she finally decides to put a stop to the exploitation and return to America—after fighting off the lecherous advances of her director—she discovers a lump in her breast and is diagnosed with cancer.

Her most dramatic moment is her last, when, the night before she is scheduled to have her breast removed, Jennifer reveals her cancer to the visiting Anne Welles. Looking fragile and lost, wrapped in a sweater and curled in a bed, Jennifer explains, "The doctor says it's not the end of the world. He says lots of women live long and happy lives after breast surgery....You know, it's funny, all I've ever had is my body, and now I won't even have that....Let's face it, all I know how to do is to take off my clothes." After a telephone call to her mother, during which she decides she cannot tell her the news, Jennifer leaves her bed, stands before a mirror and empties a bottle of pills into her mouth, staring at her reflection. Changing into a long beige evening gown and doing her makeup, she lays down on her bed, tears streaming down her face as she dies.

During breaks in the filming, Sharon gave press interviews in the commissary at Twentieth Century Fox. The impression was always memorable: "She wore a long-sleeved, white jersey mini dress with a high neckline and hemline, dainty-heeled sandals, no stockings, no make-up and super-sized, wrap around rose tinted sunglasses. Her straight, streaked, blonde hair tumbled casually past her shoulders. Every male head within viewing range swiveled in her direction as if she were pulling invisible strings; forks stayed at half-mast long after she had passed the table; bus-boys in her wake suddenly developed a clattering case of butterfingers. Sharon didn't seem the least bit aware of the commotion she was causing."[13]

Not surprisingly, many of the questions concerned Sharon's willingness to do nude scenes. "In *Valley of the Dolls*," she said, "I have a nude scene and I have no qualms about it at all. I don't see any difference between being stark naked or fully dressed—if it's part of the job and it's done with meaning and intention. I honestly don't understand the big fuss made over nudity and sex in films. It's silly. On TV, the children can watch people murdering each other, which is a very unnatural thing, but they can't watch two people in the very natural process of making love. Now, really, that doesn't make any sense, does it?"[14]

Near the end of filming, *Look* magazine sent out a writer, Betty Rollin, to do a piece on the production and its stars. Called "The Dames in *The Valley of the Dolls*," the piece flattered no one. Rollin thought little of the film, which she referred to as "that candy box of vulgarity," nor its stars, calling Parkins a mental nonentity, Duke "today's sewer mouth," and Sharon a hopelessly stupid and vain starlet. Rollin noted that Sharon had spent two hours applying make-up prior to the interview, and declared that she "doesn't go in much for underwear." Sharon complained about other people's expectations of her, and naively told Rollin, "I'm trying to develop myself as a person. Well, like sometimes on weekends I don't wear makeup." Rollin's piece did little to enhance Sharon's reputation as a serious actress in Hollywood circles.[15]

After months of work, the film finally wrapped production with the traditional cast party. "By the close of shooting," Patty Duke wrote, "everybody hated everybody."[16] Director Robson was all sweetness and light with his cast; one day, when he met Roman Polanski walking along the Sunset Strip, he said, "That's a great girl you're living with. Few actresses have her kind of vulnerability. She's got a great future."[17] But his treatment of Sharon on the set had been anything but great, and she was immensely relieved to have the whole thing, which she regarded as an ordeal, finally over.

Chapter 11
All Eyes on Sharon Tate

"THIS IS THE YEAR THAT SHARON TATE HAPPENS...."[1] THUS declared *Playboy Magazine* in March, 1967. With four major films completed, Sharon was poised on the edge of stardom. Since 1963, Martin Ransohoff had invested thousands of dollars in her training and development, guiding her career in preparation for her public launch. Although *Eye of the Devil* and *The Fearless Vampire Killers* had been filmed nearly two years earlier, neither had yet received a release date. Now, in 1967, Sharon burst upon the scene in a fury of press attention any major Hollywood studio would have envied.

During the shooting of *The Fearless Vampire Killers*, Roman had asked Sharon if she would be willing to do a semi-nude layout for *Playboy Magazine*. Despite her rather strict Catholic upbringing, Sharon had a very permissive attitude toward appearing nude. She realized that, with her beauty and her shapely figure, she was bound to be exploited for her physical assets; if someone was going to make money from her own body, Sharon reasoned, it might as well be her and, at least, in this fashion, she felt she would be in control of the environment.

"It was a pretty carnivorous thing to do," one of Sharon's friends recalled. "But I don't think she gave any thought to the idea that Polanski was simply exploiting his relationship with her. She wanted to please him, he asked, and so she reasoned it out."[2]

Ransohoff was horrified when he learned of the proposed publication. He quickly dispatched Mike Mindlin to Chicago, where the Vice President of Advertising for Filmways was charged with the impossible task of getting back the photographs. Officials from *Playboy*, however, refused to drop the layout, which had already

74

been slated for publication. After some strained negotiations, they agreed on a compromise: Mindlin was allowed to pull any photographs to which he felt Ransohoff would object.[3]

Titled "The Tate Gallery," the *Playboy* layout eventually ran in the March, 1967 issue, and included a short article which also served to publicize *The Fearless Vampire Killers*. Six stills displayed Sharon, draped in a blue towel, in various poses in the studio, revealing her breasts and buttocks.[4] It was an attempt to portray an image of Sharon which would sell to a public which, up until that time, had been largely silent on her talents.

The *Playboy* layout was the first shot in an escalating round of media attention designed to publicize Sharon as Hollywood's latest discovery. "She is unabashedly candid on subjects that are sometimes considered off-limits," wrote one interviewer, "even with her kind of publicity (not to be deliberately shocking, but simply because this is what she believes). She has obviously thought a lot about what she thinks and she presents her opinions most articulately and with an earnest intensity."[5]

Sharon was still timid around most reporters, unused to the media attention. She impressed many not only by her stunning beauty, but through an air of sophistication she managed to cultivate. "Up close," one interviewer declared, "she has a decidedly European flavor, so much so that you expect a French or Swedish accent - not the carefully rounded speech class tones, with just a tiny tinge of her native Texas."[6]

While she appeared fairly focused on the direction she wished her career to take, saying that she wanted to become "a light comedienne in the Carole Lombard style," she was also frank about her chances of breaking through as an actress.[7]

"I don't fool myself," she declared. "I can't see myself doing Shakespeare, or anything like that. I would love light comedy, but it takes so long, you know. Comedy is one of the most difficult types of acting to do, it takes so long because you have to be so serious, and that's the funny thing about it, and I haven't had the experience at the moment, but I'm getting there."[8]

"I am beginning to understand things for myself," she said during an interview in 1967. "I have no idea if I can act. I'm just discovering things about myself. I'm extremely insecure and if I can't do something honestly, I can't do it. I'm just becoming a little more sure of my judgment. I say things and I find out some other people agree. I don't mind being attached to the sex thing, but I don't want it to be mis-used. Sexiness is a very natural thing, a delicate, fluid thing, the way you do something, or nothing. I'm discovering what I can do, and what I think. I didn't think I could do anything before."9

As Sharon herself was aware, Ransohoff was trumpeting her as the next major young female star, and many of the questions she endured at interviews focused on her status as a sex symbol. "Oh, that's silly!" she told one reporter, blushing deeply. "I am not an anything...I'm just me. If I am sexy, it's just something I do naturally, like picking up a knife and fork to eat. I think people who try to be sexy are the most unsexy people in the world."10

"Sexiness," she declared, "is all in the eye of the beholder. And I think it should be. Absolutely. My sex appeal, whatever it might be, isn't obvious...at least to me." She often equated herself to her character Jennifer in *Valley of the Dolls*: "She's really got the same ideas about sex as I: She has the kind of European sex appeal—the naive, surprised type of thing, like every day is a new package to open. There is a child-like innocence; being sexy without being aware of it, without effort...and I think this makes you twice as sexy."11

That summer, *Don't Make Waves*, the third motion picture which Sharon had filmed, became the first to receive a release date. The MGM Pressbook, listing the cast biographies, declared: "And last, but definitely not least, is Sharon Tate, producer Ransohoff's new discovery whom he has been keeping under wraps but who now sheds them in *Don't Make Waves* as Malibu, Queen of the Surfers."12

Much of the film's publicity focused on Sharon. Promotional buttons showed her picture; stills showing her rescuing Tony Curtis from the ocean were sent to water safety programs across the country; and photographs depicting Sharon in skydiving gear found their ways to all branches of the Parachute Club of America. Lobbies of motion picture theatres were decorated with life-sized "Surfside Sharon" cardboard photographs depicting the actress clad in her polka-dot bikini.13 Perhaps the ultimate promotion was an add Sharon did for a tanning lotion. Shown in a blue bikini, lying atop a surfboard held by four well-built young men, she was identified as "Sharon Tate, co-starring in Martin Ransohoff's *Don't Make Waves*," and trumpeted the "better tan" achieved through the use of Coppertone.

Don't Make Waves was released to mixed reviews. Some critics praised the movie as being genuinely funny, while others warned potential viewers to stay away. By mid-1967, however, America's infatuation with California beach life was on the decline, and every-thing—from the idea of happy teenagers cavorting on the sand in the midst of the escalating Vietnam War to the title song performed by The Byrds—seemed anachronistic. "It's a terrible movie," Sharon confided to one reporter, admitting that "sometimes I say things I shouldn't. I guess I'm too outspoken."[14]

For her own role in the film, though, Sharon received rather good reviews, many commenting not only on her beauty but also on her comic talents. The impression she made in *Don't Make Waves* was enough to convince several other Hollywood directors that she had a comic talent worth pursuing, and the remaining films she would make would both be comedies.

While Sharon was filming *Don't Make Waves*, Roman had flown to Los Angeles to view the finished cut of *The Fearless Vampire Killers* with Martin Ransohoff. For six months, the film had languished on the shelf. First, there were problems with the British censors and the MGM film board. Polanski himself received several pages of written sugges-tions for cuts and changes, ranging from the brief nudity in one of Sharon's bathing scenes to the attempted seduction of Alfred by the count's son Herbert.[15] More troubling was Ransohoff's seeming reluc-tance to give the go-ahead for a final release date.

After watching the rough print with Polanski, Ransohoff and several Filmways executives, Bob O'Brien, the President of Metro-Goldwyn-Meyer, was apparently less than impressed. The dubbing made the film impossible to understand, and it was agreed that American audiences, unaccustomed to a mixture of horror and com-edy, would be too confused by Polanski's finished product. Ransohoff was left to step in and re-dub and edit the film to suit both his own standards and those of MGM as well.

Polanski was outraged. At first, he insisted that his name be removed from the film's credits; but, as he was not only the co-screenwriter and director but also a major character, this was hardly possible.

Ransohoff informed Polanski that the film was going ahead with a general American release after he himself had made final cuts, and that Roman, having signed a contract giving him this right, could do nothing to stop him. On his own, Ransohoff cut some twenty minutes from the final version, and added a cartoon prologue at the beginning to explain the history of vampires in Europe.[16]

"He tries to appear as a real artist lover, you know," Polanski later declared in anger. "He always wears the dirty sweat shirt and he always talks of the studio executives as dicks, so I believed him, you see. But then soon I realized that he's got tremendous ambition and has a real chip on the shoulder and he believes that he could do it himself with his left hand, but has got no time to do it because he is so busy with deals. So he leaves some artists to do the dirty job and when he is ready he will take it away and he will shape it right....When I saw the film I nearly fainted."[17]

Roman believed that the cuts severely damaged the film's integrity and would negatively affect its potential box office success. As things turned out, *The Fearless Vampire Killers* was a box office failure when it was released in November, 1967. The reviews were roundly bad. *Newsweek* called it a "witless travesty, this bloody bore of a take-off on vampire movies by some apprentice gagsters who will never be half the half-man Dracula was. The film gets some laughs, maybe one per reel."[18] *Time* was even less kind: "Neither spooky nor spoofy, *The Fearless Vampire Killers* never manages to get out of the coffin."[19] Only *Variety* noted that Sharon "looks particularly nice in her bath"[20] With reviews like these, the film quickly disappeared from circulation. Only many years later, in the 1980s, was Polanski's original cut restored and released, this time to some critical acclaim, and it has subsequently become something of a cult film, due, no doubt, to Sharon's presence.

Almost concurrently with *The Fearless Vampire Killers*, Filmways finally released *Eye of the Devil*. "Cumulative scenes of suspense, terror and excitement pervade *Eye of the Devil*, new Martin Ransohoff production for MGM, and one of the year's outstanding 'shock dramas,'" the Pressbook from Filmways declared. "The picture has a brilliant all-star cast headed by such distinguished veterans as Deborah Kerr, Academy Award-winner David Niven and Donald Pleasence, and also starring two exciting newcomers—beautiful Sharon Tate, who made an auspicious film debut with Tony Curtis in *Don't Make Waves*, and David Hemmings, the sensational young star of *Blow Up*." Sharon was trumpeted as "one of the screen's most exciting new personalities," and "the year's most exciting new acting discovery."[21]

Promotional posters for the film featured close shots of Sharon's eyes, staring menacingly out above captions which declared, "Look at her long enough and she may be the last thing you'll ever see!"

Unfortunately for Sharon, too many moviegoers decided to steer clear of the film. It, too, proved a failure at the box office. Only a few critics noted her bewitching presence as Odile. *The New York Times,* reviewing the film, referred to Sharon's "chillingly beautiful but expressionless" performance as one of the film's few highlights.[22]

The premiere of *Eye of the Devil* passed almost unnoticed. Most critical attention that fall, and certainly all of Sharon's hopes, focused on the imminent release of *Valley of the Dolls.* For several months, movie-going audiences had been treated to the three minute preview, which confidently announced, "Now the all-time bestseller is the motion picture you wanted it to be!"

The publicity machine at Twentieth Century Fox, already in motion, continued to roll along by promoting the film actively to Hollywood reporters. The immense wave of media attention culminated in a cruise aboard the luxury liner *Princess Italia* from Miami through the Bahamas, the Panama Canal, Mexico and on to Los Angeles. All three of the principal female leads went on the cruise, along with author Susann and her husband, writer Irving Mansfield. The ship was loaded with reporters and reviewers, and in every port of call, *Valley of the Dolls* was screened for the local journalists as well. At the premiere on board the ship, Sharon quickly got a taste of things to come. Members of the audience laughed in all of the wrong places, and Jacqueline Susann, overcome with humiliation, walked out of the ship's theatre in tears, locking herself in her cabin and refusing to come out for the duration of the voyage. Sharon and her two co-stars spent most of the cruise running from the packs of reporters on board, playing a game of cat and mouse in order to avoid having to say anything about the film, which they all thought was dreadful.[23]

Valley of the Dolls finally opened in Los Angeles in mid-December, 1967. The reviews were quick and to the point. *Time* wrote: "The story is about girls who take all sorts of pills but *Valley of the Dolls* offers only bromides....Viewers are also likely not to feel anything—except numbness—after ingesting this filmed version of Jacqueline Susann's wide-screen novel...."[24] *The Saturday Review* declared: "Ten years ago, *Valley of the Dolls* stars Parkins, Duke and Tate would more likely have been playing the hat check girls than movie queens; they are totally lacking in style, authority or charm."[25]

Columnist Bosley Crowther wrote: "Bad as Jacqueline Susann's *Valley of the Dolls* is as a book, the movie Mark Robson has made from it is that bad, or worse. It's an unbelievably hackneyed and mawkish mishmash of backstage plots and Peyton Place adumbrations....It's every bit as phony and old fashioned as anything Lana Turner ever did, and all a fairly respectful admirer of movies can do is laugh at it and turn away."[26] And *Newsweek* announced: "What a howl!...*Valley of the Dolls*, one of the most stupifyingly clumsy films ever made by alleged professionals, has no more sense of its own ludicrousness than a village idiot stumbling in manure."[27] Nor did the individual performances in the film fare much better. *The Hollywood Reporter* alone sounded a positive note: "Sharon Tate emerges as the film's most sympathetic character who takes an overdose of sleeping pills when breast cancer threatens to rob her of her only means of livelihood. William Daniels' photographic caress of her faultless face and enormous absorbent eyes is stunning."[28]

Sharon was listed fifth in the opening credits, and Jennifer exits the film roughly two-thirds of the way through the film. But her on-screen time was considerable, and the scenes allowed a certain amount of dramatic versatility which had previously been lacking in any of her roles. There was much talk in Hollywood of the irony of casting of Sharon in the role, and many felt that the untalented starlet Jennifer who makes a career out of exploiting her body was an echo of Sharon Tate herself.

Early on, Sharon had realized that the movie was not going to be her star vehicle. Although her profile in Hollywood was certainly raised by the film's publicity, the terrible reviews quickly served to counter most of the positive press. Dejected, she complained to Roman, "You're the better half," and bemoaned the fact that she had been unable to break free of the stereotypical image of the dumb blonde starlet, a role in which she seemed to be forever trapped by casting agents.[29] The year, which had begun with such promise for Sharon, came to an end with little hope that she would achieve the stardom she so wanted.

Chapter 12
The Imperfect Couple

Throughout 1967, Sharon's thoughts increasingly turned toward her personal life, and her relationship with Roman. In an interview given to the *New York Sunday News*, Sharon indicated both her devotion to Roman and her growing dissatisfaction with the direction in which her career seemed to be headed. "We have a wonderful relationship," she said. "I don't know if I'll marry him. He hasn't asked me."[1]

Sharon was absolutely convinced of her feelings for Roman. "My definition of love is being full," she explained. "Complete. It makes everything lighter. I love Roman, but I can't honestly say that right now, today, I want to marry him. I think marriage should have a true meaning behind it. I would never do it just to be quote, respectable. I feel sorry for girls who go to bed with men without any emotion. Even if you have an affair that doesn't end in marriage, it's still important to experience the feeling."[2]

Roman, however, was somewhat more reluctant to commit. "In the beginning of our relationship, I was afraid of getting too deeply involved and losing my freedom," he told *Playboy Magazine* in a 1971 interview. "But she was extremely understanding, tactful and clever. Being around me, she still made me feel absolutely free. She did not make demands, and she made it clear that she was not going to engulf me. I remember once her words, 'I am not one of those ladies who swallow a man....'"[3]

To stay with Sharon, and feel comfortable, Roman declared that he had to have complete freedom, to come and go as he wished, and to see whomever he wished. Although this ran counter to Sharon's ideas about relationships and commitment, she was so in love with Roman that she agreed to give him all that he wanted.

Their understanding, however, was completely in Roman's favor. While Sharon accepted that there might be other women, and times when Roman failed to return home, Polanski obviously did not hold the same viewpoint. He could be extremely jealous of Sharon, but, luckily for him, this fit her need to be dominated.

Sharon knew that Roman was unfaithful. "And it doesn't bother me," she declared. "I think that in the beginning, it did, a little bit. But again, you come to this European thing, where it's done very openly...very naturally. And soon you realize that this type of behavior is just part of 'The Man.' Now I've begun to think there's something wrong with a man who doesn't have the drive to want to go out and see another girl. Even after he's married—oh, yes! Any man who lets his wife tie him down or take him to task for following his natural instincts is a very meek man. He wouldn't be the man for me....Just because a man is married doesn't mean he should stop operating like a man. I would want my husband to hold down the other front as well. It's the only honest way."[4]

Such pronouncements, at least, seemed to indicate that Sharon had come to terms with Roman's behavior. But they speak more of her ability to parrot Polanski's own views than of any acceptance on her part of his style of life. For Roman and the press, she would evince a complete understanding; but secretly, she continued to hope that Polanski would come round to her own ideas of commitment.

Such acceptance was necessary, as Roman was not terribly discreet. "Roman didn't go to a lot of trouble to hide his affairs," says Victor Lownes.[5] On one occasion, when Sharon and Judy Gutowski went away for the weekend, Roman slept with a model who he had previously met. Polanski apparently bragged of his latest conquest to Gene Gutowski, who, in turn, informed his wife. At the time, the Gutowskis were in the midst of their own marital difficulties, and Judy, who despised both Roman and her husband, saw a way to strike back. "It must be nice," she said to Sharon one day, "living the way you and Roman do—I mean, allowing each other such complete freedom. Like when you and I went off to Big Sur and Roman screwed that girl and you didn't mind in the least!"[6]

Hurt though she was, Sharon never mentioned the incident to Roman. It was simply one in a string of affairs, and she had realized that there was little she could do to stop such behavior. "No matter what happens," she told a friend, "I always know that Roman will come home to me at night."[7]

When the lease expired on their Santa Monica mansion in the middle of 1967, Sharon and Roman spent several months living a semi-nomadic existence. First, they took temporary rooms at the Sunset Marquis, a prestigious apartment complex in the center of Hollywood. The stay, however, was cut short by Sharon, who disliked the atmosphere of the place. Instead, she talked Roman into renting a fourth-floor apartment in the famous Chateau Marmont overlooking Sunset Boulevard, a big Victorian building complete with turrets and oddly-shaped rooms. Sharon loved the place, with its fashionable dwellers including actors and rock stars, but Roman thought it was all too much. Walking through the hallways, he later recalled, the smell of pot hung heavily in the air, and ambulances often raced the latest suicides and drug overdoses off to the UCLA Medical Center.[8]

It was a time of seemingly endless parties, and Sharon and Roman had a steady stream of friends, business associates and acquaintances who filtered through their apartment. Inevitably, their glimpses were brief, impressionistic. Sharmagne Leland-St. John, former Playboy bunny and an occasional guest, recalled: "Sharon was the sweetest creature I had ever met, very smart, but very stupid, too. Once, she was sitting on a chair, and watering this plant. She would empty a pitcher, and go for some more water, and do it again as we sat there wondering when it would occur to her that the water was going straight through the pot down onto the carpet."[9]

After a few months at the Chateau Marmont, Sharon and Roman decided to find a house together. Polanski's contract with Paramount Studios ensured that he would be required in Hollywood for several years. After looking, however, they could find nothing suitable, and Patty Duke suggested that they rent her house above Benedict Canyon in the Hollywood Hills. Located at 1600 Summit Ridge Drive, the house was a rambling Tudor-style retreat with an enclosed garden filled with old trees and flowering vines.

To celebrate, Sharon and Roman gave a party at the Summit Ridge house. According to several sources, there was a curious incident which had ominous overtones in view of the later murders. The couple had agreed to look after Patty Duke's English sheepdog, and during the gathering it somehow managed to escape from the house, wandering down Summit Ridge Drive. Roman apparently chased the dog down the hill, only to encounter a vicious pack of Alsatian dogs belonging to members of an English cult called The

Process living nearby. The dogs chased Roman into a garage, where he became trapped until he managed to break a rear window and escape up the hillside, away from the Satanists' howling dogs, to the safety of his house nearby.[10]

Sharon and Roman frequently entertained at their new house. Roman regularly brought friends back unannounced, but Sharon never seemed to mind. She enjoyed filling the role of housewife. She was a good cook, with her specialties including Virginia ham and upside-down cake, learned from her mother Doris. Sharon relished the domestic atmosphere; it was as close as she could come to getting a commitment out of Roman.[11] Eventually, Sharon decided she needed assistance, however, and after conducting some interviews hired fifty-four-year-old Winifred Chapman as maid, at a salary of $200 a week.[12] She would later follow the couple when they moved to the house on Cielo Drive.

"This was a happy, blameless period," Roman would later recall. "There were lots of parties at people's houses, on the beach or in the mountains, and often Sharon would make dinner, and there was this magnificent group of friends who would come to our house, and we would sit outside where it was warm, with the sky full of stars, and listen to music or talk for hours—films, sex, politics or whatever."[13]

In the months following work on *Rosemary's Baby* and *Valley of the Dolls*, Sharon and Roman jetted between London and Los Angeles, dividing their time between the Eaton Mews flat and their house on Summit Ridge. They soon became among the most famous of celebrity couples in Hollywood. Photo journalist Peter Evans called them "The imperfect couple. They were the Douglas Fairbanks/Mary Pickford of our time....Cool, nomadic, talented and nicely shocking. Their Pickfair (Sharome?) was a movable mansion, a roomy rebellion. Curious, unafraid, they helped demolish the ancient Hollywood image of what movie stardom was all about. They became part of the anti-Establishment Establishment. They became rich but never regal."[14]

Polanski's influence over Sharon continued to grow, and not everyone welcomed the changes. Although Sharon seemed to be happy, there was a wilder streak in her which dd not go unnoticed. Once, Hal Gefsky and Herb Browar were dining at a restaurant in Hollywood when they happened to spot Polanski across the room. Gefsky waved him over, and asked how Sharon was doing. "Oh,

Hal," Roman answered, "I've completely corrupted her!"[15]

Indeed, their circle of friends largely encompassed those who fell somewhat beyond Hollywood's older, more established society. Jay Sebring was an intimate friend, along with such notables as Steve McQueen; Warren Beatty; Jane and Peter Fonda; Dennis Hopper; Candice Bergen and her boyfriend, promoter Terry Melcher; Jim Morrison of the rock group The Doors; Janis Joplin; and the four members of the rock group The Mamas and the Papas—John and Michelle Phillips, Cass Eliott and Denny Doherty.

Perhaps their closest friends during this period were Mia Farrow and Peter Sellers. Since her separation from Frank Sinatra, Mia had grown closer to Sharon, and often spent weekends with her and Roman. It was Roman who first introduced Mia to Sellers, whom he had met during the filming of *Rosemary's Baby*. Polanski had taken an instant liking to the rather quiet and thoughtful man who, in private, was so different from his jovial public personality. Roman later remembered both Mia and Peter as being intoxicated with the late 1960s counterculture and all that went with it—Indian clothing, beaded chains and necklaces, meditation and astrology.[16]

One weekend, Sharon and Roman and Mia and Peter went off to camp in the desert at Joshua Tree National Park near Palm Springs. They spent the weekend sitting around a fire, getting stoned and watching for UFOs in the night sky. Sharon and Roman, well aware of their friends' susceptibility, taunted Mia and Peter by throwing rocks and stones into the vast desert behind their backs, then declaring that the noise must be a paranormal experience.[17]

Recognizing Sellers' loneliness, Sharon and Roman asked him to join them on a skiing holiday for Christmas, 1967. The group traveled to Cortina, where they spent their days on the slopes and their evenings huddled round a roaring fire in the lodge. For the holiday, Sellers insisted on dressing as Santa Claus. Sharon lent him one of her long, fox fur coats, which he coupled with a red ski cap worn atop his head and a white one tied round his chin as a fake beard. Thus attired, he handed round the presents.[18]

The year ended with important career decisions by both Roman and Sharon. In Hollywood, Roman managed to buy himself out of Cadre Films' three-picture contract with Martin Ransohoff's Filmways, Inc., and instead signed up with the Ziegler Ross Agency. His new business manager and agent, William Tennant, quickly became a close friend, and he and his young wife Sandy frequently entertained Sharon and Roman at all of the fashionable Los Angeles nightspots.

Under Polanski's influence, Sharon had come to despise Ransohoff's control, believing that he was deliberately stalling when it came to her career. The debacle over *The Fearless Vampire Killers* had proved the last straw. To please Roman, she was willing to sever her connection with Filmways. Despite the evidence to the contrary, as well as the massive amount of money he had poured into her success, Sharon felt her association with Ransohoff was responsible for her lack of success.

With her career increasingly in question, she turned her thoughts to Roman, and to the idea of marriage. To this end, she apparently decided to quit the business. During a meeting with Ransohoff, Sharon told him that she wished to start a family with Polanski, and asked that she be let out of her contract's remaining three years. Ransohoff agreed, conditioned on her intention to retire. The sacrifice of her career was a high price to pay, but, at last, Sharon was free to pursue her life as she wished.

Chapter 13
Marriage

"I'LL GIVE UP ACTING THE SECOND I'M MARRIED," SHARON HAD declared in 1966.[1] Now, having freed herself of her Filmways contract, her attention turned to Roman. They had been together for two years, and most of that had been spent living either in London or in Los Angeles. Not surprisingly, Roman—who had the best of both worlds—was more than reluctant to consider marriage. There was no doubt that he loved her, but Roman feared the very idea, feeling it left him vulnerable. He knew that Sharon desperately wanted marriage and children. In spite of the fact that they had been living together for nearly two years, her deep-rooted Catholic sense of morality dictated that everything be made legal, in the eyes of not only the law but also of the Church.[2]

"What does marriage mean, anyway?" Sharon once said. "Just a legal piece of paper and a lovely financial setup. Why would I want to ruin a perfect affair by turning it into a mediocre marriage for society's sake?"[3] But, while publicly declaring that she was not ready for marriage, this was, in fact, very much on her mind. In spite of Roman's sometimes difficult nature and romantic adventures, she deeply loved him.

The idea of marriage began to pepper their conversations with some frequency through the fall of 1967. While Sharon was certain that she wanted to be with Roman, she also worried that he would be unable to remain faithful once they had exchanged vows. She once complained to Harry Falk, former husband of her friend Patty Duke: "Roman wants to marry me. I don't know what to do." When Falk apparently warned her to consider Polanski's past history as an indicator of future behavior, she said, "Thank you, I really appreciate it, you saved my life, I'm not going to throw away my life by marrying this little putz."[4]

Sharon's ambivalence was real enough, but she was also aware that Roman was not likely to remain amenable to the idea of marriage for long. One night, over dinner in a restaurant, Roman raised the subject of marriage. The proposal, such as it was, was distinctly unromantic. "I'm sure you would like to get married," he simply said to her. When Sharon quickly agreed, Roman declared, "We'll get married, then."[5] With these words, whatever doubts either partner had were temporarily banished.

The wedding was rather rushed; as a result, there were no invitations: Instead, Victor Lownes sent out telegrams to some fifty friends and acquaintances: "You are cordially invited to the Sharon Tate-Roman Polanski wedding reception at the Playboy Club this Saturday, 20 January, 1968, at noon. Informal brunch." "It was all thrown together in a day or two," Lownes recalls, "full of chaos and energy. But they seemed to live their lives that way, in a sort of spur-of-the-moment existence."[6]

Although her family were in California, Sharon agreed to Roman's suggestion that they hold the actual ceremony in London, where they had a permanent residence, and where many of their friends lived. In her happiness, Sharon also agreed to forgo a traditional religious service; her wedding was to be a simple civil ceremony in a registry office. There was a bit of a last minute wrangle over Polanski's divorce from Basia, and he had to produce the necessary legal documents from Poland before he could legally get the British Marriage Application and License forms. But, in the end, everything fell into place.

The night before the wedding, Victor Lownes insisted on throwing Roman a stag party, much to Sharon's annoyance. Attendees included the actors Michael Caine and Terrence Stamp, as well as a number of shapely beauties in various states of undress. By the following morning, Roman was bleary-eyed from too much alcohol and lack of sleep.[7]

The ceremony took place at the Chelsea Registry Office in King's Road, London, amid a crush of reporters and curious spectators. "There was a mob there," says Lownes, "with cameras jostling, flashbulbs going off, people screaming when they recognized a face."[8] Just before eleven that Saturday morning, Sharon arrived with Roman from the Eaton Mews flat, and stepped into the chill January air. She had designed her wedding dress herself: a light cream-colored taffeta mini-dress. Sharon described it to reporters: "It's

Renaissance until you get below the knees," she explained.[9] The dress was a simple, traditional one above the waist, with puffed princess sleeves, a high neck, tight bodice and rows of small pearl buttons decorating the cuffs. One reporter noted that her skirt was "so mini it was almost minus. Her long, lovely legs were displayed in their entirety and she stopped traffic."[10] She wore sheer white hose and white pumps; instead of a veil, Sharon decorated her hair with sprigs of fresh flowers which matched her bouquet, and long ribbons, "like a cloud around her exquisite face," as Joan Collins remembered.[11] Except for the dress's length, Sharon could have stepped from a Victorian afternoon tea. Roman was similarly attired, in an olive green Regency-style frock coat, bell-bottom trousers and wide cravat at his neck, at the suggestion of the owner of a Hollywood boutique, Jack Vernon.[12] He looked, declared one witness, "like a cross between Little Lord Fauntleroy and Ringo Starr."[13] Together, Sharon and Roman were very much the picture of fashionable, modern young couples of the late 1960s.

A dozen photographers had crowded into the small registry office to record the event. Roman's friend and business partner Gene Gutowski stood as best man, while Sharon selected her friend, actress Barbara Parkins, as her only bridesmaid. Parkins, too, was the picture of late-1960s fashion, attired in a long knit dress, and flowers in her hair. After the short ceremony, Sharon and Roman happily skipped down the staircase and into a sea of flashing cameras and shouted questions. "Sharon and I are very happy," Roman announced to the reporters, a wide grin on his chubby face. Sharon was clearly beside herself. "I'm so happy you can't believe it!" she declared, before running hand in hand with her new husband to a waiting car to be spirited away for the reception.[14] "The bride and groom looked like reflections in a Disneyland funhouse mirror as they posed on the Registry steps with a gawking, gaping crowd jamming the street behind them," one writer declared.[15]

Victor Lownes had arranged for the closure of the Playboy Club so that he could host the wedding reception for his friends. The rich and famous flocked to the festivities: along with Gene Gutowski and his wife Judy, and Barbara Parkins, guests included Peter Sellers, Laurence Harvey, Michael Klinger, Rudolf Nureyev, Warren Beatty, Sean Connery, Kenneth Tunan, David Bailey, Brian Jones, Keith Richards, Vidal Sassoon, Prince and Princess Radziwill, Leslie Caron, Christine Kaufman, Jacqueline Susann and Irving Mansfield, Michael

Caine, Terrence Stamp, Mia Farrow, Candice Bergen, Joan Collins, Anthony Newley, John Mills and James Fox.[16]

Lownes had invited a few reporters to the reception. The correspondent from *The Times* of London questioned Roman about his past with Sharon and their plans together. "Yeah, it's true I photographed Sharon in the nude," he declared. "Yeah, the pictures appeared in *Playboy*. But that's all over now." Sharon had previously expressed her desire to quit work and focus on her husband when she married, but Polanski had different ideas, a clear indication of the trouble which lay ahead: "No, that doesn't mean she stops working," he said. "I want a hippie, not a housewife."[17] When, at the conclusion of the brunch, the large, three-tiered wedding cake was wheeled in on a silver cart, it bore the joke inscription, "Happy Retirement, Hilda," which drew howls of laughter from the crowd.[18] On their way from the reception to return to their flat at Eaton Mews, Sharon, beaming at the gathered reporters, announced that it had all been "a very mod affair."[19] Even the staid *Sunday Times* declared that it had been "the 'turned on' wedding of the year."[20]

That evening, Sharon and Roman attended a concert by The Supremes at The Talk of the Town, before leaving for their honeymoon. As they departed, a reporter asked Sharon if she was looking forward to her time alone with Roman. "Don't be silly," she said. "We've been inseparable for two years and every day has been a honeymoon."[21]

The newlyweds first jetted across the Channel for a skiing holiday in the Swiss Alps before venturing to Paris for the French premiere of *Rosemary's Baby*. They took over several rooms at L'Hotel on the Left Bank in the St.-Germain-des-Pres quarter, and were soon joined by Peter Sellers and Mia Farrow. Sharon had broken her ankle in Switzerland and was limping in a plaster cast and on a cane, while her new husband sported a battered lip, from a fight when some Spaniards had tried to grab Sharon.[22]

Sharon loved France, and Polanski had his new red Ferrari shipped over from Los Angeles so that they could explore the countryside. Together, the two couples visited old chateaux and the locations where Sharon had earlier filmed *Eye of the Devil*. They returned to France late that spring, driving to St.-Tropez then to Cannes, where Roman was to be a juror on the panel for the 1968 International Film Festival.

Unfortunately, the visit coincided with the outbreak of riots in Paris, fueled when thirty thousand students had been locked out of the Sorbonne and taken to the street with rocks and sticks. The disturbance quickly spread to Cannes. Barriers were erected along the streets, and police in riot gear stood ready to protect the gathered celebrities. But the chaos in France politicized the proceedings. While directors such as Francois Truffaut and Jean-Luc Goddard wanted to use the festival to protest, Roman only wished to enjoy his new-found status. "He just did not appreciate what was going on," said Truffaut. "All he could visualize was Roman Polanski turning up to show everyone what a great guy he was."[23]

On 18 May, authorities canceled the film festival, and Sharon and Roman fled to Rome, driving his Ferrari across the mountains, followed by director Mike Sarne in his Rolls Royce. There was a slight hitch at the border; Roman had no Italian visa in his Polish passport. Sharon had her U.S. passport and managed to get through and Roman claimed to have lost his; Sarne eventually argued with the guards and managed to talk them through the border.[24] At the end of their long holiday, husband and wife packed up their things and flew back to California, to settle down and begin their married life in the United States.

Chapter 14
A Troubled Marriage

NINETEEN-SIXTY-EIGHT WAS A YEAR OF VIOLENCE IN AMERICA. From the intensified escalation of the Vietnam conflict with the Tet Offensive to the protests in the streets from the anti-war crowds; the rise of the Black Panthers and the Weathermen, the riots at the Democratic National Convention in Chicago; and the assassination of Dr. Martin Luther King—the country seemed poised on the edge of an abyss. The violence and growing dissatisfaction were made all the more intense for millions of Americans who sat glued to their television sets as the horrors of the year were flashed before them in rapid succession.

The world was falling apart. All of this stood in stark contrast to the previous year, the "Summer of Love," as it had been proclaimed, when everyone gravitated toward San Francisco and Haight-Ashbury. The bohemian atmosphere in the streets quickly caught on elsewhere, and crowds of hippies, brightly attired in psychedelic robes and surrounded with a haze of marijuana smoke, were soon wandering up and down Hollywood's Sunset Strip, attracting the curious attention of the rich and famous, who began to emulate their clothing, jewelry and concerns. The movement among the flower children was led by Timothy Leary, with his famous admonition to "Turn on, tune in, drop out," and by its musicians: The Grateful Dead, The Jefferson Airplane, Country Joe, Big Brother and the Holding Company, and The Doors. From the brick walls of the Fillmore in San Francisco to the sea-side thunder of the Monterey Pop Festival, the music captured both the movement and its growing anger against the establishment.

Sharon and Roman were not immune from the tenor of the times. On the evening of 3 June, they joined director John

Frankenheimer for a dinner with Senator Robert Kennedy and his wife Ethel, on the eve of the California Presidential Primary. Sharon had taken an interest in the Senator's presidential campaign, and was delighted to meet him for a few hours. The next day, having won the primary, he celebrated with a rally at the Ambassador Hotel in Los Angeles; later that night, bullets fired from Sirhan Sirhan's gun ended the dream of another Kennedy in the White House. The mood of the country increasingly turned to violence, and the growing unease threatened to tear the country apart.

"Just about the only really happily married couple I knew in Hollywood," recalled Robert Evans, "were Roman Polanski and Sharon Tate."[1] The first months of their marriage were idyllic enough, with Roman fawning and Sharon happily playing the role of wife at their rented house on Summit Ridge Drive. But, soon after returning to Hollywood at the beginning of June, 1968, the temptations of fame and fortune apparently became too much for Roman to resist. According to Zofia Komeda, "He changed when he went to America."[2]

Sharon had always known of Roman's amorous exploits in the two years prior to their marriage. During the early years in London, Roman, according to one biographer, "started playing around again on the side, mostly with old girlfriends, whenever Sharon went back to Hollywood for a part in a picture. Then, when they returned to Hollywood for *Rosemary's Baby*, Roman found a whole new field of girls that interested him. Sharon soon learned that he was playing around."[3]

Roman was quite content to carry on exactly as he had been before the marriage. To him, his numerous dalliances meant nothing, and certainly did not diminish his love for his wife. Roman was, and had always been, a womanizer, and he saw no reason to relinquish his old habits merely because he had signed a piece of paper in a London registry office.

"I am pretty sure that Sharon knew what was going on," says Victor Lownes. "Roman had always screwed around, and I don't think he made any effort to change when he married Sharon. He had always been the quintessential playboy. There wasn't a lot she could really do about it."[4]

Naively, however, Roman apparently believed that word of his extramarital affairs would not reach Sharon. But Hollywood gossip was notorious, and it did not take long before she knew what he had been up to on the evenings when he claimed to be at business dinners or meetings with studio executives. Kenneth Tynan tells of one incident in Hollywood. Polanski, who was off driving round the city, pulled up behind a beautiful girl and shouted that she had a "beautiful arse." The woman who turned round was Sharon.[5]

The uncomfortable reality of the situation began to sink in by the fall of 1968. While Sharon was prepared to devote herself to Roman and give up her career, it quickly became apparent that he had no wish to feel tied down to a happy domestic scene presided over by an attentive wife. At their wedding, he had declared as much to a reporter from *The Times* of London. These differing expectations of what their marriage would bring soon began to tear at the already fragile threads which held the union together.

Sharon and Roman had been married less than a year, and already she knew of several of his extramarital affairs. The revelation of one of these was apparently very shocking indeed. Roman had purchased a Sony videocassette camera and recorder, then very much a novelty. During one romantic encounter, he had left it running while he and Sharon made love.

One day, when Roman was away, Sharon and some friends discovered a stash of videotapes without labels. "We put them on the machine," a friend recalled, "and they turned out to be of Roman making love to someone else on their bed. Sharon turned white, and then got madder than hell. The marriage almost ended there."[6]

There is no doubt that Roman loved Sharon, but his idea of a committed relationship ran counter to hers, and there were bound to be problems. For Sharon, the whole idea of marriage was one of commitment, a lifetime partnership and trust, built around loyalty between husband and wife. Because so much of her childhood and teenage years had been spent moving from home to home, with her father frequently absent on overseas postings, Sharon longed to have the kind of stable family life which she had never really known. She had thought that in marrying Roman she would finally tame him, but the reality was difficult. "She'd call me in tears," a friend remembered, "and say, 'I know he's with so-and-so.' and I'd say, 'Well, you know where the door is. Walk out.' She didn't, of course, because I think she realized that it was just the way he was, it didn't have anything to do with her, and that he really was nuts about her."[7]

Judy Gutowski, who by this time had separated from her husband Gene, later recalled, "This was when I really began to dislike Roman....She'd cry on my shoulder, 'Why must he be this way, he's humiliating me, why can't he be faithful, I've done everything he's wanted me to do?' Then I'd talk to Roman, bawl him out, and he'd pretend to be just as unhappy. 'Oh, Judy,' he'd say, 'I can't change what I am. She knew what she was getting. If I could change, I really would.'"[8]

"I wish I had the tolerance to let everybody have complete freedom," Sharon once confided. "To be able to take a man home and make love and enjoy it without some lurking puritanical guilt interrupting the pleasure....I get frightened, I get really frightened; mentally it's what I want, but emotionally its more difficult to take."[9]

In private, Sharon repeatedly confronted Roman over his infidelities. He later recalled that his affairs were "Sharon's big hang-up." But, as quickly as she would raise the issue, he rejected it, saying, "Remember, you said you don't want to change me."[10] She had agreed to Roman's style of life with reluctance, hoping that he would change. But Roman, in no hurry to abandon his pleasures, happily took her at her word, continuing his affairs, with "an indiscretion bordering on arrogance," as one of Sharon's friends later said.[11]

Sharon worried she would drive Roman away if she insisted he put a stop to his extramarital affairs. She played along, sweetness and light on the surface, but terribly hurt on the inside. Roman had his work, his friends, his priorities and his affairs. Aside from her family and own circle of friends, Sharon had nothing except Roman and her career.

It was not in Sharon's nature to simply give up, to walk away from the situation when overcome with difficulties; if anything, her positive outlook worked against her, preventing her from grasping the realities of the situation in favor of expending effort and energy in trying to salvage what seemed to everyone else to be a doomed relationship. But her disillusion with married life began to impress itself upon those who knew Sharon best, and, for the first time that any of them could recall, she seemed very unhappy.

Increasingly, Sharon turned more and more to Jay Sebring for comfort and companionship. "Everyone knew Jay was still deeply in love with Sharon," recalls Patty Faulkner, daughter of Sebring's business partner John Madden.[12] "Jay didn't make any secret of the fact that he was still beholden to Sharon," adds friend Skip Ward.[13] Jay was careful to position himself in Sharon's life, at her side to provide friendship and consolation. According to friends, she took Jay into her confidence, telling him the details of her unhappy married life with Roman. "Jay undoubtedly filled a void in Sharon's life," a friend says. "He managed to step in where Roman had failed. I mean that emotionally, not sexually. But I know there was an intimacy between them which just wasn't there with Sharon and Roman. Jay was almost a third partner in that marriage."[14] Roman, if he resented the presence of his wife's former boyfriend, said nothing. "I don't think Roman realized how close they were," says Skip Ward, "and I doubt that he knew, maybe to the end, how serious Jay was about Sharon."[15]

On the surface, at least, Sharon and Roman seemed the perfect Hollywood couple, throwing themselves into the social scene with dizzying abandon. They haunted the clubs up and down the Sunset Strip, and the more exclusive parties in the elegant mansions high in the hills above the city.

Their constant companions were John and Michelle Phillips of The Mamas and the Papas. "John and I used to spend a lot of time with Sharon and Roman," Michelle Phillips recalls. "They were a very popular couple, a very 'of the moment' couple. Sharon was the most beautiful thing you have ever seen. She had a sweetness about her that was rare. She just did not have any kind of mean-spiritedness in her. She was very open and genuine, not particularly intellectual, but people just loved her because she was beautiful and because she made an effort to make everyone feel welcome and loved."[16]

Often, the two couples dined together at the Polanski house on Summit Ridge. "Sharon would make a big bowl of pasta, and we would all sit around the table and eat and laugh and talk for hours," Michelle Phillips remembers. "She was very social, but in a home-body sort of way. She was happier staying home, cooking, entertaining friends, than she was in going out to clubs or parties. Above everything, I think she just wanted to be a very traditional wife."[17]

Sharon frequently confided her frustrations and fears to Michelle Phillips. "She really wanted to be accepted," Phillips recalls. "She worked very hard at breaking through to people, and it bothered her that she was dismissed so often. Because she was so beautiful, she knew that she was often the butt of jokes, in the same way that attractive women in Hollywood have always been the butt of the joke."[18]

The telephone rang nearly every day in the Summit Ridge Drive house, alerting the Polanskis to the latest goings-on. The most frequent caller was Steve Brandt, a publicist with Guy McElwaine and Associates, who had been introduced to Sharon and Roman by the Phillipses. Brandt knew everyone in Hollywood, and liked to boast about his connections with the rich and famous. In reality, however, he was a loner, described by Michelle Phillips as "a rather pathetic guy," always trying to insinuate himself into the town's elite circles where he never quite fit on his own.[19]

If they grew tired of their circle of friends, Sharon and Roman might wander down to the Sunset Strip and club hop. Sharon far preferred to remain at home, cooking for her friends, watching television or reading. But Roman adored Hollywood nightlife, and Sharon faithfully accompanied him on his nightly forays, aware that her presence would at least guard against any temptation he might encounter. The most fashionable clubs—the Hullabaloo at Sunset and Vine, the Red Velvet, the Trip, Gazzari's, the Whisky A Go-Go and The Daisy—were always filled with the beautiful people of Hollywood, along with a curious mixture of struggling musicians, would-be starlets and unwashed hippies who seemed peculiarly out of place in the posh surroundings.[20] In the heat of the long summer nights, the music flowed up and down the Strip until dawn, leading the way to the watering holes and exclusive enclaves reserved for the well-to-do. The smell of marijuana wafted through the open doors of the clubs, but this was only the most prominent of the many offerings inside and down the back alleys lining the Strip.

Drugs became freely available, from marijuana and LSD—undoubtedly the most popular at the time—to cocaine and the newer thrills of mescaline and MDA. Since her days with Jay Sebring, Sharon had used drugs, mainly marijuana and LSD. But she had always done so out of a spirit of adventure and excitement rather than dependency. According to friends, Sharon occasionally continued to use drugs, but, for her, it was a matter of being social. She never became addicted, never lost her head to the temptations that came with fame and money. "Roman, on the other hand," remembered a friend, "went off the deep end. He was down on Sunset Boulevard almost every night, haunting the strip clubs and picking up girls in his car, often taking them up into the hills, snorting a few pinches of cocaine and then screwing them."[21]

Roman was too unused to American life and customs to be very discerning about the people with whom he was surrounding himself. After all, it was the era of the flower children and free love, and many of those men and women who crossed his path clearly fell beyond the bounds of the elite of Hollywood. Sharon, too, was naive in her opinions of people, completely trusting and always willing to believe the best of nearly everyone. Soon enough, with their fame and money, a house where parties were frequently thrown without regard to invitations or guest lists, and a reputation for free drugs, Sharon and Roman began to attract a disagreeable bunch of hangers-on, people on the fringes of society, users only concerned with themselves.

"Sharon and Roman were lax in a way," recalls Leslie Caron, "and their house was very available. They invited an awful lot of people there, and I always thought that there was something really dangerous about the way they lived."[22] Neither Sharon nor Roman was very aware of the situation which was rapidly developing at the house on Summit Ridge Drive, but along the Strip, it had the growing and unwelcome reputation as a place to go for both connections and drugs. According to one friend, Sharon was living "a wonderful little fantasy," in which there was never any thought as to abuse or unhappiness. She noticed the presence of unknown people in their house on several occasions, but tended to dismiss them as friends of Roman, or as hippies who had wandered in and were harmless.[23] "I love the new generation," she declared in an interview. "They're fascinating and they're fun. I think the hippies are great, they just want to be left alone and they want everybody to be nice and peaceful. That's my philosophy, to live and let live."[24] In less than a year, Sharon would be dead, killed by the nice, peaceful hippies she found so exciting.

In June of 1968, *Rosemary's Baby* was finally released to the general public after months of publicity build-up: "Pray for *Rosemary's Baby*" read the copy on the promotional posters. It was an immediate critical and financial success, and guaranteed Polanski's multi-picture deal with Paramount Studios. But the moral backlash against the film and its subject matter was just as swift. The National Catholic Office for Motion Pictures—the former Legion of Decency—rated the film with a dreaded "C" for condemned, based upon both the subject matter and the infamous dream-rape sequence with its brief nudity. A similar reaction waited in England, where the British Board of Film Censors edited out several shots before allowing the film to be released.[25] Still, Polanski had been validated as a director of major talent in Hollywood.

Sharon had declared her intention to give up her career once married. But she had previously signed to do a new film for Columbia Pictures. *The Wrecking Crew*, the fourth and last in a series of Matt Helm movies, starred Dean Martin as an American special agent, comically modeled on James Bond. The series had come from the Donald Hamilton novels of the same name, with a screenplay by William McGivern and directed by Phil Karlson. The plot was bare: a shipment of gold bullion is stolen from a train in Denmark, and Matt Helm is assigned to discover its whereabouts. It has, in fact, been taken by a Count Massimo Contini (Nigel Green), the greedy villan of the film, who, with the help of his assistants Linka Karensky (Elke Sommer), Lola Medina (Tina Louise) and Yu-Rang (Nancy Kwan), tries to prevent Helm from retrieving it. Along the way, Helm is constantly shadowed by Freya Carlson (Sharon), an agent acting as a tour guide for the visiting American.

While her role as Jennifer in *Valley of the Dolls* had been a dramatic one, the part of Freya Carlson in *The Wrecking Crew* once again called for Sharon to use her comedic talents. Freya Carlson ostensibly was a bumbling, nervous—though intelligent—woman, responsible for getting Matt Helm into trouble rather than helping him to avoid it.

In her first scene, Sharon, primly attired in a dress, vest, matching cap and a pair of thick, square-rimmed glasses, knocks into Helm while he is checking in at his hotel desk. Her bumbling behavior sets the tone for what follows: she breaks a bottle of wine intended for him; she rear ends his car; following an altercation at Count Contini's mansion, she pushes Elke Sommer into the swimming pool; and, in Helm's hotel suite, interrupts his romantic interlude with Nancy Kwan.

Helm has looked on Freya Carlson as an inconvenience. Then, in the very next scene, she disappears into his hotel suite. As he watches, suddenly a long, shapely leg arches through the air from behind a door, and Sharon, having shed her matronly uniforms and hats, now appears clad in a white mini-dress, her long hair falling about her shoulders. With a cigarette in hand, she dances round the suite, shaking her posterior, much to the enjoyment of a stunned Matt Helm.

Having temporarily escaped from Contini's agents, Freya directs Helm to take a short-cut through the country; not surprisingly, they find their way blocked by a pond. Freya decides to wade in and test the depth; she suddenly disappears, her hat floating above her. When she struggles out of the pond, she stands before Helm, takes off her wet jacket and smoothes her hair, announcing, "It's too deep."

"Too deep, huh?" Helm replies with a smile. "I want to ask you a question: Whose side are you on?"

"Well," she declares indignantly, "I'm an agent, and I also happen to be a good one...and I'm also a woman!" Frustrated, she storms off, accidentally using one of Helm's cloth-wrapped grenades to wipe her hair. When she realizes her mistake, she tosses it back to Helm, who in turn drops it on the ground before his car and, with Freya, jumps into a ditch for protection as it blows the vehicle apart. "I wanna talk to you," she declares, brushing his hair with her fingers.

"I wanna talk to you too," he answers, "after the job's finished."

She ignores this, and rolls onto Helm, kissing him passionately. Then, in the midst of this scene, she suddenly stands up and walks away, leaving a stunned Helm lying in the dirt.

Helm and Carlson return to Contini's mansion to confront the Count and his gang. While Helm is cornered by male guards, Freya finds herself accidentally trapped in a room with Nancy Kwan. The two women engage in a prolonged karate battle—a demanding scene for which Sharon did nearly all of her own stunts.

The film culminates aboard Contini's train, packed with the missing gold bullion with which the Count is attempting to flee. While Helm is embroiled in a struggle with several of Contini's agents, Freya Carlson storms into the locomotive, attempting to stop the train, only to stumble when the Count opens a trap-door in the floor. She lays straddled across the opening as the train races along, screaming for help. Finally, Helm breaks into the engine and, after a struggle, both rescues Carlson and throws Contini out the open floor and onto the tracks below.

"Mr. Helm," Freya asks coyly, "is my hair a mess?"

"You wanna know the truth?" he asks. "Yes, you're a mess!" She angrily storms off into the bathroom. While she is gone, Helm accidentally pushes several buttons, which reveal both a fold-down bed and a stereo playing romantic music. In a few minutes, the bathroom door opens, and, in a repeat of her scene in Helm's hotel suite, one of Sharon's shapely legs arches and appears round the opening. She has changed into a short pink negligee, and smiles seductively as she sprawls on the bed.

"Hey," she says, "think we can have our little talk now?" The film ends as Helm and Carlson finally prepare to consummate their relationship.

For her role as Freya Carlson, Sharon had to learn the rudiments of kung fu, and Columbia hired a young actor, Bruce Lee, to give her lessons. Sharon took an immediate liking to him, and brought him back with her to the Summit Ridge Drive house to meet Roman. Roman, in turn, was so captivated that he arranged for Lee to come over after work and teach him kung fu along with Sharon in the driveway of the house.[26]

Sharon found her work on *The Wrecking Crew* an enjoyable change from her previous film roles. Her scenes were undemanding, and allowed her a chance to showcase her comedic talents. The film was scarcely memorable, but, in retrospect, one scene stands out: as Helm and Carlson pass a dead Elke Sommer, he points at her corpse and says pointedly: "That could have been you."

Chapter 15
The House on Heaven Drive

A T THE BEGINNING OF 1969, PATTY DUKE INFORMED SHARON AND Roman that she would need her Summit Ridge Drive house back soon, and the Polanskis wanted to find something a bit more permanent. Sharon spent the last of January with real estate agent Elaine Young, driving all over Los Angeles, from Malibu to the hills above Hollywood, in search of a house. Then, in the first week of February, she learned that the Benedict Canyon estate where Candice Bergen and Terry Melcher had lived was going on the market. The property was owned by Rudolph Altobelli, an agent for several important Hollywood personalities. Sharon and Roman had previously attended several parties at the house, and she had fallen in love with its rustic charm, seclusion and sweeping views of Los Angeles.[1]

One day, while Roman was in Europe, Sharon and Young drove up to Cielo to look at the empty house. Sharon wandered from room to room, finally turning to Young and saying, "Elaine, this is my dream house." As they spoke, Sharon unwittingly revealed the troubled state of her marriage. "I was fascinated," says Young, "by the fact that she seemed frightened of Roman. She was smoking cigarettes then, and she said, 'Whatever you do, when Roman sees us, don't tell him I was smoking. He doesn't want me to smoke.' She was petrified."[2]

Roman arranged a meeting with Altobelli to discuss the lease. The $1,200 a month rent on the estate was enormous for an essentially two-bedroom house with three car garage, but, along with this came a live-in caretaker and full service by landscapers and gardeners. There was space above the garage for an office for Roman, though, and, at least according to several sources, Polanski got Paramount Studios to help pick up some of the rent for this reason.

It was also very secluded, a rarity in Hollywood, and enjoyed one of the best views in Los Angeles. On February 12, 1969, Sharon and Roman signed a one year extended lease on the estate at 10050 Cielo Drive.[3]

There was a special ambiance about the canyons above Hollywood in the late 1960s, a peculiar bohemian atmosphere tempered by the more stabilizing influences of fame and fortune. In Laurel and Benedict Canyons, the hustle of city life seemed strangely remote, sheltered by the high hills and tall trees which lent a slightly rustic, woodsy feel to the areas. Narrow roads curved through the canyons, branching off now and then to smaller roads, which in turn led to cul-de-sacs and driveways lost deep in the trees. Houses had been built everywhere: on small plots facing the roadways, on steeply sloped hills, on perilously perched mountain-top platforms. The young, wealthy and beautiful quickly bought up the cottages, bungalows and mansions, attracting a newer crowd of actors, actresses and rock stars. The Polanskis' friends John and Michelle Phillips had an English Tudor mansion high above Los Angeles, and John immortalized the hills above Hollywood in The Mamas and the Papas song, "Young Girls Are Coming to the Canyons."[4]

Benedict Canyon lies to the east of Hollywood, just above Beverly Hills and Bel Air. Slicing through the middle of the canyon is Benedict Canyon Road, winding its way from Bel Air into the hills at the top of the low mountain range, where it joins Mulholland Drive and sweeps down into the San Fernando Valley on the other side. It had always attracted Hollywood celebrities: Pickfair, the legendary home of Mary Pickford and Douglas Fairbanks, Sr., was located in Benedict Canyon, on Summit Drive; Harold Lloyd's fabled estate Green Acres perched along the top of a hillside just down the Canyon; and, overlooking the Polanskis' new house, at 1436 Bella Drive, stood Falcon Lair, Rudolph Valentino's Spanish-style mansion. A mile or so from the beginning curve of Benedict Canyon Road, on the left hand side, Cielo Drive wound up into the steep hillside, past houses lining the roadway, and smaller drives and streets leading off to hidden mansions. Near the end, just before the road climbed back along the top of the mountain, two smaller streets opened up off to either side. On the right, Bella Drive curved steeply up the side of the hill and around into the northern depths of the canyon. On the right, just opposite the entrance to Bella Drive, an unmarked cul-de-sac twisted sharply back up the rugged mountain. It was a narrow road, wide enough for only one car. To the right, the steep, wood-ed mountain rose higher; on the left, there were several houses, including a white Spanish-style mansion set at a curve in the road-way and a modern cottage perched on concrete supports at the side of the hillside. A few wide spaces, to allow motorists to pass each other, opened out to provide a spectacular view of the canyon below, before the narrow road finally came to an abrupt end at a chain-link gate centered in a similar batten-board fence stretching from the cliff to the slope of the mountain. This was the gate of 10050 Cielo Drive, the Polanskis' new home.

"It is perhaps the most difficult house in the Beverly Hills area to locate without being escorted there by someone who already knows the way," wrote one neighbor in 1969. "This is why: 10048 Cielo Drive, which has its own long, winding driveway...was built at the same time as the house Sharon Tate...later rented. But despite the fact that the number 10050 should be the next house up the road, it is not. When the builder constructed these two almost iden-tical houses with lengthy private driveways many, many years ago, property was abundant, and he placed one house way above the other, with Cielo Drive curving quite a distance between them. Each house is on a huge ledge of its own, so that the owners of both homes would have a marvelous view of the twinkling lights of the whole city below, stretching to the distant Pacific. It isn't until you get past 10070 that you see a sign for 10050; the original owner of 10050 sold off bits of the hillside for smaller houses and plots along Cielo so that in the space between a dozen houses cropped up."[5]

The house at Cielo Drive had been built in the late 1940s by French actress Michele Morgan.[6] Previous tenants had included actors Henry Fonda and Cary Grant, who lived in the house before Rudolph Altobelli purchased the three-and-a-half acre estate in 1963 and put the 3,200 square foot main residence on the rental market. Candice Bergen, who lived there for several years prior to the Polanskis, later recalled the special magic of the property: "At Terry's house on Cielo Drive, I felt at home. Surrounded by tall, thick pine trees and cherry blossoms, with rose covered rail fences and a cool mountain pool grown over with flowers, it snuggled up against the hillside—a gingerbread hideout that hung high above the city. There were stone fireplaces, beamed ceilings, paned windows, a hayloft, an attic, and four-poster beds. Built in the Forties by a French film star to resemble a farmhouse in...Normandy, it looked more Twentieth Century Fox than French....It was a fairy-tale place, that house on the hill, a never-never land far away from the real world, where nothing could go wrong."[7]

From the gate of 10050 Cielo Drive, the concrete driveway curved slightly downhill and to the right before widening out in a paved parking area next to the main house. On the right, the hillside rose steeply; on the left, from the link and batten fence, a split-rail fence edged along the downslope of the plateau on which the estate rested, marking the boundary of the property. On the other side of the split-rail fence, the hillside fell sharply away, ending several hundred feet below at the rear yards of several houses further down the canyon.

At the end of the paved parking area, just before the main residence, was a two-storied, three car garage, with barn red clapboard siding to match the main house and a cedar shake roof pierced by two dormer windows. A staircase at the side left to the loft space above the garage, which had been roughed in as an apartment, with a small kitchenette and bathroom. Roman decided to do some minor remodeling and make this his new office space. Behind the garage, a white picket fence and gate separated the rear yard from the parking area to its side. The driveway, from the gate to the end of the parking area, was lined with several old trees and flowering shrubs, which, along with the angle at which it was built, obscured the house from the other side of the gate at the end of Cielo Drive.

The rustic split-rail fence separated the front lawn of the main residence from the parking area, and continued along the eastern side of the property to the tip of the downslope of the hill. At the easternmost corner of the parking area, where the two split-rail fences from the drive and the side of the front lawn met, a dirt path skirted the tip of the hillside in front of the main residence, buffered by shrubbery, leading across the easternmost boundaries of the estate to the guest house, at the southern end of the property. The path had been designed so that visitors to the guest house would not have to walk across the front lawn of the main residence. In the center of the northern split-rail fence separating the paved parking area from the front lawn, steps beneath a tall, peaked-roof wooden gate, descended to a flagstone walkway which curved across the stretch of grass to the front door of the main house.

Two tall pine trees rose on either side of the flagstone walk on the other side of the gate. Beneath the one to the right stood a rustic wishing well, with stone doves perched on its rim. The front lawn of the main residence was long and narrow, approximately one hundred by thirty feet. The entire length of the hillside to the east was separated from the dirt path to the guest house by the split-rail fence. A deep flower bed along the inner side of the fence bordered the lawn, dotted here and there with shrubbery, rose bushes and the occasional evergreen and pine tree, shading the front lawn from the nearly incessant Southern California heat. Beyond the split-rail fence, the view opened up: down the length of Benedict Canyon, Bel Air, Beverly Hills, the sprawling city, and, on clear days, to the sparkling blue waters of the Pacific Ocean, some ten miles away. The view was a prime asset. At night, the city lights sparkled below, the glow of traffic along Sunset Boulevard creating a long strip of flickering jewels. Candice Bergen had strung the split-rail fence across the front lawn with Christmas lights one year, and left them up thereafter. The lights could be seen several miles down the canyon, blinking their bright colors in the night. Sharon thought they added a festive touch to the estate, and left them up, a beacon to guide her friends to their new house.[8]

Across the other side of the front lawn stretched the main residence itself, a long, low, one story house in wood and stone. The clapboard siding had been painted barn red, with the dark cedar shake roof, the fieldstone along the front porch and dining room, and the white trim of the numerous windows adding contrast. Near the center of the house was a twenty-five foot long fieldstone front porch, shielded by a wide overhang in the roof, supported by thick wooden beams and posts.

Just before it reached the main residence, the flagstone walk across the front lawn did a sharp turn to the right and hooked itself onto the front porch. On either side were exquisitely manicured hedges and shrubs stretching off in the distance, those to the right back along the dining room and service wing of the house, those to the left across the front of the porch and on around to the side of the house. Several iron lanterns hung from the open beams on the front porch, and twin brass carriage lamps placed high in the fieldstone wall on either side of the massive Dutch door, painted white, its top which separated from its bottom containing a large, nine-paned window.

The entrance hall of the main house was small. Directly ahead of the front door, two smaller doors opened into a walk-in closet and a powder room. On either side of the hall, wide fieldstone arches gave views of the living and dining rooms. The latter stood in its own wing; facing the front lawn were massive paned windows, looking out over the view of Los Angeles beyond. Beyond the dining room, in a smaller wing, was the kitchen, whose front windows also overlooked the lawns; a small rear hallway with a service entrance to the rear porch next to the garage, and containing the laundry area; and a maid's bedroom, set at the farthest corner of the house, a window in each of the exterior walls, looking out to both the front lawn and the paved parking area. A small bathroom was located just off the bedroom.

On the opposite side of the hallway was the living room, rising two stories into the sloped roof of the house. Three large paned windows spanned the length across the front porch, and two dormer windows set into the sloped ceiling flooded the room with light. Large, structural beams, arches and supports, all painted white to match the room's walls, ran the width of the space, reaching up to the second story loft stretching across the entire length of the western side of the room, and reached by a redwood ladder.

The thick cream colored carpet laid out across the polished hardwood floor added to the lightness and airiness of the space. A plant ledge ran round half of the room, and Sharon soon filled it with ferns, ivy and ficus. At the northwestern corner of the room, a wet bar nestled behind a set of white louvered and shuttered doors, and a French door, equipped with similar louvers and shutters, opened to the rear lawn.

Otherwise, the entire length of the west wall was taken up with a massive, floor-to-ceiling fieldstone fireplace, with bookcases and built-in seats to either side, and a raised hearth across the front.

Before the fireplace hearth stood a low trestle table, loaded with scripts, books, plants and candles; directly opposite it, facing the fireplace, was a large, three-cushioned beige sofa, with two cream and yellow armchairs set at angles to the sides, also facing the fireplace and enclosing the sitting area. An end table stood next to the sofa on the right, and a floor lamp and rattan magazine basket were next to the armchair to the left, along with a wrought-iron standing ashtray. A side table and French-style side chair stood against the southern wall, beneath a canvas calendar and a poster. Sharon and

Roman kept no television set in the living room; the elaborate and expensive stereo—one of Roman's favorite toys—stood on a shelf in the front hall closet, but its large wooden speaker cabinets were set at angles against the east wall of the room. In the southeast corner of the room stood a black baby grand piano, facing out at an angle. Sharon hung a charcoal portrait of Roman on the wall next to the piano. Pushed against the center of the east wall was a large desk for Roman, littered with a lamp, telephone, framed photographs and a white pushbutton telephone. Before the hearth and in front of the couch was a large zebra-skin rug, surrounded by piles of pillows.

A door in the center of the living room's south wall opened into a small hallway. On the left side were a set of shuttered doors opening into a linen closet, and a door to a second or guest bedroom, set at the southeastern corner of the house. Tall, paned windows looked out over the side and front lawns, shaded by a pine tree growing just beyond the corner of the house. A walk-in closet and bathroom were located just off the second bedroom, which was furnished with antique Victorian pieces.

At the end of the hallway was the master bedroom. To the north, a door opened to a small hall, which in turn led to a large walk-in closet, a bathroom with a large sunken tub, and a dressing room, with French doors leading to the swimming pool and rear lawn, which had been built onto the back of the house. Because the bedroom extended a few feet beyond the main body of the house, it had large shuttered windows on two walls, looking out over the front and side lawns. In the far corner stood a stone fireplace. Sharon and Roman brought their own queen-sized bed with them, and placed it against the west wall, balanced on either side by low tables covered with books, magazines, a princess telephone and photographs, including one of the Polanskis on their wedding day. On the opposite wall a large television set and Sony videocassette machine stood between an armoire and a tall chest of drawers.

A louvered French door led from the master bedroom to the pool area at the side of the house. The kidney-shaped swimming pool nestled up against the steep hillside, surrounded by a small flagstone terrace. A neatly manicured hedge, several tall pine trees, shrubs and a roofed gateway set amidst raised flower beds led to the guest house at the far end of the property. Here, at the end of the hillside, the split-rail fence came to an abrupt halt before the cliff fell away toward the canyon below.[9]

The lease the Polanskis signed for 10050 Cielo Drive gave them the garage, the main house and the grounds. Rudi Altobelli would continue to reside in the guesthouse at the southern end of the property. In the winter of 1969, Altobelli arranged to fly to Europe on an extended business trip; prior to his leaving, he happened to pick up a young hitchhiker in downtown Los Angeles, William Garretson, a native of Lancaster, Ohio. After a short conversation, Altobelli offered Garretson the job of caretaker to the estate at 10050 Cielo Drive. For thirty-five dollars a week, the eighteen-year old was given room and board in the guesthouse itself, for the duration of Altobelli's business trip; in return, he was required to water the lawns, arrange for the landscapers and gardeners to make regular visits, and take care of the numerous animals on the property. In addition to Altobelli's fierce Weimaraner Christopher, this included some twenty-six cats left with Altobelli by Candice Bergen and Terry Melcher temporarily; later, he was also to have charge of Sharon's Yorkshire terrier Dr. Saperstein and eventually Abigail Folger's friendly Dalmatian puppy.[10]

Although, from the front gate at 10050 Cielo Drive, neither the main residence nor the guest house was visible, Roman Polanski thought that the estate lacked a certain amount of privacy. True, it was secluded enough, just over the lip of the hill from the nearest neighbors, and the crescent shape of the property meant that one end of the estate was virtually secluded from the other. But he disliked the presence of Garretson in the guest house, feeling as if there was a live-in spy permanently on duty. Roman told Sharon that he was going to speak to Altobelli about it, but Sharon stopped him, saying, "No, he doesn't bother me. He's a very nice young man, very discreet."[11]

For both Sharon and Roman the move to Cielo Drive marked a new chapter in their lives. Busy decorating her new home, Sharon finally began to return to her former carefree self, convinced that things between her and Roman were certain to improve. On their first night at 10050 Cielo Drive, Sharon and Roman camped out, celebrating their new home and toasting the beginning of a new future. In her radiant contentment and happiness, Sharon christened 10050 Cielo Drive her "love house."[12]

Chapter 16
Pregnancy

A T THE BEGINNING OF 1969, SHARON'S FIFTH MAJOR PICTURE, *The Wrecking Crew*, was finally released. Although by no means a critical or commercial success, it did garner very good personal reviews for Sharon. While her talents as a dramatic actress might be in dispute, her sense of timing, delivery and deft physical ability marked her as a comedic actress of some potential. "Light comedy," says Herb Browar, "is difficult as hell to do. But Sharon had the facility to do it, and do it well. I thought she was brilliant in *The Wrecking Crew*. There were scenes in that movie that really pointed out where she might have gone."[1] And Hal Gefsky confirms that Dean Martin was so pleased with Sharon's performance that he wanted to do another Matt Helm film with her.[2]

The role of Freya Carlson was a fairly high profile one, which must have had something to do with her decision to take it, but it is also clear that, given the terrible reception for *Valley of the Dolls*, Sharon had made a conscious decision to return to comedic terrain. She was not disappointed; Sharon's performance was considered by many reviewers to be the movie's highlight. *The Hollywood Reporter* declared: "In a role which paraphrases Stella Stevens in *The Silencers*, Sharon Tate reveals a pleasant affinity to scatterbrain comedy and comes as close to walking away with this picture as she did in a radically different role in *Valley of the Dolls*."[3] Although she would film one more picture before her death, *The Wrecking Crew* stands as perhaps Sharon's most impressive on-screen work, a brief glimpse of what may have been had she followed a comedic path.

At the beginning of 1969, Sharon was offered a script for an Italian-French production, *Thirteen Chairs*, to be filmed on location in her beloved Italy. With five major film roles under her belt,

Sharon had become something of a recognizable commodity in Hollywood. Her great beauty ensured that people would notice and remember her, long after talk about how bad her films might be had fallen silent. She was considered one of the most beautiful women in Hollywood, and producers and directors were anxious to exploit her fame in their newest motion pictures. In the fall of 1968, Sharon was both stunned and excited to learn of the results of a poll of movie exhibitors taken by the industry trade journal *Motion Picture Herald*. In this magazine, she had been named first runner-up, among theatre owners, to actress Lynn Redgrave as the top "Star of Tomorrow."[4] With this honor, Sharon had some additional clout in the industry and, when she eventually signed on to do a sixth film, she was able to command a very substantial $125,000 salary—nearly as much money as her husband had received for directing and scripting his multi-million dollar blockbuster *Rosemary's Baby*.

The poll results, as well as the disintegration of her marriage to Roman, certainly had something to do with Sharon's eventual decision to seek a new film role. Before marrying Roman, she had declared with conviction that, once married, she would give up her acting career and devote herself to her role as wife. She had naively hoped and believed that married life would change Roman's pattern of infidelities. When it became apparent that this was not going to happen, she decided to once again pursue her career as an actress.

She was not, at the time, interested in another dramatic role. Having made a conscious decision to continue her career, Sharon decided to continue exclusively in two types of roles, which had proved so successful in the past: either sexy parts which allowed her to showcase her physical charms, or comedic roles, allowing her to further develop her growing reputation as a serious contender in the genre. Her decision reflected both her dissatisfaction with *Valley of the Dolls* and a growing realization that, no matter how hard she tried, Sharon would not score many points in the tough-to-crack dramatic market if people could see no further than her face and figure. Prior to *Valley of the Dolls*, she had desperately wanted to be taken seriously as a dramatic actress, feeling that it was necessary to prove herself in the serious roles in order to gain respect in the industry.

Her change of focus, however was, on the surface, a wise move. Sharon did not entirely abandon the idea of making a name for herself as a dramatic actress in the future, but, in order to gain the leverage she thought necessary to secure such parts, she decided to first achieve some success in other roles, allowing her more freedom of choice when the time came if she wanted to switch her energies.

The role marked for Sharon in *Thirteen Chairs* was that of female lead, a zany, comic, would-be conspirator trying to locate a fortune in stolen jewels. It was in no way a stretch for Sharon, similar to her previous role as Freya Carlson in *The Wrecking Crew*. Written into the script, however, were several semi-nude scenes, to briefly display Sharon's breasts. The intended nude footage was to be included primarily for European distribution, and Sharon was somewhat reluctant to agree to the scenes themselves until she learned that they would not appear in the eventual American cut. However, it was the prospect of working with the rest of the cast that finally convinced Sharon to take on the part. Several big Hollywood names were slated to do the picture, including Orson Welles and Vittorio de Sica.

She had few illusions as to the over-all quality of the script but, aside from her future co-stars, there was another factor which may have influenced Sharon to accept the otherwise mediocre film: it was to be shot on location in Italy, with post-production work in London, and this fact would allow her some time apart from Roman, give her back a measure of her independence and provide several months for her to consider her future, both as an actress and, more importantly, as Mrs. Roman Polanski.

Just as Sharon made a conscious decision to pursue her career again, the unexpected happened: she became pregnant. She had made no secret of the fact that she wanted a baby, but Roman, reluctant even to commit to marriage, was hardly in the mood to consider starting a family. He had previously told Sharon, according to one source, that he would never have a child, remembering his own tragic youth in war-torn Poland, and declaring, "I would never inflict the possibility of that on another human being."[5]

Sharon had been using an IUD, installed in France a year earlier. Her doctor was mystified as to how the pregnancy occured.[6] Although she knew of the pregnancy by the middle of February, Sharon did not tell Roman. Their marriage, just a year old, was already in deep trouble, an unsettling mixture of happiness and strained arguments. Uncertain about her own future, she still clung to the belief that fatherhood might change Roman's philandering ways. Yet she was also aware of his opposition to a baby.

Throughout the three years of their relationship, Sharon had always acquiesced to Roman's wishes, and he had never shown himself to be particularly sensitive to her own desires. Sharon was also aware of her own weaknesses. In the past, Roman had easily managed to influence her in matters professional and personal. She had always wanted a strong, committed marriage, and it is a measure of his power over her that Sharon had begun to parrot Roman's views about an open relationship, even though she herself was opposed to such an arrangement. Now, she apparently feared he might coerce her into having an abortion, and friends later insisted that she deliberately kept the news from her husband until such an option was too late.[7]

That Sharon made a conscious decision to hide her pregnancy was later confirmed by her mother. Rather than tell Roman, Sharon instead confided the news to Jay Sebring. It was Sebring, still on very friendly with Sharon's parents, who inadvertently became the first person to tell Paul and Doris Tate that they were soon to become grandparents.

Sharon's ability to temporarily hide her pregnancy from Roman also indicates that their physical intimacy must have been infrequent after February of 1969, further suggesting a serious strain to the marriage. "By their first wedding anniversary," confirms a friend, "a lot of us believed that things were over between Sharon and Roman. Nobody really believed that they had married in the first place, and I don't think anyone expected that it would last. But we all knew that Roman was wildly unfaithful, and Sharon had begun to learn of more incidents. She seemed to be pulling away, quietly. And then she became pregnant, and managed to convince herself that it would change Roman."[8]

A month after moving in to 10050 Cielo Drive on 15 February, the Polanskis threw a large housewarming party for a hundred friends. "The party was one of those everyone-is-here-tonight affairs," recalled John Phillips, one of the numerous guests. The evening was warm, the swimming pool glowed "like a giant turquoise stone set in the soft lawn," the "elaborate array of lights along the rail fence" glowed, as did the lights of the city behind. The evening air was scented with "pines and cherry blossoms."[9] Other guests included Warren Beatty, Peter Fonda, Tony Curtis and Danny

Kaye. Midway through the festivities of the evening, an altercation erupted between Roman's agent Willian Tennant and three uninvited guests, Harrison "Pic" Dawson, Tom Harrigan and Billy Doyle—acquaintances of both singer Cass Elliot and Roman's boyhood friend Voyteck Frykowski. The three men, who had arrived with invited guest Ben Carruthers, soon became drunk and Doyle got into a shoving match with Tennant after stepping on his foot. Angrily, Roman Polanski threw them out of the house.[10] With the tense atmosphere, John Phillips and his wife Michelle decided to leave early, at the invitation of fellow guests film director Roger Vadim and his wife Jane Fonda. From 10050 Cielo Drive, the two couples went to Vadim's Malibu beach house, where, joined by Warren Beatty, they carried on a small, private party until dawn.[11]

The day after the housewarming party, 16 March, Sharon drove Roman to Los Angeles International Airport where he caught a flight to Rio de Janeiro to attend the film festival there. Sharon remained behind, packing her things for her own trip to Europe to shoot *Thirteen Chairs*. She anticipated joining Roman in London before filming began in Rome. The Polanskis—just a month after signing the lease on 10050 Cielo Drive—therefore decided to sublet the property. One of Roman's friends, English director Michael Sarne, who had recently completed *Myra Breckenridge*, agreed to rent the house until the middle of the summer, when Sharon was due to return. But, before he was to move in, Sarne discovered a house on the beach in Malibu more to his taste and declined the Polanski house.[12]

Instead, Roman's friend Voyteck Frykowski volunteered to stay at 10050 Cielo Drive until summer. With him, he brought his live-in girlfriend, coffee heiress Abigail Folger. Roman had previously asked Warren Beatty if he would like to sublet the property. "I went up to look at the house," Beatty recalled, "and thought, Yeah, I'll stay here for a while, because I wanted to get out of the hotel, but then Abigail and Voyteck walked out from another part of the house, and said that Roman had told them to take the house. They said, 'There's plenty of room for everybody,' but I thought, No, I don't want to be in a house with other people."[13]

In late March, Voyteck and Abigail began to transfer their things from their house on Woodstock Road into the Cielo Drive property, in preparation of their move at the beginning of April. At the same time, Sharon herself was busy packing for her trip to Rome. She was scheduled to fly out of Los Angeles for Europe on March 24, along with Rudi Altobelli, who had business to attend to on the continent. The day before she left, Sunday, March 23, Sharon spent the afternoon posing for a dozen new publicity stills, taken by her personal photographer and close friend Shahrokh Hatami, a native of Iran. In the late afternoon, Jay Sebring, along with Voyteck and Abigail, arrived to have a farewell dinner with Sharon. While the four friends were chatting, Hatami noticed a strange man walking across the front lawn. He seemed unsure of where he was going, but something in his manner seemed smug to the Iranian photographer.

Irritated, Hatami walked out onto the front porch to confront the man. "I wasn't happy that he was coming on the property, and looking at people he doesn't know," he later explained. Standing in the shade of the porch was a short, casually dressed, long-haired man who appeared to be in his mid-thirties. The man said he was looking for someone—a name Hatami could not later recall, perhaps Terry Melcher. Hatami, in a loud and angry voice, told the stranger, "This is the Polanski residence. This is not the place. Maybe the people you want is back there," he said, pointing toward the guest house at the far end of the estate. "Take the back alley." Hatami indicated the dirt path on the other side of the split-rail fence which led from the paved parking area to the guest house. Just as the man was about to say something, Sharon popped her head round the door and walked out onto the front porch. "Who is it, Hatami?" she asked, stopping at the side of her friend. Hatami explained that the man was looking for someone else. Sharon watched as the stranger walked back across the lawn and down the dirt path to the guest house before she returned to the dinner party inside. A few minutes later Hatami saw the man walk back along the path and up the driveway toward the gate.[14]

The next day, on board the airplane to Rome, Sharon asked Rudi Altobelli, who had been in the guesthouse the previous evening, "Did that creepy-looking guy come back there yesterday?"[15] The stranger Sharon had watched walk across the front lawn of her house that Sunday evening was the same man who, just four months later, would order her death, Charles Manson.

Chapter 17
The Hippie Messiah

C HARLES MANSON WAS BORN ON 12 NOVEMBER, 1934, THE ILLEGITIMATE son of a sixteen-year old runaway, Kathleen Maddox. Manson never knew his father, although he was believed to be a man known by the name of Colonel Scott. In 1936, Kathleen filed a suit for child support against a Colonel Scott of Ashland, Kentucky, and was awarded a judgment of $25, plus $5 a month until young Charles reached the age of eighteen. Scott apparently never paid, and is believed to have died in 1954.[1] The surname Manson came from William Manson, a man to whom his mother was at one time briefly married.[2]

From the moment of his birth, Manson was unwanted. His mother was an alcoholic, young and unstable; when money was tight, she occasionally turned to prostitution to survive, leaving her son in the care of relatives.[3] When he was four years old, Kathleen and her brother were arrested after robbing a service station and sent to prison in West Virginia.[4] For a few weeks, Manson lived with his grandparents, a rather strict, religious couple who made no secret of the fact that they thoroughly disapproved of both Kathleen and her bastard child. After a few weeks, Manson was sent to McMechen, West Virginia, to live with his mother's sister Joanne and her husband Bill.

For Manson, home was now a large, Victorian-style house, whose wide, curved front porch looked over the town and down to the river. Although he appears to have been treated well, the boy never entirely fit in.[5] "He had just about anything he wanted," recalls childhood friend Delores Longwell. "His aunt and uncle and grandmother took him to church. He didn't like going. The only thing he really liked was the singing. Charles liked to sing."[6]

Kathleen was paroled in 1942, and returned to McMechen. "She was very, very motherly looking," Longwell remembers, "she was as motherly looking as my mother was."[7] Manson, aged eight, was returned to her custody, and Kathleen embarked upon a nomadic existence, alcoholism and abusive lovers, sharing rooms with Charles in shabby, run-down hotels and boarding houses. On several occasions, she tried to place him in temporary foster care, claiming that she was unable to care for him; when this failed, Manson was sent to Gibault School for Boys in Terre Haute, Indiana.[8] "The only thing," Manson would later declare, "my mother taught me was that everything she said was a lie. And I learned never to believe anyone about anything."[9]

Twelve-year-old Charles, according to the school reports from his time at Gibault, although on some occasions pleasant, also had "a tendency toward moodiness and a persecution complex...."[10] This was scarcely surprising, considering that, by his own account, young Manson was regularly beaten and raped. He ran away shortly after his arrival to return to his mother, only to find that she did not want him. He managed to rob several stores before being apprehended and sent to Father Flanagan's Boy's Town.

"A dead-end kid who has lived in an emotional blind alley is happy today—he's going to Boy's Town," declared an article in the *Indianapolis News*. A large photograph of a smiling young Manson, accompanied the story.[11] His stay at the legendary school, however, was brief; four days after Manson's arrival, he and another boy stole a car and drove to Illinois, committing two armed robberies along the way. They stayed for a time with the other boy's uncle, stealing from local businesses at his direction. When finally caught, thirteen-year old Charles was sent to the Indiana School for Boys at Plainfield.

During his three year term, he ran away eighteen times, hating the violence and harsh discipline. In 1951, he and several other sixteen-year-old boys stole a car and headed for California, robbing gas stations along the way. In Utah, they were finally caught. Driving a stolen car across state lines was a federal offense, and young Manson was sent to the National Training School for Boys in Washington, D.C., where he was to remain until his eighteenth birthday.

Because he had spent so much time in institutions, or on the run, Manson was barely literate. His intelligence was tested as average, with a decided interest in music, which he claimed was his favorite subject. One of his counselors later declared that Manson was an "emotionally upset youth who is definitely in need of some psychiatric orientation."[12] A psychiatrist who examined him noted a "marked degree of rejection, instability and psychic trauma."[13] But Manson somehow managed to convince the doctor that he was ready to make a go of things on the outside, and he was transferred to the National Bridge Camp. After a few months at the facility, however, Manson was charged with the homosexual rape of a fellow inmate at knifepoint, and transferred to the Federal Reformatory at Petersburg, Virginia. His early psychiatric evaluations at his latest institution stressed his sense of alienation from society, and determined that he was not only "criminally sophisticated" but also "dangerous."[14]

In September, 1952, Manson was transferred to the Federal Reformatory at Chillicothe, Ohio. Realizing that he would be eligible for parole in a few months, he studied hard to improve his education, and became a model prisoner. On May 8, 1954, at the age of nineteen—and after spending over half of his life in various institutions and correctional facilities—Charles Manson was granted parole.

Manson stayed clean for just over a year. During that time, he met and married seventeen-year old Rosalie Jean Willis, who was soon pregnant. Manson stole several cars in July, 1955, driving one from West Virginia to Los Angeles before being apprehended, having again violated the Dyer Act. At his sentencing, he declared, "I was...confined for nine years, I was badly in need of psychiatric treatment. I was mentally confused and stole a car as a means of mental release from the confused state of mind that I was in."[15] The court ordered a new psychiatric evaluation, which stated, in part: "It is evident that he has an unstable personality and that his environmental influences throughout most of his life have not been good....In my opinion this boy is a poor risk for probation; on the other hand, he has spent nine years in institutions with apparently little benefit except to take him out of circulation. With the incentive of a wife and probable fatherhood, it is possible that he might be able to straighten himself out. I would, therefore, respectfully recommend to the court that probation be considered in this case under careful supervision." The Court agreed, and Manson was given five years probation in November, 1955.[16]

In less than five months, Manson skipped out on his probation, fleeing Los Angeles with his pregnant wife. He was arrested on 14 March in Indianapolis and returned to Los Angeles for trial. The judge revoked Manson's probation and sentenced him to serve three years at the Federal Prison at Terminal Island in San Pedro, California. During Manson's trial, Rosalie gave birth to his son, Charles Jr.

During this latest incarceration, Rosalie divorced him and moved back east, taking their son with her. Manson eventually was granted some privileges, but was soon caught in the parking lot, trying to hot wire a car. For this offense, an additional five years of parole was tacked on to his sentence. A psychiatric report, dated 4 September, 1959, declared: "He does not give the impression of being a mean individual. However, he is very unstable emotionally and very insecure. He tells about his life inside the institutions in such a manner as to indicate that he has gotten most of his satisfactions from institutions. He said that he was captain of various athletic teams and that he made a great effort to entertain other people in the institutions. In my opinion, he is probably a sociopathic personality without psychosis. Unfortunately, he is rapidly becoming an institutionalized individual. However, I certainly cannot recommend him as a good candidate for probation."[17]

Three weeks after this report was filed, however, Manson was released from Terminal Island. At first, he worked a number of part-time jobs, before pimping several young girls on the streets of Malibu. He was finally arrested again six months after his parole for trying to cash a forged U.S. Treasury check for $34.50 in a local grocery store; he admitted he had stolen the check from a mailbox.[18] Although these two crimes were federal offenses, Manson arranged for a prostitute, claiming to be his pregnant wife, to plead his case before the sentencing judge; the ploy worked, and the sympathetic judge sentenced Manson to ten years, then immediately suspended it and placed him on probation.

True to form, Manson soon returned to crime. He was arrested in December, 1959 in Los Angeles for using a stolen credit card and for grand theft auto. He also took a young girl across state lines, to New Mexico, for the purpose of prostitution, another federal offense violating the Mann Act. Rather than being incarcerated, Manson was left on parole while an investigation continued. Manson took advantage of this to run; he was later picked up in Texas, having again been caught smuggling young girls across state lines for prostitution. Arrested for both this crime and for parole violation, he spent a year in the Los Angeles County Jail before finally being sentenced to the U.S. Penitentiary at McNeil Island, Washington for a period of ten years.

Manson spent some six years of his ten year sentence at McNeil Island. There, he met Alvin "Creepy" Karpis, a member of the old Ma Barker gang, and the older convict taught Charles Manson to play the steel guitar. He also began to associate with several members of the Church of Scientology, which would ultimately lead him to one of its off-shoots, a dangerous cult known as The Process. Manson would later claim that he had been put through some 150 "processing" sessions in the philosophy by fellow convict Lanier Rayner, and achieved the highest level, "theta clear."[19] Although, after his release, there is no evidence that Manson had any formal affiliation with the Church of Scientology, he certainly began to sprinkle his teachings with Scientology-influenced beliefs. Among the frequent Scientology phrases which were to reoccur consistently in Manson's later teachings were "cease to exist" and "coming to the Now." Concurrently with his interest in scientology, Manson also began to study techniques of hypnosis and mind control.[20]

Manson also appears to have been strongly infuenced by Robert Heinlein's science fiction novel *Stranger in a Strange Land.* He identified with the hero, Valentine Michael Smith, a space alien who was born on Mars and brought to Earth as a young man. Like Manson, Smith's mother was not married to his father, living, instead, with another man. And, like Manson, Smith felt alienated by the world he found, a world which did not appreciate his peculiar talents or insight. It was no coincidence that Manson would later name his second son Valentine Michael.

In prison, Manson continued to impress prison authorities and psychiatrists as a dangerous, hardened criminal. "He has commented that institutions have become his way of life and that he receives security in institutions which is not available to him in the outside world," one report declared.[21] Another report noted his "tremendous drive to call attention to himself."[22] It was obvious to most of those authorities in regular contact with him that Manson was deeply troubled, both emotionally and psychologically. Ominously, a later report made note of Manson's "fanatical interests."[23]

These interests involved both his philosophy and his music. Of the latter, Alvin Karpis recalled, "He was constantly telling people he could come on like The Beatles, if he got the chance. Kept asking me to fix him up with high power men like Frankie Carbo and Dave Beck; anybody who could book him into the big time when he got out."[24] Manson, while claiming that one day he would be bigger than his favorite musical group, at the same time listened to their music relentlessly, absorbing their songs and studying their style. A periodic correctional report in 1966 noted that Manson was spending more and more time writing his own music, practicing in his cell, and speaking of his hopes to be a musician when he was released.

Another report later that same year summed up Manson's progress and prospects: "He has a pattern of criminal behavior and confinement that dates to his teen years. This pattern is one of instability whether in free society or a structured institutional community. Little can be expected in the way of change in his attitude, behavior or mode of conduct....He has come to worship his guitar and music....He has no plans for release as he says he has nowhere to go."[25]

Adjustment to life on the outside would indeed be difficult. Manson had spent over half of his life incarcerated in institutions, reform schools and prisons. "I never realized that people outside are much different than the people on the inside," he once explained. "People inside, if you lie, you get punched, you get mis-used. You don't lie to the lieutenant, and the lieutenant don't lie to you. There's a certain amount of truth in prison, and being raised in prison, I was raised in the light of that truth."[26]

Manson was transferred from McNeil to Terminal Island in preparation of his parole. Here, he continued to study Scientology and practice his music. "I was in the Terminal Island Penitentary," recalls fellow inmate Phil Kaufmann, "and Charlie was in the yard singing. I had some friends in the music industry, and he was rather like a young Frankie Laine, he had that kind of lilt in his voice. I thought his voice was good. It was during the folk period; the young hippie stuff, and the new music, and I thought he would fit in."[27]

On the morning he was to be released, Manson begged the prison officials to let him remain. He had nowhere to go on the outside, he told them. He did not think that he could stay straight. The officials refused his request. On the morning of March 21, 1967, after spending over half of his life incarcerated, Charles Manson, aged thirty-two, was turned loose on society.[28]

Chapter 18
Beginnings of the Family

A FTER HIS RELEASE FROM TERMINAL ISLAND, CHARLES MANSON eventually settled in San Francisco. It the middle of 1967, the height of the "Summer of Love." The city was rapidly becoming the focus of all counter-culture, with its prominent psychedelic bands, protests, and abundance of illegal drugs. "Haight Ashbury," recalls Larry Melton, a former associate of Manson, "was a grey, foggy street where we totally ruled; where most of us kids wore army surplus coats and bell bottom jeans. The Haight was intense emotion, the Haight was our show. A place where straight people were in the minority, and we were the rulers of what ever we wanted to do....We had far-out places to hang out, like the Drug Store, the Psychedlic Shop, the God's Eye, the Hip Job Coop. The Haight was a refuge for rejects and throwaways who were not wanted by their parents....We could be anyone we wanted to be, and do anything we wanted. It was our world, and the Haight Ashbury was our wonderland."[1]

While wandering through the streets of nearby Berkeley, Manson met twenty-three-year-old Mary Brunner, a recent graduate of the University of Wisconsin, who worked in the library at the University of California. "He opened me up," Brunner later declared. "I was living with my dog in an apartment, and having just a real...go to work, go home, go shopping, go to work, go home, go to movies, to bed, go shopping...you know, it was so routine, it was truly a drag...and it was getting to me, and when he came in, I just dropped it, whatever was happening."[2]

Manson quickly moved in to her apartment. Brunner was not only the first of Manson's female disciples, but would also be the first to bear him a child, Valentine Michael Manson. One day, Manson brought home a second woman, Lynnette Fromme, whom he apparently seduced while telling her, "I am the God of Fuck."³ Like Brunner, Fromme came from a middle-class background, but felt alienated as she grew older. Mary Brunner objected strenuously to this peculiar living arrangement, and it says something for Manson's powers of persuasion that she eventually relented, allowing Fromme to move into her apartment as well.

In the middle of 1967, at the height of the "Summer of Love," Charles Manson and his two female followers moved to the center of the Haight-Ashbury district. The house soon had a reputation for free sex and drugs, and Manson began to attract a following among the runaways who flocked to the city. He purposely cultivated those things which he had not previously had: a family, albeit one of his own making; freedom; and easy access to drugs.

"When he came out," recalls Roger Smith, Manson's parole officer, "he initially told me that there was nothing I could do, that he could go back to prison, that he was not afraid of it, he was not going to do parole, that parole was going to be onerous. He was clearly an anti-social personality, he was superficial and he was very adaptable...Charlie was what he needed to be at any given time."⁴

It was this very ability to adapt to his surroundings that now served Manson so well. Early on, he recognized his considerable influence, and began to make a name for himself on the streets of Haight-Ashbury. His early gospel was simple: love was the most important thing, and in trying to share his love with everyone else, Manson was simply following in the footsteps of other prophets. He began to associate himself with Jesus Christ, and, through drugs, sex, and countless, mind-numbing pronouncements on the state of the world, Manson indoctrinated his followers to his own peculiar view of the world and how things should be. As future Family member Paul Watkins later described them, these followers were seeking "a new awakening of consciousness; a generation utterly alienated from their parents by the seemingly unbreachable gap of time and acid."⁵ Thus, in the summer of 1967, the Family was born.

In the summer of 1967, Charles Manson and his still relatively small number of followers lived for a time at a house located at 636 Cole Street, in the Haight-Ashbury district of San Francisco. Scarcely two blocks away, at 407 Cole Street, lived a man named Victor Wild, who sold leather goods by profession. But Wild and his residence also sheltered a curious organization called The Process, of The Church of the Final Judgement.

The Process had been founded by a former Scientologist, Robert Moore, who used the name Robert DeGrimston within the organization. Moore broke from the Church of Scientology in 1963 after reaching a very high level at their London headquarters. Eventually The Process produced several splinter groups around the United States, but Moore kept most of his energies focused on the ripe ground of San Francisco and the seemingly endless parade of runaways and drug addicts crowding the Haight. "De Grimston," wrote one author, "was the subculture's worldly philosopher, its Karl Marx. Manson was its Lenin."[6]

Victor Wild, who went by The Process name of Brother Ely, was frequently seen on the streets of the Haight-Ashbury district. Manson himself apparently knew Wild, and purchased several outfits from him. Given his interest in both Scientology and in other, more bizarre philosophies, it is not surprising that Manson pursued the ideas of The Process to some degree.[7] At the time of the murder trials, prosecutor Vincent Bugliosi was visited by two members of The Process, a Brother Matthew and a Father John, who apparently came for the express purpose of declaring that Manson had had absolutely no ties with their organization, either in San Francisco or at any other location. The following day, both men went to visit Manson in prison. Although what they may have discussed is not known, this very action seemed to indicate some prior link.[8]

Further evidence that there was a connection with The Process came from Manson himself. When Bugliosi asked if he knew who Robert DeGrimston was, Manson denied any knowledge. But he admitted having met Robert Moore, which was DeGrimston's true name. Manson went even further, telling Bugliosi, "You're looking at him. Moore and I are one and the same." By this, Bugliosi believed, Manson was declaring that his and Moore's philosophies were identical. After this conversation, however, Manson suddenly became evasive, and refused to discuss The Process again.[9]

There is no doubt, however, that much of Manson's philosophy was derived from his contact, however brief it may have been, with The Process. The similarities are simply too numerous to be coincidence. The Process, like Manson, preached that the end of the world was very near, and that only a chosen few would survive the destruction and chaos. Both Manson and The Process used the Book of Revelation to support these views, and both believed that motorcycle gangs would play an active role in bringing about the destruction of the end of civilization. Where Manson would speak of the bottomless pit, The Process referred to a bottomless void. Within the organization itself, members of The Process were called The Family, and referred to as brother, sister, father or mother.

The Process held that there were three controlling forces in the universe, three gods: Jehovah, Lucifer and Satan. Jesus Christ served as the mediator among the three, bringing them together. There was thus little distinction between the forces of good and evil.[10] Manson was almost certainly influenced by this when he later declared to his followers that he was both Jesus and the Devil. According to The Process, "Through Love, Christ and Satan have destroyed their enmity and come together for the End: Christ to judge, Satan to execute the judgements."[11] Manson put a further spin on this by declaring that this time around, it would be the Romans—the Establishment—who were crucified. "Now it's the pigs' turn to go up on the Cross," he said.[12]

Manson's views on fear and death seem also to have been derived from some of what he was exposed to in The Process literature. In one special issue of The Process magazine concerning fear, the organization stated: "Fear is beneficial....Fear is the catalyst of action. It is the energizer, the weapon built into the game in the beginning, enabling a being to create an effect upon himself, to spur himself on to new heights and to brush aside, the bitterness of failure."[13]

Manson, in fact, himself contributed a feature to the issue of The Process which followed the "Fear" edition; its theme was "Death." Manson wrote, in part: "Death goes to where life comes from. Total awareness, closing the circle, bring the soul to now. Ceasing to be, to become a world within yourself. Locked in your own totalness....Death is peace from this world's madness and paradise in my own self. Death as I lay in my grave of constant vibrations, endless now. Prison has always been my tomb. I love myself as I love death, as being alone with self the words I send you bore me and bring me from my death only to play in your illusion and bring down the Christian thought placing new value on life being death and death being life. Your world is not your world as you may think."[14] This was a shattering, ominous hint of things to come.

Eventually, Manson grew tired of San Francisco, and the Haight in particular. Ironically, he disliked the criminal element which was rapidly taking over the district. He felt confined by the city.

Then, too, there were other fringe groups coming to the surface: Jesus freaks, the Satanists, the endless stream of bikers who poured into the city in long lines of motorcycles. There was simply too much competition, too many others trying to attract the attention of the flower children, and too much freedom of thought for Manson's liking.

In September, 1967, Manson, Brunner and Fromme moved south, renting a house in Santa Barbara. Here, they met eighteen-year-old Patricia Krenwinkel, daughter of a respected, middle-class insurance salesman from Inglewood. A serious young woman, Krenwinkel was a former Sunday school teacher and Bible student; at one point, she had considered becoming a nun. Manson Family member Charles Watson later recalled: "Even though she was the sweetest of the girls, none of the men except Charlie ever got involved with her sexually. She was a little stand-offish....When Charlie started Krenwinkel trying to get bikers involved with the Family by offering them girls, they all complained that Katie was too hairy."15

By the time she reached Manson, Krenwinkel suffered from low self-esteem, which led to her heavy involvement with various drugs. "I never felt like I had a sense of who I really wanted to be or who I wanted to become," she later declared. Cannily, Manson recognized her insecurities, and managed to turn them to his advantage, paying attention to her. "That night," Krenwinkel remembers, "we slept together. And I felt really loved by him, almost immediately, mostly because I think at that point I was really desperate for someone to care. When we made love, all I remember is just crying and crying to this man, because he said, 'Oh, you're beautiful.' I couldn't believe that, I just kept crying."16 Soon, Krenwinkel became a convert, and quit her job as an insurance clerk to join the Family.

In much the same way as Mary Brunner had allowed Lynette Fromme to share her bed with Manson, both girls now welcomed Krenwinkel. "It was awkward," recalls Fromme of the situation, "but it easily became familiar."17 Manson and his female followers headed north in a Volkswagon van, through San Francisco and up the coast into Oregon and on to Seattle. They stayed for several weeks; Manson wanted to look up some former fellow inmates, and also to try to locate his mother, who had moved to the Pacific Northwest a few years earlier. On this trip, Manson met twenty-five-year-old Bruce Davis, a former editor of his high school yearbook and student at the University of Tennessee. By the time he met Manson, Davis had been heavily involved with drugs. Davis joined Manson and his women, and became his principal male disciple.

During one of their frequent trips around California, the Family discovered an old school bus for sale. Manson traded his Volkswagon van as a down payment and took possession. He and his followers removed the seats from the rear two-third of the bus, creating a living space complete with refrigerator, portable stove and numerous pillows. They painted the exterior of the bus, including the windows, black. At the helm of the bus, Manson and his group of followers set off for Los Angeles.

On the way, they stopped in San Francisco, where, at a party, they met nineteen-year-old Susan Atkins. Atkins was an extremely troubled young woman. Her mother had died of cancer when Susan was fourteen, and the following years had been marked with family quarrels, involvement with drugs and sex, and ended when she ran away at the age of sixteen. Atkins became a waitress in San Francisco, staying with several habitual criminals who made a living holding up convenience stores. In 1966, she was arrested by Oregon State Police for riding in a stolen car, and spent three months in jail. Placed on probation for two years, she headed back to San Francisco, where she worked as a topless dancer. Occasionally, she danced at Anton LaVey's Church of Satan, participating in his Black Masses.

Atkins' first meeting with Manson made a deep impact. She listened to his music and was enchanted. They had sex that first night, and Manson told her to imagine that she was making love with her father, which, according to Atkins, heightened the experience immeasurably. Rechristened Sadie by Manson, Susan Atkins became the newest member of his roving Family. "Susan," recalled Watson, "was the evangelist of the group, always praising Charlie, repeating his teaching, urging the rest of us to give ourselves to him totally, even while her own ego was fighting back sometimes, asserting itself against his domination. It wasn't so much that she resisted doing what Charlie told her; she just wanted to be special; she refused to be annihilated."[18]

Manson picked up another female follower, Ruth Ann Morehouse, the teenage daughter of former Methodist minister Dean Morehouse. Called Ouisch by the Family, she had run away from her family in Ukiah to join up with Manson after meeting him on a previous visit to the Bay area. Her father, understandably upset, called the police and tried to have Manson arrested for harboring a teenage run-away, but Manson managed to save himself by convincing Morehouse that he meant his daughter no harm, talking of his ideas of peace and love. He capped this triumph by turning the former minister on to LSD. Thereafter, Morehouse not only allowed his daughter to join the Family, but also himself became one of its fringe members.

One of the most amazing aspects in the early years of the Manson Family is the sheer number of important contacts which they had made. On arriving in Los Angeles in the fall of 1967, Manson managed to secure recording time for his music at Universal. He made several demos; these brought no attention but, he claims in his autobiography, he was allowed free run of the studios, and became friendly with numerous celebrities. Manson asserts that he had sex with many of these important personages, heavily implying that their tastes were far from wholesome. "I could authenticate experiences with some of those in Hollywood that would make the sexual practices I enjoyed look pure and innocent," he later declared.[19]

Eventually, the Family settled in the Topanga Canyon area, in a house known as the Spiral Staircase. While in residence at the Spiral Staircase, the Family first became involved with the numerous Satanic groups operating in the area. Cultists gravitated to the house, which was owned by a woman apparently involved in both Anton LaVey's Church of Satan in San Francisco and several other fringe groups, and the rituals the Family witnessed included Black Masses, animal sacrifice and blood drinking.[20]

Once Manson took up residence in Los Angeles, his contacts with the occult—and the contacts of those who surrounded him—continued. Manson himself acknowledged that the time he and his Family spent at the Spiral Staircase, and the people they encountered there, was the beginning of the darker side of their existence. "I think I can honestly say our philosophy—fun and games, love and sex, peaceful friendship for everyone—began changing into the madness that eventually engulfed us in that house." [21]

Manson met another group of people whom he described as the "Devil's Disciples," and accompanied several members north on a trip to Mendocino. Just how heavily involved Manson and his followers were in these groups is difficult to determine. But, in spite of Manson's later claims that he disliked the activity surrounding the Spiral Staircase, a wealth of secondary evidence suggests just the opposite—that he and his followers went far beyond anything they ever encountered at Topanga Canyon.

One of the attendees at these parties was twenty-year-old Robert Beausoleil. Author Truman Capote would later describe him as handsome, "but in a rather husterlish camp-macho style."[22] He ran away when he was twelve, after suffering, according to his account, years of sexual and physical abuse. At fourteen he was made a ward of the Court and sent to reform school.[23] Wandering in Los Angeles, he made a living as a rock musician and occasional actor. In 1968, he appeared in two low-budget films: a "western-porno" called *Ramrodder*, starring with soon-to-be fellow Manson family member Catherine Share, and, a documentary called *Mondo Hollywood*, which, ironically, also featured a segment on Jay Sebring.

"To me, Devil-worship was a lot of shit," Beausoleil once declared.[24] But gradually, he became indoctrinated, and through the use of acid came to at least accept the basics of Satanism. When first meeting Manson, Beausoleil told him that he was the devil, and he himself was on an all-meat diet. His most obvious Satanic link was to film director Kenneth Anger.

Kenneth Anger was an avant-garde filmmaker who used experimentation and intense visuals to create dream-like images on screen. His works were nightmarish mixtures of psychedelic pictures, violence, music and color. Anger himself had been a follower of the infamous Aleister Crowley, the self-proclaimed Great Beast and England's premier occult figure in the early years of this century. In the late 1960s he joined Anton LaVey's Church of Satan in San Francisco.[25]

Anger met Beausoleil in 1967, while he was preparing to film the second part of a Satanic trilogy, *Lucifer Rising*. The first installment, *Invocation*, had been released the previous year. Anger hired Beausoleil to star in his new film, playing the part of Lucifer. In addition, Beausoleil formed an eleven-piece band, the Magick Powerhouse of Oz, which provided the score for the film. Before filming was complete, however, Anger and Beausoleil got into some kind of disagreement, and the latter reportedly made off with a chunk of the completed footage. Nevertheless, Anger was able to complete *Lucifer Rising*, and had enough stock footage left to do the third installment, *Invocation of My Demon Brother*, which again featured Beausoleil as Lucifer.[26] Anger declared at the film's premier, "My reason for filming has nothing to do with 'cinema' at all. It's a transparent excuse for capturing people....I consider myself as working Evil in an evil medium."[27]

The stay at the Spiral Staircase was brief; after a few months, Manson moved his Family out, and, at Beausoleil's invitation, they camped out at the ruins of a burnt-out mansion he had recently rented in Topanga Canyon. Together with Beausoleil, Manson formed a band called The Milky Way. They had one, short-lived performance at a country-western club in the Canyon, but were fired after a single set. The owner claimed that they were attracting the wrong kind of crowd to his establishment.[28]

Charles Manson and Bobby Beausoleil were, in spite of their musical connection, largely at odds with each other. Each was a powerful, determined personality, and each had his own set of female followers. But Beausoleil, unlike Manson, was not obsessed with the idea that he was a latter-day prophet sent to preach a new way of life to the younger generation. Although Beausoleil became a member of the Family, and later committed murder on Manson's behalf, he was always on the fringe of the group, coming and going at will, and was never caught up in the Helter Skelter philosophy.

During this time, the Family continued to grow. One new convert to Manson's way of life was Dianne Lake. Known in the Family as Snake, Lake had joined the famous Hog Farm Commune at the age of thirteen, and left with Manson when he visited the encampment. Catherine Share, called Gypsy within the Family, also came into Manson's orbit. The daughter of Hungarian-German-Jewish parents, she had been born in Paris in 1942, and was brought to the United States eight years later when she was adopted by a California family. By the time she joined the Manson Family, Share had attended several years of college, been married and divorced, and acted in several small film roles.

Other new members included Sandra Good, daughter of a well-to-do California stockbroker; Brooks Poston; Kitty Lutesinger; and sixteen-year-old Paul Watkins, known in the Family as Little Paul; and Nancy Pitman, called Brenda within the Family, who had come to Manson through the latter's friendship with Deirdre Lansbury, daughter of actress Angela Lansbury. By this time, too, Manson had become a father again, when Mary Brunner gave birth to a son, Valentine Michael Manson, whom they called Pooh Bear.

In the summer of 1968, Sandra Good, through a friend, arranged for the Family to visit the Spahn Movie Ranch, just above the town of Chatsworth in the Simi Hills at the northern fringe of the San Fernando Valley. The ramshackle collection of decaying sets stood as scenery for films like *Duel in the Sun* and the television series *The Lone Ranger.*[29] It was owned by eighty-year old George Spahn, who, crippled with arthritis and nearly blind, was no longer up to its day-to-day running. Manson arranged for the Family to move into the collection of collapsing, haphazard movie sets and shacks; in return for this housing, he and his Family would take care of the ranch and the horses which were rented out to visitors, and cook and clean for George Spahn. Contrary to popular belief, however, the Family's residence at Spahn Ranch was never continuous for very long. They stayed for several months at a time, alternating between it and other houses for the next year-and-a-half.

The Spahn Movie Ranch stood just off the old Santa Susanna Pass Road, sprawling across a stretch of desert snuggled between the Simi Mountains and Topanga Canyon. A number of dry creeks and a freshwater stream crossed the land, which was filled with enormous rocks and boulders. At some distance from the main buildings was a waterfall and a large rock formation with a shallow cave in the side of a cliff. The movie set itself was near the roadway, a fake western town, with a boardwalk along which such buildings as the Longhorn Saloon, a jail, a hotel, the Rock City Cafe, an undertaker's parlor, a carriage house filled with dusty old vehicles, and a number of smaller stores were constructed. A barn and coral stood off to one side, along with several bunk houses and trailers used by the ranch hands. A little further up the fire road stood a large ranch house, and several shacks into which the Family first moved.

Aside from a number of those who would come and go, the Manson Family was now almost complete. By the end of the summer, Leslie Van Houten, Steve Grogan and Charles Watson would join. And, by the end of the summer, Charles Manson would be back on his quest to conquer the musical world.

Chapter 19
Wilson and Melcher

I N THE SUMMER OF 1968, CHARLES MANSON MADE HIS MOST IMPORTANT social and business contacts, two men who were to be deeply involved with the Family during the following eventful year. The first of these was Dennis Wilson, drummer of the rock group The Beach Boys. The second man, Terry Melcher, would play an even greater and, for Sharon Tate, ultimately more fatal role in Manson's life.

Dennis Wilson, singer and drummer for The Beach Boys, lived at the time in a large house set in the middle of a three-acre estate at 14400 Sunset Boulevard. Formerly the hunting lodge of Will Rogers, the house was surrounded with manicured lawns and a swimming pool in the shape of the state of California.[1] Wilson, having gone through a messy divorce, frequently picked up hitchhikers while driving through Los Angeles, taking them back to his house for sex and drugs. One day, he picked up two female hitchhikers, Ella Bailey and Patricia Krenwinkel, both members of the Manson Family. Back at his Sunset Boulevard residence, Wilson listened for several hours while the two women spoke almost exclusively of a man they knew named Charlie.

Wilson had a recording session that evening, but he allowed the two girls to stay at his house in his absence. When he returned at three in the morning, he discovered a black-painted school bus parked in his driveway. On entering his own house, he found the living room full of a dozen or more scantily clad women; in the middle of the group was Charles Manson. Frightened, Wilson asked, "Are you going to hurt me?" Manson approached him and said, "Do I look like I'm going to hurt you, brother?" while he knelt down and began to kiss Wilson's feet, a favorite action to demonstrate his humbleness. Wilson was suitably impressed: he allowed Manson and his Family to stay with him for several months.[2]

Manson and Wilson spent a good deal of time discussing song-writing and singing duets. Although Wilson sat through these long musical sessions, and tried to promote Manson heavily to others he knew in the industry, he later told Vincent Bugliosi that "Charlie never had a musical bone in his body."[3] While Wilson and Manson chatted happily, the women of the Family cleaned the house, shopped, and cooked. At night, they provided Wilson with sexual entertainment, but soon enough, the singer put a stop to this. Most of the Manson Family had a number of venereal diseases, and Wilson took them all to his Beverly Hills doctor for penicillin shots—"probably the largest gonorrhea bill in history," he later said.[4]

Soon, Wilson had cause to regret his generosity. The Family members simply appropriated anything and everything they wanted. Manson continually asked for money, to pay off creditors, to buy new musical instruments, to pay for studio time, to buy drugs. Most of Wilson's clothes disappeared as well, worn by the family or simply given away by them to people they met on the streets. Then, too, there was the occasion when several members of the Family took Wilson's uninsured $21,000 Ferrari and smashed it into the side of a mountain near Spahn Ranch, totaling the vehicle.[5] Susan Atkins' teeth needed to be fixed, and Wilson paid the bill for her dentist. He even gave Manson a number of gold records which had been awarded to him as a member of The Beach Boys. Altogether, Wilson later estimated that he ended up losing about $100,000 of his money or belongings to the Manson Family.[6] After the murders in the summer of 1969, Wilson commented, "I'm the luckiest guy in the world, because I got off only losing my money."[7]

The other important personage introduced to Charles Manson that summer was Terry Melcher. Melcher was the son of Doris Day, and worked as a producer at Columbia Records. His interests had included the groups The Byrds and Paul Revere and the Raiders. In addition, he also headed a number of smaller music publishing and television related businesses. If anyone could pull the strings in Hollywood for Manson, it was Melcher.

Melcher first met Manson at a party at Dennis Wilson's house. He walked into a room to find Manson sitting in the middle of a group of admiring females, gently strumming his guitar. Whether or not Melcher was impressed by Manson's disputed musical abilities, he agreed to his friend Wilson's suggestion that he arrange for some studio time for Manson in the near future.

Manson also met Gregg Jakobson, an associate of Melcher, who was to eventually serve as liaison between his boss and the Manson Family. Jakobson, who was married to the daughter of comedian Lou Costello, became rather deeply involved with the goings-on at Spahn Ranch, but luckily managed to avoid any of the murderous activity which occurred at the end of the summer of 1969.

There were to be three more additions to the Manson circle that summer. Seventeen-year-old Steve Grogan had been living at Spahn Ranch since the spring of 1967. Grogan had dropped out of school in the tenth grade and spent a year wandering round California, staying at various communes and monasteries.[8] "There was a point in my life," he later recalled, "where I was being real romantic about the meaning of life. I was a real philosopher, philosophized a lot about life and its meaning, deep meanings in my life, my purpose in life, you know, what I imagine every teenager goes through that same period in his life."[9]

Grogan had a lengthy juvenile criminal record. In 1967, he was arrested for possession of marijuana, counseled and released. A few months later, he was apprehended while attempting to steal a pair of socks. His parents put up the money for bail, and Grogan walked.[10] Shortly after this, he was arrested for indecent exposure. "The pants I was wearing," Grogan later explained, "had the crotch ripped out of them from riding on the horses and things at the ranch. So when I was playing with the kids on the lawn I guess one of the mothers had viewed it from one of the windows and had called the police thinking that I was exposing myself to their children."[11] As a result of this incident, Grogan was placed on probation.

Through his wanderings, he eventually came to Spahn Ranch. Although he was only fifteen, and a runaway, Grogan managed to get a job working with the horses and cleaning the property in exchange for room and board. When Manson and the rest of the Family arrived at Spahn Ranch, they quickly befriended Grogan, rechristening him Clem.

Leslie Van Houten was a very pretty, eighteen-year-old whom Bobby Beausoleil had picked up hitchhiking while on a trip in Northern California. Van Houten had been born in 1949 in Altadena, California, and grew up in Monrovia, where she excelled in her school activities including band. Although her parents divorced when she was young, Van Houten seems to have done well in school and had few problems. In high school, she had been her freshman class treasurer, a volunteer in the Job's Daughters service organization and a member of her church choir.

"I was always a very creative girl," Van Houten recalls, "as a young girl artistic, but for a while I wanted to become a school teacher. Somewhere along the line I got distracted and lost the motivation. I believe that I was desperately seeking someone that I could love and hold on to and call my own. That somehow my dad leaving had left a space there."[12]

Van Houten eventually moved in with her sister Charlene, and was exposed to the latter's frequent drug use. Her increasing interest in both religion and philosophy, mixed with the freely-flowing drugs of the late 1960s, left Van Houten open to the Manson Family's sphere of influence.

But by far the most important newcomer to the Manson Family was Charles Denton Watson, who, a little over a year later, was to become Manson's main instrument of murder. Watson, a tall, handsome twenty-two-years old, hailed from Copeville, Texas. He was a gifted athlete, a member of his high school's football and track teams, a well-liked, charming boy with good manners and a studious attitude toward his education. All of this changed when Watson left his hometown to go to school at the North Texas State College to study Business Management.

During his three years at North Texas State, Watson gradually declined. The athlete and scholar joined a fraternity, where he encountered both drugs and alcohol. On a dare, he broke into a high school some fifty miles away and stole several typewriters; his mother managed to hush up the affair and convince the police not to press charges. After three years at North Texas State, he suddenly quit school. He moved to Dallas with a friend who got him a job with Braniff Airlines. Here, he continued to both use and deal drugs, slept with numerous girls he met, and, while under the influence of either drugs or alcohol, wrecked several automobiles. Deciding that there were bigger and better opportunities—including, in Watson's own words "much better grass"—in California, he left for the state in 1967.[13]

In Los Angeles, Watson applied for but never attended college; his application, however, ensured a supply of money from his parents back home, which allowed him to engage in other ventures.

Contrary to what Watson would later claim, he was heavily involved with drugs long before meeting Manson. He later admitted to taking LSD up to five times a day on a regular basis before joining the Family.[14]

Watson first met Manson through Dennis Wilson. According to Watson, he picked up the singer while the latter was hitchhiking along Sunset Boulevard. Wilson had Watson take him back to his mansion up the Strip. Wilson told Watson that there was someone he should meet in the living room, and Charles dutifully followed. Through a cloud of thick blue hashish and marijuana smoke, Watson saw Manson, guitar in hand, sitting in the midst of a group of semi-nude women. Watson joined Manson and Wilson as they smoked more pot, while Manson strummed away at his guitar, talking all the while about love and peace and music. When Watson stumbled out of the house later that afternoon, Wilson told him that he could come back at any time to use the pool. Watson took him at his word, returning the following day, and again spoke with Manson.[15] Watson also accompanied the women on their frequent garbage runs, when they ransacked refuse bins behind grocery stores, picking out bruised or damaged vegetables and canned goods to take back to Wilson's house or Spahn Ranch. Eventually, Watson, because of failing finances, moved into Wilson's house permanently. After a few weeks in this setting, with the freely available sex and the even more frequent drug use, Watson voluntarily decided to join Charles Manson and his followers. He was promptly rechristened "Tex."[16]

Chapter 20
Spahn Ranch

I N THE SUMMER OF 1968, DENNIS WILSON ARRANGED FOR MANSON
to record some demo tracks. Wilson's brother Brian had split the
cost of installing a studio in his house on Bellagio Road in Bel
Air with his record label, Capital, on the understanding that The
Beach Boys would then scout out new talent and record them for
Capital's benefit. Dennis accompanied Manson and several of his
women to his brother's house, where they spent the night recording
several songs. The first night stretched into a second, and then a
third, leaving Brian Wilson distinctly uncomfortable. "I never saw
them," he recalled; "the bad vibes filled the house and I locked
myself in the bedroom....They had weird names, they were dirty,
they showed little respect for our property."[1]

On August 9, 1968—exactly one year before Sharon was murdered—Gregg Jakobson arranged for Manson and some of his followers to record in a Van Nuys studio. This resulted in several additional demo tapes, to add to Manson's growing collection. Jakobson
was impressed enough with Manson and his lifestyle to sit through
endless philosophical discussions and even considered joining the
Family himself.

In the fall of 1968, Manson succeeded in selling The Beach Boys
one of his songs. Called "Cease to Exist," Manson allegedly wrote it
as a fable for the group, then in the midst of disagreements. But they
tampered with the song before they recorded it, much to Manson's
anger. The words of the chorus, "Cease to Exist," were changed to
"Cease to resist," thereby giving the song a vaguely sexual connota-
tion which was the last thing Manson had intended. They changed
the title, too, calling the song, "Never Learn Not to Love." As eventually recorded, with the typical Beach Boy harmonies and back-up

instrumentals, the song was a far cry from what Manson had first written. The song went on to The Beach Boys album 20/20 and was eventually released as a B-side to another single, "Bluebirds over the Mountain," on December 8, 1968. The single reached sixty-one on the *Billboard* charts before disappearing into obscurity. Manson, in payment, received an unspecified amount of cash and a BSA motorcycle.[2]

Throughout the summer and fall of 1968, Manson was continually after Terry Melcher to cut him a deal, to pull some industry strings. Melcher was to make a few half-hearted attempts, but his interest in Manson had never been very great. But Manson and members of his Family persisted in cultivating a relationship. In late summer, 1968, Manson Family members Charles Watson and Dean Morehouse both apparently attended several parties given by Melcher and his girlfriend, actress Candice Bergen, at their house at 10050 Cielo Drive—the same house in which Watson would slay Sharon a year later.[3]

On another occasion, Watson hitchhiked to Beverly Hills and walked up Benedict Canyon Road, Cielo Drive and the cul-de-sac which ended at the gate to 10050. Having let himself in to the property by pushing the automatic gate control button, Watson made his way to the back door and rang the bell. A maid answered and recalled that he had made an earlier visit with Dean Morehouse. She left Watson sitting in the kitchen while she herself went off to find Melcher. In a few minutes, Candice Bergen walked in to the kitchen and demanded to know who he was and what he wanted. Watson explained that Gregg Jakobson had been arrested on drug charges, and that he needed bail money, but Bergen, apparently annoyed by the fact that Watson was covered in grime, eyed him suspiciously. When Melcher entered the room, he told Watson that he was unable to help, saying that there was no way for him to come up with the money as it was a Saturday.[4]

Sometime in the fall of 1968, Terry Melcher lent Watson and Dean Morehouse his Jaguar, which they picked up at 10050 Cielo Drive and then drove to Ukiah to pick up Mary Brunner's baby Pooh Bear, Manson's son. Melcher even gave Watson his Standard Oil credit card to use.[5] After returning to Los Angeles, Watson apparently took advantage of this fact to fill up the Family's schoolbus as well.

Manson himself visited the property at 10050 Cielo Drive on numerous occasions. Once, he sat in the back seat as Dennis Wilson drove Melcher home. Manson did not leave the car, but continued to sit inside, strumming his guitar.[6] Manson also became involved with the property on Cielo Drive not only because of Melcher but also because Rudi Altobelli, the owner of the estate and permanent resident of the guest house, was a major agent in the city. If Wilson and Melcher could not come through for him, Manson reasoned that Altobelli could pull all of the right strings. Altobelli later described how, in the late summer of 1968, both Melcher and Jakobson had talked excitedly about Manson and his Family, and were anxious to arrange a meeting.

Altobelli eventually did meet Manson, but it was not at Cielo Drive. One evening he attended a party at Dennis Wilson's Sunset Boulevard mansion, and Manson and his followers naturally formed a large portion of the invitation list. Wilson introduced the pair. Altobelli agreed to listen to one of the demo tapes which Manson had recorded that summer. But he was not interested in Manson's philosophy, incessantly spilled out during the course of the evening. Jakobson had spoken of Manson's great ideas about love and peace and life, but Altobelli, uninterested, apparently brushed him aside.

Another Hollywood personality introduced to Manson was the Polanskis' good friend John Phillips. Both Dennis Wilson and Terry Melcher approached Phillips with tapes of Manson and asked him to listen to their new discovery. Phillips wasn't very enthused, but Wilson tried to draw him in. One day, he rang Phillips and told him: "This guy Charlie's here with all these great-looking chicks. He plays the guitar and he's a real wild guy. He has all these chicks hanging out like servants. You can come over and just fuck any of them you want. It's a great party."[7]

"Terry Melcher and Dennis Wilson," Phillips later said, "and the people who were living with Manson at Dennis Wilson's house used to call me all the time, you know, and say, 'Come on over, it's incredible.' I'd just shudder every time. I'd say, 'No, I think I'll pass.'"[8]

By the beginning of August, 1968, Dennis Wilson had had enough. He moved out of his house on Sunset Boulevard and into a small apartment with Gregg Jakobson. He left it up to his business manager to throw out Manson and his followers. Manson immediately went back to Spahn Ranch, asking if they could stay at the outlaw shacks—small wooden huts that had formerly been used as set pieces for the numerous westerns filmed at the Ranch. George Spahn agreed, and the Manson Family moved in, staying for just over two months.

Manson's relations with George Spahn always remained good, and Manson made sure that the girls took care of the old man, ensuring that he never had the opportunity to find out what was taking place at the ranch. But, for other residents of the Spahn Ranch, having Manson and his band of followers living in their midst was a less than comfortable experience. The ranch hands in particular disliked him, and never trusted either Manson or his Family. Randy Starr, Donald Jerome "Shorty" Shea and Juan Flynn were all witnesses to the comings and goings at the ranch, many of them illegal. In time, as Manson became more comfortably ensconced at Spahn, he arranged to make drug deals at a high level. For a time, the ranch served as a kind of mid-way point, between the stretch of Death Valley and the sprawl of Los Angeles, a place where bikers converged to leave their stashes, and where Manson, in turn, sold to those from the neighboring areas.

For Manson, Spahn Ranch represented a pratice Utopia, a place where he could remain firmly in control and steer the destinies of those around him. "I see the young love coming and getting free of all the programs," he once told follower Paul Watkins.[9] At the Ranch, Manson was able, to a large degree, to separate his Family members from their previous lives.

"Being at Spahn's made it easier," Watkins later wrote. "We were isolated from society. We had no TV sets, no newspapers, and we rarely left the ranch except to drive into town on garbage runs or into the valley to pick up a truckload of corn for the horses. We were nearly always together: sleeping, eating, making love, playing music, working on the ranch. There was nothing more important to any of us than putting Charlie's scene together."[10]

"It was a great place, actually," recalls Lynette Fromme of the Spahn Ranch. "We could make anything we wanted out of it. It was like having the *Our Gang* set. You could turn it into anything."[11]

"It was all very fun in the beginning, innocent," Van Houten later declared of their time at the Ranch. "At first, the Magical Mystery Tour was that we would be cowboys, or gypsies or pirates, and every day, it was to wear a different role, so that we would get more out of ourselves. Every day was Halloween."[12]

Life at Spahn Ranch was a more or less leisurely existence while Manson waited for his big recording contract to come through. The Family helped take care of the horses Spahn kept to rent out to weekend visitors, cleaned the barns and occasionally acted as guides to curious tourists. Several of the women were detailed to look after the group's children: by this time, Manson's son Pooh Bear had been joined by Susan Atkin's bastard son, who she named Zezo Ze-ce Zadfrack, as well as several other infants. The Family doted on these offspring, but Manson in a determined effort to sever all links between parents and children, pointedly refused to let mothers care for their infants, instead charging other female members with the task.

In time, the Family spread over the ranch, erecting tents, building lean-tos, and trying to find secret hiding places. The women would borrow ranch hand Johnny Swartz's 1959 yellow and white Ford and go on garbage runs to Hughes Market at Chatsworth Plaza, just down the road, spending the rest of the afternoon preparing the food for the evening meal. Dinner was a communal event, often taken outdoors, sitting around a campfire while Manson sang or rambled on about philosophy.

After dinner, the drugs came out: pot, hash, LSD, peyote, mushrooms—whatever the Family happened to have on hand. "They came in different, various ways," recalled Steve Grogan. "Some people just brought in a bag of weed. Other times one or two members of the group would go out and buy drugs. It was all bought so everybody would ingest them at the same time. That was one of the rituals, that no one would be taking any drugs without everybody else being able to participate at the same time."[13]

"The evening ritual," said Paul Watkins, "was always the same: we'd eat dinner, listen to Charlie rap for an hour or two, play music together, then make love—either in small groups or as a Family. Once or twice a week we'd set aside an evening to take acid. Use of drugs in the Family was never indiscriminate or casual. Rarely did we smoke grass during the day, and Charlie forbade anyone taking acid on his own. Drugs were used for a specific purpose: to bring us into a higher state of consciousness as a Family, to unify us."[14]

Some nights there were orgies, which, in later literature, assumed truly gigantic proportions. Former Family member Linda Kasabian, for example, testified that Manson directed the couplings, picking out partners and supervising initiations. Sometimes, orgies were staged to impress visitors if Manson wanted them to join his group, and the women were occasionally used as bargaining chips, with sex in exchange for money or drugs with the bikers who hung out at the ranch. That Manson eventually came close to dominating the sex lives of his followers is without dispute, although it would be incorrect to think that the only sexual encounters on the ranch were those which occurred at Manson's direction. But the numerous tales of nightly orgies, rapes, and even necrophilia which later surfaced—all of these seem, in retrospect, to have been greatly exaggerated by the contemporary media reports hungry for any details of the seedier side of life at the Spahn Ranch prior to the murders in August, 1969. Even Charles Watson later admitted: "Despite some of what has been written about Manson's methods of breaking down inhibitions, I never saw any male homosexual activity in the Family; in fact, I heard Charlie preach against it several times. I never saw or heard anything about the sexual initiations that were reported, either—Charlie supposedly performing perverse sexual acts with a new member while the rest of us watched."[15]

For the most part, however, these evenings were filled with talk about death of the ego and loss of individualism in favor of the group. "I am you and you are me," Manson told his Family. "What we do for ourselves, man, we do for everyone. There's no good in life other than coming to the realization of the love that governs it....Coming to 'Now,' dig? People, you know, wear all kinds of masks to hide their love, to disguise it, to keep themselves from conquering their own fear. But we have nothing to hide...nothing to be ashamed of. There is no right and wrong."[16]

Steve Grogan later recalled how Manson repeatedly told the group "to get rid of our egos, because if our egos were involved in anything we do, it would bring in confusion."[17] "To lose the ego is to die," Manson once said. "And when you die or a part of you dies, you release that part to love. So what it means is overcoming your fear of death. Fear is the beginning of growth. Yet, it's what holds us back. Fear is a higher form of consciousness, 'cause it gives us a glimpse of the love. So it's like you have to submit to your fear...your fear is your pathway to love."[18]

Manson became expert at testing his followers. Watson later recalled how Manson would walk up to him, gun in hand, and say, "Go ahead, shoot me." When, inevitably, Watson refused, Manson would take the gun back, declaring, "Well, now I have the right to kill you."[19] To a large extent, this was, as Paul Watkins recalled, "a game of awareness, being aware primarily of what Charlie wanted, anticipating Charlie. My success in the Family was based on my ability to play the games. I learned to pick up on Charlie's signals, knew when he moved a certain way or assumed a certain expression just what he wanted."[20]

Such pronouncements were quickly absorbed by the various Family members. "Whatever is necessary to do, you do it," Sandra Good later declared. "When somebody needs to be killed, there's no wrong. You do it, and then you move on. And you pick up a child, and you move him to the desert. And you pick up as many children as you can, and you kill whoever gets in your way. This is us."[21]

Manson's philosophy duly impressed many of those he encountered. David Smith, who ran the Haight-Ashbury Free Clinic and knew Manson, collaborated with Al Rose on an analysis of Manson and his followers which was written before the murders in 1969. Titled "The Group Marriage Commune: A Case Study," the article eventually appeared in *The Journal of Psychedlic Drugs* in 1970.

Rose and Smith described Manson as:

a thirty-five-year-old white male, with a past history of criminal activity....He was never arrested or convicted of a crime of violence, and, in fact, during the study expressed a philosophy of non-violence....He was an extroverted, persuasive individual who served as absolute ruler of this group marriage commune....Tales of Charlie's sexual prowess were related to all new members....Charlie would get up in the morning, make love, eat breakfast, make love and go back to sleep. He would wake up later and make love, have lunch, make love and go back to sleep. Waking up later, he would make love, eat dinner, make love, and go back to sleep—only to wake up in the middle of the night to have intercourse again. Such stories, although not validated, helped him maintain his leadership role. Charlie had a persuasive mystical philosophy placing great emphasis on the belief that people did not die and that infant consciousness was the ultimate state....Charlie used the words of Jesus, 'He who is like the small child shall reap the rewards of Heaven,' as a guide for the group's child-rearing philosophy....However, Charlie's mysticism often became delusional and he, on occasion, referred to himself as 'God' or 'God and the Devil.' Charlie could probably be diagnosed as an ambulatory schizophrenic....Charlie set himself up as 'initiator of new females' into the commune. He would spend most of their first day making love to them, as he wanted to see if they were just on a 'sex trip'...or whether they were seriously interested in joining the group....An unwillingness, for example to engage in mutual oral-genital contact was cause for immediate expulsion, for Charlie felt that this was one of the most important indications as to whether the girl would be willing to give up her sexual inhibitions....Charlie felt that getting rid of sexual inhibitions would free people of most of their problems....The females in the group had as their major role the duty of gratifying the males. This was done by cooking for them and sleeping with them....Of the fourteen females in the 'immediate family,' two were pregnant at the time of our observations. Both said that Charlie was the father, although there was no way to verify the claim, as sexual relations in the group were polygamous. It should be noted that Charlie was held in such high regard by the girls that all of them wanted to carry his child."[22]

Very early on, Manson was concerned with breaking inhibitions and standards, crushing the moral and psychological barriers in his followers. Part of this philosophy was designed to break the ego of the initiates, to reduce them to a common level, on which they became emotionally dependent on Manson. Once their resistance was broken, it was much easier for him to indoctrinate them to his way of thinking.

Manson also used humiliation and violence. "If someone didn't do something just exactly the way he said it," recalls Steve Grogan, "he would go into a tirade, break something or slap somebody around or slug them. And a lot of times—when I look back on it— it looks like he was using the girls to talk to different people through, people who just came to the group, like men. He would yell at the girls and tell them, 'You're stupid. Why don't you do it this way?'"[23]

Manson was certainly crafty enough to recognize and play on his followers' emotional weaknesses, but his eventual command of their bodies and minds rested more with their own inabilities to come to terms with life outside the Family than with any mythological powers which Manson purportedly possessed. Manson, for all of his influence and power, simply managed to manipulate in each of his followers that which already existed. He himself would always claim, in his self-serving fashion, that he had ordered no one to do anything, and that every one of his followers was free to come and go at will, to choose freely what to do and what not to do. Even though the evidence does indicate the large degree to which

Manson was able to manipulate his Family, on this issue, at least, it is generally correct to take him at his word. All of the Family members were free to make their own decisions. That they all decided to believe Manson's bizarre philosophy speaks more for their own disturbed states of mind than for Manson's power over them.

Many of the Family members were later to claim that it was only after they met Manson, and he broke down all of their previously held beliefs, that they came to such a state of dependence and unquestioning trust. Often—and particularly in the cases of two of the most prominent future murderers, Susan Atkins and Charles Watson—they insisted that it was a combination of Manson's powerful hold over them, along with his incessant distribution of drugs, which led them to commit their crimes. In effect, they presented themselves as good-hearted, all-American youths, corrupted through both Manson's evil influence and by the use of mind-altering drugs.

At the time of their trials, much was made of their seemingly ordinary backgrounds: Leslie Van Houten, a former church choir member and honor student; Patricia Krenwinkel, a Bible student; Charles Watson, a gifted athlete and scholar in high school. Only through such terrible factors, they, their defenders and the media proclaimed, could such normal, average and decent youths—who might have come from any family across America—become mindless killers. Defense attorney Paul Fitzgerald, for example, took great pains to tell the media that the members of the Family on trial for murder "had not so much as smoked a cigarette before they met Charles Manson." It was a comfortable, convenient view which eased the minds of many parents unable to come to terms with the fact that their own children might also be capable of such horrible crimes.

None of Manson's followers, however, came to him without the fundamentals upon which he himself capitalized to launch the murders. They were not zombies, controlled through their leader and through drugs, lacking the elements within themselves to become criminals. Those who participated in the eventual murders had all been heavily involved with multiple sexual partners and engaged in frequent drug use long before they came into Manson's orbit. As Dr. Clara Livsey has pointed out in her study of the Manson Family, Susan Atkins, "after telling of her gross promiscuity, her abuse of drugs, her disavowal of any decent conventions before she met Manson...states that Manson 'worked on ridding us of our inhibitions.' What inhibitions, one wonders, did she have left before she met him?"[24] Thus, it is impossible to ascribe their enthusiastic willingness to murder simply as a symptom of their lives with, and influence by, Manson.

"These men and women who came to Manson brought an element within themselves which he was later able to exploit to his own criminal ends," says Vincent Bugliosi. "None of them had to be coerced to commit their crimes. There was something in them which reveled in their crimes, which refused to fight against the notion of right or wrong as you or I would do. It was Manson's ability to recognize this ingrained willingness to kill which led to the murderous events of the summer of 1969."[25]

Chapter 21
The White Album

B
Y THE FALL OF 1968, MANSON'S DISILLUSION WITH HIS Hollywood circle of friends was growing. He approached both Dennis Wilson and Gregg Jakobson at the latter's Malibu beach house and demanded that they make a choice: either join his Family or stop playing with them. Both men were startled by the demand. Wilson, although he continued to associate with Manson, was certainly not about to run off to Spahn Ranch and abandon his career; and Jakobson, still attracted to much of what Manson said, luckily had the more stabilizing influence of his wife to dissuade him from making the move. Both men refused. Thereafter, Manson's relationship with them took a turn for the worse.

In late October, 1968, Manson moved his Family to Death Valley. There, they divided their time between two remote, ramshackle properties, the Barker and Myers Ranches. "Death Valley," wrote Paul Watkins, "marked a turning point for the Manson Family. It is not easy to make sense of what happened there....But I do believe that coming to the desert stamped the fate of the Family, and subsequently, the fate of its victims."[1]

It was Catherine Gillies, known in the Manson Family as Capistrano, who first suggested a move to Death Valley. Her grandparents Bill and Barbara Myers owned the motley collection of buildings which comprised Myers Ranch, and she obtained permission for the Family to temporarily stay there. The remote location suited Manson: in order to reach either of the two ranches, which stood a half-mile apart, he and his Family had to leave what little civilization existed in Death Valley and traverse Goler Wash, a desolate and dangerous ravine at the edge of the Panamint Mountains where once an old mining road had cleaved its way through the rocks.

Barker Ranch stood at the head of the Wash, an old stone house with a wide porch, surrounded by cottonwood and cactus. The only heat came from an oil-drum wood stove and a wood-burning kitchen range. A bunkhouse, constructed of old railroad ties, stood at the back of the main house. Myers Ranch was even more rustic: a small stucco building heated by a fireplace and facing a seemingly endless stretch of bare desert.[2]

Isolated in these new desert outposts, Manson began to speak of a coming race war, with blacks pitted against whites. "Dig it, man," he told his followers. "This shit can't go on forever with black-ie ...pretty soon he's gonna revolt and start kickin' whitey's ass. I've seen it buildin' up for years. It was bad enough at Watts and San Francisco, but now that they wasted that jive-ass Martin Luther...well, that's a heavy number, man. I mean, you gotta figure whitey's karma's gotta turn one of these days...it's just a matter of time. Yeah, it's gonna come down hard...a full on war. And when it does, we're gonna be glad we're out here."[3]

In time, Manson grew increasingly convinced that the apocalyptic vision of the end of the world foretold in the Book of Revelation in the Bible was at hand. Although he himself would later claim that he had never really believed the idea, he certainly spent time and money searching Death Valley for the entrance he thought was there, a portal to The Hole, the bottomless pit spoken of in the Bible. Manson thought it was a buried paradise; but scripturally, the bottomless pit was another name for hell, one of many mistakes Manson was to make in his interpretation of both the Bible and the music of The Beatles.[4]

At the end of 1968, members of the Manson Family were scattered among various houses and apartments in Los Angeles, shacks at the Spahn Movie Ranch, the desert ranches in Death Valley and a rented house on Gresham Street in Canoga Park which they dubbed the "Yellow Submarine" because of its color. Manson disliked having his followers so dispersed, and gradually tried to round them up and bring them to Canoga Park. Among those who voluntarily returned to the Family was Charles "Tex" Watson, who had, for a time, been living on his own, away from the Family. The group now included several new members, including Straight Satan motorcycle gang member Danny De Carlo, who was later to provide important information during the murder investigations.

❖❖❖❖❖

In December, 1968, Capital Records released their *White Album* by The Beatles, their follow-up to the highly successful *Magical Mystery Tour* album. It was a double album, with two discs containing thirty songs. For Manson, everything about the album was of incredible significance. Even the stark album cover, unadorned except for a slightly embossed name of the group, carried a message: the *White Album*, according to Manson, was a declaration of the beginning of a race war between the whites and the blacks, and The Beatles had fired the first shot by proclaiming their allegiance to the white race.

During the first months of 1969, Manson spent hours at the house in Canoga Park, listening to the White Album over and over again. Many of the songs seemed to convey—or affirm—special messages to Manson and his Family. That The Beatles wrote a song called "Sexy Sadie" long after he had christened Susan Atkins with the nickname was, for Manson, proof that he and the musicians from Liverpool were psychically connected. Manson also saw warnings about the upcoming race war in songs like "Blackbird," and "Rocky Racoon." In the first, the lyric, "Blackbird singing in the dead of night, take these broken wings and learn to fly; all your life, you were only waiting for this moment to arise," meant, for Manson, The Beatles were aware of the coming black revolution—that they were saying that it was time for the black man to arise. Later, at the LaBianca house, the killers would print the word Rise in blood at the scene of their second set of murders with which they hoped to ignite "Helter Skelter." In the song "Rocky Racoon," Manson believed The Beatles were referring to black people as "coons," and sending out secret messages for the attuned.

The song "Piggies" was also significant for Manson. It described the wealthy members of the establishment, "piggies," getting rich on suffering and poverty, dining out with their knives and forks, interspersed with the sounds of snorting and screams. One line in the song declared that what the "piggies" needed was "a damned good whacking." Manson took this to heart, believing The Beatles were again declaring that the establishment figures needed to be taught a lesson.

There were two songs that Manson took as deliberate urgings to blacks to begin an uprising, "Revolution," and "Revolution 9." In the first, the lyrics declared, "You say you want a revolution, well you know, we all want to change the world....But if you talk about destruction, don't you know that you can count me out." On listening to the version on the *White Album*, however, Manson discerned the scarcely audible word "in" immediately following "out." It was but one of the hidden messages buried in the album's songs, and Manson believed the group was declaring that they were all in favor of the coming revolution. "Revolution 9" was a peculiar song, containing no lyrics, but rather comprised of an unnerving collection of shouted phrases, bits of classical music, machine gun fire, pigs snorting, people screaming, spoken dialogue and car horns, interspersed with a frequently repeated chant of "Number 9, number 9, number 9...." Manson believed this song was a preview of the coming revolution, what the race war would sound like: total anarchy. He also matched up the song's title with Chapter 9 in the Bible's Book of Revelation, which predicts the end of the world.

For Manson, however, the most important song was "Helter Skelter." Although a "Helter Skelter" in England is a giant slide, Manson took the word at its American meaning of total chaos and confusion. The chorus, "Look out, Helter Skelter...she's coming down fast!" was, for Manson, a pure declaration that the race war was on, and that it was happening right now. Only those people hip to what was going on—those attuned to what Manson and The Beatles were saying—would escape the coming slaughter.

Before the release of the *White Album*, Manson had spoken in vague terms of a possible race war. The album reinforced his vision, and made it concrete. He began to speak confidently, describing the scenario he felt would unfold. According to Family acquaintance Paul Watkins, "He used to explain how it would be so simple to start out. A couple of black people—some of the spades from Watts—would come up into the Bel Air and Beverly Hills district...up in the rich piggy district...and just really wipe some people out, just cutting bodies up and smearing blood and writing things on the walls in blood...all kinds of super-atrocious crimes that would really make the white man mad...."[5] Another Manson acquaintance, Brooks Poston, told Vincent Bugliosi the same thing, describing how Manson said the victims would be killed, with messages written in their own blood on the walls of their houses. "He said a group of real blacks would come out of the ghettos and do an atrocious crime in the richer sections of Los Angeles and other cities. They would do an atrocious murder with stabbing, killing, cutting bodies to pieces, smearing blood on the walls, writing 'pigs' on the walls...in the victims' own blood."[6] This would prove to be a powerful link during the murder investigation.

Soon, Manson began to couple the songs on the *White Album* with his own unique interpretation of the Bible's Book of Revelation. For Manson, the four angels spoken of in the scripture were the four Beatles—John Lennon, Paul McCartney, George Harrison and Ringo Starr. The Bible's fifth angel, Abadon, was, according to Manson, himself. This fifth angel held the key to the bottomless pit—Manson's fabled hole in Death Valley, where, during the race war—Helter Skelter—he and his followers, who would number 144,000 according to the Bible, would live, thus escaping the eventual slaughter of all the white race. At the end of the war, total confusion would reign; the blacks would be unable to make a go of things, and Manson and his followers would then present themselves, taking over and ruling the world.[7]

This talk was a constant factor in the daily lives of Manson and his Family, and they made continual preparations for what they believed was the unavoidable coming slaughter. They poured over the desert in search of the entrance to the bottomless pit, outfitted dune buggies to use as Helter Skelter vehicles to make trips around the desert, and began to arm themselves with a massive supply of artillery. If Manson, as he later claimed, was only playing a game, then it was proving to be a very expensive, mind-consuming game.

By spring of 1969, the Family was safely back at the Spahn Ranch, with Squeaky—Lynnette Fromme—having sweet-talked elderly George Spahn into their return to the property. With the addition, in July, of twenty-year-old Linda Kasabian—who left her husband and brought with her to the ranch her infant daughter Tanya—the Manson Family was complete. The wheels were now set in motion for the momentous events of the summer of 1969.

Chapter 22
The Storm Builds

TERRY MELCHER AND CANDICE BERGEN MOVED OUT OF 10050 Cielo Drive over the Christmas holidays in 1968 and into his mother Doris Day's beach house in Malibu. The main house stood vacant from January until the middle of February, when Sharon and Roman signed their lease with Rudi Altobelli. During those six weeks, Gregg Jakobson arranged for Manson Family member Dean Morehouse to temporarily stay in the main house. Fellow Manson follower Tex Watson apparently visited Morehouse there frequently during that time.[1] Author Bill Nelson has also discovered that Manson Family members Catherine Share and Susan Atkins visited the property to swim in the pool.[2]

On Sunday, March 23, Manson himself drove to 10050 Cielo Drive. He went first to the main house, the occasion on which he was met by Shahrokh Hatami, Sharon Tate's photographer, who told him Melcher no longer lived at the house and that he should try the guest house. As soon as he saw Sharon walk onto the front porch, Manson fled back down the flagstone walk to the paved parking area, turned round, and strode up the dirt path toward the guest house at the far end of the estate. No one was home, and Manson left. This took place in the afternoon. Several hours later, he returned.

Rudi Altobelli was taking a shower in the guest house when he heard his dog Christopher barking. He jumped out, grabbed a robe and walked into the hall, only to find Manson standing in the enclosed screened porch. Altobelli was immediately angry that Manson had opened the door and walked in uninvited.

Manson began to introduce himself but Altobelli cut him off, saying, "I know who you are, Charlie. What do you want?"

When Manson said he was looking for Terry Melcher, Altobelli quickly declared that he no longer lived on the property. Manson asked for his new address, but Altobelli replied that he did not know it—a lie. Manson then began to question Altobelli about his business contacts, saying he would like to talk about his music career, but Altobelli again cut him short, saying that he was in the middle of packing for an extended trip and that he would not be returning for a year—another lie. He asked Manson, in the future, not to disturb his tenants in the main house, and coldly said goodnight, closing the door in Manson's face.[3]

Facing Altobelli's rejection, Manson tried to rebound. He and his Family made concerted efforts that spring to land a recording contract. Bobby Beausoleil apparently visited musician Frank Zappa in an effort to find support for Manson's quest. But Zappa, frequently exposed to an endless stream of freaked out would-be stars, had no time for this newest request, particularly after Beausoleil tried to explain that the Family was busy building a tunnel to Death Valley to escape the coming race war. Another Family member, Catherine Share, known in the Family as "Gypsy", arranged for The Doors' producer Paul Rothschild to listen to Manson's demo tapes; after hearing the offered product, Rothschild passed.

Manson was persistent, and Wilson, Melcher and Jakobson could not put him off forever. In April, they arranged for Manson to record several more tracks in a studio in Santa Monica. He arrived with several of the women, Beausoleil and Watson to provide backing vocals; Dennis Wilson also lent his voice to this latest effort. While sitting in the studio, Manson composed a couple of impromptu songs, including one seeming bit of gibberish while he mindlessly strummed his guitar. The repeated refrain of "digh-de-day, digh-dow-doi, digh-tu-dai" evolved into "digh-tew-day, digh-tew-day," and, finally, became a sinister chant of "Die today, die today, die today."[4] Melcher, amongst others, was unnerved, and soon left the building.

Together with his previously recorded demos, both from Brian Wilson's home studio and from the set in Van Nuys, Manson now had a collection of a dozen songs. Some were still in very rough stages, but it was enough raw material for an album—Manson's only real desire all along. Dennis Wilson and Terry Melcher both seemed sympathetic, and Wilson went so far as to discuss Manson in an interview he gave to a British music magazine called *Rave*. He referred to Manson as "The Wizard," and said The Beach Boys would be producing and releasing his first album later that year on their own record label, Brothers Records.[5]

Unknown to Manson, he and his songs were the subject of several intense discussions between Wilson, Melcher and Jakobson that May. Wilson was eager to push Manson's album, but Melcher, after his recording studio scare, was quickly losing interest. Jakobson, the only one who knew Manson well and had spent any considerable time with him, proposed a documentary about Manson, his followers, their way of life at Spahn Ranch and their music.[6] Jakobson tried to convince Melcher that he should both finance and produce the documentary; but Melcher put off any decision for the time being.

Jakobson went to Spahn Ranch to discuss the idea with Manson, who was immediately taken with the thought of starring in his own story. But he had other ideas as well, which ran contrary to Jakobson's vision of a peaceful, loving commune. Manson apparently wanted scenes of destruction; of garbage runs by Family members; of his Helter Skelter philosophy; and of Satanic worship. Jakobson knew that such a film would never win approval, but did not directly contradict Manson's own aspirations.

On May 18, 1969, Terry Melcher drove out to Spahn Ranch to meet with Manson. On his way he picked up Bobby Beausoleil and his girlfriend Kitty Lutesinger. At Spahn, Manson gave Terry Melcher a guided tour by dune buggy of the various buildings and fire roads. But the main purpose of the visit was to hear Manson and the Family perform several new songs. "After hearing them sing a dozen or so songs I may have singled out one and said, 'That is a nice song,' just to be polite," Melcher later said. "When someone performs for you, you don't want to simply not respond to their whole presentation, and to be polite, I probably said something."[7] At the end of the session, Melcher gave Manson fifty dollars—all of the money in his wallet—to buy some hay for the horses.[8]

After Melcher's visit, Manson had little contact with him. Eventually, he called up Jakobson and asked if Melcher had made up his mind, a clear indication that no deal had as yet been reached. Manson repeatedly asked for Melcher's private telephone number at his Malibu house, but Jakobson would only give him the listing for his answering service.

A few weeks later, Melcher and Jakobson were back at Spahn Ranch. There was trouble at the ranch when they arrived. Two policemen were questioning Manson about the alleged rape of a young girl from Reseda. That morning, Manson had gone to Los

Angeles to find Melcher and discuss his recording contract. A witness recalls overhearing a violent argument take place between
Manson, Melcher and Jakobson as they stood on the boardwalk of
the Rock City Cafe. Jakobson had previously shot some footage for
his proposed documentary, and garnered some interest from NBC-
Studios. But both Jakobson and NBC wanted a film about a hippie
commune, dealing with love and peace. Manson was outraged and
refused to cooperate if the movie would not devote itself to his
vision of Helter Skelter and his music. Eventually, both Melcher and
Jakobson angrily left the ranch.

Manson was livid. He approached a hanger-on known as
Sunshine Pierce and asked if he would be interested in a bit of work.
Pierce thought it might be robbery, and said yes. But what Manson
had in mind was murder. "If you ever want to get anything and you
want it bad enough, you can't let anybody come between you when
you are going to do something," Manson declared. He told Pierce
that there was one person in particular that he wanted killed,
although it might be necessary to kill others as well. He thought he
could come up with about $5,000 if Pierce was interested. Pierce
was not, and left Spahn Ranch the following day. Although he did
not mention any names, it seems obvious that Manson had decided
to kill either Terry Melcher or Gregg Jakobson, or both men.[9]

In the middle of July Manson finally had his last falling out with
Melcher. By this time, Manson was in trouble on several fronts. He
went to see Dennis Wilson at his offices, but found him away. Instead,
he was greeted by Wilson's agent, who, in answer to Manson's
request for money, threatened to call the police, and threw him out,
telling Manson to never come back. Manson next went to see Melcher.

By this time he was beyond anger. "Goddamn, Terry!" he
recalled screaming. "We've been going through this kind of crap for
the last year. Is it ever going to happen or not?" To this, according
to Manson, Melcher answered slowly: "Look, Charlie, there's mixed
emotions about promoting you. You're unpredictable. You amaze
me at times, and at other times, disappoint the hell out of me."[10]

Manson left Melcher aware that his dream of becoming a
recording star was now over. He had tried to win members of the
industry over to his side with his music and failed. Dejected, Manson
allegedly told a friend that summer, "How are you going to get to
the establishment? You can't sing to them. I tried that. I tried to save
them, but they wouldn't listen. Now we've got to destroy them."[11]

Chapter 23
Murder

B
Y EARLY SUMMER OF 1969, MANSON AND HIS FAMILY HAD
reached the point of no return. It was apparent that neither
Wilson nor Melcher was going to come through on any of
their proposed business deals, and Manson, at first depressed with
the situation, quickly became angry. His anger was directed not only
at the men who had rejected him, but at the symbols which represented their culture: the establishment, Hollywood, fame and
money.

Manson's paranoia had been growing steadily over the last few
months. He was certain that something was about to happen. In
preparation for a possible outbreak of Helter Skelter, the Family,
under his direction, began to assemble a caché of arms for use in
their future struggles. While in residence at the house in Canoga
Park, the Family became heavily involved in a number of illegal ventures, including auto theft and drug dealing. A small car theft ring
operated out of the house, and, when the Family moved to Spahn
Ranch, it followed. Family members and many of the bikers who
stayed at the ranch regularly stole vehicles, stripped and then sold
them. At Manson's directive, dune buggies were particularly prized,
for use in the desert during Helter Skelter.[1]

Straight Satan biker Danny De Carlo helped the Family assemble an impressive collection of arms. He set up a special gun room
at Spahn Ranch, appropriately enough in the former Undertaker's
Parlor, where he slept to guard this caché of weapons. It included a
303 British Enfield, a .22 caliber rifle, a .30 caliber carbine, a .20
gauge shotgun, a .12 gauge riot gun, an M-1 carbine and a subma-
chine gun. Manson himself had a long, sharp sword which was kept
here, along with a number of buck knives, which were sharpened

down both sides of their blade, creating a double edge. Finally, there was a .22 caliber revolver, called a Buntline special, modeled after a pair of guns which Ned Buntline made for Wyatt Earp. The gun had a long barrel, wooden grips, and its chamber held nine bullets. Sometime in June, Manson went to a Jack Frost Surplus Store in Santa Monica and purchased several hundred feet of white nylon, three ply rope.[2]

Manson's philosophy, already violent, took a more immediate, dramatic turn in the middle of July, 1969. He predicted to several people that soon members of the establishment would be slaughtered in their Bel Air mansions, their bodies scattered across the front lawns, with messages written in blood on the walls of their houses. To Danny De Carlo, Manson declared that the "pigs ought to have their throats cut and be hung up by their feet."[3] Talk of violence was spurred by his impatience. He had been talking about Helter Skelter, making his plans, buying supplies, waiting for the crisis to erupt, but, so far, nothing had happened. The blacks in Los Angeles had not risen up against the white establishment. One day, Manson took Paul Watkins aside and announced, "Helter Skelter is ready to happen...it's gotta happen soon. All the piggies are gonna get their jolt of where it's really at. We have to stock supplies at the desert and be ready to boogie....I'll tell ya, blackie never did anything without whitey showin' him how....Helter Skelter is coming down. But it looks like we're gonna have to show blackie how to do it."[4] To ranch hand Juan Flynn, Manson complained: "The only way I'm going to show them niggers how to do it is to go down and kill a bunch of those motherfucking pigs."[5]

Family member Leslie Van Houten later recalled: "Manson had started changing his talking about surviving the Helter Skelter war and that perhaps we would have to do something to instigate it, because it wasn't coming along as quickly as he had anticipated. I didn't know, specifically, when it would be starting."[6]

"Being around Charlie during that time," remembers Van Houten, "was like playing a game of Scrabble. He never labeled anything as exactly like it was. He'd say, 'The question is in the answer,' and 'No sense makes sense'—things that would make your mind stop functioning. Then it wasn't a matter of questioning when things began to get bad. We'd stopped questioning months before."[7]

For some time, Manson had been instructing his followers on ways to slip into the mansions of the wealthy in the dead of night, using credit cards to trip the door locks. Sometimes, they would steal jewelry or money; other times, dressed in black clothing, Family members would simply wander through the house, perhaps rearranging an item of furniture here or there to startle the owners when they awoke. They referred to these nightly forays as "creepy-crawling."[8]

One of Manson's apparent targets that July was the house of John and Michelle Phillips on Bel Air Road in Beverly Hills. Earlier, Phillips had expressed disinterest in meeting or assisting Manson. Certain members of the Family are believed to have at least been acquaintances of Cass Eliott, one of the two women in Phillips' The Mamas and The Papas, and Manson himself—friends with Melcher and Jakobson—was aware that Phillips, too, had rejected him. Michelle Phillips recalls: "One night John and I were in bed. He had become very paranoid recently, and begun to sleep with a gun beneath his pillow, which really angered me. In the middle of the night, he heard something, and got up to investigate. I remember telling him to go back to sleep, but he grabbed the gun and went off. When he came back a few minutes later, he told me that in the garage he had seen a number of people dressed in black, walking like penguins. He was pretty heavily involved with drugs at the time, and I thought he was imagining the whole thing. 'Go back to bed, John,' I told him, and he eventually settled down. Only later did we suspect that Manson had sent his followers out to our house."[9]

Such activities were possible as members of the Family increasingly came to trust Manson, losing their individuality as the group melded together to form a collective conscience. "When it came time to play Helter Skelter," write Flo Conway and Jim Siegelman, "life in the Family had become a game with no borders on fantasy and reality, an extended 'trip' that kept up long after any chemical effects had worn off."[10]

By the beginning of the summer of 1969, the Family was deeply involved in criminal activities. Through a source in Santa Monica, they fenced stolen vehicles and other smaller goods. But they seem to have made most of their money from illegal drug activities, which were widespread.

Perhaps the biggest participant was Tex Watson. Before joining the Family the previous summer, Watson had regularly dealt drugs as co-owner of his wig shop on Santa Monica Boulevard. Significantly, for someone who would claim to be completely under Manson's influence and unable to escape when the time for murder came, Watson divided his time between Spahn Ranch and his drug-dealing girlfriend. He had actually left the Manson Family during late 1968 for several months, and made his own choice to return in March, 1969. And, although he would later insist that it was his drug use with Manson which had led to the murders, Watson—even away from the Family—continued to be heavily involved with the selling and using of illegal drugs.[11]

"It was strange," Watson would later admit, "but even though I truly believed that Charlie knew everything, I could sometimes ignore what he said, even disobey him." He detailed, for example, his secret stash of speed, which he kept hidden from Manson and shared with fellow members Bruce Davis and Susan Atkins. "I was willing to kill for Manson," he said, "but I wasn't willing to give up my speed."[12] This admission of selective control hardly supports Watson's view of himself as a mindless zombie who belonged body and soul to Manson.

Watson remained in control enough to be trusted with organizing the Family's drug orders. They were involved not only in dealing marijuana, but also apparently LSD, hashish, coke and mescaline.[13] One of their prominent drug contacts was black dealer Bernard Crowe, known as Lottsa Poppa. Manson mistakenly believed that he was a member of the Black Panthers organization.

On the evening of June 30, 1969, Watson, accompanied by his girlfriend Rosina, went to Bernard Crowe's house in an effort to swindle him out of both drugs and money. Crowe gave Watson $2,400 to make a marijuana purchase; he later claimed that the deal involved a total of $20,000, and that the money he gave to Watson that night was only an initial payment.[14] Watson took the money, excused himself, and, with Rosina sitting in the living room with Crowe, dashed out the rear of the house and fled back to Spahn Ranch. How and why Watson ever thought he could get away with such a piece of obvious thievery is not known. Within a few hours, Crowe had cornered a terrified Rosina, who finally rang Spahn Ranch, pleading for Watson to come back and settle up. Finally, Manson himself got on the telephone and told Crowe that he would be on his way in a few minutes.

It is not known if Manson was aware of the deception beforehand. He took Family associate Thomas Walleman, known as T.J. the Terrible, with him; Bobby Beausoleil has also claimed that Bruce Davis accompanied the pair.[15] Manson drove ranch hand Johnny Shwartz's yellow and white 1959 Ford; on the front seat lay the .22

caliber Buntline Special. Once at the apartment, Manson got into a heated exchange with Crowe, claiming he had not been responsible for Watson's action. After this went on for several minutes, Crowe was joined by several friends. Manson pulled out the gun and offered it to Crowe, telling him that he could shoot him. Crowe replied that he was not interested in hurting Manson, just Watson. Manson, according to the witnesses, did a kind of ritualistic dance around the apartment and grabbed the gun, aiming it at Crowe and pulling the trigger. The chamber was empty, and nothing happened. Crowe looked relieved, but Manson, with a smile on his face, pulled the trigger a second time, and the gun went off, the bullet fired almost directly into Crowe's stomach. He fell over onto the floor, silent. Manson bent down and kissed his feet, then picked up the gun and calmly walked out of the apartment.

Back at Spahn Ranch, Manson told Watson and Danny De Carlo about the shooting. Manson believed he had killed Crowe; but Bernard Crowe was only wounded, and was taken to the hospital for emergency surgery—a fact which, if known, might have prevented the bloodshed in the coming months. Instead, Manson's paranoia increased dramatically. There were witnesses to the shooting, and Manson feared a Black Panther backlash against the Family.

In the next few days, Manson ordered guard posts set up around Spahn Ranch, and had regular dune buggy patrols of the fire roads leading to the back ranch house where most of the Family stayed. Sometime earlier that summer, several members of the Family had stolen a green telescope from Terry Melcher's Malibu beach house; now, they used the spyglass to scan the hills surrounding Spahn Ranch, fearing that the Black Panthers were going to attack.[16] Manson became fanatical about the start of Helter Skelter, waiting for a chance to move his Family out to Death Valley. But they still needed money.

Manson got some cash when Linda Kasabian joined his Family on 4 July. Kasabian, twenty, had spent several years wandering from commune to commune; in the process, she married twice, the second time to a fellow hippy Robert Kasabian with whom she had a daughter, sixteen-month-old Tanya. Within a day, Kasabian, having stolen some $5,000 from a friend of her husband, had duly turned over the cash, along with her own wallet and driver's license. The money helped, but Manson needed more. It was now that the Family's associations with musician Gary Hinman became deadly.

Hinman, a thirty-two-year-old former musician and friend of Bobby Beausoleil, had always been helpful to Family members, giving them money when he could and allowing them to stay at his house. Hinman also apparently was involved in the manufacture of mescaline and LSD, work he carried out in a small, make-shift laboratory in the basement of his hillside cottage in Topanga Canyon.[17]

There are several versions of what led to the eventual confrontation between Hinman and Manson. On the surface, it was a conflict over money, with Manson expecting the musician to apparently hand over the cash which the Family wanted. According to several sources, however, someone in the Family had purchased 1,000 tabs of acid from Hinman, for distribution to Danny De Carlo and his Straight Satan motorcycle gang; a day later, members of the gang claimed that the acid was bad, and complained to Manson that Hinman had deliberately swindled them.[18]

On 25 July, Manson dispatched Beausoleil, Mary Brunner and Susan Atkins to Hinman's Topanga Canyon house. At first, Hinman welcomed them. Then, after they demanded the pink slips to his cars as well as his money, he told them to get out. Beausoleil, Brunner and Atkins threatened and pleaded with him for several hours before Beausoleil pulled out a nine millimeter Radon pistol which Bruce Davis had purchased a few weeks earlier. After waving the pistol in the air for a few minutes, Beausoleil hit Hinman in the face, and the musician spit out a mouthful of blood and a piece of chipped tooth. A struggle ensued, during which time Hinman eventually got the gun away from Beausoleil and turned it on the three. Unbelievably, he then did something which was to cost him his life: Hinman handed the gun back to Beausoleil, saying that he did not believe in violence. After asking them to leave, he wandered off into the living room. Uncertain what to do, Beausoleil called Manson at Spahn Ranch.[19]

Around midnight, Manson, accompanied by Bruce Davis, arrived at Hinman's house. Manson waved his sword in Hinman's face, threatening him and demanding money, but the musician continually begged to be left alone. Finally, Manson raised the sword and brought it down on the side of Hinman's head, cutting off part of his ear. After this, Manson and Davis quickly left for the ranch.[20] The rest of the Family members, however, remained behind, tying up Hinman and taking turns watching him all night. Susan Atkins later admitted that she walked down the canyon to an all-night store and bought some food, bandages and white dental floss so that they could sew up the wound in the side of Hinman's head.[21] While she was gone, Beausoleil and Brunner turned the house upside down, searching for money and the pink slips to Hinman's cars.

For two days, the trio of Mansonites tormented Hinman, with the girls offering him food while Beausoleil repeatedly beat him. Finally, Hinman signed over his Volkswagon minibus and his Fiat. Beausoleil reported back to Manson at the ranch, who told him to kill Hinman, saying "He knows too much."[22]

Atkins was in the kitchen when she suddenly heard Hinman screaming, "No Bobby!" She saw Hinman stagger into the kitchen, clutching his chest, and Beausoleil followed, holding a knife which he had used to stab him twice.[23] Beausoleil and the women moved Hinman into the living room; he was a Buddhist, and they placed him before his Nichiren Shoshu shrine, handing him his prayer beads. The trio stood over him, watching as Hinman lay on the floor, covered in blood, chanting his prayer until he fell silent.[24]

With clear heads, and under instructions from no one, the three spent the next few minutes running through the house, wiping it down for prints.[25] They covered Hinman's body with his green bedspread; above him, on the living room wall, they printed the words "Political Piggy" in his blood, drawing a paw which was supposed to point toward the Black Panthers as the culprits. They locked all the doors and climbed out a side window.

As they stood on the deck outside the house, they heard Hinman moaning. Beausoleil went back inside, followed by the women. They took turns holding a pillow over the struggling musician's face until he again fell silent. They left in Hinman's VW bus, Manson and Bruce Davis having already taken the Fiat. On their way back to Spahn Ranch, they stopped at the Topanga Kitchen Restaurant for cherry cake and coffee, paid for with a twenty dollar bill Mary Brunner had stolen from Hinman's wallet.[26]

A day later, police raided Spahn Ranch. It was not in connection with Gary Hinman's murder, but with reports that an auto theft ring was operating out of the property. Manson managed to effectively threaten the officers by saying that he had armed troops hidden in the hills above the ranch. But the police left after arresting only Johnny Schwartz, whose 1959 Ford had invalid registration. Manson and his followers remained at the ranch.

On 31 July, worried at not having heard from their friend for several days, Hinman's friends went round to his house and found his mailbox full of mail. As they wandered round the deck, they noticed hundreds of flies swarming at the windows. When they broke in, they found Hinman's body, covered with maggots and rapidly decomposing in the heat.[27]

Manson was away from Spahn Ranch when, on Tuesday, August 5, Bobby Beausoleil left in Hinman's stolen Fiat, on his way to San Francisco. There was a police bulletin out on the vehicle, and it only took a few hours before a California Highway Patrol car pulled Beausoleil over near San Luis Obispo. Although Beausoleil declared that he had purchased the car the previous week from an unknown black man, the police were suspicious enough to have his fingerprints sent down to Los Angeles for comparison with those found in Hinman's house. When they matched, Beausoleil was shipped south to Los Angeles, charged in the murder of Gary Hinman. He admitted that he had been in Hinman's house, and that Gary had told him he had been attacked by some black militants. Beausoleil said he and two unnamed female friends had helped sew up the musician's face, and that a grateful Hinman had given them the pink slips to his cars.

The police bought none of it. On August 7, Beausoleil arrived in Los Angeles and made his one telephone call, to Spahn Ranch. A few hours later, on the morning of Friday, August 8, 1969, Charles Manson returned to the ranch from a trip north and learned what had happened. In less than twelve hours, he would order his followers to kill everyone at 10050 Cielo Drive.

Chapter 24
Thirteen Chairs

S HARON ARRIVED IN LONDON ON TUESDAY, 24 MARCH, 1969. SHE was scheduled to begin work on *Thirteen Chairs* the following month, in both England and in Italy. She joined Roman, who had arrived earlier for business meetings, at their Eaton Place Mews house. That same week, John and Michelle Phillips flew in from the United States, and the two couples accepted an invitation from producer Alfred "Cubby" Broccoli to stay with him at his country estate.

On Saturday night, while Roman and John Phillips were talking, Sharon pulled Michelle aside and disappeared into a bathroom to have a cigarette. "Roman hated her smoking, and was always trying to get her to quit," recalls Michelle Phillips. "She used to sneak cigarettes behind his back." In the bathroom, Sharon told Michelle that she was pregnant. "She said that she hadn't yet told Roman, and began to laugh about it. She seemed very happy, very giddy."[1]

By the last week of March, however, Sharon could no longer conceal the truth. She finally told Roman. She had waited until the last possible moment, fearful perhaps that he would try to force her to have an abortion, and uncertain what his response would be. To Sharon, the prospect of a baby meant a chance to save her marriage, to reform her husband's troubling behavior, and to finally settle down to the role which she had always wanted most: that of wife and mother.

Roman's response to the news was apparently less than enthusiastic. He had not wanted a child, and, now that the choice had been taken from him, he panicked. One of his first remarks was to remind Sharon that she was scheduled to do *Thirteen Chairs*, and that, by the time production actually began in a few weeks, she would almost certainly be visibly pregnant. Sharon dismissed this with a calm, "Everything's going to be fine."[2] To every objection, she answered with assurances.

It took Roman several months before he began to warm up to the idea of being a father. Finally, however, he began buying books on fatherhood and babies, talking to doctors about what to expect from his wife's pregnancy, and making plans for the future of the child.

Now that she did not have to hide the fact, Sharon was transformed by her pregnancy. Suddenly, everything else—her career, her troubled marriage to Roman—took a back seat to the child growing within her. The prospect of motherhood fulfilled a deep need in Sharon, and her sense of expectancy over the impending birth overshadowed her other concerns. "She was really happy," remembers Michelle Phillips, "and seemed at peace with herself."[3]

Very quickly, Sharon was wrapped up in shooting *Thirteen Chairs*. There was a month long rehearsal period, and the picture itself was on a relatively short six-week shooting schedule, with another month slated for post-production work in London. Director Nicolas Gessener had to shoot around Sharon's pregnancy, especially since she was to be semi-nude in several scenes filmed for the European release. Gessener slated these scenes for early shooting, before work began on the rest of the film; even so, Sharon masked her rapidly-growing stomach with a succession of purses, long coats and scarves. By the time the production wrapped in late May, she was visibly pregnant.

Sharon played the role of Pat, an assistant in an antique store in England. Mario, played by Vittorio Gassman, flies from New York, where he works as a barber, to England to collect an inheritance left by an aunt. Expecting great wealth, he instead finds a crumbling house, empty but for a dozen old chairs. Needing money to return to America, he takes these to the local antique shop and sells them. Sharon's role called for not only comedic talents and timing, but a brusque, almost sarcastic delivery. Her first scene, set in the antique shop, had her selling a chamber pot to visiting American tourists. The pot is one of many, but she craftily tells the couple that it might have belonged to Queen Victoria, allowing her to raise the price. Once they leave, the shop owner, Mr. Greenwood, confronts her.

"When you first came to work here," he says, "it was because I thought we needed maybe a little trans-Atlantic efficiency. But now, sometimes, Pat, I feel that you are sometimes a little...."

"Mercenary?" she answers. "Sure I am, Mr. Greenwood. "I think money's sexy, sexier than people."

"That means you haven't met the right person," Greenwood tells her.

"All that means," she declares, "is I haven't met the right money."

Mario brings his twelve chairs to Mr. Greenwood's shop and asks the owner for $264.

"How much did you say you wanted?" Greenwood asks.

"Two-hundred-sixty-four dollars," he answers.

"That would be about...."

"One hundred twenty six pounds, eleven and eight," Pat interjects. "Why?"

"London to New York economy flight," Mario replies.

"Well, now," Greenwood answers, "if you want to leave them with us on a commission basis, I am sure that within a few days...."

"How much is London-New York by boat?" Pat asks.

"About ninety dollars, I guess," Mario tells her.

"In that case," Pat announces, "I hope you don't get seasick."

Only after he has sold the chairs does Mario discover that his aunt has hidden a fortune under one of the seats. By the time he returns to Greenwood's shop, the chairs have already disappeared, on their way to London. Pat, suspicious, quickly decides to follow him, announcing that she has the name of the buyer on a piece of paper, and that he must share the money with her if he wants to find the chairs. In their London hotel, Mario corners her, trying to take the paper away, but Pat eats it. In the struggle, however, he rips off her shirt, and she is forced to run, arms crossed over her bare breasts, through the hotel corridor to her own room. The following morning, stealing a raincoat, she sneaks away, hoping to locate the chairs herself. Thereafter, she and Mario pursue the chairs from London to Paris to Rome, through a series of misadventures and deceptions, in a futile attempt to find the hidden treasure.

For much of the filming, Sharon was unwell, suffering from morning sickness. Nevertheless, Gessener was on a tight schedule and could not wait, and much of Sharon's performance in the movie appeared strained and uneasy. Her mental state, too, was not the best. She had gone off to Rome radiantly happy, but soon, depression set in. She missed Roman, who was busy working on a script for a film version of the novel *Day of the Dolphin*. Although she made regular telephone calls to him, this brief contact did little to lessen her loneliness.

Sharon frequently asked Roman to join her in Italy, but he continually replied that he was too busy in London to get away. She knew it was an excuse, and became depressed, worrying not only about her husband's activities but that she was becoming unattractive to him.

At the beginning of the summer, she finally joined Roman in London, to complete the dubbing of the film. Things were tense from the start. The novelty of her pregnancy had, at least for Roman, apparently worn off. He was accustomed to Sharon's undivided attention; now, he found her increasingly focused only on her pregnancy. According to one of her friends, "The summer did nothing to improve their relationship. God knows, Sharon tried, she tried almost too much. But he was bored with her being pregnant. He treated her like she was a piece of excess baggage. He was even pointedly cruel to her in front of others at times, calling her a dumb hag and criticizing her whenever she expressed an opinion."[4]

For the time being, Sharon ignored the uncomfortable reality of the situation. As the baby grew inside of her, her need for Roman lessened; all of her energies, enthusiasm and expectations concentrated solely on the birth of her child. She haunted the fashionable shops in Knightsbridge and Regent Street, buying a layette for the baby, and spent hours reading every book on childbirth and babies she could find.[5]

Sharon wanted an English nanny for the baby. After placing an advertisement in *The Times*, she spent the next few weeks interviewing the various candidates who applied and were willing to move to Los Angeles to take up the post. Eventually she settled on a young girl named Marie Lees and arrangements were made with the proper authorities to get the necessary work papers and permits. There was no question but that the baby would be born in the United States, and Sharon spent her last few days in London on the telephone, planning her return to America.

While she had been in Italy, Roman had purchased a belated birthday gift for his wife: a vintage Rolls Royce Silver Dawn, which he drove up to the mews house one day to surprise her.[6] Sharon loved it, and happily posed before it while Roman snapped a few pictures. The car then disappeared, to be shipped, along with Roman's Ferrari, back to Los Angeles.

One day, while Sharon was out, Roman received a telephone

call from his friend Voyteck Frykowski, who, along with Abigail Folger, had been living at 10050 Cielo Drive during the Polanskis' absence abroad. Voyteck, while backing out of the driveway, had accidentally run over Sharon's pet Yorkshire terrier, Dr. Saperstein. "A terrible thing happened today," he explained. "I killed Saperstein. I heard a squeak under the wheels and he ran under the bushes. I ran after him and found him and took him to the vet, but it was too late. The only thing I ever got from you was goodness, and now I feel very bad."[7]

Knowing that his wife would be heartbroken, Roman immediately bought another Yorkshire puppy and gave it to Sharon, who named the dog Prudence. He told her that Voyteck could not find Dr. Saperstein and that he had probably run away. She never knew the truth.[8]

In her final days in London, Sharon did a photo shoot for the British fashion magazine *Queen*. She was slated to appear on the cover of an upcoming issue, in connection with the future release of *Thirteen Chairs*. She finished reading Thomas Hardy's novel *Tess of the d'Urbervilles*, which she left for Roman to look at, explaining that she thought it would make an excellent motion picture.[9]

Sharon was eight months pregnant when she left London—too far along for any of the commercial airlines to fly her. Instead, Roman booked her into a stateroom on the ocean liner *Queen Elizabeth 2*. At first, Sharon wanted to wait the week or so Roman said he needed to finish up his script, and accompany him back to America. It appears that initially they were both slated to travel together on board the ocean liner but, at the last minute, Roman changed his mind. Sharon was angry, but there was nothing she could do.[10]

On their last night together in London, Sharon and Roman went to a party at a restaurant overlooking the Thames. The following morning, they drove to Southampton, where they wandered over the vessel before last call was sounded.[11]

"Okay, go now," Sharon told Roman, wiping tears from her eyes. As he later recalled, Roman began to cry, and held his pregnant wife tightly. He was overcome with the feeling that something tragic was about to happen. Finally, he walked down the gangway and climbed into his borrowed Alfa Romeo for the drive back to London. With his pregnant wife safely on her way home, however, Roman quickly returned to London where, he later admitted, he decided to "call Victor Lownes, have a ball, see some girls."[12] It was the last time Roman ever saw Sharon.

Chapter 25
Voytech and Gibby

O N THE DAY BEFORE HIS THIRTY-SIXTH BIRTHDAY, SUNDAY, August 17, 1969, a shattered Roman Polanski wandered through the blood-stained rooms of his house at 10050 Cielo Drive, just a week after the murders of his wife, his unborn child and his friends. He had asked Voyteck Frykowski to remain at the Cielo Drive house until he returned, to look after Sharon. Now, as he entered the corner bedroom which Voyteck and Abigail Folger had shared, he commented bitterly, "I should have thrown him out when he ran over Sharon's dog!" A reporter at his side asked how long Frykowski had been staying at 10050 Cielo Drive. "Too long, I guess," was Polanski's sad reply.[1]

Since coming to America, Roman had taken an intense interest in a growing circle of friends, all former Poles like himself, now expatriates trying to find fame and fortune. "Roman became sort of a Polish Y.M.H.A. in America," a friend later declared. "He loaned them money, he even borrowed money to loan them money, he read their scripts and got them jobs, and it didn't matter if some of them had no talent and no promise. What was important was that they were Polish. There was this incredible bond."[2]

Jerzy Kosinski was one of these arrivals. The author made an immediate and favorable impression on American audiences with his highly successful works *The Painted Bird* and *Steps*.[3] Another, less successful and not always welcome, addition to the Polanski circle was Voyteck Frykowski, who tried his hand at several ventures, but with no marked achievement.

The tall, handsome Frykowski had made something of a career in following Polanski round the globe, from Poland to Paris, London to Hollywood. According to Zofia Komeda, Roman "wasn't very pleased," at his friend's continual pursuit.⁴ In the process, Frykowski married and divorced twice, leaving his young son Bartek in Poland when he eventually left his homeland in 1967. Determined to fit into American society, Frykowski spent long hours studying English, and kept large notebooks filled with his observations on culture and customs. He tried his hand at poetry, hoping to become a writer, an aspiration encouraged by his friend Jerzy Kosinski.

It was Kosinski, in fact, who, during a party in New York City, first introduced Voyteck to Abigail Folger. At the time, the pretty, twenty-five-year-old heiress to the coffee fortune was working at the Gotham Book Store, a large art house on Forty-Seventh Street.⁵ Frykowski could barely manage in English, but he found that Folger spoke fluent French, a language in which he was also proficient, and Abigail agreed to show Voyteck round the city. During their days together, she tutored him in English; soon, Voyteck was calling her "Lady Folger."⁶ According to Roman, Abigail Folger "was very good for him."⁷

Born in 1943, Abigail Anne Folger, known to friends and family as Gibby, was the product of a privileged, cloistered upbringing. Her father Peter was Chairman of the Folger Coffee Company, the multi-million dollar corporation which had made the family very wealthy. After her parents' divorce, she had been closest to her mother Inez, inheriting her sense of *noblesse oblige*. Abigail grew up in the rarified atmosphere of San Francisco society, educated at the exclusive Catholic School for Girls in Carmel, California. Her debutante ball, held in the ballroom of San Francisco's elegant St. Francis Hotel a few days before Christmas, was one of the social highlights of 1961. After graduating from Radcliffe College, she took a job as publicity director for the University of California Art Museum at Berkeley, before doing graduate work at Harvard University, where she was awarded a degree in art history.

Abigail was a wealthy woman. After her death, investigators would report that her estate was worth some $500,000.⁸ Frykowski, although he had a genuine affection for her, also shrewdly realized that Abigail's vast riches and powerful network of social contacts could open many important doors, doors which even Polanski could not enter. After several months of living together in New York City, Voyteck and Abigail moved to Los Angeles. In August 1968, they rented a car and drove across the country, from the east coast to the west. Rather than settling in her native San Francisco, the pair instead took a house in Hollywood, at 2774 Woodstock Road, just off Mulholland Drive. Their neighbor across the street was Cass Elliot.

When Frykowski first arrived in Los Angeles, he expected Polanski to get him a job. "I resented him in a way," Roman later admitted. "He was a loser in a way. Whatever he started, he would fuck it up. He was always writing me letters...asking me for a job."[9] But Roman had few illusions as to his friend's abilities, and managed only to locate a position as a set constructor at Paramount. This apparently lasted for only a few days. "Fryko," recalled Zofia Komeda, "told them he wasn't going to spend his life knocking nails in the fucking floor and quit."[10]

In Los Angeles, Abigail threw herself into social work. She registered as a volunteer for the Los Angeles County Welfare Department, a position which she kept until the day before she and Voyteck took up residence at 10050 Cielo Drive, on April 1, 1969. She reported to her department at dawn each morning, then drove to the ghettos of Watts and Pacoima to work.[11] Although she entered into the work with great enthusiasm, soon enough, Abigail fell victim to depression. "A lot of social workers go home at night, take a bath and wash their day off," she told a friend. "I can't. The suffering gets under your skin."[12]

She was generous with her fortune. Abigail contributed large sums of money to the unsuccessful election campaign of Thomas Bradley against opponent Samuel Yorty, and volunteered her time as well. She also worked closely with the Haight-Ashbury Free Clinic in San Francisco. The clinic was nearly always short of funds, and liberal San Francisco society had taken the cause, promoting a rock concert at the Carousel Ballroom featuring Big Brother and the Holding Company with Janis Joplin and the Quicksilver Messenger Service. Abigail's mother Inez Folger was instrumental in helping the Free Clinic to receive a grant from a charitable trust, along with some $25,000 from another corporate group, and herself volunteered her time to aid in drug counseling. She gave several fundraising parties for the clinic's benefit, with Abigail, as well as Sharon's parents Paul and Doris, in attendance.

In Los Angeles, Abigail came into the Polanskis' orbit through Voyteck. The two Polish expatriates often left Sharon and Abigail more or less on their own. When together, Roman and Voyteck would speak only Polish, often in a deliberate effort to exclude the women. Abigail, like Sharon, endured this humiliation in relative silence. Although pretty, Abigail knew she was not stunning, and constantly worried that Frykowski would leave her for a more attractive paramour. This, coupled with her sense of guilt over her vast fortune and depression over the situations of those she encountered during her social work, left Abigail increasingly unhappy. With her low self-confidence, she easily let Frykowski take advantage of both her good nature and her wealth.

Not surprisingly, Sharon and Abigail quickly became friends. According to Jerzy Kosinski, who knew all four of them well, Sharon and Abigail were so close because "they shared impossible conditions, [Polanski and Frykowski being] two egotistical narcissists. Each one contributed knowledge of her difficulty to the other."[13]

"Voyteck," recalls Michelle Phillips, "had a kind of weird vibe about him, a hustler-like feeling. No one really wanted to be around him that much. I never really got to know Abigail very well. She was considered a sort of 'little rich girl,' and, at least among our circle, there was a great snobbery which kept them both at arm's length."[14]

As members of the Polanski circle, both Abigail and Voyteck soon became friends with Jay Sebring. Jay himself was heavily involved with expanding his business interests. Together with manager and business partner John Madden, he worked out a scheme which would ensure his financial stability for years to come. He kept his original salon at 725 North Fairfax in Los Angeles, but also opened a number of franchise boutiques under the corporate name Sebring International. Abigail had recently become a business partner in the company, having invested $3,500 in Sebring International.[15] In the last weeks of his life, Jay had a new will drawn up, leaving everything to Madden; his contact with his own family was infrequent and strained, and Jay wanted to reward his partner. The document was slated to be signed on Monday, 11 August—ironically, two days after Jay was killed.[16]

During the four months that Sharon was away, the situation at 10050 Cielo Drive rapidly disintegrated. Voyteck Frykowski and Abigail Folger entertained regularly, and their guests of choice seemed to be drug dealers and the seedier elements of Hollywood society. Voyteck was too new to American culture and society to distinguish between the innocent hangers-on who always surrounded the rich and famous, and the more dangerous fringe elements in Los Angeles. Abigail Folger was just as lost in this milieu, and her dependency on her lover ensured her silent acquiescence.

During their tenure at 10050 Cielo Drive, Voyteck and Abigail allowed one of his friends and fellow emigrés from Poland, artist Witold Kaczankowski—known as Witold K.—to live in their house on Woodstock Road. With their permission, Kaczankowski invited a friend named Harrison "Pic" Dawson to share their house. Dawson. whose father worked for the United States State Department, occasionally dated Cass Eliott, who lived just across Woodstock Road.

It was through these two men that Frykowski met Ben Carruthers, Tom Harrigan and Billy Doyle. Dawson, Carruthers, Harrigan and Doyle were all heavily involved in the distribution of illegal drugs in Los Angeles, and all four were to become major suspects in the LAPD investigation into the murders at 10050 Cielo Drive.

Doyle and Harrigan had come to Los Angeles from Toronto in January 1969, bringing with them an estimated two pounds of cocaine. Quickly, they began to seek Hollywood connections, a quest which brought them, through Cass Eliott, into Frykowski's orbit.[17]

The extent of Frykowski's involvement in the Los Angeles drug scene is not known. Police investigations after the murders disclosed any number of possible suspects in drug rings operating in the city. Voyteck is alleged to have set up a ring outside of a recognized group, a definite breach of drug protocol, and a move which is said to have angered established dealers. He also transgressed accepted standards by becoming a heavy drug user. He seems to have been the one to first introduce Abigail to the illegal drugs which both were soon consuming. Certainly, it was Folger money which bought the endless supply of marijuana, LSD, cocaine, hashish and mescaline throughout the summer of 1969.

Frykowski took advantage of his tenure at 10050 Cielo Drive to throw lavish parties, designed to impress important members of the motion picture industry. These events seem to have attracted not only people on the fringe of show business but hangers-on, drug dealers and alleged pornography industry contacts. Much of the mythology concerning wild goings-on at 10050 Cielo Drive stems from the Frykowski/Folger residence there. After the murders, rumors of witchcraft, sex orgies and drug dealing proliferated.

"There were a lot of parties without any planning," an acquaintance recalled. "An enormous number of people came and went, and you never saw them again. You felt you were in a very volatile, dangerous world."[18] Los Angeles detectives would note ominously: "During April, May, June and the first part of July, Frykowski and

Folger had many impromptu parties. An open invitation policy existed at the house. Drug use was prevalent. They used hashish, marijuana, mescaline, cocaine and the stimulant MDA."[19]

However, William Garretson, the young caretaker hired by Rudi Altobelli to look after the property in his absence, would later recall only one major party given at 10050 Cielo Drive during Sharon's time in Europe. "There were cars parked all the way down Bella, and they had a band there...and they had ten cases of champagne; they had...three parking lot attendants parking cars, and then about—I don't know how many people serving drinks and everything."[20] But Garretson was also careful to distinguish between large parties such as this one, and the "usual" gatherings, which could include several dozen people.

In July, Harrison Dawson, in the midst of a heated argument with Witold Kaczankowski, pulled a gun on the artist. When Frykowski heard of this, he drove over to the house on Woodstock Road and threw Dawson out. In return, Dawson apparently threatened Frykowski's life. Even with this threat hanging over him, however, Voyteck continued his illicit association with Dawson's three friends as the summer progressed.

In early July, Harrigan returned from Toronto with samples of the synthetic drug Methlenedioxyl-amphetamine, or MDA, a euphoria-inducing stimulant new to the Los Angeles market. Harrigan met with Frykowski at 10050 Cielo Drive and offered him the exclusive rights to deal MDA in the Los Angeles drug market. With Frykowski's agreement, Harrigan flew to Toronto and purchased a fairly large quantity of the drug which, on his return to Los Angeles, he handed over to Voyteck.[21]

Just before Sharon returned from Europe, Jay Sebring telephoned Roman in London and asked if he could use the property at Cielo to host a business party. Guests, invited to invest in Sebring International, included Warren Beatty and John Phillips. Two drunken males crashed the party, and quickly became abusive. Frykowski, with the assistance of several friends, managed to eject them, hustling the pair up the driveway. As Frykowski closed the gates behind them, one of the men shouted: "You fucking son of a bitch! We'll be back and we'll kill you!"[22]

With Roman
Polanski in *The
Fearless Vampire
Killers*

Poster for *The Fearless
Vampire Killers*

An atypical portrait of Sharon

Chapter 26
Sharon Alone

AFTER HER LINER DOCKED IN NEW YORK, SHARON RETURNED TO Los Angeles, where Jay Sebring picked her up. She was back at Cielo Drive in time to watch the moon landing live on television, on July 20. Her parents were down from San Francisco for the weekend to work on their house at Palos Verdes, and they joined their daughter, Jay, Abigail and Voyteck as they watched the scenes from the moon that afternoon. With her, Doris had brought a large wooden rocking chair, in which she herself had rocked and nursed her three daughters. Sharon placed it in a corner of the living room until the nursery was finished. It was the last time Paul and Doris Tate would see their daughter alive.

Sharon selected the maid's room at the northern corner of the house as the nursery for her baby. Winifred Chapman, the middle-aged lady whom Sharon had hired as maid while she and Roman still lived in Patty Duke's house on Summit Ridge Drive, did not live-in, and the room had been left empty. "I was at the house a few weeks before the murders," recalls Michelle Phillips. "Sharon seemed happy, relieved to be home, but tired. We talked about the baby, and her plans. She didn't know if it was a boy or a girl, and so had some trouble picking out a scheme to decorate the nursery. She showed me the fabric she had decided to use, yellow with a pattern of little birds on it. That was the last time I saw her."[1]

Sharon wanted Roman home, not only because she worried about what he might be doing and who he might be seeing in London without her, but also because she disliked the atmosphere she found on her return at 10050 Cielo Drive. Although she personally liked Abigail Folger, she made no secret to Roman that she could barely tolerate the arrogant Frykowski. In addition, Voyteck frequently invited numerous friends to the house for small parties after her return, and they were almost always drunk, or using drugs, or both. Sharon had quit using drugs as soon as she found out she was pregnant. Voyteck and Abigail seemed to be in constant arguments, too, and Sharon became so upset that she worried her own stress might harm her baby. According to Doris Tate, "Whatever was going on at that house prior to her going home bothered her a great deal. She wasn't so naive that night that she called [me] and said she wanted these people out of the house. Roman couldn't get home quick enough for her to be settled and have that baby."[2]

Sharon expected Roman to arrive at any time. But, after placing a few telephone calls to him, she realized that he had no intention of following her back to Los Angeles. He claimed that he had to be in London to finish working on the script for *Day of the Dolphin*. To a friend, however, he allegedly admitted, "I can't stand seeing Sharon blown up the way she is. This pregnancy has made her such an insecure, nagging bitch. If I could, I'd wait until she gives birth. Then maybe I could go back and find Sharon the way she used to be."[3]

His reluctance to return to Los Angeles hurt Sharon deeply. During the last weeks of her pregnancy, at a time when she desperately wanted Roman at her side, he refused to abandon his own plans. Instead, and against Sharon's wishes, he asked Frykowski to remain at Cielo Drive, to look after his wife. Roman finally told Sharon that it would be another two to three weeks before he could get away. He promised, however, that he would be home before his birthday, August 18, which was, incidentally, the expected date for their baby's arrival.

One of the reasons Sharon had been so eager to take on the role of Pat in *Thirteen Chairs* was the chance it gave her for time away from Roman. Initially, she had wanted to think things through regarding the troubled state of their marriage. She was unhappy enough to seek the advice of many of her friends, who, in turn, encouraged her to hold on; when she found out she was pregnant, the change in her state of mind had been almost immediate. Once Roman began to show enthusiasm for the baby, Sharon hoped that all of the problems between them would become things of the past. This hope was shattered soon after she returned to Los Angeles. Sharon learned that Roman, while in London, had had another affair. To make things worse, it had been with a mutual friend, Michelle Phillips. "It was a stupid thing to do," Michelle Phillips says. "We

Sharon Tate in Hollywood

Sharon Tate as a senior at
Vincenza American High School

Philippe Forquet (left)—with Robert Morley, Sandra Dee and James
Stewart—as a romantic interest in his brief Hollywood career, in the
film *Take Her, She's Mine* (Universal Pictures 1963)

Poster for *Valley of the Dolls*

Leno LaBianca (center) signing a Gateways Market contract
(photo courtesy of Alice LaBianca)

The words "Death To Pigs" written in blood on the wall of the
LaBianca residence

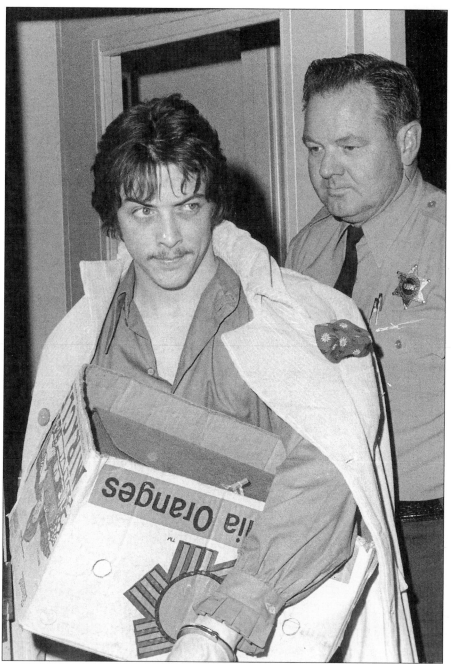

Robert "Bobby" Beausoleil (AP/Wide World Photo)

Mary Brunner, mother of
Manson's son
(AP/Wide World Photo)

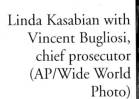

Linda Kasabian with
Vincent Bugliosi,
chief prosecutor
(AP/Wide World
Photo)

Manson, clean-shaven, with a swastika carved on his forehead, March 1971
(AP/Wide World Photo)

Three smiling girls prior to being sentenced to death—(from left to right) Susan Denise Atkins, Patricia Krenwinkle, and Leslie Van Houton. (Corbis Images)

Before conviction, Manson gags with newsmen in court (AP/Wide World Photo)

A crew cut Manson after conviction
(AP/Wide World Photo)

A postcard (front and back) sent by Manson in 1998 from State Prison in Corcoran, California

"Do you want to wright (*sic*) one of the guys here—you know I can't keep up with ALL & or Everyone. So I just ride and help it roll in a (illegible) thing. Do you want to HOOK up with somebody. Cool— Easy, Charles Manson."

Mrs. Doris Tate being interviewed (with Bill Nelson) about her frequent battles for victims' rights

The grave marker

Publicity shot of Sharon at the apex of her career

were both drunk, it just happened, and I regretted it."[4] Word of it reached back to Hollywood. John Phillips knew of it soon afterward, and Sharon's friends, belonging to the same circles as the Phillips, alerted her to what had happened.[5]

Sharon was crushed by this latest development. She had put up with Roman's philandering before their marriage and even during their marriage. When she became pregnant, she hoped that he would change. Against her wishes, Sharon found herself in the midst of a crisis. She had no doubt that Roman loved and cared for her, but she could no longer ignore his infidelities, which hurt her deeply. Worse still was his lack of discretion, a selfish determination to live as he wished, without alteration or consideration of Sharon's feelings. His wife's pregnancy, she now realized, had not changed Roman at all. The humiliation of facing friends who knew of her husband's promiscuity was simply too much to bear.

In London, Roman was apparently continuing his amorous exploits. According to several sources, he regularly picked up girls at either the Playboy Club or in the fashionable night spots he haunted with his friends, taking them back to the house at Eaton Place. Sharon, through mutual friends in London, learned of this.

Previously, Sharon had taken only minimal steps to confront Roman. Each time, he would remind her that she had once agreed to allow him his freedom. But Sharon had matured in the year of her marriage to Roman. His infidelities had hardened her, made her more resolute, more determined. The pregnancy simply cemented her own growing self-respect. She now realized that, if she was to salvage anything of her future happiness, she would have to make an uncomfortable decision. Roman would never change. Sharon began to seriously consider the idea of divorcing Roman.

A divorce had long been expected by many of the Polanskis' mutual friends. Yet this easy solution came hard for Sharon: it was an admission of failure, that those things she most prized—a happy marriage and loving husband—had eluded her. She had always suffered from doubts, seeking approval from powerful and influential men and subjugating her will to theirs. The almost total subversion of her values and wishes to those of Roman had not come easily, but she had been willing to sacrifice her own personal desires in the hope that the marriage would succeed. Now, she realized that no matter what she did, she would never be able to change Roman; she still loved Roman, but was too hurt to remain his wife.

Sharon seems to have been adamant. She told several friends, and, at least among her intimates, her resolution was well-known.[6] "We knew she planned to divorce Roman," says Patty Faulkner, daughter of Jay Sebring's business partner John Madden.[7] Whether she ever told Roman that she was considering divorce is not known; his autobiography, not surprisingly, is silent on the question. After the fact, he would scarcely have admitted that the marriage had been all but over.

From the moment of her return to the United States, her constant companion had been Jay Sebring. Jay had rushed to meet her in New York, escorted her back to Los Angeles, and remained by her side through the last week of July and into August. Now, she apparently confided her thoughts of divorce to her former boyfriend.[8]

Jay's closest friends knew that he remained in love with Sharon. A succession of casual affairs and beautiful girls had all been a futile attempt on his part to ease Sharon from his mind. But now, having positioned himself as Sharon's most intimate friend, he cannot have but considered the future, and the possibility that she might return to him. Sharon, who had always valued Jay's gentle qualities and sincere love and concern, at least knew that she would have his support no matter what happened with Roman.

Such knowledge only strengthened her resolve. Sharon apparently decided to wait until the baby was born, perhaps to see if fatherhood altered her husband's extra-marital activities. If there was no change, she would institute divorce proceedings. In anticipation of this she made arrangements to star in the erotic, soft-core pornographic adaptation of *The Story of O*. Allied Artists was set to produce the film, and Sharon was to begin work several months after the birth of her baby.[9] With her newly-found confidence and independence, Sharon would be ready, if necessary, to make a fresh start to her life.

Jay flew north to San Francisco to attend a cocktail party to publicize the grand opening of his new shop at 629 Commercial Street. Sharon did not feel like traveling with him, but Abigail Folger, who had invested several thousand dollars in Sebring International, was there, as well as Sharon's parents. Both Paul and Doris Tate remained devoted to Jay. Paul Tate was finishing up his Army career at nearby Fort Barry at the Presidio, before permanently retiring to the house in Palos Verdes Estates which he and Doris had purchased.

Sharon's pregnancy, in the last few weeks of her scheduled term, began to tire her easily. She preferred staying home at 10050 Cielo Drive, watching television or escaping from the incessant heat in the cool waters of the kidney-shaped swimming pool. She purchased several rings and floats, so that she could comfortably drift around the pool propped up on her expanding stomach. Nearly every afternoon, she took a short nap; down the middle of the queen-sized bed, she lined up a row of pillows, which she hugged in place of her absent husband. Occasionally, she would telephone friends, or drive down to Dolores's Drive-In, her favorite haunt, for one of their special hamburgers, which she loved.[10]

William Garretson, the young man who lived in the guest house, recalled seeing Sharon occasionally sunning herself on the lawn, or swimming in the pool. "Once, when I was swimming, she came out of the house," he remembers, "and sat down on the edge of the pool, chatting with me. She was very nice, quiet, and seemed very down to earth. She told me that I could swim in the pool whenever I wanted. After she came back from Europe, I never saw any parties going on at the main house."[11]

During these last weeks of her life, Sharon found herself the center of her sisters' inquisitive attention. "They were probably the happiest days on earth to our family," Sharon's youngest sister Patti later recalled. "We'd finally come together. She was often gone, so those times were very far and few between that we got together, and this was our time. It was a time that she was going to be home for a while now with the child coming, and it was wonderful because we were all united as a family."[12]

Occasionally, sixteen-year-old Debbie and eleven-year-old Patti would come up to Cielo to stay the night, sleeping in the loft above the living room. "My sister was everything to me," Patti recalls. "She was so sweet and such a gentle soul. She was a movie star and beautiful, and in my eyes she was just so big. There wasn't anything I wouldn't have done for her." The two girls would swim with Sharon, laugh with Abigail Folger, and put their hands on their sister's stomach to feel the baby kicking inside.[13]

On Friday, August 1, Voyteck Frykowski threw a small luncheon party at 10050 Cielo Drive. Both Sharon and Abigail were away from the house at the time. His guests, including several young girls he had reportedly picked up on Sunset Strip, enjoyed a lunch of chicken and champagne served by Mrs. Chapman at the side of the pool.

The maid later recalled that the guests spent some time perched on the edge of Sharon's bed, watching television.[14]

Jay Sebring returned from San Francisco late Saturday night, and spent Sunday, August 3, with Sharon at the house on Cielo Drive. One afternoon, she happily posed for him on the front lawn. Dressed in flowered bikini panties and a loose, flowing halter top, she stood before the split-rail fence, holding her Yorkshire terrier Prudence, and perched at the edge of the swimming pool. She also posed with Jay while Voyteck took a number of photographs, leaving a pictorial hint of their feeling for each other. Jay, wearing only a low-cut pair of bikini trunks, smiled broadly at the camera, one arm cradled round Sharon.

The intimacy suggested by the pictures was no secret in Hollywood. Kirk Douglas later wrote: "There was talk that their romance still continued, even that the baby might have been Jay's."[15] While there can be no doubt of Jay's love for Sharon, and, indeed, her deep feelings for him, there is no evidence whatsoever that Sharon's baby was not Roman's. That such talk ran high amongst their circle of friends, though, is clearly indicative of the depth of the relationship between Sharon and Jay.

Jay, in fact, was with Sharon nearly every day that first week of August. On Monday, he drove her to the offices of Airways Rent-a-Car, where Sharon picked up a 1969 Chevrolet Camaro, which she leased until the following Saturday, August 9.[16] Her Rolls had not yet arrived from London, and she had had a small accident in Roman's Ferrari, which was to be in the repair shop for the next five days. He saw her again on Tuesday, Thursday, and finally Friday.

On either Sunday or Monday, Thomas Harrigan visited 10050 Cielo Drive to deliver drugs to Voyteck Frykowski. To friends, Voyteck explained that he was receiving supplies of MDA, and that he was in the middle of a ten-day experiment with the drug. That night, publicist Steve Brandt met Voyteck at a club in Hollywood. He later declared that Frykowski seemed "unfocused, staring." When he asked if he was taking drugs, Voyteck quickly replied, "Yes, it's mescaline. Want to buy some?"[17]

Voyteck himself, in the last week of his life, appeared at times out of control. One day that week, he showed up unannounced at John Phillips' house in Beverly Hills, banging on the door and loudly demanding to be let in. "He seemed slightly incoherent and had a bizarre presence about him," Phillips recalled. "I wouldn't let him in, but he insisted. I just didn't feel right about it. He was rumored to have had weird drug connections and was part of the crowd that had been feeding off Cass. I apologized and closed the door in his face."[18]

On Tuesday evening, Sharon threw a party for a few dozen of her friends, in honor of French film director Roger Vadim and his wife Jane Fonda. After the murders, the party became the subject of an immense amount of speculation, the source of a number of bizarre rumors involving nefarious activities taking place at 10050 Cielo Drive.

A few days earlier, Jay Sebring had complained to one of the receptionists in his salon that he had been burned for $2,000 worth of cocaine. The dealer who perpetrated the burn was Billy Doyle, one of Voyteck's friends, and a regular source for drugs for both Frykowski and Cass Eliott.[19]

When Frykowski heard of this, and of Sebring's desire for vengeance, he allegedly invited Doyle to the party at 10050 Cielo Drive on Tuesday evening. During the course of the evening, according to the stories, Doyle was tied to a chair, sodomized by both Jay and Voyteck, and then whipped, the whole sordid affair taking place before the invited audience and the event being captured on videotape.[20]

Allegations to this effect were first aired by actor Dennis Hopper. In an interview with an underground Los Angeles newspaper, he reported: "They had fallen into sadism and masochism and bestiality—and they recorded it all on videotape, too. The L.A. police told me this. I know that three days before they were killed, twenty-five people were invited to that house to a mass whipping of a dealer from Sunset Strip who'd given them bad dope."[21]

Years later, Manson Family member and convicted murderer Bobby Beausoleil told author Truman Capote: "They burned people on dope deals. Sharon Tate and that gang. They picked up kids on the Strip and took them home and whipped them. Made movies of it. Ask the cops; they found the movies. Not that they'd tell you the truth."[22]

Tales of pictures and videotapes allegedly discovered at 10050 Cielo Drive after the murders are legendary. Paul Krassner, editor of the underground journal *The Realist*, wrote in his memoirs that Warren Hinckle, the editor of *Ramparts Magazine*, "brought me to the renowned private investigator Hal Lipset, who informed me that not only did the Los Angeles Police Department seize pornographic films and videotapes they found in Sharon Tate's loft but also that certain members of the LAPD were selling them. Lipset had talked with one police source who told him exactly which porn flicks were available—a total of seven hours' worth for a quarter-million dollars....Sharon Tate with a popular singer. There was Sharon with Steve McQueen. There was Sharon with two black bisexual men."[23] Terry Melcher later declared: "I knew they had been making a lot of homemade sadomasochistic-porno movies there with quite a few recognizable Hollywood faces in them. The reason I knew was that I had gone out with a girl named Michelle Phillips, one of the Mamas and Papas, whose ex-husband, John Phillips, was the leader of the group. Michelle told me she and John had had dinner one night, to discuss maybe getting back together, and afterward he had taken her up to visit the Polanskis in my old house. Michelle said that when they arrived there, everyone in the house was busy filming an orgy and that Sharon Tate was part of it."[24]

According to Michelle Phillips, however, the story is apocryphal. "That's absolutely untrue," she says. "It's totally false. It never happened. I never said anything like that to Terry."[25]

In spite of such allegations, it seems that the truth was less sensational. Roman had purchased a Sony videotape machine and camera, for use in his work. Occasionally, the machine was used for other purposes, and one videotape which the police seized did indeed show Sharon and Roman making love. When and why Roman had filmed this event is not known. The only photographs which the police discovered at 10050 Cielo Drive were publicity shots of Sharon.

In the four months that Sharon and Roman were absent, Voyteck was involved in some questionable activities, which, after the murders, became linked forever to Sharon's reputation. He is known to have picked up girls from the Sunset Strip in Abigail's absence and photographed them at 10050 Cielo Drive. It seems likely that this itself was the basis for the many rumours that summer.

As for the events of Tuesday evening, 5 August, not one single reliable piece of evidence has surfaced to support the allegations of a mass videotaped humiliation and rape. The story, in fact, was a confused version of an event which had not even occurred at the Polanski house. "We investigated the incident," says Mike McGann, one of the police team later assigned to the murders. "It hadn't taken place at Cielo Drive, but at Cass Eliott's house, and didn't involve either Sharon Tate or Jay Sebring."[26]

On Wednesday, August 6, Sharon, Voyteck and Abigail drove over to director Michael Sarne's beach house in Malibu for a quiet dinner. Halfway through the meal, however, Sharon complained that she was not feeling well. After finishing dessert, she had Voyteck drive her home.[27]

The following afternoon, Tom Harrigan again visited Voyteck at Cielo Drive. He, Voyteck and Abigail shared a bottle of wine, while Harrigan discussed the distribution of MDA. Sharon, Harrigan recalled, was not present.[28]

She had, in fact, spent most of the day with Jay. Late that afternoon, Ib Zacko, one of Sebring's neighbors on Easton Drive, heard a car gunning its engine on the road. The noise was so loud that the windows in his house were rattling. When he went outside to investigate, he found Sharon sitting on the passenger side of Sebring's Porsche, which was idling loudly.

"What the hell are you doing sitting there by yourself, Sharon?" he asked.

She explained that she and Jay had driven up to his gate, but that someone had parked their car in front of it, and that now they couldn't get through. In a few minutes, Jay returned to the Porsche, climbed in and honked his horn, trying to attract the attention of the unknown owner. Finally, however, after knocking on several doors, he acted on his own initiative: jumping into the abandoned car, he eased the emergency brake off, slipped it into neutral, and rolled the vehicle down the length of Easton and out into the middle of Benedict Canyon Road, where he left it for the owner to claim.[29]

That evening, after Jay had returned her to Cielo, Sharon made a rare date to attended a screening at Universal Studios of a new *Marcus Welby, MD* television episode featuring one of her friends, actor Robert Lipton. "She was so pregnant that I'm sure it tired her just sitting through an hour episode," he later recalled.[30]

In the last week of July, Sharon had given a promotional interview to Italian journalist Enrico di Pompeo in anticipation of the European release of *Thirteen Chairs*. During the interview, Pompeo asked if Sharon believed in fate. "Certainly," she told him. "My whole life has been decided by fate. I think something more powerful than we are decides our fates for us. I know one thing—I've never planned anything that ever happened to me."[31]

Chapter 27
The Last Day

FRIDAY, AUGUST 8, 1969 DAWNED HOT AND MUGGY IN LOS Angeles. The city was in the middle of a heat wave, and over the past few days, the temperatures had remained consistently in the unbearable nineties. At 10050 Cielo Drive, high above the sweltering city, the heat was less oppressive, and there was the additional relief of a breeze sweeping fresh, cooling air to the privileged residents of the canyons. Even so, it promised to be a warm and miserably humid day.

Around eight that morning, Mrs. Chapman arrived at 10050 Cielo Drive. She normally worked full days on Friday and Saturday, a half day on Sunday, and full days again on Mondays and Tuesdays. She took the key to the back door from above the rafters of the rear porch, and entered the kitchen, where she found a few dishes left over from the previous evening. After washing these, she went on to begin her regular work for the day.[1]

About half an hour later, Frank Guerrero arrived to paint the intended nursery at the northern corner of the main house. Before he began, he removed all of the screens from the exterior windows. He was to return a day later to give the room another coat of paint. Sharon had hired interior decorator Peter Shore to come the following week and begin furnishing the room; the weekend would give the paint the opportunity to dry.[2]

Sharon awoke that day around nine. When it was hot, she preferred to be as comfortable as possible. This morning, she dressed in a bikini panties and bra, decorated in a small, blue and yellow floral print. After greeting Mrs. Chapman, she took an early morning swim. She was still lounging near the pool when, at eleven that morning, Roman called from London. According to Roman, she sounded nervous and edgy, suffering from the intense heat. He also gathered from the broad hints she dropped that she was rapidly becoming irritated with Voyteck and his constant drug use.

Roman informed Sharon that he was in the process of packing his things and would return shortly; two steamer trunks, containing his and Sharon's wardrobes, had already been sent from London. He had to get a U.S. Visa, and, although this was a mere formality, he had to wait until Monday, when the consulate would be open. He told Sharon to expect him home on Tuesday, August 12. Before hanging up, Sharon told Roman that a stray kitten had wandered on to the property; she was feeding it with an eye-dropper.[3]

Just as Sharon finished her telephone call with Roman, Mrs. Chapman noticed that the dog had left paw prints on the front door of the main house. She washed the Dutch door with a solution of vinegar and water. A few days earlier, on Tuesday, she had done the same thing to the set of French doors leading from Sharon's bedroom to the pool area at the side of the house.[4]

Just after noon, two of Sharon's friends, actress Joanna Pettit and Barbara Lewis, arrived for lunch. There was a small group of wrought iron lawn furniture beneath a pine tree near the swimming pool, and the three women sat in the shade, talking, as the two visitors later recalled, mostly about the expected arrival of the baby, which was due late the following week.[5]

Sharon seemed disillusioned, worn out. She allegedly complained "that Roman was a bastard for leaving her alone with Frykowski," adding that, without Jay's support, she "would have gone out of her mind." Roman's apparent disinterest in their baby hurt her deeply. Above all, she clearly felt that he was deliberately avoiding her, unwilling to put aside his own schedule to accommodate her feelings. "That's probably why the little rat is still in London," she added sadly.[6]

Abigail Folger had left the property earlier that morning with Voyteck. She purchased a bicycle from a shop on Santa Monica Boulevard and arranged for it to be delivered to 10050 Cielo Drive later that afternoon. She and Voyteck then drove back to the house, where they joined Sharon and her guests as Mrs. Chapman served luncheon. Pettit and Lewis left just after three.[7]

Two of the gardeners from the landscaping service Altobelli used were scheduled to trim the lawns, weed the flower beds, clip the hedges and water the plants. One of the men, Dave Martinez, walked over to the guest house and asked William Garretson to water the lawns over the weekend. Tom Vargas, Martinez's partner, arrived around half-past three that afternoon. As he drove through the gates, he saw Abigail Folger climb into Sharon's rented yellow Camaro and drive out. She was going to keep her regular 4:30 PM appointment with her psychiatrist, Dr. Marvin Flicker. A few minutes later, Voyteck also left, in Abigail's red Firebird.[8]

During her appointment with Dr. Flicker that afternoon, Abigail confided that she had reached her limit with Frykowski. As Flicker listened, she declared that his various affairs and wild drug use had finally become too much to bear. She left his office early that evening, having decided to leave Voyteck the following week.[9]

Shortly before four, Jay Sebring called Sharon. He was at home, having spent most of the day in bed with his current girlfriend, Susan Peterson. He told Sharon that he would be over to see her in a few hours. He then called his business manager, John Madden, to discuss details of a trip to San Francisco he was to make the following day to do some work at his salon there.[10]

A few minutes later, Voyteck arrived at Jay's house on Easton Drive. He picked up Peterson and drove downtown to see Witold Kaczankowski at the latter's Beverly Wilshire Hotel gallery, which was set to open the following week.[11] On seeing his friend, Kaczankowski burst out laughing. Frykowski was attired in a pair of purple bell bottom pants with tiny flowers on them, a purple shirt, a dark vest and black boots. Voyteck pointed out his pants as being his latest purchase, but Kaczankowski was not impressed, finding Frykowski's choices too effeminate for his taste. "If you want to be a fag, go ahead," he told Voyteck. "But the fags are going to be after you." Unflustered, Voyteck asked his friend to have dinner with him, Abigail, Sharon and Jay. Kaczankowski refused the invitation, however, saying that he had too much work to do at his gallery. Frykowski later called him from Cielo Drive, again inviting him to stop by. Kaczankowski told Voyteck that he and his girlfriend might stop by the house later that evening.

Voyteck then called another Polish friend, Professor Stanislav Wohl, one of his former teachers at Lodz, and asked him to dinner. Wohl, saying that he had a previous dinner engagement with friends, also declined.[12]

After leaving Kaczankowski's gallery, Frykowski and Peterson drove to the house Voyteck shared with Abigail on Woodstock Road, where he unloaded a few boxes of clothes. They stayed at the Woodstock Road house for around an hour, listening to records.

Back at 10050 Cielo Drive, gardener Dave Martinez was getting ready to leave. Mrs. Chapman told Sharon that she had finished her work for the day, and that, unless there was something else she wanted done, she was going to leave. Sharon, thinking how hot it might be in Mrs. Chapman's central Los Angeles apartment, asked if she would like to stay over at 10050 Cielo Drive for the night, especially as she was due to work the following morning. After a few seconds of thought, however, Mrs. Chapman declined Sharon's offer. She picked up her purse, and Martinez drove her to her bus stop down Benedict Canyon Road.[13]

Sharon decided to lie down for a short nap before Jay arrived. She was still asleep when, around 4:30 PM, a delivery truck from the Air Dispatch Company arrived at 10050 Cielo Drive with the two blue steamer trunks containing both Sharon's and Roman's belongings from London. Gardener Tom Vargas, knowing that Sharon was asleep, did not want to disturb her, and signed for the trunks himself. Vargas placed them in the living room, just to the side of the wide opening into the entrance hall. A few minutes later, Vargas left the property.[14]

At half-past five, a neighbor saw Jay Sebring leave his house on Easton Drive. He sped down Benedict Canyon Road in his black Porsche, turned right at Cielo Drive, and drove up the hill to 10050.[15] Neither Voyteck nor Abigail were in when he arrived.

Sharon's sixteen-year old sister Deborah telephoned shortly after Jay's arrival. Since her return from London, Sharon had usually tried to spend a part of the weekend at her parents' house in Palos Verdes Estates, or have her mother and sisters up to 10050 Cielo Drive for a night. She had not done so the previous weekend, however, because both her mother and father had been in San Francisco, packing up their belongings for the final move when Major Tate retired in two weeks. This weekend, her mother Doris was in Los Angeles but her father was at his base in San Francisco. Sharon, physically tired at the end of the week, decided not to stay with her mother that Friday night. Instead, Debbie had earlier discussed the possibility of coming to stay with Sharon at 10050 Cielo Drive. When she called, however, Sharon told her that she was tired, and asked if they could make it another time.[16]

Sharon, in fact, had been expected at a small dinner party being thrown that evening by her friend Sheilah Wells. Sharon would have gone with Jay, and joined Sheilah and her husband Fred Beir, Joanna Pettit, Alex Cord, Stella Stevens and Skip Ward. Just after Sharon's sister Debbie called, Sheilah Wells rang and asked her not to park in her driveway when she arrived because her neighbors had been complaining about the noise. But Sharon told her that she was too tired to go out. She thought that she and Jay might drive down the Canyon to fetch some hamburgers for dinner, but, otherwise, she simply wanted to remain at home. "I tried to persuade her to come afterwards and spend the night," Sheilah recalled. "It was a very hot summer night—but she said she wanted to wash her hair and get to bed early. This was the last time we ever spoke."[17]

Although Sharon wanted to have a quiet evening at home, shortly after the murders, nearly half of Hollywood would describe how Sharon had called them and invited them to 10050 Cielo Drive that night. Columnist Steve Brandt and Cass Eliott later said that they turned down invitations from Sharon that evening. Author Jacqueline Susann, then staying at the Beverly Hills Hotel, said that Sharon called and asked her to stop by, but Susann had already committed to having dinner that night with friend Rex Reed.[18]

Sometime after seven, both Abigail and Voyteck returned from their separate errands. According to the later police investigation, Joel Rostau, boyfriend of one of Sebring's employees, delivered cocaine and mescaline to 10050 Cielo Drive for either Jay or Voyteck, or both.[19] This in itself would not have been an unusual occurance, however. Although Sharon had stopped using any drugs since learning of her pregnancy, she knew Jay and Voyteck continued to do so. Apparently, the amount Rostau brought was minimal, since Sebring and Frykowski asked if he could get more. Rostau was unable to do so, and did not return.

After some discussion, Jay made dinner reservations for Sharon, Abigail, Voyteck and himself at El Coyote, a fashionable Mexican restaurant on Beverly Boulevard. The four drove down the Canyon to the restaurant, where, after a fifteen minute wait at the bar, they were seated and had dinner. Around a quarter to ten, they finished their meal and left.

It was dark by the time they returned to 10050 Cielo Drive. The lights on the property were fixed to a timer; as they drove through the gates, the yellow bug light on the side of the garage and the Christmas lights strung across the split-rail fence bordering the lawn glowed in the night. Landscape lights, positioned around the lawn and behind the shrubbery, cast eerie shadows against the house as the foursome followed the flagstone walk across the lawn to the front porch.

Abigail went off to the bedroom she shared with Voyteck and changed into a mid-length white nightgown. Sometime after returning, she took a fairly large dose of the MDA Voyteck had purchased a few days before.

Within a few minutes, the telephone rang; it was Abigail's mother Inez. Abigail was due to catch a 10 AM flight on United Airlines the following morning, to spend the day in San Francisco. The conversation, which lasted for only a few minutes, was unexceptional; Inez Folger did note, however, that her daughter sounded "a little high."[20]

After saying goodnight to her mother, Abigail climbed into the antique, carved bed nestled in a corner of her bedroom. Above her perched a large stuffed rabbit, gazing down from the headboard. Relaxing into a drug-induced euphoria, she settled back into the bed to read before going to sleep.

Voyteck was in the living room, listening to the stereo in the hall closet. He, too, had taken MDA on their return to 10050 Cielo Drive, and happily dozed off on the long couch. The only light in the living room came from the small table lamp on the desk.

At the southern end of the house, Sharon and Jay had retired to her bedroom. After returning from the restaurant, Sharon changed out of her minidress, revealing the bikini panties and bra which she had worn all day. It was still hot outside—eighty degrees at eleven—and she was uncomfortable. She still wore her gold wedding band and a pair of gold stud earrings.[21] Sharon kept the refrigerator at 10050 Cielo Drive stocked with Heineken, Jay's favorite beer, and he had grabbed one on their return. He sat on the edge of the bed, talking with Sharon, and smoking a marijuana joint he had brought with him. Beyond the open windows of the bedroom, the lights of the swimming pool shimmered in the night.

A hundred feet away, past some low shrubbery, beneath an open, roofed gateway and down a curving flagstone walk, sat the guest house. The previous night, after drinking four cans of beer, smoking two marijuana joints and taking a dexedrine capsule, caretaker William Garretson had been sick.[22] He slept late on Friday, cleaned the guesthouse and spoke with Dave Martinez, promising to water the lawn over the weekend.

Around seven that evening, Garretson walked down Cielo and Benedict Canyon to Turner's Drug Store, where he purchased a TV dinner, a pack of cigarettes and some Coca-Cola. As he walked back up the canyon, he noted the Christmas lights strung across the split-rail fence, sparkling in the distance.[23]

Just after eleven-thirty, eighteen-year-old Steven Parent drove his father's white 1966 Nash Ambassador through the gate at 10050 Cielo Drive. Six feet tall, with short red hair and glasses, Parent lived with his parents, sister and two younger brothers in the Los Angeles suburb of El Monte. Parent had been something of a loner in high school, focusing his attention on choir. His sister Janet recalls that "Steve didn't date much, and he didn't have many close friends."[24]

His recent past had been troubled. He had been arrested several times for petty theft, and had spent some time in a youth correctional facility.[25] According to Parent's sister Janet, his trouble stemmed from his passion for electronics: "Steve was fascinated by electronics and mechanics, and he stole several radios, bringing them home and tearing them apart to understand how they worked." Parent's interest seems to have been real enough: "When he was at the correctional camp," his sister recalls, "Steve tested at near-genius level for electronics."[26] Having graduated in June from Arroyo High School, Parent began to prepare for college. To save money, he worked two jobs: as a delivery boy for Valley City Plumbing Company in Rosemead during the day, and, in the evening, at Jonas Miller Stereo on Wilshire Boulevard.

Two few weeks earlier, Parent had stopped for Garretson when the latter was hitchhiking in Beverly Hills. When Garretson warned the young man that he lived up in the hills, Parent replied, "That's okay, I don't have anything to do," and motioned him into his father's Ambassador. During their ride, the caretaker told Parent of his job, mentioning that he looked after a house in which a famous movie star lived. Garretson directed Parent up Benedict Canyon Road, left on Cielo Drive, and then left again on the cul-de-sac to the gate of 10050. Before saying goodbye, he gave Parent his telephone number, and said that the young man should call him if he was ever coming up to the canyon.[27]

Late that Friday night, Parent had indeed rung Garretson, saying that he was in the area and asking if he could drop by. Garretson, who had no plans, said yes, and gave Parent instructions on how to operate the electronically-controlled front gate.[28] As he walked down the dirt path in front of the main house, Parent noticed, through the open windows, Abigail Folger sitting in bed reading, and, a little further on, Sharon perched on the edge of her bed.

He asked Garretson about the identities of the women. Garretson, who had little contact with the residents of the main house, thought that Voyteck Frykowski was Roman Polanski's younger brother. To Parent, he described Folger as the "younger Polanski's" girlfriend, while the other lady was Polanski's wife. Parent burst out laughing. "You mean Polanski has a girlfriend and a wife?" he asked in astonishment. After a bit more explaining on Garretson's part, Parent finally understood.[29]

Parent had brought a clock radio, hoping to sell it to the caretaker. Garretson, who had been listening to the stereo, turned it off so that Steve could demonstrate his. Garretson listened, but he had no use for the device. "I don't need any clocks, man," he told Parent. "I got clocks all over the place here."[30]

After drinking a beer with Garretson and calling a friend, Parent decided to leave. He unplugged the clock radio, wrapping the cord round it.[31] As he got up to leave, Christopher, Altobelli's Weimaraner, began to bark. When Parent asked if anything was wrong, Garretson dismissed it, saying that the dog always barked. Garretson watched as Parent started his walk up the dirt path toward the parking area and his white Ambassador, before he himself closed the door and returned to the living room, to write letters to friends and family back in Ohio.

It was late, just after midnight, when the 1959 Ford with its headlights turned off, took a left and climbed the steep cul-de-sac toward the high gate of 10050 Cielo Drive.

Chapter 28
Now is the Time For Helter Skelter

CHARLES MANSON RETURNED TO SPAHN RANCH ON THE MORNING of Friday, August 8. He quickly learned that Bobby Beausoleil had been arrested earlier that week. Manson was furious. If Beausoleil talked, the police would almost certainly come after him as an accessory in Gary Hinman's murder. The investigation would undoubtedly lead the police straight back to Spahn Ranch. In either case, the situation looked hopeless for Charles Manson.

While Manson considered what to do, Mary Brunner and Sandy Good drove to a nearby Sears store to purchase a few things with a stolen credit card. The card, however, showed up on a list while they were making their purchases, and both were apprehended after an extended car chase through the streets of the San Fernando Valley. They were booked into custody around 6 PM.

When Brunner and Good did not return as usual, Manson began to worry. After dinner, the Family gathered around a camp-fire. At ten that evening, Manson got a telephone call: it was Sandy Good, informing him of the arrest earlier in the day.

According to his own account, when he hung up the telephone, Manson was "in a rage. I walked away from the buildings, stood beside a tree and pounded my fists against it....All I could focus on was, 'What the fuck is happening here? One by one this fucked-up society is stripping my loves from me. I'll show them! They made animals out of us—I'll unleash those animals—I'll give them so much fucking fear the people will be afraid to come out of their houses....' Every abuse, every rejection in my entire life flashed before my eyes."[1]

Although things had not been going Manson's way for several months, by Friday, 8 August, it must have seemed as if his world were falling apart. On that day he found out that Bobby Beausoleil had been arrested for Hinman's murder—an arrest which he believed would eventually lead the police back to Spahn Ranch. This was followed by the news of Brunner's and Good's arrest that evening. Dennis Wilson had rejected him; Terry Melcher had rejected him; Rudi Altobelli had rejected him; the Establishment had rejected him; his Family was on the verge of being destroyed.

Much ink has been spilled on the events of that August weekend, in an attempt to make sense of what surely must rate as one of the most senseless of the twentieth century's mass murders. The tendency to seek the fantastic, the most bizarre explanation for the Tate-LaBianca murders, flows naturally enough from the very nature of the crimes. It is difficult to assign to such a savage rampage the most logical conclusions, and this difficulty in accepting the obvious has plagued historians of the case for thirty years.

It is apparent that the murders were not planned; these were random acts of violence, undertaken on a criminal whim. And that whim can only have been brought about by the momentous events of Friday, 8 August. Manson's plans for the future were disrupted; his very freedom was threatened should Beausoleil be traced back to Spahn Ranch. Two of his most ardent disciples were in jail. Manson had been unable to exert any control over the Establishment, and had been rejected by them. Now, he was fast losing control of his own Family. It does not stretch credulity to believe that the resulting murders were as much an attempt by Manson to re-assert his authority over the group at Spahn as they were to instigate a race war.

Manson undoubtedly believed that a race war, Helter Skelter, was indeed on the horizon. He may very well have believed that two nights of murder would help speed the process along. It was also later claimed during the trial by various Family members that a series of crimes, committed in a manner similar to Gary Hinman's murder—that is, vicious knife wounds, messages left in blood at the scene, the use of the word "Pig" in the phrases—would at least give the police pause that they might have arrested the wrong suspect.

But Manson's determination to maintain his hold over his followers cannot be underestimated as a motive for the crimes which took place. Certainly the very act of committing the various crimes solidified, at least for a time, not only Manson's position as head of the Family, but the bonds among the Family members themselves.

The two nights of murder once again restored Manson to what he perceived as his rightful place: that of leader, of seer, of manipulator, of master over life and death.

Seething with anger over his own tenuous position, and facing not only the months of rejection at the hands of others but the disintegration of his Family, Manson struck out. His target, the residents of 10050 Cielo Drive, represented the establishment in abstract, and, in particular, a substitute for Melcher, Wilson, Altobeli and all of those who had turned their backs on him and ignored their promises to promote Manson and his music.

When Manson returned to his followers, his mood had changed. He began to complain about the establishment. Everyone in Hollywood, he said, was too busy with their own lives to notice what was going on around them. No one was interested in anyone else. No one was interested in Manson anymore. With this, he turned to his followers and declared flatly, "Now is the time for Helter Skelter."[2]

Manson pulled Tex Watson, Susan Atkins and Linda Kasabian aside. He told each to get a knife and a change of clothes, and to meet him at the front ranch when they were ready. He asked both to dress in dark clothes.[3]

According to his own account, earlier in the day, Tex Watson had taken a large dose of acid.[4] He and Susan Atkins also allegedly had their own stash of Methedrine, which they had been snorting for several days.[5] Prior to Manson's annoucement, Atkins again used the crystal speed. Once he had a moment after receiving his instructions from Manson, Watson, too, went to their stash and snorted Methedrine.[6] According to Atkins, "We were both stoned, but our senses were keen. We were alert. We knew what we were doing."[7]

Patricia Krenwinkel was asleep in the children's trailer, when Manson came in and woke her. "Get up," he said. "I want you to go somewhere." On his instructions, she grabbed a knife, and joined Watson and Atkins on the boardwalk in front of the Longhorn Saloon.[8]

On her way to the Saloon, Manson told Kasabian to stop at the bunkhouse to retrieve her California Driver's License, which he had confiscated when she had joined the Family only a month earlier.

Within fifteen minutes, Watson, Atkins, Krenwinkel and Kasabian stood waiting on the boardwalk. Considering this group, Family member Ruth Ann Morehouse later declared that Manson had "sent out the expendables."[9]

Watson wore black cowboy boots, black jeans and a black velour turtleneck over a white cotton tee shirt. Atkins and Krenwinkel were dressed in blue denim jeans and black tee shirts. Linda Kasabian wore a dark skirt and purple shirt. All the women were barefoot.

They had three knives between them, two Buck knives and a larger kitchen knife with a taped handle. Manson had brought out the .22 caliber Buntline Special, with which he had shot the drug dealer Bernard Crowe just over a month before. Watson had a pair of red-handled bolt cutters and around forty feet of the white nylon three strand rope which Manson had purchased earlier that summer, coiled over his shoulder.

Manson took Watson aside. "I want you to go to that house where Terry Melcher used to live...and totally destroy everyone in that house, as gruesome as you can. Make it a real nice murder, just as bad as you've ever seen. And get all their money."[10] According to Manson, the house was occupied by "some movie stars."[11]

Manson was explicit in his instructions. First, he told Watson to cut the telephone lines, so that no one could call for help. Watson was not to use the electronic gate either, even though both men were familiar with its operation, having previously been to 10050 Cielo Drive. Manson feared that there might be some kind of new security alarm. He wanted the bodies mutilated. "Pull out their eyes and hang them on the mirrors!" he exhorted Watson. He also told him to leave messages written in blood.[12] "If you don't get enough money at the Melcher house," Manson told Watson, "then go to the house next door, and then to the house after that...."[13]

"There is no reason to suppose," writes journalist David Cooper, "that the wily Manson was unaware of what he was doing or of the illegality and commonly accepted immorality of his actions....Even if Manson's disciples had become unthinking zombies, brainwashed into automatic obedience to their master's commands, Manson himself was no zombie incapable of not giving those commands. And Manson, moreover, displayed in all his behavior a scheming canniness and sharp instinct for self-preservation, which are incompatible with the picture of a man who is victim to unshiftable, unalterable intentions."[14]

Watson, Atkins, Krenwinkel and Kasabian all climbed into ranch hand Johnny Schwartz's 1959 white and yellow Ford. Watson drove, although Kasabian had been brought along specifically because she was the only one at the ranch who possessed a valid driver's license. Instead, she sat in the front passenger seat, with Atkins and Krenwinkel crouched on the rear floor; the back seat had been removed earlier that year to make room for more food on the Family's garbage runs. Watson had enough self-possession to tell Kasabian that there was a gun in the glove compartment, and that, if they were stopped by the police along the way, she should throw the gun, and all of the knives—which she carried in her lap—out the window.[15] As the car began to drive away, Manson ran up to the open passenger window and leaned in. "Leave a sign," he told them. "You girls know what to write. Something witchy." With that, the four drove off into the night.[16]

Chapter 29
Cease To Exist

WATSON DROVE DOWN THE SANTA MONICA FREEWAY. IT WAS just past eleven when he finally told the women what they were going to do. He explained that they were going to the house where Terry Melcher used to live, and once there, they were to get all of the money that they could, and then kill whoever was in the house.[1] "It would make no sense at all to argue that the Family could not have had any idea of what acts they might perpetrate," writes Peter French, "especially after months of indoctrination in ritual slaughters and Manson's 'Helter Skelter' vision."[2]

They got lost on the way to Hollywood. Watson missed a turn, and ended up in downtown Los Angeles. He drove until he came to Santa Monica Boulevard, then followed it through West Hollywood and up into Beverly Hills. At the edge of Beverly Hills, he turned onto Sunset Boulevard and followed it until it met Benedict Canyon Road. A few miles later, he turned and began the ascent up the steeply winding length of Cielo Drive.[3]

He drove straight to the end of the cul-de-sac at 10050 Cielo Drive and got out of the car. Kasabian saw him take the red bolt cutters from the rear of the car, walk to the right side of the gate, and climb up the high telephone pole.[4] At the top were three different sets of wires. Watson had to guess which ones to cut. He used the bolt cutters to sever two of the three sets, and, with a splat, they fell across the metal and chain-link gate. From the top of the telephone pole, he could see that the lights at the side of the garage and the Christmas lights along the front lawn remained on.[5]

Watson returned to the car, backed it up against the hillside and, with the headlights off, drove back down the cul-de-sac and out onto Cielo Drive, parking the Ford just off the side of the road in a wide space nearly hidden by trees. Taking the gun from the glove compartment, he hoisted the coil of white rope over his shoulder, and, motioning to the women to follow, set off back up the cul-de-sac on foot.

When they arrived at the gate to 10050 Cielo Drive, Watson stopped. The gate itself, twelve feet long and six feet high, sat in the middle of a six-foot high chain-link and board fence stretching from the edge of the cliff on the left to the sharp upslope of the hill on the right. To the left of the gate and a few feet before it, on a metal pole, was an electronic gate control button, which allowed a driver to open the gate without having to leave their car. A similar device was located on the inner side of the gate. Although Watson had been to the property before, and knew how to use the gate mechanism, he finally decided to scale the embankment at the right of the fence and follow the hill down the other side and on to the driveway.[6]

Atkins stood silent, waiting and watching for Watson to make a move. "Suddenly," she later wrote, "that whole section, number 10050, was cut out of the rest of the world and lifted into another existence. We were separated from the whole world. Perhaps for the first time in my life I was deeply aware of evil. *I* was evil." As they climbed over the hill, she noticed the Christmas tree lights twinkling across the front lawn.[7]

On the other side of the gate, at the end of the paved parking area, Steve Parent approached his car, carrying the clock radio in his hand. The night was quiet, warm, the lights of Los Angeles spread out and sparkling below. As he climbed into his car, it is likely that he spotted the foursome, clad in their dark clothes, climbing over the hillside at the top of the driveway. He started the car and turned on the headlights. He obviously feared for his life: he backed the Ambassador out of the drive so quickly that he crashed into the split-rail fence bordering the parking area; police would later discover paint scrapings from his car on the fence, and crushed pieces of wood still attached to the Ambassador's bumper.[8]

Watson had seen the headlights of the approaching car as he and the women were stashing their bundles of clothing in the bushes next to the gate. "Lay down! Stay here!" he whispered to the women, as he bolted toward the gate and the approaching car.[9]

Parent had his driver's side window rolled down, to allow him to reach the gate control button. Watson ran up to the car, a knife in one hand and a gun in the other. Atkins, hiding in the bushes, heard him yell, "Halt!"[10]

Watson thrust his hand into the open window, trying to reach the keys. Parent must have been terrified. He looked at glassy-eyed Watson and pleaded, "Please, please, don't hurt me! I'm your friend! I won't tell!"[11] In answer, Watson raised the knife and sliced at the open window. In an attempt to shield his face, Parent raised his left hand. The knife went down, slicing between Parent's little and ring fingers and running down the length of his palm. His Lucerne wrist-watch flew from his arm, its band slashed in half, and landed in the rear seat.[12]

In reaction, Parent pulled down his arm. Watson aimed the .22 caliber Buntline through the open window and fired four shots in quick succession. One shot went cleanly through Parent's descending left arm, another through his left cheek, exiting out of his mouth and crashing into the dashboard. Stunned, Parent was unable to move. The other two shots hit him in the chest. He slumped toward the space between the front bucket seats, covered in spreading blood. Parent became the first of what Watson would later refer to as "impersonal blobs."[13]

On the other side of the gate, some 100 feet north of 10050, was 10070 Cielo Drive. Mr. and Mrs. Seymour Kott, the residents, had just finished hosting a dinner party. At midnight, they said goodnight to their guests; as they stood on their doorstep, the Kotts could see the gate of 10050 and the yellow bug light burning on the side of the garage, as well as the string of Christmas lights along the split-rail fence. They were just getting ready for bed when Mrs. Kott heard four shots, all in rapid succession. She thought that they came from the direction of 10050 Cielo Drive, but was not certain. She listened for a few more minutes. Hearing nothing further, she went to bed. She later estimated the time as about 12:30 AM.[14]

The four shots apparently had not been heard in the main house at 10050 Cielo Drive. The stereo in the hall closet was on, playing at a moderately high level, but it, along with the curious echo patterns in the canyon itself, was apparently enough to buffer the shots from the drive.

Watson reached inside the Ambassador, turned off the ignition and the headlights and motioned for the women in the bushes to join him. He flipped the car into neutral and, together, the four of them pushed the car down the driveway. Watson felt that the car would be less conspicuous if it was parked away from the gate.[15] They left it parked at an odd angle, to the left of the drive, about twenty-five feet beyond the gate.

According to Linda Kasabian, on watching Watson shoot Parent, she immediately went into a state of shock. "My mind went blank," she recalled later. "I was aware of my body, walking toward the house."[16] The four walked past Jay Sebring's black Porsche and Abigail's red Firebird parked next to the split-rail fence at the end of the drive. They followed the curve of the flagstone walk across the front lawn, Watson noting "the shimmering lights of the whole west side" of the city below.[17]

They stopped at the front porch. The white Dutch door was closed, the carriage lights on either side shining brightly. Watson told Kasabian to go round to the rear of the house and check to see if any of the windows or doors were open.[18] She went off, but, still horrified at the shooting she had just witnessed, walked past the two open windows of the freshly painted nursery-to-be, past the rear entrance door, and as far as the French door to the living room, before returning to the front lawn. On telling Watson that everything was locked and closed, he walked to the multi-paned dining room windows, stood in the flower bed behind the neatly trimmed hedge, and, with his knife, made a long, horizontal slash through the screen, allowing him to reach up inside and remove it. He set the screen at the side of the window and slipped his fingers into the crack, raising it up enough to allow him to hoist himself over the ledge and into the dark room. Once inside, he walked through the room to the entrance hall and opened the Dutch door leading to the front porch. As the women walked toward him, he pulled Kasabian aside, telling her to go back to the gate and wait there, to watch in case anyone approached the estate.[19] Atkins and Krenwinkel disappeared inside the house; before Kasabian turned to leave, Watson ominously whispered that she should "listen for sounds."[20]

Watson, Atkins and Krenwinkel entered the living room. A table lamp on the desk filled the room with dim light. In front of them stretched a long, beige couch whose back was draped with an American flag. Although there would be speculation as to its meaning later, Mrs. Chapman told police investigators that it had simply been placed on the back of the couch as a decorative touch a few weeks earlier.[21]

When they walked round the couch, they saw for the first time that there was a man asleep there. It was Voyteck Frykowski. Watson stood over Frykowski and said, "Wake up!"[22] Voyteck stirred, looked up at the curious trio gathered in the darkened living room, and asked "What time is it?"[23]

"Be quiet!" Watson answered. "Don't move or you're dead."[24]

"Who are you?" Frykowski demanded, rising from the couch. "What do you want?"[25] In response, Watson kicked him in the head, and Frykowski fell back against the couch, stunned.[26]

"I'm the Devil," Watson chillingly announced, "and I'm here to do the Devil's business."[27] According to Atkins, his tone was disturbing, "guttural."[28]

Watson told Atkins to look for something with which to tie up Frykowski. She looked through several rooms, finally grabbing a towel from the linen closet in the hallway. When she returned, Watson told her to tie Frykowski's hands. "I did the best I could with the towel," Atkins recalled, "but I knew it wasn't very secure."[29]

Frykowski continued to question these invaders, but Watson cut him off, saying, "Another word and you're dead!" He asked for his money, and Voyteck nodded toward the desk. In fact, his wallet contained only a few dollars.[30]

Watson ordered Atkins to search the rest of the house. She walked into the small hallway leading to the bedrooms at the southern end of the house. The doorway to the corner bedroom shared by Abigail and Voyteck stood open. As Atkins came to a halt, she saw Abigail Folger perched on a pile of pillows against the headboard, reading a book. Noticing the motion in the hallway, Abigail looked up. Like her boyfriend in the living room, she did not express any alarm at seeing this strange girl, dressed all in black, wandering through the house in the middle of the night. Instead, she smiled, and waved. Atkins smiled and waved back. Abigail turned her attention back to her book.[31]

Adjacent to Abigail's bedroom was a half-closed door. Atkins opened it slowly, and peered through the crack. Sharon was lying on the bed, propped up against the headboard; Jay sat on the edge of the bed, his back to the door. Neither noticed the opened door, and continued to talk. Atkins pulled the door closed. As Atkins turned, Abigail again saw the motion, looked up, and smiled.[32]

Standing in the living room, Krenwinkel suddenly realized that she had no knife. She walked out of the house and back up the driveway, where she found Kasabian kneeling in the bushes near the gate. She took Kasabian's knife, whose broken handle had been wrapped in tape, and returned to the house.

In the living room, Atkins told Watson that she had found three more people in the house. He grabbed the length of white nylon rope he had brought with him and handed it to Atkins, telling her to re-tie Frykowski's hands. "I had him put his hands together in a crisscross fashion," she later testified. "I have never been very good at tying knots, and I wrapped the rope around his hands a couple of times, and I was shaking and everything was happening so fast that I did a very poor job of tying him up."[33]

When she had finished, Watson told Atkins to go back and get the others.[34] She walked down the hallway to the first bedroom and stepped inside. When Abigail looked up from her book, Atkins stood at the foot, a knife shining in her hand. "Get up and go into the living room," she said. "Don't ask any questions. Just do what I say."[35] Abigail did as told, entering the living room with Atkins following, knife held out before her. Krenwinkel stepped forward and cornered the heiress with her raised knife.

Atkins returned to the closed door at the end of the hallway and flung it open. "Come with me," Atkins said. "Don't say a word or you're dead."[36]

Sharon looked up, startled. The long-haired woman standing in her bedroom doorway, dressed in black and barefoot, held a knife. Without a word, Sharon and Jay rose from the bed and followed Atkins down the hallway. "She was very pregnant," Atkins recalled, "and with the bikini panties and flimsy top she was wearing, it showed plainly."[37] Sharon, she later remembered, "couldn't believe what was happening."[38]

As Sharon approached the door from the hallway into the living room, she stopped. She looked at Abigail, who stood in the corner by the fireplace, next to another unknown woman dressed in black who held a knife menacingly in front of her. Voyteck lay on the couch, a white rope around his arms. Her gaze finally landed on Watson, tall, wild-eyed, bushy-haired and bearded. She hesitated for a few seconds. Watson ran forward and grabbed her roughly by the arm, pulling her in to the room. As he did so, he brushed against the light switch, using his elbow to avoid leaving fingerprints, and throwing the hallway into darkness.[39]

"What are you doing here?" Jay demanded.[40] Jay began to protest against the rough treatment Sharon had received, but Watson told him that if he said anything further, he would die. From the couch, Voyteck mumbled, "He means it."[41]

Watson grabbed the coil of rope from the floor and threw one end over the long ceiling beam which ran the length of the room and supported the loft above. Once the rope dangled from the ceiling, he approached Jay and tied his wrists in front of him. He looped the rope round his neck, pulling it tight, then pushed him down into the lemon yellow armchair to the left of the couch.[42]

Turning to Sharon, Watson took the end of the rope hanging from the beam and wrapped it tightly round her neck. When he had finished, Watson ordered the prisoners to lie down on their stomachs in front of the fireplace. Terrified, Sharon began to cry. "Shut up!" Watson screamed at her.[43]

"Can't you see she's pregnant!" Jay demanded, rising from the chair. "Let her sit down!"[44] He began to move toward Sharon, in an attempt to place himself between her and the unknown man. His effort to protect Sharon proved fatal.

"I told you, 'One more word and you're dead!'" Watson screamed. Without bothering to aim, he pulled out the .22 caliber Buntline revolver and fired at Jay.[45] The bullet entered just beneath Sebring's left armpit and angled down, smashing through his left fifth rib, puncturing his left lung and exiting out of his back midway down on the left side. Jay spun to the floor, collapsing atop the zebra skin rug before the fireplace. Watson ran over and kicked him viciously in the bridge of the nose.[46] He did not move, but lay still on the floor, blood rapidly spreading across his dark blue shirt and black and white striped pants.

Sharon and Abigail both screamed as Jay fell to the floor.[47] This was no empty threat. These people were willing to kill them. For a few minutes, Sharon was hysterical sobbing loudly. Then, overcome with fear, she was silent again.[48]

"I want all the money you've got here!" Watson barked out.[49] Abigail, terrified, said that she had some money in her purse in her bedroom. Atkins, went with her, guarding her with a knife, as she walked back into the bedroom and grabbed her black canvas shoulder bag. She nervously handed Atkins seventy-two dollars—all of the cash she had. "I've got some credit cards," she offered in a pleading voice.[50] But Atkins shook her head. While they stood alone in the bedroom, Abigail, in a shaking voice, begged, "Please don't hurt me. You can have everything." Atkins' only reply was a harsh, "Shut up!"[51]

When they returned to the living room, Atkins handed Watson the seventy-two dollars. "You mean that's all you've got?" he yelled.

"How much do you want?" Frykowski asked from the couch.

"We want thousands!" he answered.[52]

But, if robbery was the motive, the murderous trio made some curious oversights. An expensive Cartier wristwatch remained on Jay's wrist. His wallet was in his leather jacket, hanging over the back of a chair in the living room. On the nightstand next to Sharon's bed was $18 in cash, lying in plain view. The trio ignored any number of expensive items in the house itself—a videotape machine, a television set, stereos and camera as well as the cars parked in the driveway.[53]

Through her terror, Sharon managed to draw herself together to explain that, although they did not have any more money in the house, she could get them some if they just gave her some time. Watson merely yelled back at her, "You know I'm not kidding!" Sharon, numb with fear, sobbed softly, "Yes, I know."[54]

Watson grabbed Abigail and tied her hands with a loose strand of the rope with which he had bound Sharon. He then looped the other end of the rope a few more times around Jay's neck as he lay bleeding on the floor. When he pulled on the free end dangling over the heavy beam above, Sharon and Abigail had to stand on their toes, to avoid being strangled.

Suddenly, Jay began to stir. He was moaning, trying to crawl across the living room floor. Screaming, Sharon watched as Watson ran over and stabbed him several more times in the back and side with his double-edged knife, piercing his lungs. As he rose, he continually kicked Jay in the face until, finally, his movement ceased.[55] Watson's maniacal laugh filled the room, an evil grin across his face, his face, hands and shirt covered with blood. "In that flash," Atkins later wrote, "I knew that Tex was not a human being. He was another creature."[56]

Watson told Krenwinkel to go through the house and turn off the lights.[57] The only ones found on the following morning were the small table lamp on the desk in the living room, and the light in the hallway leading to the bedrooms.[58]

"What are you going to do with us?" Sharon asked.

"You're all going to die," Watson declared.[59]

Sharon, Abigail and Voyteck began to plead for their lives. Within a few seconds, Voyteck was struggling with his bonds as he lay on the couch. Seeing him, Watson looked at Atkins and ordered, "Kill him!" She ran over to the couch and raised her knife, but, according to her own account, hesitated for a second.[60]

It was all the time Frykowski needed. He managed to free his hands and jumped up against Atkins, who fell with him onto the floor in front of the fireplace. In the struggle, they knocked over the low trestle table before the hearth, rolling round in a jumble of books, movie scripts, candle stubs, flowers and a bowl filled with matchbooks. Atkins stabbed Voyteck several times in the leg before he rose and tried to crawl away. She was on him quickly, continuing to stab, but he reached round behind his back and, grabbing her long hair, pulled hard, sending them both sprawling back against the armchair on the opposite side of the fireplace from where Jay Sebring lay dying.[61] In the struggle, she lost her knife. The police would later find it, blade up, lodged between the seat cushion and rear of the chair. They continued to roll round on the floor. "Blood was everywhere," she would later remember. "Above everything, I could hear Sharon Tate crying, sobbing."[62]

Voyteck struggled down the side of the living room, toward the entrance hall and the open front door of the house. Atkins clung to him, beating at him with her fists. Watson had watched in silence. He wanted to use his gun, but was afraid, as Frykowski and Atkins were twisted round each other in their struggle. Instead, he jumped over Sebring's body and tackled Frykowski. They knocked against the two blue steamer trunks standing by the arch to the entrance hall, sending them collapsing one on top of the other, and leaving smears of blood. Watson later recalled how "enormously powerful" Frykowski proved to be.[63]

As Frykowski struggled on toward the open front door, Watson aimed his revolver and fired twice. The first bullet struck Voyteck just below his left armpit, lodging in his back. The second shot, badly aimed, penetrated Voyteck's left right thigh. Still, Frykowski stumbled toward the entrance hall.

Watson pulled the trigger a third time, but the gun, which had previously mis-fired when Manson used it to shoot Bernard Crowe, jammed. Instead, Watson turned the revolver wrong-way round and began to beat Frykowski relentlessly over the head, smashing away again and again. "I heard the crack of bone - Frykowski's skull," Atkins recalled.[64] The wooden gun grip disintegrated under the heavy battering, its shattered pieces falling to the living room floor.[65]

Voyteck was almost at a stop by the time he reached the entrance hall, but Watson held on, stabbing repeatedly now, each blow and swing casting an arc of blood across the walls and floor.

Watson later recalled "the whole world spinning and turning, as red as the blood that was smearing and spattering everywhere."[66]

"Help me, O God, help me!" Voyteck screamed as he reached the open door.[67]

Still kneeling in the shadows by the gate, Linda Kasabian suddenly heard "horrible sounds" coming from the house down the driveway. A man shouted, "No, no!" and a woman was screaming. She started running down the driveway. "There were no words," she recalled, "it was beyond words, it was just screams."[68]

She ran across the flagstone walk on the front lawn. Just as she reached the porch, Frykowski staggered out of the front door, covered in blood. He leaned against the door frame for a second before stumbling a few steps across the porch, reaching out to one of the heavy posts for support. Through the blood pouring down his face, he looked Kasabian in the eye. "Oh God! I'm so sorry!" she cried as he finally lost his balance and spun round the post, falling into the hedge at the side of the porch.[69]

Within seconds, both Watson and Atkins appeared in the door. While Watson ran over to Frykowski and began to stab him, Kasabian turned to Atkins, saying, "Sadie, please make it stop! People are coming!" It was not true, but Kasabian was desperate to put an end to the slaughter taking place. Atkins simply looked at her and said flatly, "It's too late."[70]

In the living room, Sharon was screaming. While Krenwinkel watched the struggle with Frykowski, Abigail, who had not been tied well, managed to slip the bonds round her hands and stumble across the room. Shouting for help, Krenwinkel ran after her, trying to wrestle her to the floor. But Abigail, bigger and stronger, proved more than equal to the barefoot Krenwinkel, managing to grab hold of her long hair and pin her against the living room wall.

Still on the porch, Watson heard Krenwinkel's cries, and, with Atkins in hot pursuit, he ran back into the house. As Atkins watched, he cornered the heiress, who, seeing him approaching, raised knife in hand, loosened her grip on Krenwinkel. For a split second, there was a dreadful, silent anticipation. Abigail knew that it was over. She let her arms drop to her sides, looked at Watson, and said, "I give up, take me."[71] With a vengeance, Watson repeatedly swung his knife until Abigail, clutching her stomach, collapsed in the doorway from the living room to the bedroom hallway.[72] "It was total chaos," Atkins recalled.[73]

"People were running everywhere," Watson later admitted. "But
I was perfect, like a machine.....I had no control, like an animal,
making noises, happiness noises. They were saying things but
sounds didn't have meaning....I was jumping around, perfection, like
from space, making happiness noises....I don't remember any of the
persons. Their faces were unreal. They didn't look like people."[74]

On the porch, Voyteck somehow managed to struggle to his
feet. He took a few uncertain steps, falling on the lawn as he left the
flagstone walkway. As he crawled across the lawn, he began to
scream, "Help me! O God! Help me!"

His screams attracted Watson's attention. Shouting at Atkins to
watch Sharon, he ran out of the open door and across the blood-
stained front porch. A few feet ahead of him, Voyteck, half-crawling,
half running, made his way across the lawn, screaming down the
canyon, "like a chicken with its head cut off," Watson later gleefully
declared.[75]

Voyteck looked back for a moment and saw Watson running
after him, a knife in one hand and the gun in the other. "Oh God,
no! Stop! Stop! Oh God, no, don't!" he screamed.[76] Watson jumped
Frykowski, forcing him to the ground, stabbing him repeatedly in
the back, the chest, the arms, and the legs, "until my wrist disappeared in the mess," he later wrote.[77] Again and again, he brought
the heavy gun butt down against Voyteck's head, smashing his skull
open. As he stood over the lifeless body, Watson violently kicked
him in the head with his heavy cowboy boot.[78]

Unnoticed, Abigail Folger rose to her feet, staggering down the
hallway and into Sharon's bedroom. Krenwinkel saw the motion out
of the corner of her eye and gave chase, catching Abigail just as she
reached the French door opening to the swimming pool. Abigail
clawed at the doors smearing the white louvers with blood,
Krenwinkel stabbing her with a knife in one hand while, with the
other, trying to hold the door closed. In spite of being wounded,
however, Abigail was taller and stronger, and managed to open the
door. Running outside, she splattered blood across the flagstone
walk, the shrubbery, and the coiled green garden hose at the side of
the house.

The Christmas lights sparkled against the split-rail fence separating the lawn from the steep cliff, and Abigail, her freedom within sight, stumbled on, Krenwinkel's knife slicing into her chest and
stomach, her white nightgown turning crimson. She had almost

reached the fence. "She was running," Krenwinkel recalled. "When I caught up to her, I stabbed her. I don't know how many times. She fell immediately. She fell down, but she was still moving."[79]

"Stop! Stop!" Abigail begged as Krenwinkel continued to stab.[80] "I remember her saying, 'I'm already dead,' Kenwinkle later admitted.[81]

Watson, standing over Voyteck's body some thirty feet away, saw the struggle at the end of the lawn between the two women. In response to Krenwinkel's cries for help, he jumped over the motionless Frykowski and sprinted toward them. Abigail lay at the edge of the lawn, near the base of a large pine tree. Krenwinkel held her down as Watson slashed, his knife slicing the left side of her face, and ripping her abdomen and chest. "I felt nothing," he later wrote.[82]

As he rose from Abigail's bloodstained, lifeless body, Watson saw the lights of the guest house, a hundred feet across the lawn. He ordered Krenwinkel to search it, and kill whoever she found. She approached the silent building, following the ribbon of concrete walk past the swimming pool, beneath an open, roofed gateway to the closed glass door. "I just stood there and looked in," she recalled. "I never saw anyone. I never went past the door. I just saw a lamp and I just stood there."[83] As she stood at the door, she later said, "I knew this is wrong. It was like an echo from way back that said, Wait a minute, this has finally gone into total madness."[84]

"I had no idea of even how to connect a thought together at that point," Krenwinkel later declared. "I had absolutely no way to put together the kind of rational thinking, because there was no rational thought in my head. Everything was out of my control. I felt helpless, I felt hopeless to do anything. All I was doing was carrying through a macabre dance that was horrible and I never knew how to stop it."[85]

❖❖❖❖❖

The house at 10050 Cielo Drive was silent. Blood was smeared across the living room's cream-colored carpet; on the couch and nearby chairs; on the walls of the hallways; on the door leading from Sharon's bedroom to the swimming pool; on the floor of the foyer; on the front porch. Voyteck Frykowski and Abigail Folger lay dead on the lawn, the latter stabbed so many times her white nightgown had turned red. Jay Sebring's dead body was curled before the fireplace, his face battered and frozen in torment.

In the midst of this carnage, Sharon remained untouched in the living room. Atkins had forced her on to the couch, the rope still looped round her neck, trailing over the beam and down to Jay. She held Sharon's arms, preventing escape. Terrified, Sharon pleaded for her life. "Please don't kill me! Please don't kill me! I don't want to die! I want to live! I want to have my baby! I want to have my baby!" But Atkins, who had left her own ten-month-old son in the care of others back at Spahn Ranch, had no mercy.

"Look, bitch," she sneered, looking Sharon straight in the eye, "I don't care about you! I don't care if you're going to have a baby! You had better be ready. You're going to die, and I don't feel anything about it."[86] Sharon, Atkins later told a fellow Manson Family member, "was the last to go because she had to watch the others die."[87]

"I didn't relate to Sharon Tate as being anything but a store mannequin," Atkins admitted. "She just sounded like an IBM machine....She kept begging and pleading and pleading and begging, and I got sick of listening to her."[88]

Watson and Krenwinkel re-entered the living room.[89] The chaos of the evening had thwarted their plans. They had intended, according to Atkins, to rip out their victims' eyeballs and smash them against the walls, cut off their fingers, mutilate them. The excitement of the slaughter, the screams down the canyon and gunshots shattering the night, however, brought with them the fear of being caught.

Knowing that the trio were about to turn on her, Sharon again begged for her life, repeating that she was pregnant and she wanted to have her baby. Watson told her to shut up. Sharon then asked them to take her with them when they left, to keep her until she gave birth, then they could kill her. Watson said nothing. Finally, realizing that she was about to die, Sharon pathetically begged the killers to take the baby from her, so that it might have a chance to live.[90] Her composure finally gave way, and she began to sob. She was, according to Atkins, "out of her mind."[91]

"Kill her!" Watson yelled at Atkins.[92]

Atkins hesitated. "If you're going to kill her, then do it, for God's sake," Krenwinkel finally said. "I mean, we have already killed everyone else here. What's the point? Either do it, or let her go, or just bring her with us and let her have her fucking baby."[93]

Sharon was silent as the murderous trio continued to argue. Finally, Watson lunged forward. He would later torment his mother "by going on and on about how beautiful Sharon's face had been as she was pleading for her life, just before I cut her."[94]

He swept his knife across Sharon's face, leaving a small gash in her left cheek. She screamed out as the knife struck her.[95] Although

Watson stabbed first, Atkins later recounted how she, too, had joined in. "I got sick of listening to her, so I stabbed her," she chillingly declared.[96]

"It felt so good the first time I stabbed her," Atkins gushed to a cellmate, "and when she screamed at me it did something to me, sent a rush through me, and I stabbed her again....I just kept stabbing her until she stopped screaming....It was just like going into nothing, going into air....It's like a sexual release. Especially when you see the blood spurting out. It's better than a climax."[97]

The pair continued to slash out at Sharon. Sixteen times, their sharp knives pierced her body: through her pregnant stomach, through her breast, through her heart, her back, her lungs. The knives caught her arms as she raised them in a vain effort to protect herself from the blows. Finally, her resistance weakened. Moaning "Mother, mother!" Sharon fell forward and collapsed onto the floor in front of the couch, covered in blood.[98]

Standing over Sharon's body, Atkins noticed that she had blood on her hands. She lifted her fingers to her mouth and licked it off. "To taste death and yet give life," she told a friend. "Wow, what a trip!"[99]

Watson ordered Atkins and Krenwinkel from the house. As they left, he ran from Sharon to Jay, stabbing repeatedly at their bodies. He did the same with Voyteck and Abigail on the lawn, unwilling to take any chance that they might survive the wounds already inflicted upon them. The trio, their dark clothes covered in blood, were halfway up the driveway when Watson turned to Atkins and told her to go back to the house and leave a message in blood. "Write something that will shock the world," he said.[100]

Atkins approached the silent house, leaving a bloody footprint on the front porch as she stepped through the pools of Voyteck's blood. She grabbed the beige towel with which she had tied up Frykowski's hands, and walked round the couch. Sharon, she recalled, "seemed to have been cut up a lot more than when I had last seen her. I never actually saw her face. Her hair was covering her face and there were sounds coming from her body...like blood flowing into the body out of the heart."[101]

She reached down and touched the towel to Sharon's chest. The blood, she noted, was "still warm."[102] Once the towel was saturated, Atkins returned to the front porch. The white Dutch door stood open. Kneeling down, she wrote "Pig" in Sharon's blood across its bottom half. She threw the bloody towel back into the living room and ran up the driveway to her friends, leaving behind five dead bodies littered with seven gunshots and 104 stab wounds. "I felt so elated," she would later declare; "tired, but at peace with myself."[103]

Chapter 30
That s How the Day Went. Hell.

T HE SLAUGHTER AT 10050 CIELO DRIVE TOOK JUST OVER HALF AN hour. When the murderous trio arrived at the bottom of the cul-de-sac, they found Linda Kasabian cowering in the 1959 Ford. When she tried to start the car, Watson pushed her aside. "What do you think you're doing?" he yelled. "Get over on the passenger side. Don't do anything unless I tell you to do it."[1]

Watson drove the car down Cielo and took a left onto Benedict Canyon Road. Along the way, the killers changed out of their clothing and into the second sets they had brought with them. Kasabian steered the car as Watson pulled his black turtleneck and jeans off. The girls and Watson handed the wet, bloody clothes to Kasabian, who rolled the black tee shirts, denim shirts and jeans into a ball and pushed them beneath her seat.

The killers' faces, hands and arms, however, were still spattered and smeared with blood. A little over a mile up the canyon from the scene of the murders, Watson took a right on Portola Drive, just one block north of Easton Drive, where Jay had lived. He stopped the car before a house perched against a steep hillside to the right, using a garden hose he spotted to wash off any blood which remained. The noise woke the occupants, Rudolph and Myra Weber, who angrily confronted the foursome. Watson and the girls explained that they had merely wanted a drink of water, and hurriedly retreated to their car. Weber, after attempting to reach through the open car window and grab the keys from the ignition, quickly wrote down the license plate as Watson stepped on the gas and fled into the night.

Turning right off Portola, Watson drove up Benedict Canyon, following the road as it twisted and turned along the crest of the mountains. When he reached a wide shoulder, he eased the car to a temporary stop and Kasabian took the bundle of bloody clothes and flung it over the hillside. Watson continued along Mulholland and Beverly Glen, pausing briefly as Kasabian tossed the knives and the gun from the open car window down the sides of embankments. Throughout the ride, Kasabian listened as the trio complained about the murders. Atkins said that her hair hurt, from where Voyteck had repeatedly pulled it in an effort to win his struggle with her. Watson had hurt his leg, and Krenwinkel said that, as she had stabbed Abigail Folger, she had repeatedly struck bone, bruising her hand.[2]

Watson followed Beverly Glen down into the San Fernando Valley. He pulled the car into a gas station, where the killers took turns checking for bloodstains in the bathroom.[3] As he stood before the mirror, Watson later recalled thinking: "I wasn't anyone. I wasn't Charles Watson. I was an animal. The end of the world was there. I was the living death."[4]

Charles Manson and Nancy Pitman were dancing naked in the moonlight on the boardwalk in front of the Longhorn Saloon when Watson and the car of killers pulled into Spahn Ranch.[5] Manson was surprised to see them so soon. "What're you doing home so early?" he demanded.[6]

Watson explained that they had gone to Terry Melcher's former house. There had been a lot of panic, and that had caused the killers to panic. But everyone in the house was dead. "Boy, it sure was Helter Skelter!" he added, a grin on his face.[7]

But Manson was beside himself with anger. "Man!" he yelled as Watson described the scene, "I told you to go to every house on that street! Now we'll have to go back!"[8] Watson just shrugged. Manson then faced each of the four and, in turn, asked if they felt any remorse. "I felt no remorse for the murders," Watson later wrote, "no revulsion at the incredible brutality of the killings."[9] And Atkins added: "I felt as though I, too, were dead. I wasn't alive anymore."[10] Kasabian alone seemed shaken, looking at Manson and saying quietly, "Charlie, they were so young...."[11]

Manson, accompanied by at least one other member of his Family, hopped in the car and drove off to Cielo Drive. "I went back to see what my children had done," he told a lawyer at his trial.[12] This seems to have been an open secret among members of the Family; Watson has recently confirmed Manson's return to the crime scene.[13] They entered the grounds as the killers had, climbing over the fence to the right of the gate. Fearing fingerprints, Manson wiped down the car where Steven Parent lay dead, before continuing on to the main house.

Once he had surveyed the carnage, Manson apparently decided to create an even more nightmarish scene. He and his followers moved through the darkened, bloodstained house, carrying the battered, lifeless bodies of Sharon and Jay out onto the front porch. Here, Manson seems to have intended to enact one of his darker fantasies: hanging his victims upside down, like pigs in a slaughterhouse, and slicing them to pieces.[14]

By this time, however, daylight was approaching. The police would later log reports of a loud argument coming from the direction of 10050 Cielo Drive which filtered through the canyon early that morning, and it is possible that the voices came from Manson and his comrades, engaged in a heated discussion concerning the scenario.[15] In the end, they were unwilling to risk discovery. The bodies were carried back into the living room and placed in approximately the same positions in which they had died. Sebring's face was carefully covered with the blood-soaked beige towel Manson had found lying on the living room floor where Atkins had thrown it a few hours earlier, tucked beneath the strands of white nylon rope looped round his neck.[16] Once again, 10050 Cielo Drive was silent.

Early on the morning of Saturday, August 9, 1969, *Los Angeles Times* delivery boy Steve Shannen rode his bike up the steep cul-de-sac to the gate of 10050 Cielo Drive. He immediately noticed the cut communication wires hanging over the gate.[17] As he looked further on, down the drive and past the white Ambassador which was parked at an odd angle, he saw that the yellow bug light on the side of the garage was still on; this in itself was hardly unusual, for it was just beginning to get light. Noticing nothing else out of the ordinary, he pedaled his bike back down the road.[18] A few hours later, Seymour Kott, the neighbor at 10070 Cielo Drive, also noticed both the downed wires and the bug light shining in the distance.[19]

Just after eight that morning, Mrs. Winifred Chapman, the Polanskis' housekeeper who had turned down Sharon's invitation to stay at 10050 Cielo Drive the previous evening, left her bus at the corner of Santa Monica and Canyon Drive, at the end of Benedict Canyon Road. She was already late for work, although, under normal circumstances, it was unusual for anyone to be up that early at the house. But Abigail Folger had mentioned the day before that she would be flying to San Francisco at 10AM to visit her mother. Mrs. Chapman considered calling a cab for the rest of the journey, but, just then, a friend saw her, pulled his car over and gave her a ride to the gate of 10050.

As her friend drove off, Mrs. Chapman turned to the gate to get the newspaper out of the mailbox. She immediately noticed the fallen wires across the gate. At first, she thought that the electricity might be out but, when she pushed the control button at the right side of the gate, it swung open. She walked down the driveway as the gate automatically closed behind her. Mrs. Chapman saw three cars in the driveway. One was Jay Sebring's black Porsche, which she knew by sight. Next to it was Abigail Folger's Firebird. But, farther up the driveway, halfway to the gate, was an unfamiliar car, a white Ambassador, which was parked at a curious angle in the middle of the road.[20]

Mrs. Chapman entered the house by the rear door, using a key secured on the rafter above. She did not see the front lawn, which was hidden both by the angle of the estate, and by the split-rail fence and the shrubbery lining the end of the parking area. After setting her purse down in the kitchen, she picked up the telephone. It was dead.[21]

Wondering if any of the residents knew that the phone was out of order, she walked through the dining room and into the entrance hall. Then she abruptly stopped. The fieldstone floor was covered with pools of blood. There was blood on the stone surrounding the opening to the living room, blood on the walls, a trail of blood across the cream-colored living room carpet. The front door stood half open. As Mrs. Chapman looked out, she saw that the front porch, too, was covered with pools of blood. Farther out, halfway across the lawn, she saw a body.[22]

She ran back through the house the same way in which she had come in, grabbing her purse on the way out. As she ran up the driveway, she crossed to the left hand side of the gate, so that she could push the gate control button and flee from the property. This time, she saw that there was a body in the white Ambassador as well.

Once out of the gate, she ran to 10070 Cielo Drive, banging on the door and screaming at the top of her lungs. When no one answered, she ran further down the cul-de-sac, to 10090, shouting, "Murder! Death! Bodies! Blood!"[23]

Fifteen-year old Jim Asin was standing outside the house, waiting for his father to drive him to the West Los Angeles Division of
the LAPD, where he was to work the desk as part of his involvement
with the Law Enforcement Unity of the Boy Scouts. He rushed to get
his parents when Mrs. Chapman appeared, but they had already
heard her screams and run to the door themselves. While they tried
to calm her down, Jim Asin called the LAPD emergency number.[24]

When Officer Jerry De Rosa arrived, he tried to talk with Mrs.
Chapman, but she was too hysterical to do more than repeat her
story about seeing the blood and the bodies. She did, however, calm
herself enough to tell him how to work the electronic gate control
button so that he could gain access to the estate.[25]

Taking his rifle from his squad car, De Rosa nervously
approached the white Ambassador, where, through the open driver's
side window, he saw Steven Parent, slumped toward the space
dividing the bucket seats in front. His jeans and red and blue plaid
shirt were soaked with blood.[26]

As De Rosa straightened up, a second police car, this one driven by Officer William Wisenhunt, arrived. Wisenhunt carried a
shotgun as he joined De Rosa in searching the other cars at the end
of the paved parking area and the garage. They found nothing. As
they were about to approach the main residence, a third officer,
Robert Burbridge, joined them, and together, the trio cautiously
walked on to the front lawn.[27]

They could see the two bodies which lay ahead. As they
approached Voyteck, they noted the terrible condition of his body.
He lay on his right side, his head against his outstretched right arm,
his left hand still clutching a clump of lawn. Not only was his clothing covered in blood, but his neck and arms had been stabbed
repeatedly, and his head and face were battered, scarcely recognizable. Abigail Folger lay on her back, beneath a pine tree some twenty-five feet beyond her lover. She had been stabbed so many times
that her once white nightgown was red.[28]

The officers did not know if the killers were still inside the
house. Two of them went around back while the third stayed on the
front lawn. The two officers found a raised window in the nursery,
and carefully entered, guns drawn. They made their way to the
entrance hall, where they were joined by their partner from the front
lawn. Aside from the pools and spatters of blood covering the front
porch, they saw the ugly epithet "Pig," scrawled in Sharon's blood
on the lower half of the white Dutch door.[29]

The living room had spots of blood on the carpet, blood on the steamer trunks which had been knocked over in the struggle the night before, and blood near the doorway leading to the rear hallway, where Abigail had first fallen. A length of white nylon rope still hung looped over the long beam crossing the underside of the loft. As the police made their way around to the side of the couch, they saw Jay. He lay on his right side, his legs tucked up toward his stomach, and his still-bound hands bunched near his face. His face itself was covered with the beige bath towel, and the rope had been twisted round his neck several times. When the officers removed the towel, they saw that his face was horribly battered, his nose broken, flattened and swollen, large hematomae across his forehead where Watson had repeatedly kicked him.[30]

One end of the rope crossed from Jay's body, up around the ceiling beam, and then down again to Sharon. She lay on her left side in front of the fireplace, her back against the couch. Her legs were drawn up toward her round stomach in a fetal position. Her left arm rested next to her body, bent at the elbow as if in death she had clutched at the noose around her neck. Her right arm crossed her head, partially obscuring her features. A few wisps of blood-caked blonde hair fell across her face where it had escaped from the rope around her neck. Blood had poured from the ugly gashes in her chest and stomach, soaking the carpet onto which she had fallen, surrounding her in a large pool of crimson.[31] "It was very quiet," De Rosa later said, "and the only thing that I can recall hearing was the sounds of the flies on the bodies."[32]

The discoveries shocked the three policemen, but they continued with their search, noting bloodstains and signs of a terrible struggle. As they exited the house by the blood-smeared French doors leading from Sharon's bedroom to the swimming pool, they saw the guest house. Thinking that there might be further bodies, they cautiously approached. They heard a dog barking, and then, unbelievably, a male voice, whispering loudly, "Be quiet!"[33]

When the officers kicked in the door to the guest house, they found William Garretson, holding Christopher, Rudi Altobelli's Weimaraner. The police, according to Garretson, roughly handcuffed him, as he repeatedly asked what had happened. In answer, they dragged him out of the guest house and across the front lawn, from Abigail Folger to Voyteck Frykowski. Garretson thought that Abigail was actually Mrs. Chapman, and identified her as such, while he thought that Voyteck was, as he had told Steven Parent the evening before, Roman Polanski's younger brother. By the time he reached the parking area, he apparently was in such a state of shock that he completely failed to recognize Parent.[34]

Garretson, the only person found alive on the entire estate, at first seemed like the prime suspect. He was taken downtown for further questioning. Mrs. Chapman, suffering from the strain of discovering the bodies, was quickly placed in a police car and driven to UCLA Medical Center, where she was treated for shock and released later that day.[35]

By mid-morning, the estate at 10050 Cielo Drive was swarming with police, special criminal investigators, and, beyond the gate, dozens of reporters and curious spectators. As soon as the word spread that a murder had been committed at the exclusive address in Hollywood, newsmen flocked to Cielo Drive, eager for a story. Throughout the morning and afternoon, they were fed details by police officers entering and leaving the premises.

Throughout the rest of the morning and into the afternoon, investigators arrived. The crime scene photographer took a hundred color and black and white prints of the house, the bodies, the bloodstains and anything which the police thought looked suspicious. A fingerprint expert arrived and dusted the house. Blood specialists took samples from spots all over the house and grounds. The detectives, examining Sharon's corpse, noted in their report: "There was dried blood smeared over the entire body. It appeared to investigating officers that someone had handled the victim, as in moving her from one location to another and the blood from the stab wounds had been smeared over other parts of the body."[36]

Indeed, the smeared blood pattern was consistent only with the actions of Manson and his trusted followers having moved Sharon's body in the early morning hours. The evidence supporting this gruesome nocturnal visit was copious. On the front porch, police discovered a large blood spot of type O-MN blood, which could only have come from Jay. A second pool of blood was typed as O-M, Sharon's blood group. In addition, her blood was found smeared on the door surround in the entrance hall. As none of those involved in her death—Watson, Atkins and Krenwinkel—placed her anywhere near the front door during the murder, the blood had to have come during the time her body was moved, as if it had been knocked against the door frame when in transit. The police also found that a mixture of types O-M and O-MN—Sharon's and Jay's blood—had dripped on to the two blue steamer trunks. The quantity of this sample, as well as the pools on the front porch and smears in the entrance hall, was such that it could only have come had the bodies been present in those locations for several minutes. Lastly, the towel found over Jay's face had been carefully tucked beneath the rope round his neck; as Atkins had simply tossed it back into the house after using it to write "Pig" in Sharon's blood on the front door, someone had to have come into the residence, as Manson later claimed, and placed the towel in the manner in which it was discovered by the detectives.[37]

Investigating officers also discovered pieces of a broken wooden gun grip near the desk in the living room, which had fallen from the .22 caliber Buntline as Watson hammered repeatedly at Voyteck's head the night before. A pair of eyeglasses, which belonged to no one in the residence, was found lying on the floor of the living room; it is likely that they belonged to either Manson or one of his accomplices, deliberately placed at the crime scene to cause confusion. Finally, the police saw the Buck knife which Atkins had lost in her struggle with Frykowski, blade up, wedged between the cushion and back of one of the living room's overstuffed chairs.

There was a considerable quantity of drugs found at Cielo. A gram of cocaine was found in Sebring's Porsche, plus 6.3 grams of marijuana and a partially smoked joint. There were 6.9 grams of pot in a plastic baggie in a cabinet in the living room. In the Folger/Frykowski bedroom were 30 grams of hashish, plus ten capsules of MDA. There was also marijuana residue in the ashtray next to Sharon's bed, as well as a partially smoked marijuana cigarette in the ashtray on the living room desk.[38]

Mrs. Chapman, having recognized his Porsche parked in the driveway, mentioned Jay Sebring to the police. The police, in turn, apparently mentioned this fact in one of their reports which went out over the police radio. A reporter heard it and, recognizing the name, called Sebring's house and asked his butler Amos Russell if he was at home. Alarmed, Russell called John Madden, President of Sebring International and Jay's business manager and partner. Madden had not spoken with Jay since the previous afternoon.

Madden rang Doris Tate. He mentioned that there were reports of some deaths on Cielo Drive. Mrs. Tate had not heard anything about a crime, and quickly hung up the telephone. "We got a call early in the morning that something had happened up on Benedict Canyon where Sharon lived," Sharon's sister Patti remembered. "We knew that something was wrong up there, but everything was very vague."[39] Heart sinking, Doris immediately dialed her daughter's number. The telephone rang and rang, but there was no answer.[40] Truly scared, Doris Tate called Sandy Tennant, wife of Roman's business manager William Tennant. Sandy had spoken with Sharon the previous afternoon. Abigail and Voyteck, Sharon had told her, would be staying at 10050 Cielo Drive that night, and Jay would also be visiting. She had not heard from Sharon since. Sandy Tennant told Doris Tate that she would call her husband, and try to find out what was happening. With growing unease, Doris waited by her telephone all morning.[41]

William Tennant was playing tennis at his club when his wife reached him. He immediately left and drove over to 10050 Cielo Drive, informing the police stationed at the gate that he was Roman Polanski's business manager. They led him through the gate and down the driveway, to the first body in the white Ambassador. He did not recognize Parent, whom he had never met. On the front lawn, he identified Voyteck and Abigail, and was then led inside to the living room. Crying, he identified Sharon and, he thought, Jay, although the man's face was so badly beaten and swollen that it was impossible for him to be sure. The sight of the bodies in the living room was too much for Tennant: he ran outside and vomited repeatedly.[42]

The reporters were in a frenzy at the front gate as Tennant left. By now, everyone knew who lived in the house. He ignored the shouted questions: "Were they murdered?" "Is Sharon dead?" "Has anyone informed Roman Polanski?"[43] They got better results from the incautious police. "It looked like a battlefield up there," one officer declared.[44] Another, unwittingly laying the basis for weeks of rumors to come, said, "It seemed kind of ritualistic."[45]

By mid-afternoon, after hours of nerve-shattering silence, the telephone finally rang in the Tate house in Palos Verdes. An LAPD spokesman had reached Paul Tate in San Francisco and told him the devastating news. Immediately, Paul rang his wife and told her that Sharon had been murdered the night before at Cielo Drive, along with Jay, Abigail, Voyteck and an unidentified young man. "I was never notified by the police," Doris recalled, "and I'm not sure that I don't thank God that I wasn't notified first because I could have been."[46]

The shock was immediate. Sixteen-year-old Deborah and eleven-year-old Patti were in the family room when their mother appeared in the doorway. "I remember her empty gaze and her anguished expression when she looked at me and my sister, when we were playing on the sofa," Patti later recalled.[47] Gripping both sides of the door, Doris cried, "My daughter's dead!" and fell to her knees.[48] "That's how that day went," Patti remembered. "Hell. And hell continued for years."[49] It was the beginning of a nightmare.

❖❖❖❖❖

Roman Polanski spent Friday, August 8, working on the script for the movie *Day of the Dolphin* in London. He had called Sharon around seven that evening from the Eaton Place mews, reassuring her that he would be returning home on Tuesday. He went out to dinner that night with friend Victor Lownes and then to The Revolution in Bruton Place, a fashionable nightclub.[50] According to Lownes, Roman picked up a girl he described as "a bimbo" and spent the night with her.[51]

It was William Tennant who finally called Roman from Los Angeles around eight-thirty Saturday night, London time. The connection seemed bad to Polanski, and it was made worse by the fact that he could barely understand Tennant, who sounded as if he were crying. Finally, the horrible news came out.

"There's been a disaster at the house," Tennant told his friend.

"Who's house?" Polanski asked.

"Yours," Tennant answered. "Sharon's dead. Voyteck's dead, too. And Gibby and Jay. They're all dead."

"No, no, no!" Roman screamed. At first he thought he didn't understand.

"Roman, they were murdered," Tennant said sadly. Roman dropped the telephone in shock and began wandering around his living room in circles. A friend happened to be with him and called Gene Gutowski, who rushed over to look after Roman. He found him moaning, "No, no!" and punching the walls of the flat. He cried all night long as Gutowski held him, whispering now and then through his sobs, "Did she know how much I loved her? Did she? Did she?"[52]

Gene Gutowski, Victor Lownes and Warren Beatty were among those in London who took turns watching over the sedated Roman Polanski. "Roman was utterly devastated," recalls Lownes. "He kept muttering things to himself, crying. I had to go to the American Embassy on Sunday and get a special Visa so that he could immediately return to the United States—he was in no condition himself to go."[53]

Still heavily tranquilized, he was escorted aboard a Pan Am flight from Heathrow to Los Angeles on Sunday, spending most of the flight sleeping or crying. A large contingent of the press knew of his imminent arrival and waited for him in the terminal in Los Angeles. The only glimpse they got of him, however, was a brief one as Roman, in dark glasses, was escorted off the plane and into a waiting car, which sped away rapidly into the night. "I was with Roman, holding his arm, trying to help push him through the crowd at the airport," remembers Victor Lownes. "Reporters were shouting questions about Sharon, about their marriage—it was horrible."[54] He stayed in a small apartment on the Paramount Studio lot, away from all reporters. Aside from the telephone calls to Sharon's parents and the constant company of a few friends who watched over him, Roman was left alone with his grief.[55]

Earlier that Saturday, across Los Angeles from the Hollywood Hills, in the quiet, middle-class suburb of El Monte, Juanita Parent had been nervously awaiting the return of her son Steven since the previous evening. After leaving his regular job earlier that Friday night, the eighteen-year-old had telephoned home, mentioning to his mother that he might be late, as he was going to visit a friend in Beverly Hills.

Parent should have been home shortly after midnight. By one early that Saturday morning, according to Steven's fifteen-year-old sister Janet, "My mom was in a panic. My brother always called if he was going to be late."[56]

When Saturday morning came, Parent had still not arrived home. His father Wilfrid telephoned his son's friends, but no one knew where he had gone. "We were all upset," Janet Parent remembers. "We knew something was wrong, but we didn't know what."[57]

At noon, Wilfrid and Juanita Parent drove down to their local church, where a Knights of Columbus meeting was taking place. The parish priest, Father Robert Byrne, was one of their son's closest friends, and they thought he might have some idea where Steven had gone.

Janet Parent was home with her two younger brothers when she heard a loud knocking. Two men stood at their front door. Both identified themselves as police reporters, and asked if her parents were at home.

"No," she replied, "you'll have to come back."

"Well, we have a report that your brother's car was stolen," one of the men told her.

When Janet tried to close the door, one of them men put his arm in, and pushed her back against the frame. "They both barged in," she recalls, "and ran across the living room to the television set. On top of the set were a lot of photographs of our family, and they found one of Steve, taken at his prom earlier that year, and started to snap pictures of it."

Uncertain what to do, Janet telephoned her mother and father at the Parish Hall, asking them to return. When Wilfrid Parent arrived home, he quickly telephoned the El Monte Police Department, who told him that they had not sent anyone out to his house.

The long hours of the afternoon passed in an agonized wait. The Parents still had no news of their son. "We sat down and watched television," Janet remembers. "We saw the news reports about Sharon Tate, but it didn't really mean anything to us. We were all so worried about Steve, and trying to figure out what had happened to him."

Juanita Parent called Father Byrne, and asked him to come to their house. A few minutes after the priest arrived, a policeman knocked on the door. When Juanita opened it, he simply handed her a business card, and told her to call the number at the bottom. It was a card from the Office of the Deputy Coroner of Los Angeles County. "That's the morgue!" she screamed, and passed out in the middle of the open doorway.

Wilfrid Parent picked up his wife and carried her to the couch. While Janet and Father Byrne looked after her, Parent dialed the Coroner's Office. He was put on hold; after a few minutes, he was transferred, before being again being put on hold. Finally, his composure gave way. "If my son is lying up there dead," he yelled, "by God, somebody is going to give me some information!"

Father Byrne volunteered to drive down to the morgue and see if they had Steven's body. Juanita went to the bedroom to lay down, and Wilfrid, Janet and her brothers turned on the television to watch the news. "We still hadn't found out anything," Janet remembers.

"Then the news came on. They were showing footage from the Tate house. And we saw them pulling my brother's body out of my dad's car. We all looked at one another in shock, and just collapsed. That's how we found out he was dead. Thank God my mom didn't see it. I think if she had, it would have killed her."[58]

Sharon's death made headlines around the United States and in Europe. The fame of the victims, and the gruesome manner in which they had been killed, guaranteed expansive media coverage. As reporters grasped for any information, gossip and innuendo were often repeated as truth. It was to become the one consistent factor in the aftermath of the tragedy.

"There were odd things going on around town," recalled Joan Didion. "There were rumors. There were stories. Everything was unmentionable but nothing was unimaginable. This mystical flirtation with the idea of 'sin'—this sense that it was possible to go 'too far,' and that many people were doing it—was very much with us...A demented and seductive vortical tension was building in the community. The jitters were setting in....On August 9, 1969, I was sitting in the shallow end of my sister-in-law's swimming pool in Beverly Hills when she received a telephone call from a friend who had just heard about the murders at Sharon Tate Polanski's house on Cielo Drive. The phone rang many times during the next hour. These early reports were garbled and contradictory. One caller would say hoods, the next would say chains. There were twenty dead, no, twelve, ten, eighteen. Black masses were imagined, and bad trips blamed. I remember all of the day's misinformation very clearly, and I also remember this, and wish I did not: I remember that no one was surprised."[59]

The *Los Angeles Times* devoted a large section of its front page to Sharon's death. Even the staid *New York Times* reported the murders on its front page. They made every national newscast in America that evening. The early details of the tragedy were often erroneous: it was widely reported, for example, that Sharon's unborn baby had been cut out of her womb; that her breasts had been cut off; that the victims had been sexually assaulted; that Jay Sebring had been found with a hood over his head.

Sharon's friend John Phillips later recalled how, that afternoon, he went out and waited in line at a sporting goods store on Wilshire

Boulevard to buy a handgun. He already had a Beretta at home. In his house on Bel Air Road, he hid knives underneath cushions, behind books, in drawers, ready to defend himself if the killers struck at his address next.[60] Michelle Phillips also armed herself with a gun, which she carried in her purse whenever she left the house.[61] "In the aftermath of the Tate murders, paranoia swept through Beverly Hills and Bel Air....Everyone was terrified, waiting to see who would be sacrificed next. No one felt safe."[62]

Ken's Sporting Goods Shop in Beverly Hills sold 200 guns in the two days following the murders, where previously they had sold three or four a day.[63] The exclusive and private Bel Air Patrol hired dozens of additional men and added them to their nightly security patrols. John Phillips even recalled older Eagle Scouts being hired as extra watchmen.[64] Guard dogs, which had sold for around $200 prior to the murders, now went for as much as $1,500, and locksmiths told customers that there was up to a two-week wait for additional security installations.[65]

Celebrities were terrified that they might be next. There were rumors that Jerry Lewis had suddenly installed an expensive security system complete with cameras and monitors.[66] Frank Sinatra was said to be in hiding, protected by bodyguards. Mia Farrow allegedly declared that she could not attend Sharon's funeral, so fearful was she that the killers would be after her next. Connie Stevens spent thousands of dollars turning her Hollywood mansion into an armed fortress. Sharon's friend Leslie Caron vividly remembers "the horror in Hollywood that day. No one knew why it had happened, why such horrible, bestial murders had taken place."[67] Fearful not only of the killers but also of police investigators, many celebrities rid themselves of illegal drugs. "Toilets are flushing all over Beverly Hills," one actor said. "The entire Los Angeles sewer system is stoned."[68]

Amidst the frenzied reactions of both the media and the Hollywood community, investigators at 10050 Cielo Drive concluded their work. Earlier, someone had taken bedsheets from the linen closet in the hallway leading to the bedrooms and finally covered the bloody bodies, preventing the circling helicopters from capturing the grim scene on the lawn. By two o'clock that afternoon, in the 94 degree Los Angeles heat, Coroner Thomas Noguchi and his assistant were wandering from body to body, checking their conditions. Paper bags were placed over their hands and the rope between Sharon and Jay was cut.[69] Finally, one by one, stretchers were unloaded from the white medical examiners' vans and wheeled across the front lawn. Sharon's body was carefully lifted from the bloody floor and placed in a bag on the stretcher, covered with a sheet and wheeled from her house for the last time, before being driven down to the medical examiner's office in Los Angeles.

As night fell over Los Angeles, everyone was on edge. "In the great houses of Bel Air," one reporter later wrote, "terror sends people flying to their telephones when a branch falls from a tree outside."[70] Benedict Canyon was strangely silent; the cars filled with reporters and the morbidly curious, which had clogged the twisting length of Cielo earlier that afternoon, had disappeared now, replaced with the peaceful sound of crickets, the rustle of leaves in the breeze. A lone policeman paced uneasily before the gate at 10050 Cielo Drive, standing guard over the empty, blood-stained house. Just after nine, a neighbor across the canyon happened to look out her window. No one had bothered to turn off the automatic timers which controlled the exterior lights at 10050 Cielo Drive. "As if a belated celebration

were taking place, all the brightly colored Christmas lights that surround the entire property of the Tate-Polanski home suddenly came alive and began to twinkle their merry colors."[71]

Chapter 31
The Second Night

T HE ONLY TELEVISION SET AT SPAHN RANCH WAS LOCATED IN George Spahn's trailer. Family members eagerly crowded around to watch the news the following morning, excited by what had taken place, and at all of the press coverage the crimes were generating. Everyone at the ranch knew what had happened. To one of the bikers at the ranch, Danny De Carlo, Family member Steve Grogan bragged, "We got five piggies."[1]

"I have no explanation for how hardened I had become in only a few hours," Susan Atkins later admitted. "As I watched the TV reporters, I even laughed as they described the details of the horror."[2] Charles Watson took immense pleasure in telling Dianne Lake how much "fun" he had had the previous night.[3] Only Patricia Krenwinkel seemed bothered by the murders. "I was very dead inside, very empty, very frightened," she later recalled.[4] Talking to Leslie Van Houten, she again expressed surprise at how young the victims had been. It had "seemed wrong, and not right," she said.[5]

Van Houten, however, regretted that she had not been able to go the night before. "I felt that what we were doing was a mission that needed to be done," she declared. "I felt that if they went again, that I wanted to go. I wanted to go and be a good soldier and surrender myself for what I believed in."[6]

That afternoon and evening, Manson seemed on edge. After leading the Family in song and smoking some pot, he suddenly announced, "Last night was too messy. This time I'm going to show you how to do it." He told Watson, Atkins, Krenwinkel and Kasabian to get a change of clothing and their knives.[7] "Charlie definitely had me go the second night," Krenwinkel recounts. "At that point, I felt so dead inside it didn't really matter."[8] On her way to the car, Atkins turned to ranch hand Juan Flynn and bragged, "We're going to get them fucking pigs."[9]

This time, he also took Steve Grogan and Leslie Van Houten. "I didn't walk right up and say, 'May I go,'" Van Houten remembers. "But I think everything in my face said that."[10] She recalled that Manson "came up to me," asking if she "believed enough" to "go with them." "I made it very clear," she admits, "I wanted to go."[11] "I knew that people would die," Van Houten later declared. "I knew that there would be killing."[12]

This time Kasabian drove the killers. At first, no one in the car spoke. "I was completely numb from the night before," Krenwinkel later recalled.[13] They appeared to be headed nowhere in particular, Manson occasionally directing Kasabian to stop as he considered conducting murders at various houses. "Manson," Van Houten remembers, "was very agitated, and Kasabian was very nervous and upset, and he was yelling at her a lot."[14]

Once, Manson had her pull up at a church, saying he wanted to go inside and kill the priest on the altar. But, finding the door locked, he soon returned, having accomplished nothing. At a traffic light, he intended to kill the driver of the car next to them, but the signal suddenly changed. Suddenly, Kasabian recalled, his directions became very precise. He ordered her to take lefts and rights, until the car finally reached Waverly Drive, skirting the crest of a hillside in the fashionable Los Feliz section of Los Angeles near Griffith Park.

Several of the killers were familiar with the area. For nearly a year, Watson had lived just two miles away, ironically only a half-block from the daughter of his soon-to-be latest victim.[15] Kasabian herself recognized the house where they stopped, a big, Tudor-style mansion where she had formerly been to a party. Manson had also been to the house on several occasions, and met the owner, Harold True.[16] But Manson said they were going to the house next door, a smaller Spanish-style home perched at the top of a long driveway.

The house belonged to forty-four-year-old Gateway Markets owner Leno LaBianca and his thirty-eight-year-old second wife Rosemary. Leno, the son of Italian immigrants, had taken the reins of the successful Gateways Market chain on the death of his father when he was twenty-six, built on his hard work, and enjoyed the financial rewards which accompanied that expansion. He owned a string of racehorses and indulged his passion for gambling.

He had married twice: his first wife, Alice Skolfield, bore him three children, daughters Cory and Louise, and son Anthony. They divorced in 1957. "Leno was one in a million," Alice remembers. "We went our separate ways amicably, and never fell out of love with each other. We found as we matured that we wanted different things from life and never alienated the children toward one another. I wanted a career and Leno wanted someone more like his mother."[17]

Two years later, Leno met Rosemary Struthers. A dark beauty, she was believed to have been born in Mexico of American parents. Following their premature deaths, Rosemary was placed in an Arizona orphanage, from which she was eventually adopted by a California family. In the late 1940s, she met Frank Struthers, and the pair soon married. By the time of their eventual divorce in 1958, Rosemary had given birth to two children, a daughter, Suzan who was conceived in an extra-marital affair, and a son, Frank Struthers, Jr. Leno LaBianca first met Rosemary Struthers while she was working as a hostess at the Los Feliz Inn. They soon married, and, in November of 1968, moved into Oak Terrace, a Spanish-style house at 3301 Waverly Drive. It was the house in which Leno himself had been raised, and he purchased it from his mother Corina. Here, he lived with Rosemary and her two children. Leno's first wife, Alice, later remembered Rosemary as "an attractive woman, more sophisticated than I had ever been."[18]

That second weekend of August, 1969, the LaBiancas had gone to Lake Isabella with Rosemary's children for a quick holiday. To avoid the Sunday traffic, they left Lake Isabella at nine that Saturday night, taking Rosemary's twenty-one-year-old daughter Suzan with them; fifteen-year-old Frank decided to return the following day, and remained at the lake with friends. It was a long drive; behind his green, 1968 Thunderbird, Leno pulled a speedboat on a trailer, which further slowed them.

They arrived back in Los Angeles around one that morning. Leno drove the Thunderbird across town, dropping Suzan off at her apartment on Greenwood, before heading to the corner of Hillwood and Franklin, where John Fokianos ran a news stand. Leno greeted the news vendor, and purchased a copy of Saturday's *Los Angeles Times* as well as a racing form. Rosemary, Fokianos later recalled, seemed unnerved by the Tate murders. After a few minutes, Leno eased the Thunderbird back onto the street and drove through the Los Feliz district to the house at the top of Waverly Drive. Because it was so late, Leno left the speedboat on its trailer, still attached to the Thunderbird.

Rosemary LaBianca had good reason to be nervous. Strange things had been taking place at Oak Terrace. A few weeks earlier, she had complained to a friend that someone must have been inside the residence, as their dogs had been found wandering round outside when they had been left locked in the house.[19]

The LaBiancas' arrived at Oak Terrace round one-thirty early that Sunday morning. Leno changed into pajamas and remained in the living room, reading the newspaper and drinking a can of Apple Beer, while Rosemary retired to their bedroom to unpack. A half hour later, Kasabian pulled to a stop before the long, curving driveway leading to Harold True's house at 3267 Waverly Drive.

Manson and Watson walked up the driveway to the True house, then hopped the low wall separating its grounds from the LaBianca residence. On the east side of Oak Terrace, a French door opened to a small terrace; when Manson turned the door handle, it opened. He and Watson entered the dining room; through an open archway to the left was the living room. As they crept in, they saw Leno. He had fallen asleep sitting on the L-shaped sofa facing the fireplace, his newspaper folded in his lap. Suddenly, he stirred.

"Who are you? What do you want?" he asked.[20]

"We're not going to hurt you," Manson assured him. "Just relax. Don't be afraid."[21] Manson took a leather thong from round his neck and handed it to Watson, telling him to tie the man's hands behind his back, while he himself searched the rest of the house. Manson found Rosemary, attired in a nightgown, in the bedroom. On Manson's instructions, she grabbed a striped dress and quickly pulled it over her nightgown, before he brought her into the living room. She sat on the sofa next to her husband, while Manson tied her hands behind her back. He then left, whispering to Watson, "Make sure the girls get to do some of it, both of them."[22]

Manson returned to the car. According to Kasabian, he explained that he had assured the couple inside that they would not be harmed. Motioning to Krenwinkel and Van Houten, he instructed them to join Watson inside the residence. "Go do what Tex says," he told them as they climbed from the rear of the car.[23] As they headed up the hill, he whispered, "Don't let them know that you are going to kill them."[24]

As soon as the two women reached the house, Manson climbed back into the car and, together with Kasabian, Atkins and Grogan, drove off into the night.

231 GREG KING

"We went in the house," recalls Van Houten, "and I would say that was when I first really understood what was happening."[25] There was an eerie stillness. Leno LaBianca, clad in a pair of blue pajamas, sat on the living room sofa, his hands tied behind his back. Beside him, Rosemary gazed at the women, terrified.

After whispering with Watson, Krenwinkel and Van Houten walked over to the sofa. "Pat and I took Mrs. LaBianca into the bedroom," Van Houten remembers.[26] Once in the bedroom, the women stripped the pillows of their cases. Along with Watson, they placed one of the cases over Rosemary's head. Watson took a massive lamp from the table at the side of the bed, unplugged it, and wrapped the cord round and round Rosemary's neck and through her mouth. He then returned to the living room with the second pillow case, and did the same to Leno, taking another lamp and wrapping its cord round the terrified man's neck.

Leaving Rosemary on the bed, Krenwinkel and Van Houten walked into the kitchen. The silence was shattered by the rattle of knives, as the two women rummaged through the drawers for weapons.[27] Hearing this, Leno realized what was about to take place. He began to scream, "You're going to kill us, aren't you? You're going to kill us!" Watson pushed him back against the couch and told him to shut up.[28]

As Leno yelled and struggled, his wife, in the bedroom, joined in his cries for help. Watson told Krenwinkel and Van Houten to go and keep her quiet. He himself turned on the helpless Leno. He stabbed the struggling man repeatedly in the stomach and chest.

"Don't stab me anymore!" Leno managed to howl. "I'm dead! I'm dead!"

Watson took no notice. He stabbed Leno in the throat so violently that he broke off the blade of the steak knife he was using, leaving it lodged in Leno's windpipe. "The room began to explode with color and motion," he later recalled. To finish the job, he grabbed a double-tined carving fork from the kitchen and stabbed Leno in the stomach over and over again, ripping his pajama top open in the process.[29]

In the bedroom, Rosemary LaBianca, hearing her husband's screams—"horrible, guttural sounds" in the words of Van Houten—began to struggle with the women.[30] "What are you doing to my husband?" she yelled.[31]

"I remember her screaming for him...." Van Houten has said. "I remember thinking to myself, how much she loved him, that, that was her thought, her concern for him. You could hear the—you could hear the guttural sounds of him dying. And I tried to hold Mrs. LaBianca down while Pat [Krenwinkel] stabbed her."[32]

Krenwinkel plunged her knife deeply into the white pillowcase; it struck Rosemary LaBianca's collarbone, and bent. Although Krenwinkel tried again, her knife was damaged, and she could not deliver any further blows.

"I was confused and torn inside," Van Houten remembered. "I wanted to do what Manson had asked us to do and I was battling with my own sense of I was in something that I was—was not capable of handling. And I didn't hold her down well and she picked the lamp up and I don't really know if she even knew she had the lamp. She was struggling for her life...."[33]

"Leslie was still trying to hold her," Krenwinkel remembers, "because she was still struggling, and I went and got Tex [Watson]."[34] Van Houten was not strong enough, however, and Rosemary managed to pull away. Watson entered the room to see her, head cloaked in the pillowcase, backed into a corner like a wounded animal, swinging the lamp in her hands blindly before her in a futile effort to keep her killers at bay. Watson ran forward, stabbed her, and she fell. As she lay on the floor, kicking and screaming, he continued to stab.[35]

Van Houten and Krenwinkel were both attempting to hold her down to the floor. Later, Van Houten claimed that she had left the room. "I stood in the hallway and I looked in to a blank room that was like a den. And I stood there until Tex turned me around and handed me a knife and he said, 'Do something.' I went back in the bedroom and Mrs. LaBianca was laying on the floor, on her stomach, and I stabbed her numerous times in the back."[36] Watson later wrote that Van Houten showed "none of the enthusiasm" demonstrated by Krenwinkel.[37] Van Houten, as she later admitted both to her own lawyer and on the witness stand during her trial, had no idea if Rosemary LaBianca was alive or dead as she stabbed her repeatedly in the lower back and buttocks. Rosemary's autopsy would later show that one of the wounds in her lower back had indeed been a fatal one, administered while she was still alive.[38] She had, Van Houten later said, "No mercy" for Rosemary LaBianca.[39]

In the living room, Krenwinkel noticed the double-tined carving fork lying on the floor next to Leno's body. She picked it up and thrust it into his exposed stomach. Giving it a twang, she watched it wobble back and forth, fascinated.⁴⁰ As she looked at the body, she thought, or so she later said, "You won't be sending your son off to war." Taking one of the knives, she bent down and carved WAR into the exposed flesh of Leno's stomach.⁴¹ The killers left several bloody messages, helped themselves to food from their victims' refrigerator, and took a shower in their pink-tiled bathroom. Before leaving, Van Houten, worried about prints, spent a considerable amount of time wiping down the rooms in which the murders had taken place.⁴² The killers left Oak Terrace, walking down the long driveway and turned left, following Waverly Drive down the hillside to an overpass, where they hid in some bushes. At dawn, they hitchhiked back to Spahn Ranch.

Sunday evening, fifteen-year-old Frank Struthers returned with friends from the weekend at Lake Isabella. As he walked up Waverly Drive, he noticed that his stepfather's speedboat was still on its trailer, and still attached to the Thunderbird on the street. This was unusual, for Leno generally never left the boat out at night. He also saw that the shades of the house had been drawn, but that the lights inside were on. This, too, was unusual. Rather than enter, he nervously knocked on the door. There was no answer.

He walked to the nearest pay telephone, at a drive-in located at the corner of Hyperion and Rowena, nearly a mile down the hillside. He first called Oak Terrace. The telephone rang and rang. Next, he called the restaurant where his sister Suzan worked; she was not there, but the manager offered to call her apartment, and took the number of the pay phone. Just after nine, she called back. Frank explained that he was worried about entering the house, as no one answered his knocks; everything seemed odd at the house on Waverly Drive. After a quick discussion, she told her brother to remain where he was until she could join him.

Suzan Struthers arrived just after ten, accompanied by her boyfriend, Joe Dorgan. Together with Frank, they drove back up the hill to Oak Terrace. They entered the house by the kitchen door, Dorgan telling Suzan to remain in the kitchen while he and Frank looked through the rest of the house. They got no farther than the living room before they found Leno LaBianca, sprawled on his back, dead. Without bothering to search the rest of the house, the trio ran from the property and immediately called the police.

Soon, the house at Waverly Drive was swarming with detectives. They found Leno LaBianca in the living room, lying on his back beside a couch. A pillowcase had been placed over his head, and the cord from a heavy lamp had been tied round his neck. His hands were bound behind his back with a leather thong. He had been stabbed repeatedly, and the broken blade of a kitchen knife was later found in his throat. The pajama top he wore had been ripped back, and a carving fork rose from his stomach. Carved in large letters across his full belly was the word "WAR". His wife Rosemary was lying face-down in their bedroom, a pillowcase over her head as well as a lamp cord knotted round her neck. Her dress and nightgown had been pulled up over her back, and she had been stabbed repeatedly, over forty times the autopsy would reveal. Smeared in Leno LaBianca's blood on the northern wall of the living room were the words "Death to Pigs;" on the southern wall, just to the left of the front door, "Rise" had been written in his blood. On the door of the refrigerator in the kitchen was written a misspelled "Healter Skelter."

Alice LaBianca, Leno's first wife, had spent that Sunday at the beach with her children. Late that night, the telephone rang. Leno's eldest daughter Cory took the call. She hung up the telephone and turned to her mother.

"Suzan just called," she said slowly, "Suzan just called."

"Well, so?" Alice asked.

"She said dad's been shot."

"Don't be ridiculous," Alice replied. "Who'd want to shoot your father? Call her back. Did she leave her number?"

The LaBiancas, however, were unable to reach Suzan Struthers. "We didn't know what it was all about," Alice recalled. "My stomach was just in knots, wondering what had gone on." Alice's brother quickly phoned the police, who acknowledged that there had been a homicide in the neighborhood, but refused to confirm any details. "It was five or six hours later," Alice continues, "while we were all keeping vigil all night, before we heard from one of Leno's very close friends, who happened to be in the police department. He called and told us what had happened. He said it was pretty awful. From that moment on, we didn't turn on the news, we didn't look at a newspaper, we didn't do anything, because we didn't want to know what awful thing had happened to Leno, because the children loved him dearly, and he was a very good father to them. I'd loved him dearly."[43]

"Leno had just had his forty-fourth birthday when he was murdered," says Alice. "He was the financial expert as well as the

President of Gateway Markets, and when he was murdered, it left the company without a knowledgeable leader. The creditors took it over six years after his death. Leno's mother died of a broken heart soon after."[44]

Although the police tried to keep many of the details of these crimes from the press, the leaks were sufficient enough to raise questions. Two different sets of murders in Los Angeles, on two different nights and in two different locations. Both sets of victims were wealthy. There was no apparent motive in either set of crimes. Both sets of crimes had been committed with terrible savagery. Victims in both sets of murders had been stabbed repeatedly, with apparently similar weapons. There was no evidence of robbery at either crime scene. And, at both crime scenes, the killers had left messages printed in the victims' own blood.

"I don't see any connection between this murder and the others," Los Angeles Police Department Inspector K. J. McCauley told reporters. "They're too widely removed. I just don't see any connection."[45] As much as the LAPD tried to deny any linkage between the murders on Cielo Drive and those on Waverly Drive, however, the evidence seemed to indicate that both crimes had been committed by the same set of killers.

Chapter 32
You Wouldn t Believe How Weird These People Were.

S HARON HAD DIED WITH A SLIGHT, ALMOST WISTFUL SMILE ON HER face, a perverse mockery of the brutal wounds which had savaged her body. Her half-open eyes stared vacantly, a stream of tears having washed a path through the trickle of blood which had escaped from her lips. Her long, honey-blonde hair was still partially tucked into the nylon noose twisted round her neck, its strands matted with crimson.

Her body had been logged into the admission books at the downtown Los Angeles Medical Examiner's Office early that Saturday afternoon. A photographer circled the metal table, every flash illuminating a new, horrific wound, before the body was stripped of its blood-spattered bikini panties and bra, and carefully washed. The autopsy would not take place until the following day, Sunday, and her body was stored in a refrigerated drawer until that time.

Dr. Thomas Noguchi, Chief Coroner for the City of Los Angeles, performed the post mortem examination, assisted by several deputy coroners. The autopsy began at 11:20 A.M. Sunday morning. Cause of death was listed as "Multiple stab wounds of chest and back penetrating heart, lungs, and liver causing massive hemorrhage." Of her wounds, four of these were to the chest, one to the abdomen, eight to the back, and one to the back of her right thigh. Her upper right arm and upper left arm both bore defensive stab wounds, obtained in her desperate, futile attempt to fight off her killers and protect the life of her unborn baby. Most of the wounds to the chest and abdomen had penetrated to a depth of four inches, causing massive internal injuries to the liver, lungs and heart. Those to the back had struck her ribs, chipping at the bone.[1] On her left cheek, Noguchi noted a small rope burn, suggesting that, prior to her death, she had been hung.[2]

Barium-sulfate paste was carefully squeezed into each of the wounds, allowing their exact dimensions to be measured and carefully examined in x-rays.[3] The knives which had made many of the wounds had been sharpened along not only the cutting edge, but also along the top half of the blade, making them twice as deadly. Portions of her organs were sectioned and saved in formalin; separate jars were labeled and filled with pieces of skin extracted from three of the back wounds to preserve the dimensions of the wound pattern. Her liver, kidneys and stomach were also removed, examined and sectioned. Finally, Noguchi did a vaginal smear, determining as a result that Sharon had not had intercourse within the last twenty-four hours.[4]

In spite of the fact that she had been pregnant, Sharon had not put on much weight: at the time of her death, she weighed 136 pounds. During the course of the autopsy, Noguchi carefully removed the perfectly formed fetus from the womb. It was a boy, of eight-and-a-half months gestation. The fetus had not been harmed at all by the numerous stab wounds the mother received. Noguchi thought that the fetus probably lived for about fifteen to twenty minutes after its mother's death before it, too, had died.

The autopsy took three hours. While television broadcasts and the front pages of newspapers round the world had featured film clips and photographs depicting her great beauty, this was not how Thomas Noguchi saw her. For him, Sharon Tate would always be Victim No. 69-8796.

Throughout the afternoon, the autopsies of the other Cielo Drive victims were carried out, revealing the terrible condition of the bodies. Steven Parent had been shot four times: once in the left cheek, twice in the chest, and once on the left arm. He had also been stabbed once in the left hand, a slice which cut deeply between his fingers.

Jay Sebring had been shot once, the bullet penetrating the left side of his chest and piercing his lung. The wound was, in and of itself, fatal. He had been stabbed six times, wounds primarily to his left chest, causing massive internal hemorrhage to the aorta. He had also suffered a defensive stab wound to his left hand. His face bore mute witness to the brutality of his death: repeated kicks and blows had broken and flattened his nose, and caused ugly swellings below his right eye and cheek.

Abigail Folger had been stabbed twenty-eight times, and died from massive blood loss. While the stabs to the chest and aorta had caused death, several wounds to her lower right stomach had resulted in an open wound, some six inches long, through which her intestines protruded. Her face had also been violently slashed. Her left cheek was sliced by a diagonal incision, running from her hairline to her mouth, some six inches long. It continued across her lips and curved just above her chin. A second slice, running several inches, crossed her upper left chin.

Voyteck Frykowski had struggled hardest for his life. He had been shot twice, struck over the head thirteen times with a blunt object, and stabbed fifty-one times. The blunt-force trauma to his head had left his skull smashed in several places. Several of his stab wounds were to the back; nearly a dozen to the chest; sixteen wounds to his upper left arm; and eight to his left leg, as if they had been administered while he lay on his right side on the lawn. Noguchi noted that many of the stab wounds were post-mortem, inflicted as Voyteck was already dead. "In my entire experience," wrote Noguchi, "I had never seen such savagery applied to one person."[5]

The mournful parade of funerals took place on Wednesday, 13 August. Victor Lownes, under police escort, had gone up to 10050 Cielo Drive to select a dress from Sharon's closet to bury her in. "It was very quiet, no one around except for a few policemen," Lownes recalls. "I remember walking up the walk and to the porch and seeing pools of blood all over the place. And 'Pig' on the door in Sharon's blood." There was blood all over the place—in the living room, in the bedroom. I went through the closet in a hurry—I just wanted to get out of there."[6] He eventually settled on a blue and yellow Emilio Pucci print mini dress, which had been one of her favorites.[7] This was taken to Cunningham and O'Connor, the funeral home handling the arrangements. Once she was dressed, her body was carefully placed in a satin-lined silver casket; also in the coffin, wrapped in a shroud, lay her unborn baby, Paul Richard Polanski. On Roman's instructions, the casket was closed; the only person to view Sharon's body after it was placed in the coffin was her father.[8]

She was buried at the Holy Cross Memorial Cemetery at Baldwin Hills in Culver City, overlooking Los Angeles near the San

Diego Freeway. Her grave was located on a bluff near a serene grotto, just up the hill from that of actor Bela Lugosi. A memorial service was conducted in the cemetery chapel by a friend of Sharon's family, Father Peter O'Reilly. Sharon had frequently gone to Mass at Father O'Reilly's Catholic Church, and he had known her well. Some two hundred persons attended the service, including John and Michelle Phillips; Peter Sellers; Kirk Douglas; Robert and Peggy Lipton; Warren Beatty; Yul Brynner; James Coburn; and Lee Marvin. Even in his drug-induced stupor, Roman noted the absence of one of Sharon's friends, actor Steve McQueen, who, fearful of the unknown killers, had remained away. "I never forgave him for that," Polanski later commented bitterly.[9]

"Black-clad," recalls Joan Collins, "the celebrity mourners, many of whom were weeping uncontrollably, looked strangely out of place under the azure sky."[10] A hundred members of the press, kept away from the chapel, still managed to capture the agony of Roman Polanski and Sharon's family with their long lenses. As the silver casket, covered with white and pink tea roses, was carried into the chapel, Roman, dressed in black and his eyes hidden behind dark sunglasses, followed behind, clutching the arms of Sharon's mother Doris and a family doctor. Sharon's two sisters, Deborah and Patti, their heads covered, like that of their mother, with lace mantillas, walked with their father Paul. "I will never forget the scene," Doris Tate later recalled. "The mourners couldn't all get inside, and the crowd was standing outside the little chapel, where flowers lined the walkway to the road."[11]

"I had never been to anything so sad, so horribly unreal," remembers Michelle Phillips. "It seemed totally unbelievable, overwhelming. I remember at one point I just went out of the church, walked to the lawn, and laid down on the grass, staring up at the sky. I couldn't handle what was happening."[12] Through his own tears, Father O'Reilly said, "She was a fine person, and we were in no small measure devoted to her....Goodbye, Sharon, and may the angels welcome you to heaven, and the martyrs guide your way."[13]

Later that afternoon, a memorial service was held for Jay Sebring at Forest Lawn Memorial Park in Glendale. This time, Steve McQueen did attend, along with Henry Fonda, James Garner, Warren Beatty and John and Michelle Phillips. "We had a bottle of Crown Royale in the car," Michelle Phillips remembers. "By the time we got to Jay's service, I think I was probably drunk. I just couldn't face the reality of what had happened to Sharon and Jay. It was an awful period for all of us."[14]

No one knew what to expect, and a sense of unreal tension hung in the air. Neile McQueen recalled, "Steve carried a gun in his breast pocket. Just in case. At the church at Forest Lawn I was shocked to find Jay in an open casket. But considering his violent death, the morticians had done a masterful job. As we sat waiting for the service to start, a strange man climbed up to the altar where Jay's body lay and began a bizarre chant. Nobody knew who he was and it galvanized everyone present to attention. Warren Beatty, who was sitting next to me, was ready to throw me onto the floor, fearful that some sort of altercation was about to occur. He was aware Steven had a gun and was concerned what might happen if anybody opened fire. But somebody removed the man who was chanting in front of Jay's body and order resumed."[15] Later, his body was buried in Southfield, Michigan.

Abigail Folger's body was returned to San Francisco, for a Catholic requiem mass that same morning at Our Lady of the Wayside Catholic Church in Portola, followed by interment at a nearby cemetery, while Steven Parent was buried by his family in El Monte that afternoon. Voyteck Frykowski's body was cremated; on 29 August, his ashes were finally returned to his native Poland, where he was interred in the St. Josef Cemetery in Lodz.

The day before her funeral, Sharon finally received in death what she had worked so hard for in life: stardom. Eager to cash in on the prevailing interest in her murder, distributors rushed to re-open *Valley of the Dolls* and *The Fearless Vampire Killers*. These were soon followed by some of her other films, all sharing one common factor: in death, Sharon's name was billed in large letters, before the films' titles. No one in Hollywood ever paid so great a price for fame.

Once Sharon was laid to rest, the speculation began anew: who had killed her and her friends, and, perhaps more curiously, why? The uncertainty weighed heavily on everyone around her. Not only did the chance remain that the killers might strike again, but, for Roman, Doris and Paul Tate and their surviving daughters, it was impossible to begin the healing process as long as the questions remained unanswered. Fearful for their safety, Doris took Deborah and Patti back to Texas, where they stayed with relatives, away from the glare of the media. "We didn't know who did it," Doris Tate recalled. "If they wanted to kill one, they could kill another."[16]

The situation was made even worse by the ceaseless press attention, speculation and erroneous reporting which was a consistent feature of the months following the murders. Everyone who had known Sharon in life seemed to want to talk about her in death, and often unfavorably. Rumors of wild orgies and massive drug dealing at 10050 Cielo Drive became legion. Those who did remember her kindly were largely ignored in the sensationalistic rush to dig up anything potentially "relevant" to a possible motive.

In an attempt to stem the tide of speculation, Roman's friend and business partner Gene Gutowski released a statement to the press on Monday, 11 August:

> Roman Polanski is understandably too overcome by grief and shock to speak to the press. In speaking to me and other friends, however, he has expressed some thoughts which I feel should be made public. Nobody or anything can give him back his lovely wife and the unborn child or his dear friends Voyteck Frykowski, Jay Sebring and Abigail Folger, who were murdered so brutally by some sick person or persons.
>
> Mr. Polanski wishes to make it very clear that there was no rift between his wife and himself as some irresponsible journalists here have suggested even before the tragedy. I personally know how devoted to each other they were...the few weeks they were separated they phoned each other every day; last time Roman phoned her a few hours before she was murdered. The reason that Sharon went to California ahead of Roman was to avoid a long air journey in her last full month of pregnancy. In fact, she traveled by sea. Roman had to stay behind in order to accept in person the Donatello Award in Taormina from the Italian Government and to finish off work on a new screenplay. He planned to join Sharon in Hollywood this week...she was planning a birthday party for him on Monday, the 18th. In the meantime, he asked Voyteck Frykowski, an old friend from Poland, and Abigail Folger to stay in the house in Cielo Drive with Sharon. I doubt if anyone knows Roman better or has been closer to him in the last five years than I have. Not only are we working partners, we are also close friends as were Sharon and my wife....I was with him when he first met Sharon, when they fell in love. I was his best man at their wedding a year and a half ago. They were a storybook couple, deeply in love and expecting a much-wanted baby.[17]

But such pronouncements did little to fill the public appetite for gossip. "You wouldn't believe how weird these people were," a detective on the case commented to a reporter from *Life* magazine. "If you live like that, what do you expect?" He was referring to the prominent rumors of sex and drugs circulating about the residents of 10050 Cielo Drive—and Jay Sebring and Voyteck Frykowski in particular. But Sharon's family was horrified, reading the words of a detective on their daughter's murder case saying, in effect, that she herself had brought about her own death through some imagined lifestyle. Very quickly, the victims ceased being victims, and soon became the catalysts of their own deaths in the eyes of many on the scene. "The same abject details are cited again and again," the same reporter noted, "always proving something different, until one collects an impression of the victims murdered again and again by relays of fresh marauders....The rumors read like a graph of community paranoia. Every story promotes the murders into assassinations, crimes of logical consequence in which some vision of the victims' way of living makes them accomplices in their own deaths...."[18]

Joe Hyams wrote in one article that Sharon had been a student of black magic and voodoo and the occult. Another writer reported that he had attended a black mass at Jay's house. He said Sharon greeted him at the door and led him into a dark, candlelit room filled with people in white robes where he was handed two goblets. "One contains wine, the other rat poison," Jay is alleged to have told him. "Take your pick."[19]

A week after the murders, an article in *Newsweek* strongly hinted that there were serious problems in the Polanskis' eighteen-month-old-marriage.[20] There was much speculation as to Jay Sebring's presence that evening in his former girlfriend's house during her husband's absence. "The reporting about Sharon and the murders was virtually criminal," Roman said in 1971. "Reading the papers, I could not believe my eyes. I could not believe my eyes! They blamed the victims for their own murders. I really despise the press. I didn't always. The press made me despise it....The victims were assassinated two times: once by the murderers, the second time by the press."[21]

Two weeks after the murders, an article in *Newsweek* declared:

> Nearly as enchanting as the mystery was the glimpse the murders yielded into the surprising Hollywood subculture in which the cast of characters played. All week long the Hollywood gos-

sip about the case was of drugs, mysticism and offbeat sex—and, for once, there may be more truth than fantasy in the flashy talk of the town. The theme of the melodrama was drugs. Some suspect that the group was amusing itself with some sort of black magic rites as well as drugs that night, and they mention a native Jamaican hip to voodoo who had recently been brought into Frykowski's drug operation. Some such parlor rites might account for the hood found over Sebring's head and the rope binding him to Miss Tate. Indeed, a group of friends speculates that the murders resulted from a ritual mock execution that got out of hand in the glare of hallucinogens.[22]

A curiously consistent pattern, right up to and even through the murder trials themselves, was the mention of Roman Polanski's sometimes bizarre and gruesome films. The implication was obvious: Polanski had sunk to such levels of depravity in his career that now the deaths of his wife and his friends not only echoed his penchant for the macabre but may have been influenced or inspired by his on-screen images of terror. Referring to Sharon, *Newsweek* wrote that, "In the end, she took the lead role in a murder mystery far more tragic and macabre than Polanski could ever have crafted for her on the screen."[23] It was a statement repeated by such respectable periodicals as *Life*, *Newsweek* and *Time*.

The latter magazine, in fact, was singularly responsible for promoting a wealth of inaccuracies. A week after the murders, *Time* reported: "Police said that every room in the house showed signs of a struggle."[24]

The following week, an article titled "The Night of Horror" devoted much space to a grisly retelling of what they claimed to be the truth of the matter:

> There was evidence of a wild struggle with the killer or killers as Sharon and another victim, hair stylist Jay Sebring, 35, were slashed repeatedly while they fought for their lives. A large number of pistol bullets were embedded in the walls and ceiling....Sharon's body was found nude, not clad in bikini pants and a bra, as had first been reported. Sebring was wearing only the torn remnants of a pair of boxer shorts. One of Miss Tate's breasts had been cut off, apparently as a result of indiscriminate slashing. She was nine months pregnant and there was an X cut on her stomach. What appeared to be the bloody handle of a paring knife was found next to her leg, the blade broken off. Sebring had been sexually mutilated, and his body also bore X marks.

Not content to stop here, the writer went on to include some groundless speculation: "Sharon and Sebring were the prime objects of the mayhem: the deaths of the other three victims seemed almost incidental....Frokowski's [sic] trousers were down around his ankles.[25]

On Sunday afternoon, August 17, Roman drove to 10050 Cielo Drive to look at his house. The estate was still under constant LAPD guard. With him, he took a writer and friend who worked for *Life* magazine, Thomas Thompson, who he had agreed could do a story. Thompson had brought a photographer. At the front gate, they were met by famous Dutch psychic Peter Hurkos, who had been sent by friends of Jay Sebring to see if he could gather any information from the scene. Roman reluctantly allowed him inside.

"This must be the world-famous orgy house," Roman declared angrily to Thompson as they drove through the front gate and down the driveway.

On the front lawn, the blood-stained blue bedsheet with which the police had covered Abigail Folger lay in a heap.[26] The blood on the walkway and the front porch had dried into a dark brown stain, but the letters "PIG" in Sharon's blood on the front door were still visible. The living room was a mess—cushions piled end on end, drawers opened, papers sorted through, black smears from the fingerprint powder on every surface. Before the couch, Roman paused at the crimson spot where Sharon had fallen, overwhelmed.

He wandered through the house all afternoon, picking up objects now and then, fighting back tears at times, searching through the havoc, trying to make sense out of the carnage, re-enacting what he thought must have happened that night.[27] The French doors in the master bedroom were still smeared with dark blood and black finger-print powder, the sheets on the bed pulled back as Sharon had left them that night. His eyes wandered from place to place: above the armoire stood the bassinet for the baby, still wrapped in plastic. He stumbled on a cache of Sharon's publicity photographs, and collapsed in sobs. It was too much for him to take in, too much to understand. "Why, why?" he kept repeating to himself, seeking an answer which was nowhere to be found.[28]

Hurkos, who had consulted with the police on the Boston Strangler case, immediately held a news conference and declared that he had received vibrations at the house and knew the identity of the killers. "Three men killed Sharon Tate and the other four," he said, "and I know who they are. I have identified the killers to the police and told them that these men must be stopped soon. Otherwise they will kill again." Hurkos declared that the killers, "although friends of Sharon," had become "frenzied, homicidal maniacs" through use of LSD. "The killers were not high on marijuana. They were high on LSD, which is the most unpredictable drug in the world."[29]

Truman Capote went on *The Tonight Show* with Johnny Carson and announced that only one person had killed the Cielo victims. "The killer was in the Tate house earlier," he declared, "and something happened to trigger a kind of instant paranoia. So this man leaves the house, and he goes back. He comes back, maybe an hour later, with a gun and a knife." Capote said he believed the murders were triggered by a real or imagined insult to the killer. "It's like these men you read about in the papers who are in a bar and having a drink and somebody insults them. They go out and get a gun and shoot everybody in the place. It was that kind of instant paranoia. By the time the killer came back, the house was quiet. Sharon Tate and the other girl had gone to bed. The house was rather dark and the two men, Sebring and Frykowski, were having a drink. The killer cuts the phone lines, then he rings the bell and walks inside with a gun in his hand. He forces the men to go and wake up the two girls and they are brought down into the room. Now the murderer ties Sharon Tate and Jay Sebring together with a rope he brought." According to Capote, Parent was the last to die.[30]

Any number of other alleged experts took to the airwaves, giving their versions of events at 10050 Cielo Drive. Louise Huebner, the "officially appointed witch" of Los Angeles County, told reporters: "In my opinion, they were having a sadistic-masochistic orgy. They were innocent victims of someone else's sadistic-masochistic whims. I believe they were having an orgy that got out of hand."[31] Leader of the Church of Satan Anton LaVey declared: "They were all the objects of a lust murder. The penetration knife wounds duplicate the sex act." And Jim Slaten, an astrologer, told the media: "My friend and I...said that there would be some kind of bloody murder in Hollywood because of the position of the planet Mars. Sharon Tate was a member of a devil-worship black magic cult, but she was thrown out because she was getting too involved with animal sacrifice and they were afraid that she was going to draw too much attention to them."[32]

The day after his thirty-sixth birthday, August 19, Roman held a news conference at the Beverly Wilshire Hotel. He was still visibly shaken, but his anger at what was being reported about his late wife drove him to address the "multitude of slanders" in the press. To Polanski, the real villans were the media, "who for a selfish reason write horrible things about my wife. All of you know how beautiful she was and very often I read and heard statements that she was one of the most, if not the most, beautiful woman of the world, but only a few of you know how good she was. She was vulnerable." He added that there had been no problems in their marriage. "The last few years I spent with her were the only time of true happiness in my life...." Referring to the rumors of the wild sexual escapades at 10050 Cielo Drive, he declared, "The house is now open, the police have released it, and you can now go and see the orgy place. You will see innumerable books on natural birth, which she was planning, and I was hurrying home because I had to go to some kind of school with her, I never understood what it was, but apparently I had to be present at this lesson or whatever it was, but I was going along with whatever she said." The bitterness in his voice barely concealed the tears he choked back throughout the interview.[33]

Although Roman found it an emotional ordeal, he had to deal with the aftermath of Sharon's death. She had no will, and her estate went into probate. According to the papers filed, Sharon, at the time of her death, had been worth $45,400; in the probate papers, this was broken down as $37,200 in cash; $5,700 in automobiles; and $500 in personal property—clothes and jewelry. Her annual income was estimated at $2,000 if she did no further film work.[34]

Roman, as next of kin, had to file claims in a Los Angeles court. William Tennant constantly telephoned him from 10050 Cielo Drive, as he and others went through the Polanskis' belongings there, but, no matter what the object was—from Sharon's clothing to their furniture—Roman would always sadly reply, "Give it away. I don't want it. I wish I had spent more. I wish there had been more dresses," before collapsing in sobs.[35] For probate purposes, Roman had to file a waiver with the Court. On 1 February, 1970, he signed a letter addressed to Sharon's father: "Dear Paul...I have decided not to accept any benefits derived from the estate of Sharon and I direct them....to your family." Paul Tate was duly appointed Executor of his daughter's estate.[36] Roman did not even want his own cars: he gave away the Silver Rolls Royce which had been his birthday present to Sharon, and, to his father-in-law Paul Tate, he sent his own red Ferrari. He wanted nothing to remind him of the past.

With Roman's cooperation and approval, but without the blessing of the LAPD investigators, several of his friends, including Victor Lownes, Peter Sellers and Warren Beatty, announced that they had formed a reward fund for information leading to the arrest and conviction of any of those responsible for Sharon's death:

Reward

$25,000

Roman Polanski and friends of the Polanski family offer to pay a $25,000 reward to the person or persons who furnish information leading to the arrest and conviction of the murderer or murderers of Sharon Tate, her unborn child, and the other four victims...[37]

Chapter 33
The Investigation

THE POLICE INVESTIGATION INTO SHARON'S MURDER WAS HEADED by Lieutenant Robert Helder, and was assisted by five sergeants: Michael McGann; J. Buckles; E. Henderson; D. Varney and Danny Galindo. These men had the unenviable task of sorting through the flotsam which had once formed the lives of the victims, trying to find both a motive and a suspect.

The most obvious suspect, caretaker William Garretson, was given a lie-detector test on the Sunday afternoon following the murders. He was shown to be answering truthfully as to any involvement in the crimes, and apparently he knew nothing as to their causes. Questioned at length about the events of that Friday night, Garretson declared:

> Well, I just—I just stayed inside the house and everything; and I was kind of scared that night. I don't know why, you know, I was kind of scared, and I stayed in the house and everything, and I started to write letters, you know....And I—I tried to call—I wanted to know what time it was because, you know, I had quite—you know, Christopher had barked that night and everything else, and I wanted to know what time it was. And just before, you know, it got daylight, I called the time and then, you know, I found out the phone was dead, and then I went to the room and got another phone, and I plugged it into the wall, and then, you know, to—and there was nothing, and so then I really got kind of worried then, you know, what happened and wasn't giving it too much thought. It wasn't daylight yet because, you know, it was still dark. But it was just beginning to get daylight. And I got kind of, you know, I really got kind of scared then, and then I stayed up until it did get daylight; and when it did get daylight, then I went to sleep and the next thing I knew I woke up and there was an officer pointing a gun at me.[1]

248

Garretson's story that he had remained in the guest house all night, writing letters, however, is open to doubt. In jail, Patricia Krenwinkle declared that, on Watson's instructions, she had gone to the guest house and found no one there. As they chased both Voyteck Frykowski and Abigail Folger across the front lawn of 10050 Cielo Drive, the killers could not have helped but noticed the lights burning in the little house just a hundred feet away. It was not hidden at all. Conversely, it is nearly impossible that Garretson, sitting in the living room with a stereo whose volume was set between 4 and 5—as he testified—would not have heard the screams and gunshots coming from the lawn just outside his windows.

"How could he have not heard that commotion," Doris Tate later questioned, "how could he have been in that house?"[2] The First Homicide Report, in fact, stated: "In the opinion of the investigating officers and by scientific research...it is highly unlikely that Garretson was not aware of the screams, gunshots and other turmoil that would result from a multiple homicide such as took place in his near proximity. These findings, however, did not absolutely preclude the fact that Garretson did not hear or see any of the events connected with the homicide."[3]

Contrary to this, Prosecutor Vincent Bugliosi writes: "Using a general level sound meter and a .22 caliber revolver, and duplicating as closely as possible the conditions that existed on the night of the murders, Wolfer [an LAPD acoustics expert] and an assistant proved (1) that if Garretson was inside the guest house as he claimed, he couldn't possibly have heard the shots that killed Steven Parent; and (2) that with the stereo on, with the volume at either 4 or 5, he couldn't have heard either screams or gunshots coming from in front of or inside the main residence."[4]

Under intense questioning, Garretson finally admitted that, at some point during the night, he had looked at the door to the guest house and saw that the handle had been turned.[5] He went no further, and does not seem to have been questioned on the point. In the intervening years, Garretson has altered his version of events that night a number of times. In 1997, he told author Bill Nelson: "I did hear a scream. I walked down the hall and into the closet. It had a window facing the pool area and there was a curtain over the window. All the windows in the house were closed that night and the doors were locked. I had lights on everywhere. The whole house was lit up. As I stood there at the window I said to myself, 'What the fuck is this? What the fuck is going on?' Something impressed me not to open those curtains. I don't know why, Then I walked down towards the living room because the three dogs were at the front door barking loudly. I stopped at the bathroom door. I thought, This doesn't make sense. I heard footsteps running the other way. Something impressed me again not to move. They could not see me because I was in the hall and there was no window right there. When I saw the front door I saw the handle. Someone had moved it and it was turned."6

In 1999, in his first television interview, he declared that he had not only heard the four shots which killed Steven Parent, but that he had looked out of the guest house window facing the main residence and saw Patricia Krenwinkel chasing Abigail Folger across the side lawn. According to Garretson, he ducked back down, out of sight, but listened as he heard screams followed by a woman saying, "Stop! Stop! I'm already dead!" He froze, and within a few minutes saw that the handle to the front door had been turned. He then heard footsteps running in the opposite direction, back toward the main house.7

"The problem with Garretson," says Prosecutor Vincent Bugliosi, "is that, as a lawyer, you have to look at what he first told the police. I spent a number of hours with him, questioning him at length about what he had seen and heard that night. At that time, he never deviated from the story that he was listening to the stereo. As a prosecutor, you always want to go with the first statement of a witness, which is usually the most accurate and unhindered by time and enhancement. It is possible that he heard something, but highly unlikely, and I would still think his 1969 version of events is most likely to be the truth."8

Garretson has said that he tried to use the telephone and found it dead. He later admitted to the police that he may have gone out onto the rear lawn, on the far side of the guesthouse. It is possible that he remained there for some time, fearing for his life. Perhaps he did try to leave when enough time had passed and the house was quiet, only to do so at the same time Manson and his friend were coming to or were in the main house. He may have thought the killers were still on the premises, and waited until morning, falling asleep, only to be woken by the barking of the dogs at the approach of the police. As Vincent Bugliosi points out, however, it is highly suspicious that Garretson has continued to alter and enhance his

version of events with the passage of time. In the end, we are left
with no definitive account of Garretson's experiences. Despite the
contradictory stories, Garretson apparently told the truth to the
police when he said he had no part in the murders, and the following day they released him from custody. He quickly returned to his
native Ohio.

The police had their suspicions, too, about Roman Polanski. In
the swirl of rumor and innuendo surrounding the murders, there
were whispered allegations of a love triangle between him, Sharon
and Jay, of jealousy and revenge, of a hired killer. In addition,
Polanski's reputation for the macabre did not serve him well in the
eyes of many of the police. Two days after the murders, on Monday,
11 August, he submitted to a lie detector test, conducted at Parker
Center by Lieutenant Earl Deemer.

Throughout the proceedings, Roman seemed curiously light-
hearted, a possible symptom of both his sedated state and also of
his denial of the tragedy which had taken place. He joked with
Deemer, "I will lie one or two times, but I will tell you when."[9]
According to one of his friends, Deemer had little taste for this. He
knew that Roman, within a day of learning of Sharon's death, had
begun a series of casual sexual relationships. This was typical behavior for Roman, an attempt to temporarily forget his troubles through
a meaningless sexual encounter, but Deemer, who knew nothing of
Polanski's deeply traumatic past, was horrified. He found Polanski's
lack of obvious grief disturbing.[10]

"Have you dated any airline stewardesses since Sharon's death?"
he finally asked the director.

"I haven't dated any," Roman replied. "I just...fucked them."[11]

The majority of the interview concerned the motive for the murders. "I think target could be myself, maybe just some kind of jeal-
ousies, or something," Roman volunteered. "Target couldn't be
Sharon directly....Could be Jay the target, could be Voyteck." Asked
about the possible drug connection, Roman admitted that Jay had
been involved with drugs on and off for years. He added that he had
recently discovered that Jay owed a large amount of money to his
dentist, and may have been in debt. "He might have been entangled
in some peculiar business....For this reason he might have gone into
some kind of dangerous area to make money."[12]

Roman passed the test, and the police had no indication that he
knew anything at all about the crimes. He added, however, as he

was leaving the interview: "The whole crime seems so illogical to me. If I'm looking for a motive, I'd look for something which doesn't fit your habitual standard, under which you are used to work as police. I would look for something much more far out...."[13]

Polanski later recalled that Lieutenant Robert Helder had "told me about this group of hippies living at that ranch with this guy they called Jesus Christ. Bob said they were suspected of being involved in the killing of some musician and writing a note on his body, and there was a possibility that these people had something to do with it. I said, 'Come on, Bob, you're prejudiced against hippies.' And I remember his words: 'You should suspect everyone. Don't dismiss it so easily.'"[14]

Polanski, too, had his suspicions. "He suspected a lot of his friends," recalled Richard Sylbert, one of the director's associates. "He had either fucked their girlfriends or their wives."[15] The police had discovered a pair of eyeglasses lying frame-up on the floor of the living room at 10050 Cielo Drive. As they had not belonged to any of the victims, the presumption was that they been dropped by one of the killers. Polanski actually borrowed the glasses from the police and crept round trying to find out if they fit anyone he knew. Although he could find no one who fit the prescription (and the glasses had apparently been left by Manson as a false clue), Roman had a lingering fear that his friend John Phillips might have had a hand in the murders as a way of getting revenge against Roman for the brief affair the director had with Michelle Phillips in London earlier that year. Roman actually went through Phillips' automobiles to check for bloodstains, and eventually confronted the singer, holding a knife to his throat and demanding to know if he had been involved in Sharon's death. Phillips told him no, and Roman dropped the weapon, believing his friend.[16]

The investigators into Sharon's murder faced a number of mistakes which, from the beginning, compromised the integrity of the case. First and foremost were the continual leaks made by various officials to members of the press, depriving the investigators of an important element in interrogating witnesses and potential suspects. The murder scene at 10050 Cielo Drive had been mishandled: blood on the front porch had been tracked about by officers, creating new prints; blood typing and sub-typing was not done on many of the pools and stains found in the house; the pieces of the gun grip discovered on the living room floor had been kicked beneath the desk by one of the police; and the potentially damning bloody fingerprint on the inside gate control button had been smeared when an exiting officer superimposed his own print over it on pushing the button.[17]

Both the Tate and LaBianca investigators submitted preliminary reports at the end of August, outlining the progress made and their theories as to why the crimes took place. The reports were never made public and they revealed little of importance. As to motive, the Tate detectives still held to what had been their first theory, that the slaughter at 10050 Cielo Drive was somehow connected to a drug burn, and involved Voyteck Frykowski as the primary target.

The police first began to formulate a possible drug-related motive for the murders on Cielo Drive a few days into the investigation, when they learned of Voyteck Frykowski's numerous drug connections in Los Angeles and beyond. Although the drug link would eventually be dismissed when the killers began to confess, it remained the strongest possibility in the investigators' opinions throughout the fall of 1969. "Roman didn't know what the hell was going on at his house," a friend told Thomas Thompson. "All he knew was that one of his beloved Poles was staying there. Sharon probably knew, she had to, but she was too nice or dumb to throw him out. If any creeps or weirdoes went up, it wasn't by Sharon's invitation."[18]

The investigators quickly learned of Voyteck's friendships with Pic Dawson, Ben Carruthers, Tom Harrigan and Billy Doyle, all four of whom were apparently known to LAPD drug investigators. The incident at the housewarming party at 10050 Cielo Drive, when Roman Polanski had ejected them, was related by William Tennant. The police also learned that Pic Dawson had threatened the lives of both Voyteck Frykowski and his friend Witold Kaczankowski, and there were rumors of the alleged drug burn at 10050 Cielo Drive and whipping of Billy Doyle a few days before the murders themselves. All of this was strong circumstantial evidence of a possible motive and possible killers.

Witold Kaczankowski volunteered further information to the police, and, at their request, set about translating the numerous and lengthy diaries which Voyteck had kept in Polish, suspecting that there might be a vital clue hidden in the pages. At one point, apparently, the artist told LAPD officials that he thought he knew who the killers were, and pointed the finger of guilt at the foursome who had been Frykowski's drug connections. The LAPD eventually tracked down Dawson, Harrigan, Carruthers and Doyle and interviewed each of them as to possible motives and whereabouts on the night of the murders.

The police still had their suspicions. While there was no doubt that Frykowski, Dawson, Harrigan, Carruthers and Doyle had been involved in the drug underworld of Los Angeles, there was nothing found to indicate a connection with the deaths on Cielo Drive. "We looked at the drug angle long and hard," says former Tate murder investigator Mike McGann. "In the end, there just wasn't anything there."[19]

Although nearly everyone in Los Angeles believed that there was a link between the Tate and LaBianca murders, the police continually pointed out the dissimiliarities, noting, for example, the drugs found at 10050 Cielo Drive. Many police officers who spoke to reporters declared that they thought the LaBiancas had been killed by a copy-cat murderer, a common enough occurrence. The Tate homicides fell under the jurisdiction of the Los Angeles Police Department, while the LaBianca inquiry was undertaken by members of the Los Angeles Sheriff's Office. Thus, there were two separate investigations, rarely sharing information. This lack of communication and insistence that the two murders were unrelated undoubtedly prolonged the eventual solution of the crimes.

At times, there were various advances. On 1 September, ten-year-old Steven Weiss discovered the .22 caliber Buntline used by Watson during the Tate murders, lying in some bushes in his rear yard. The yard sloped up a steep hillside to Beverly Glen Drive, from which Kasabian had apparently thrown the gun as the killers returned across the Hollywood hills to Spahn Ranch. The gun was taken by police, logged into evidence, and then ignored. As summer slipped into autumn, no one knew with any certainty if the killer or killers would strike again, and the fear, which had vanished briefly amidst the promising news reports of August, once again took hold of Los Angeles.

❖❖❖❖❖

Acting on a tip that an auto theft ring was operating on the premises, over seventy-five members of the Los Angeles Sheriff's Office raided Spahn Ranch on 16 August, just a week after the murders. Twenty-six people, including Manson, members of his Family, and various ranch hands, were arrested and incarcerated. The search warrant, however, signed and dated on 13 August, was good only for that particular day. As a result, Manson and his followers were released from jail.

Manson was convinced that ranch hand Donald Jerome "Shorty" Shea had had a hand in alerting the police to possible illegalities taking place at the Spahn Ranch. As soon as Manson returned to the Ranch, recalls Steve Grogan, members of the Family had "a growing hostility" toward Shea. "They didn't like him," Grogan says. "Charlie didn't like him because he was always drinking, and he thought he was a slob. He was always talking about messing with the girls that were there....It was kind of subtle at first, the way he voiced his dislike and disapproval of the man. He would bring it up on conversation at dinner when we all sat around and ate. Over a period it grew worse until we were raided by the police, where everything we had was taken, that we had bought legitimately. All our tools and cars and all the possessions that we had accumulated. And plus the children were taken, too. Everybody was arrested on the ranch. In fact the only person left was George Spahn, and he was blind....We spent three days in jail, and we were released. And we didn't get back none of our property. The pink slips were confiscated, along with our property, to four or five dune buggies that we couldn't get back from them; the children were put into foster homes. And what it really did is made everybody really upset at this guy, because I was led to believe that he was doing it to get us evicted off the ranch, to get us thrown off the ranch. And that was the only place we had to stay at the time. And it was through his actions that he caused us this trouble."[20]

On returning to Spahn Ranch, Manson, Watson, Bruce Davis and Steve Grogan killed Shea, believing that he was working to get them evicted from the property, and fearing that he knew too much about the Family's involvement in the murders. Family member Barbara Hoyt happened to be in the back bunkhouse, sitting near an open window which overlooked the dry creek bed below, when she heard Shea's agonized screams and cries for help. Terrified, she remained crouched out of sight.[21] After the murder, Grogan bragged that Shea had been decapitated, and his body cut into nine pieces and buried in separate graves. He did this, he later explained, on Manson's instructions, "to make the crime more threatening and use the psychological tool of fear among the other people that were there at the time."[22]

Shea's murder was an open secret among those at the ranch. Barbara Hoyt recalled how Manson laughed that "Shorty committed suicide with our help. We stabbed him, and kept cutting him. He got to now. It was hard to kill him, sure hard to kill him, when he got to now."23

Shortly after Shea's murder, most of the Family left Spahn for Death Valley. The situation was rapidly becoming too intense, and too many people knew too much. Often, this was a direct result of the inability of Manson and his various Family members to keep their mouths shut. Just before he took his followers out to the desert, Manson turned to ranch hand Juan Flynn, pushed a knife beneath his chin, and yelled, "You son-of-a-bitch, don't you know I'm the one who's doing all these killings?"24

In Death Valley, the Family spread themselves between two ranches, Myers and Barker. Those who remained continued to speak openly about their participation in the Tate-LaBianca murders. "Sadie [Susan Atkins] and Leslie [Van Houten] were bragging about how they killed them, and how much fun it had been," remembers former Family member Dianne Lake. "Krenwinkel was the only one who seemed bothered by what she had done." Watson took great delight in telling Lake that it had been "fun to tear up the Tate house."25

On 19 September, Ranger Richard Powell, on patrol through the Panamint Mountains of Inyo County, discovered the charred remains of a Michigan Articulated Skip Loader. Suspecting arson, he began a series of regular patrols round the area. Three days later, he happened across a red, four-wheel drive Toyota occupied by five ragged-looking hippies. The isolation of the area meant that Powell could do nothing but question the group and let them go; when he returned to Death Valley National Monument Headquarters, he ran the license plate and discovered that the Toyota was registered to Gail Beausoleil, wife of Bobby Beausoleil, then in jail in Los Angeles in connection with the murder of Gary Hinman.

Concerned that the individuals in the Toyota might have a connection with the burning of the earth moving machine, Powell began to coordinate an investigation. On 29 September, California Highway Patrol Officer James Pursell joined him on a patrol which encompassed Goler Wash and the surrounding area. At Barker Ranch, the pair discovered some scantily-clad young women, along with local miner Paul Crockett and Manson Family member Brooks Poston. Crockett, whose previous run-ins with Manson had infuriated him, promptly informed the officers that the group and its leader were staying in the desert, indulging in frequent sex orgies and indiscriminate illegal drug use.

It took just over a week to coordinate a proper raid. California Highway Patrol officers, joined by Inyo County District Attorney Frank Fowles and several other officials, divided into two groups and circled the area where Crockett had warned they would find Manson and his followers. Both Barker and Myers Ranches were raided, during the course of which the remaining members of the Family were arrested and booked into custody in Independece on suspicion of arson. Manson himself, discovered crouched inside a narrow cabinet beneath a sink, was arrested as well. Other members of the Family had fled: Linda Kasabian to the east coast, Charles Watson back to his native Texas, Mary Brunner to Wisconsin.

A few hours before the police raids, Kitty Lutesinger—Bobby Beausoleil's pregnant girlfriend—and Stephanie Schram, also pregnant, managed to sneak away and hitchhike out of Death Valley before a police car picked them up. Ominously, they began to talk of murders the Family had committed. Lutesinger told the police that Beausoleil had not been alone in killing Hinman, and named Atkins as one of the participants. Investigators came to Independence to interview her, and Atkins readily admitted her role.[26] She was transferred to Los Angeles and arraigned for the murder of Gary Hinman.

Atkins was incarcerated at the Sybil Brand Institute for Women in Los Angeles. While there, she bragged to two of her cellmates, Virginia Graham and Ronnie Howard, of her participation in the Tate murders as well. She took a perverse delight in their horrified reactions as she described stabbing Sharon Tate and watching the blood gush from her full stomach. The two women made some speedy calls, conveying details of Atkin's conversations to various authorities.

Unknown to the public, however, police were fast closing in on the solution to the crimes. By the middle of October, the Tate and LaBianca investigations, brought together by the officers working on the Hinman case, began to realize that the three crimes all seemed to be connected. Although the various investigations were plagued with unusual difficulties, it would be wrong to conclude that the case would not have been broken, as has often been claimed, had it not been for Atkins' prison confessions.

Tate murder investigator Mike McGann confirms that, prior to Atkins' confession, he and his fellow sergeants had begun to link the activities of the Manson Family to the three crimes.[27] Indeed, this is itself confirmed by Roman Polanski's own account of his interview with lead investigator Lieutenant Robert Helder, during which the officer mentioned a group of hippies living at a nearby ranch. Police first interviewed Atkins the last week of October, and became suspicious that members of the Manson Family might be involved in the Tate-LaBianca murders. Six members of the Manson Family were interviewed on 6 November and, on 13 November, Danny De Carlo told police that he had overheard conversations at Spahn Ranch which led him to believe that the Family was involved in the Tate and LaBianca murders. That same day, the Hinman, Tate and LaBianca investigatory teams were combined into one unit. Five days later, police first learned that Atkins, in jail, was openly bragging that she herself had stabbed Sharon Tate to death.

The horror and emotional uncertainty of the last several months for the victims' families finally came to an end on December 1, 1969. On that day at 2 PM, Los Angeles Police Chief Edward Davis walked into an auditorium at Parker Center in downtown Los Angeles and announced that police had finally solved the murders of Sharon Tate, Jay Sebring, Voyteck Frykowski, Abigail Folger, Steven Parent and Leno and Rosemary LaBianca. The suspects, all members of a group of hippies known collectively as the Manson Family after their criminal leader Charles Manson, were either under arrest or awaiting indictment or extradition for the murders.

A few days later, on Friday, 5 December, 1969, Susan Atkins sat before a Los Angeles County Grand Jury and gave a lengthy account of the murders. She had been promised that, in return for her truthful testimony, the state would not seek the death penalty against her, nor would they use any of her testimony against either her or her co-defendants. Atkins loved an audience, and she left out no brutal detail during her multi-hour interview. It was enough for the Grand Jury. On December 8, they handed down indictments against Manson, Watson, Atkins, Krenwinkel and Kasabian, for seven counts of murder and one count of conspiracy to commit murder. It was the beginning of the end for the Manson Family.

Chapter 34
The Trials

V INCENT BUGLIOSI, THE DEPUTY DISTRICT ATTORNEY ASSIGNED TO
co-prosecute the Tate-LaBianca defendants along with Aaron
Stovitz, was only thirty-five when he received this most
important of cases.

Over the next two years, he was to demonstrate again and again
the wisdom of the choice. Building upon the work of the LAPD, he
sought out information with a passion and devoted long hours trying to tie down a motive for the crimes. More importantly, he managed to convey the incredible sense of what had taken place, and
also to convince a jury of the guilt of not only those who had killed
for Manson but of the complicity of Charles Manson himself.

"It was very difficult," Bugliosi recalls, "because in no sense was
this an ordinary murder case. I had to convince the jury that even
though Manson hadn't been present when Sharon Tate was killed,
the crime had his fingerprints all over it."[1]

Throughout the course of the trial, Bugliosi was assisted by a
team of equally dedicated and talented men. Aaron Stovitz, who was
to have argued the case with Bugliosi, left mid-way through the trial.
Replacing Stovitz was a pair of young, driven Deputy District
Attorneys, Donald Musich and Stephen Kay. It would be Stephen
Kay who continued his deep association with the killers and the victims' families long after his duty ceased.

Finding a jury pool which had not been unduly exposed to the
massive press coverage surrounding the crimes proved to be an
ordeal. On 14 July, 1970, however, seven men and five women were
sworn. They included a retired sheriff's deputy; a state employee; a
former drama critic; an electrician; and a telephone repairman. The
majority were over the age of forty, and married. As their foreman,

they selected Herman C. Tubick, who held the ironic position of funeral director in Whittier, California. For the duration of the trial, they were sequestered at the Ambassador Hotel in Los Angeles.

On Friday July 24, 1970—two weeks short of the first anniversary of Sharon's death—the Tate-LaBianca trial opened in Department 104 in the Hall of Justice in downtown Los Angeles. Presiding over the trial was Judge William Older. Appointed to the bench by Ronald Reagan, Older had a distinguished military record, having been a member of the Flying Tigers and a fighter pilot in World War II.[2]

Thirty-eight days of jury selection and pre-trial motions had already taken place. Charles Manson had desperately tried to convince the court that he should be allowed to represent himself in *propria persona*, but Judge Older would not allow this potential miscarriage of justice. Instead, Manson was represented by Irving Kanarek. "If I can't defend myself," Manson told Judge Older in chambers, "I want whoever gives you the worst time. He gives you the worst time. I want him."[3]

Kanarek was renowned for his obfuscation, lethargy and obstruction in court. The Prosecution was stunned; Bugliosi and Stovitz pleaded with their office to intervene. Eventually, Los Angeles District Attorney Evelle Younger appealed to the California State Supreme Court to order Judge Older to hold a competency hearing for Kanarek. The motion was dismissed, but is clearly indicative of the strong feeling roused by Kanarek's presence in the court.[4]

Susan Atkins was represented by Daye Shinn; Patricia Krenwinkel by Paul Fitzgerald; and Leslie Van Houten first by Ronald Hughes and later by Maxwell Keith. Charles "Tex" Watson, still fighting extradition in Texas, would be tried at a later date.

On the first day of the trial, Manson walked into the court room with an X carved into his forehead. His followers who remained free passed around a statement, in which Manson declared:

> "I am not allowed to be a man in your society. I am considered inadequate and incompetent [sic] to speak or defend myself in your court. You have created the monster. I am not of you, from you, nor do I condone your unjust attitude toward things, animals and people that you won't try to understand. I haved [sic] Xed myself from your world. I stand in the opposite to what you do and what you have done in the past. You have never given me the constitution you speak of. The words you have used to

trick the people are not mine. I do not accept what you call justice. The lie you live in is falling and I am not a part of it. You use the word God to make money....I know what I have done. Your courtroom is man's game. Love is my judge.....No man or lawyer is speaking for me. I speak for myself. I am not allowed to speak with words so I have spoken with the mark I will be wearing on my forehead."[5]

In a grey business suit, Vincent Bugliosi rose and addressed the twelve jurors. "What kind of diabolical, satanic mind would contemplate or conceive of these mass murders?" he asked the jury. "What kind of mind would want to have seven human beings brutally murdered? We expect the evidence at this trial to answer that question and show that defendant Charles Manson owned that diabolical mind....The evidence at this trial will show defendant Manson to be a vagrant wanderer, a frustrated singer and guitarist, a pseudophilosopher, but most of all, the evidence will show him to be a killer who cleverly masqueraded behind the common image of a hippy, that of being peace loving. The evidence will show Manson to be a megalomaniac who coupled his insatiable thirst for power with an intense obsession for violent death."[6]

Bugliosi went on to admit, "There was more than one motive" for the crimes, but he concentrated his energies on trying to explain the intricacies of the Helter Skelter theory. "Besides the motives of Manson's passion for violent death and his extreme anti-establishment state of mind, the evidence at this trial will show that there was further motive which was almost as bizarre as the murders themselves. Very briefly, the evidence will show Manson's fanatical obsession with Helter Skelter, a term he got from the English musical recording group, The Beatles. Manson was an avid follower of The Beatles and believed that they were speaking to him through the lyrics of their songs. In fact, Manson told his followers that he found complete support for his philosophies in the words sung by The Beatles in their songs. To Manson, Helter Skelter, the title of one of The Beatles' songs, meant the black man rising up against the white establishment and murdering the entire white race, that is, with the exception of Manson and his chosen followers, who intended to escape from Helter Skelter by going to the desert and living in the Bottomless Pit, a place Manson derived from Revelation 9, the last book of the New Testament from which Manson told others he found further support for his philosophies. The evidence will show that although Manson hated black people, he also hated the white establishment, whom he called 'Pigs.' The evidence will show that one of Manson's principal motives for the Tate-LaBianca murders was to ignite Helter Skelter, in other words, start the black-white revolution by making it look like the black people had murdered the five Tate victims and Mr. and Mrs. LaBianca, thereby causing the white community to turn against the black man and ultimately lead to a civil war between blacks and whites, a war Manson foresaw the black man winning. Manson envisioned that black people, once they destroyed the white race and assumed the reins of power, would be unable to handle the reins because of inexperience and would have to turn over the reins to those white people who had escaped from Helter Skelter, that is, turn over the reins to Manson and his followers." He ended by warning that, although at times the trial would almost certainly prove to be both a physical and emotional ordeal, he trusted that the jurors would have no problem finding the defendants guilty.[7] Following the defense opening statements, Bugliosi called the first witness to the stand: Lieutenant-Colonel Paul Tate.

Since his daughter's murder, Paul Tate had left his career in military intelligence and devoted himself to a personal search for her killers. He let his army crew cut grow long, grew a beard and submerged himself in the anti-establishment world from which he thought his daughter's killers had come. He had regularly spent long nights wandering through the Haight-Ashbury District and along the Sunset Strip in Los Angeles in search of clues.

Tate's presence at the trial greatly worried not only members of the Manson Family and the defendants but courtroom security as well. He was, after all, a trained military man, capable, if he wished, of exacting his own vengeance against those accused of Sharon's death. Prior to being allowed in the courtroom, Paul Tate was subjected to a thorough body search in the event that he had come to the Hall of Justice armed with more than just his testimony.

Manson himself later said: "They whisper so I can hear it, 'Sharon Tate's father is in court!' And then they go over and shake him down to see if he has a gun, and they're just putting that idea into his head. He has a nice face. I saw him the first day in court. He doesn't want to kill me. They're putting that into his head. You know, they say things like, 'We wouldn't want you to shoot the defendant.' And every day I see him in court, his face gets a little harder, and one day he's gonna do it."[8]

Despite the emotional build-up, Paul Tate's testimony was limited to identifying pictures of his daughter, Jay Sebring, Abigail Folger and Voyteck Frykowski, and confirming that the last time he had seen Sharon alive was when he and his wife had visited 10050 Cielo Drive to watch the moonlanding with their daughter on 20 July. He occasionally cast long, emotionless glances at Manson and the other defendants, but they rarely met his gaze. When he left the witness stand, he did not leave the courtroom, but rather took up a seat in the spectators' section. He would sit through long portions of the trial off and on for the next several months. On one occasion, while walking through the hallway outside of the courtroom, he was approached by Family member Sandy Good. "I don't know how to tell you this," she said. "I'm sorry, but we're not guilty." Tate ignored her and quickly escaped into a telephone booth.[9]

Wilfred Parent immediately followed Sharon's father to the witness stand. "We went to court the first day," remembers Janet Parent, "when my dad had to testify. When we came off the elevator, the reporters were there. They kept sticking a microphone in my mom's face, and then my dad's face, shouting questions at them pushing at us. Finally, my dad hauled off and hit one of the reporters who kept after my mom."[10]

Seeing the fracas, Bugliosi slipped through the press mob and hustled the Parents into a small room just off the courtroom. "In the beginning," Janet Parent recalls, "we didn't know anything about Steve's death. We didn't know how fast he died, how many times he was shot. One paper said one thing, another wrote something else. I remember that once we were alone in that room, my mom turned to Bugliosi in tears and asked, 'Can you tell me if my son suffered?' He told us no, that it had had all been over in a few seconds."[11]

On the witness stand, Wilfred Parent was asked to identify a photograph of his son. As soon as he picked it up, Parent broke into sobs. He continued to cry as he identified photographs of the family car, telling the court that he had given Steven permission to drive it that fateful Friday night. "I remember sitting in the courtroom," Janet Parent says, "and looking at Manson and the others. Mostly I remember Susan Atkins, because she just stared at us with this cagey smirk."[12]

The highlight of the trial came early, with the testimony of former Manson Family member Linda Kasabian. The only indicted defendant who had not actively participated in the actual murders,

Kasabian had the good fortune of obtaining a lawyer who managed to cut her an extraordinary deal: if she testified truthfully at the trial, the District Attorney's Office would petition the Court for immunity. Although Kasabian began her testimony on 27 July, and the Grant of Immunity was not signed until 10 August, her lawyer had applied for the petition before his client took the stand. There was little doubt, therefore, that Kasabian would testify and, at the end, win her complete freedom.

The prosecution deal did not satisfy everyone. If Kasabian had not actually murdered anyone, she had also not acted to prevent either set of murders. Following the shooting of Steven Parent, she was left alone by the other killers; although undoubtedly in a state of shock, she had ample opportunity to summon help. She later tried to explain that she had feared for the safety of Tanya, her young daughter who was back at Spahn Ranch. Such concerns, however, did not prevent Kasabian from abandoning Tanya to the very Family members she herself had witnessed engaged in murder when she fled California a few weeks after the crimes. It is arguable that, had Kasabian acted, the lives of Sharon and the others at 10050 Cielo drive might have been spared; certainly the LaBiancas would never have fallen victim to the murderous spree of the second night. "That she was totally cleared in return for her testimony," writes Dr. Clara Livsey, "gives one a glimpse of how doubtful the prosecutors must have been of otherwise getting a conviction for the Defendants Manson, Watson, Atkins, Krenwinkel, and Van Houten."[13]

"As a prosecutor," Bugliosi explains, "I had to do everything within my power to get a conviction against those defendants who were most culpable. Kasabian hadn't actually killed anyone, and was cut from a different cloth than the rest of Manson and his followers. It's difficult in retrospect to say if we could have won without her testimony, but at the time, I wanted to make sure that those jurors heard her voice as she described the Tate murders. It was certainly the most powerful evidence we had at the trial."[14]

Kasabian took stand on Monday, 27 July. A line had formed for curious spectators eager to hear her first-hand account of the murders. As soon as Kasabian raised her right hand to swear her oath, Kanarek was on his feet. "Object, Your Honor, on the grounds this witness is not competent and she is insane!"

"Wait a minute, Your Honor!" Bugliosi shouted, while jumping to his feet. "Move to strike that and I ask the court to find him in contempt of court for gross misconduct. This is unbelievable on his part."[15]

Fitzgerald argued on behalf of the Defense "that Linda Kasabian, due to prolonged extensive illegal use of LSD is a person of unsound mind, is mentally ill, is insane, is unable to differentiate between truth and falsity, right or wrong, good or bad, fantasy and reality, and is incapable of expressing herself concerning the matter so as to be understood."[16]

After much discussion, Judge Older over-ruled Kanarek's objection, and allowed Kasabian to testify. Those who had crowded into the courtroom to hear the graphic details of the murders were not disappointed. Over the next few days, Kasabian told all that she knew and had seen. Paul Tate sat silently as she recalled hearing screams and moans coming from the house. "There were no words," she sobbed, "it was beyond words, it was just screams."[17] She described watching as Watson and Atkins chased Voyteck Frykowski across the lawn; and saw Krenwinkel chasing Abigail Folger as the heiress ran for her life toward the freedom on the other side of the split-rail fence.

At many points during her testimony, Kasabian broke into sobs, sometimes continuing barely above a whisper. She was not alone. Several spectators in the courtroom were also crying by the time she had finished. It was a devastating moment for the defense. "Her answers were sincere," recalled Juror William Zamora, "and to the point. She left no trace of doubt in our minds that she was telling the truth."[18] From that moment on, no matter how many witnesses they called or how many objections were raised, the trial was lost. This fact was not lost on the defendants, nor on the remainder of the Family. Manson was seen to draw a finger slowly across his throat as Linda testified, an apparent threat, while Sandy Good was more explicit, running up to Linda in the hallways and screaming, "You'll kill us all! You'll kill us all!"

A number of other witnesses testified, including a very scared Terry Melcher, who still believed that he had been the target of the murders and feared for his life. The press attention was constant, and updates on the latest developments were common features on all three of the network nightly news broadcasts. Entire front pages of the day's newspapers were filled with headlines screaming the latest sensationalistic revelation.

Much of the trial was devoted to the presentation of the "Helter

Skelter" motive. Although certain Family members would dismiss the entire idea as the work of prosecutor Vincent Bugliosi, the weight of the evidence demonstrates that Manson and his followers believed at least elements of the idea.

While certain members of the Family may have believed Manson's frequent talk of a "bottomless pit," it is unlikely that such delusions fueled the murders. Here, it is important to separate Manson's fanciful lectures on The Beatles and Biblical prophecy from the very real belief that a race war was likely to erupt. Belief in the latter was visibly and repeatedly demonstrated by the Manson Family: they spent hours converting dune buggies into assault vehicles for the coming conflict; purchased surveyors' maps of Death Valley in order to plot their escape routes; and practiced both defending themselves and killing others. "Helter Skelter," Manson's envisioned race war, was a constant companion in the lives of his Family members. But the less fantastic elements of revenge and an attempt to reassert control over his crumbling Family seem to have had at least an equal part in motivating the crimes. It speaks volumes of Bugliosi's brilliance that he managed to convince the trial jury that the "Helter Skelter" motive was the correct one.

If the murders of Sharon and the others had stirred up a storm of rumor and controversy, it was nothing compared to the actual, incredible facts of the Manson Family. The apparent utter normalcy of the killers prior to their meeting Manson—high school athletes, choir girls, Sunday school teachers—sent waves of fear through an entire generation of parents already agonizing over the rebellious and seemingly reckless spirit of the youth in America. That these defendants all possessed arrest records, had used illegal drugs and been sexually promiscuous prior to meeting Manson was forgotten. Thus, more than anything else, the trial came to symbolize the violent nature of the hidden 1960s, and the dreadful uncertainty that somewhere out there, lost among the hippies who still wandered the streets, might be more Mansons, waiting to claim the spotlight of murder.

"This will be remembered," declared Defense Attorney Paul Fitzgerald, "as the first of the acid murders; our changing social structure is making more people turn on and we're on the brink of a whole new concept of violence...violence perpetrated against society by people who have reached a different plateau of reality through LSD."[19] The most famous of all commentators on the proceedings was undoubtedly the President himself. During a visit to

California, Richard Nixon, in remarks to a group of reporters, referred to Manson. "As we look at the situation today," the President said, "I think the main concerns that I have are the attitudes which are created among many of our young people in which they tend to glorify and make heroes out of those who engage in criminal activities. I noted, for example, the coverage of the Charles Manson case when I was in Los Angeles. Here is a man who is guilty, directly or indirectly, of eight murders without reason, a man who as far as the public is concerned appeared to be rather a glamorous man."[20]

The comments made headlines across the nation the next day, and the President was roundly criticized for offering this opinion which seemed to ignore the fact that the defendants had not yet been proven guilty. Manson somehow got hold of a copy of the *Los Angeles Times* whose headline declared the Nixon verdict and flashed it to the jury before being dragged from the courtroom. It nearly caused a mistrial, and each juror had to be individually polled to ensure that it would not influence his or her decision.

At times, it all seemed to be a game. Paul Fitzgerald commented: "The girls manifest no sense of guilt in prison. They laugh and sing and are generally happy; they drive the matrons crazy. People up on murder charges, especially if they have seven counts like Patricia [Krenwinkel] has, tend to be morose and filled with remorse or foreboding. These girls are not like that. It's not a put-on. They genuinely do not feel a sense of guilt."[21]

Manson himself created a few headlines during the course of the trial. At one point, after much protesting that he was not being allowed to make any statements in his defense, Judge Older let him speak to the court at length, albeit with the jurors removed from the scene. As he spoke, he turned from a soft-spoken, humble man to an angry, black-eyed criminal, denouncing society and the establishment:

> I never went to school, so I never growed up in the respect to learn to read and write too good, so I have stayed in jail and I have stayed stupid, and I have stayed a child....I have nothing against none of you. I can't judge any of you. But I think it is high time that you all started looking at yourselves, and judging the lie that you live in....Helter Skelter is a nightclub. Helter Skelter means confusion. Literally. It doesn't mean any war with anyone. It doesn't mean that those people are going to kill other people. It only means what it means. Helter Skelter is confusion.

Confusion is coming down fast. If you don't see the confusion coming down fast around you, you can call it what you wish. It is not my conspiracy. It is not my music. I hear what it relates. It says, "Rise!" It says, "Kill!" Why blame it on me? I didn't write the music. I am not the person who projected it into your social consciousness....To be honest with you, I don't ever recall saying, "Get a knife and change of clothes and go do what Tex said." I am not saying that I didn't say it, but if I said it, at that time, I may have thought it was a good idea. Whether I said it in jest and whether I said it in joking, I can't recall and reach back into my memory. I could say either way. I could say, "Oh, I was just joking." Or I could say I was curious....These children that come at you with knives, they are your own children. You taught them. I didn't teach them. These children, everything they have done, they have done for love of their brother....I have killed no one and I have ordered no one to be killed. I don't place myself in the seat of judgment. I may have implied on several occasions that I may have been Jesus Christ, but I haven't decided yet who I am or what I am. I was given a name and a number and I was put in a cell, and I have lived in a cell with a name and a number....You see, you can send me to a penitentiary; it's not a big thing. I've been there all my life anyway. What about your children, just a few, there is many, many more coming in the same direction; they are running in the streets and they are coming right at you!"[22]

Eventually the frequent disruptions became too much for the court to bear. Manson, although he was allowed to make his long, rambling statement, continually stood up in the middle of a witness's testimony and began to question the bench. Once, when he did this, Judge Older angrily told him, "If you don't stop, I will have to have you removed."

"I will have to have you removed if you don't stop!" Manson shot back. "I have a little system of my own!"

When Older ignored him and turned back to the prosecuting attorney, Manson shouted, "Do you think I'm kidding?"

"Mr. Manson," Older finally declared, "I'm going to have you removed if you don't stop it immediately."

In answer to this, Manson simply jumped up, across the defense table, a sharpened pencil in one of his raised hands, and ran toward the bench. A bailiff tackled him to the floor and, with the assistance of some other wardens, handcuffed him and led him from the court

as a shaken Older looked on. As Manson was led from the courtroom, he snarled, "In the name of Christian justice, someone should
cut off your head!"[23] Eventually, the behavior of both Manson and
the female defendants was such that Older barred them from the
courtroom during the remainder of the guilt phase of the trial.

Finally, after nearly four months of testimony, Vincent Bugliosi
drew the State's case to a close on November 16, 1970, and rested
the prosecution. The following day was day one-hundred fifty-eight
in the trial. At first, as the court convened that day, the collective
defense argued that all charges against their clients be dropped.
When Older refused this request, Paul Fitzgerald, speaking on behalf
of the other attorneys, rose and said simply, "The defense rests."[24]

The decision to offer no defense was not only a recognition of
the lack of a cohesive strategy but also an acknowledgment that
everyone thought the case was lost. Older called all the attorneys
into his chambers to discuss the move, but the defense, other than
making a few selected statements to the jury, would not be pushed.
Older realized the potential ground being laid for an appeal based
on inadequate defense, and did all in his power to thwart the measure. In the end, however, no defense strategy was formed, and
there was nothing left to do but sum up the case.

Bugliosi began his summation on January 13, 1971. It was a
moment of intense, effective theatre. "Charles Manson is not a defendant in this trial," he observed, "because he is some long-haired
vagabond who made love to young girls and was a virulent dis-
senter. He is on trial because he is a vicious, diabolical murderer
who gave the order that caused seven human beings to end up in
the cold earth. That is why he is on trial." After running through the
lengthy list of evidence and witnesses to support his case, he began
to wind up his case in dramatic fashion:

> On the hot summer night of August 8, 1969, Charles Manson, the
> Mephistophelean guru who raped and bastardized the minds of
> all those who gave themselves so totally to him, sent out from the
> fires of hell at Spahn Ranch three heartless, bloodthirsty robots
> and—unfortunately for him—one human being, the little hippie
> girl Linda Kasabian. The photographs of the victims show how
> very well Watson, Atkins, and Krenwinkel carried out their mas-
> ter Charles Manson's mission of murder....What resulted was per-
> haps the most inhuman, nightmarish, horror-filled hour of savage
> murder and human slaughter in the recorded annals of crime. As

the helpless victims begged and screamed out into the night for their lives, their lives, their lifeblood gushed out of their bodies, forming rivers of gore. If they could have, I am sure Watson, Atkins and Krenwinkel would gladly have swum in that river of blood, and with orgasmic ecstasy on their faces. Susan Atkins, the vampira, actually tasted Sharon Tate's blood....The very next night, Leslie Van Houten joined the group of murderers, and it was poor Leno and Rosemary LaBianca who were brutally butchered to death to satisfy Charles Manson's homicidal madness....Ladies and gentlemen of the jury...Sharon Tate Polanski...Abigail Folger...Voyteck Frykowski...Jay Sebring...Steven Parent...Leno LaBianca...and Rosemary LaBianca...are not here with us now in this courtroom, but from their graves they cry out for justice! Justice can only be served by coming back to this courtroom with a verdict of guilty.[25]

Monday, January 25, 1971 was the day after what would have been Sharon's twenty-eighth birthday and ironically her parents 29th wedding anniversary. On this day, the courtroom was packed, the press on the edges of their seats, the defendants looking uninterested, the spectators silent. Word had come back that the jury had reached their verdicts. As the jurors filed into the room and took their seats, there was little doubt as to what their decision would be. Nevertheless, when the foreman handed the verdicts to the clerk to read, the sense of anticipation was real.

The first charge was the death of Abigail Folger; Sharon and the other victims were listed alphabetically. Each of the defendants was also listed in the different charges of murder. The clerk grimly announced, "We, the jury in the above suited action find the defendant, Charles Manson, guilty of the crime of murder, in violation of the penal code 187, a felony, and we further find it to be murder in the first degree."[26]

On and on the list went, Manson guilty of the deaths of all seven victims in the first degree and of conspiracy to commit murder; Susan Atkins, guilty of seven counts of murder and one count of conspiracy to commit murder; Patricia Krenwinkel, guilty of seven counts of murder and one count of conspiracy to commit murder; and Leslie Van Houten, guilty of two counts of murder and one count of conspiracy to commit murder. The defendants were led from the courtroom, Manson shouting at the top of his lungs at Older, "You're all guilty! We weren't allowed to put on a defense, old man! And you won't forget it for a long time!"[27]

The sense of relief was palpable. For over seventeen months, Paul and Doris Tate had awaited justice for the murder of their daughter and unborn grandson. Amidst the media celebration of Manson and his murderous band of followers, Sharon and the other victims had been all but forgotten. The guilty verdicts, recalled Doris Tate, were "handed down on our [wedding] anniversary like a gift."[28] "For the first time," she later said, "I slept in peace that night."[29]

The first phase of the trials was over. The defendants' guilt had been proven. Now came the penalty phase, with Bugliosi seeking the death penalty in all cases. This was a relatively short process compared to the actual prosecution of the case. The girls took the stand, and each testified that she felt no remorse or guilt for the murders. It did not take the jury long to reach a decision. On Monday, March 29, they announced that the penalty for all defendants had been set at death. Manson and the female defendants, with shaved heads and large Xs carved into their foreheads, responded by shouting at Judge Older and the jury. "Better lock your doors and watch your own kids!" Atkins warned before being led from the court.[30]

"I hope this verdict will be a lesson to the young people of this country that you just can't go into a person's house and butcher them up," said Juror Marie Mesmer. Seventy-four-year-old retired deputy sheriff Juror Alva Dawson told reporters: "I just hope this will teach all these other young people not to make trouble, not to go out and kill people." Jury Foreman Herman C. Tubick added that the death sentences were "retribution" for the crimes, and that he would be disappointed if they were not carried out.[31]

Even this was not the end. Charles "Tex" Watson had resisted extradition so that he could stand trial separately. He sat in jail in the Collin County Sheriff's Office in Texas, provided with a TV, radio, record player, a cooler, and food provided by his mother who also did his laundry.[32] He was finally extradited to California in September, 1970, too late to be included with the other defendent in their trial. Instead, Watson stood trial alone.

At first, it seemed that Watson's defense would portray him as a clean-cut, all-American boy, who had been influenced through drugs and Charles Manson to commit unspeakable crimes which never would have come about otherwise. When it appeared that this would not work, Watson suddenly regressed, perhaps in genuine shock, perhaps in an effort to simulate insanity. His weight dropped dramatically and at one point he had to be fed by tubes inserted through his nose. "These physical symptoms Tex experienced were, in part, a reaction to the stress he was experiencing," writes psychiatrist Ronald Markman, who examined Watson at the court's order. "I suggested that he was also exaggerating in order to develop a psychiatric defense."[33]

Watson was examined by nearly a dozen psychiatrists. "When asked what should be done with him," noted Dr. John M. Suarez, "he at first considered that he should be killed for what he has done, but then alluded to the fact that the killings had really been done not by himself. In other words, he says that his body had carried out the deeds but that he had not been a person at that time."[34] In discussing the actual crimes with Dr. Ira Frank, he declared: "I had no feelings then or now. It doesn't affect me, although I can see how others can feel it is wrong."[35]

Watson was eventually confined at the Atascadero State Hospital for psychiatric observation, where, in the opinion of those in charge, he tried to "feign amnesia."[36] He conveniently claimed to have forgotten most of the details of the murder nights and insisted that the girls had been in charge. "He indicates that the girls gave him a wire cutter and told him to cut all the telephone wires," noted Dr. Vernon Bohr. "He attempted to climb up the fence but because of intoxication, he fell backwards. However, they aided him in pushing him up onto the fence. At that time a car was coming out. One of the girls said, 'Get it'....He states: 'When the girls said to do something, I would do it. They would call me from one person to another. I would start stabbing. I didn't have any control.'"[37]

"He was very sensitive to discussion of the act of killing," writes Dr. Markman, "and became angry when pushed to talk about it. 'I could kill you easily,' he once retorted to an examiner."[38] Another report, by Dr. Keith Ditman, declared that, while he spoke of his crimes, "This is not to say he did not evade somewhat, talking of intimate personal details, and of attempting to avoid accepting responsibility and blame for the crimes in question. I felt he consciously and unconsciously attempted to present himself as a 'good boy,' who had fallen into evil hands, been duped and taken advantage of by Manson."[39]

On 10 May, 1971, Watson pled not guilty by reason of insanity before Superior Court Judge Adolph Alexander. His trial began on 2 August, 1971, two years to the week of Sharon's murder. Vincent Bugliosi and Stephen Kay again acted as prosecutors. Watson's trial was largely a rehash of the Manson proceedings: Sharon's father was again called as one of the first witnesses. Kasabian again appeared to give her description of the two fatal nights. Paul Tate and Steven Parent's father Wilfred were the first witnesses. The most notable difference, however, was that, unlike Manson and the female defendants, Watson took the stand in his own defense.

On the stand, Watson clung to his defense that he had been a mindless zombie, under Manson's total control. "I had no feelings," he told one psychiatrist. "I did exactly what I was told. No more than I was told."[40] Bugliosi carefully destroyed this defense, showing that Watson had been perfectly willing to commit the killings; that he had been involved with drugs prior to meeting Manson; and that he had left the Family after the murders of his own accord, not on Manson's instructions. Although Watson tried to later claim that he had been suffering from paranoid schizophrenia at the time, on the stand, he had enough self-possession to lie about his participation in the crimes, and hide certain details which would further implicate his guilt.[41]

On 12 October, 1971, Watson was found guilty on seven counts of murder and one count of conspiracy to commit murder. The question of his sanity was addressed by Dr. Joel Fort, who reported: "I conclude he was sane at the time of the offenses. In knowing what he was doing and understanding that society considers it wrong to kill. Although his specific and general behavior and life style are not such that they would be considered normal, mature, or healthy in terms of psychiatric standards, Watson probably had no mental illness at the time of the crimes that would prevent him from forming a specific intent to perform murder. He demonstrated the mental capacity to deliberate, to premeditate, to hyper-malice and to meaningfully reflect upon the gravity of his actions to the extent that he knew what the result would be for his victims, and what it could be for himself if caught. The killings showed malice aforethought in that the defendant showed an intention to kill his victims and this intention preceded the act of killing."[42] Jurors took only two-and-a-half hours to weigh the psychological evidence and find Watson sane. Two days later, on 21 October, 1971, he was sentenced to death.

The trials were over; justice had been served. The judgments brought an end to the reign of the notorious Manson Family, as well as a sense of grim satisfaction. The death penalty verdicts promised closure. Sharon's father Paul told a reporter after they had been delivered: "That's what we wanted. That's what we expected. But there's no jubilation in something like this, no sense of satisfaction. It's more a feeling that justice has been done. Naturally I wanted the death penalty. They took my daughter and my grandchild."[43]

Chapter 35
The End of the Manson Family

T HE ULTIMATE FATES OF THE MANSON FAMILY HAVE YET TO BE completely played out. Although Manson, Watson, Atkins, Krenwinkel, Van Houten, Beausoleil and Davis were all found guilty and condemned to death, the United States Supreme Court voted in February 1972 to abolish capital punishment. The convicted killers were thus spared the gas chamber.

Immediately after the Tate-LaBianca verdicts, Manson, Bruce Davis and Steve Grogan were tried for the murder of ranch hand Donald Jerome "Shorty" Shea. All three were found guilty of first degree murder, and sentenced to death. After reviewing his psychiatric evaluations, however, the presiding judge reduced Grogan's sentence owing to his admittedly diminished mental capacity. Charles "Tex" Watson, who had also assisted in Shea's murder, was never tried for his participation.

During the Shea trial, a group of Manson's followers robbed a gun store in Hawthorne, planning to steal a cache of weapons with which to both rescue their leader and kidnap the judge. The robbery attempt ended in a vicious gun battle with the police, who arrested several former Family members, including Catherine Share and Mary Brunner. The latter, having participated in the murder of Gary Hinman, had been granted immunity in exchange for her testimony against Manson, Atkins, Davis and Beausoleil in their trial on that charge, and had, until this time, been free to wander the streets.

The intricacies of the Manson Family's crimes after the murders in the summer of 1969 would fill many pages. It is alleged that several of the Family members murdered defense attorney Ronald Hughes. Numerous other murders have taken place over the last few decades, most in the years surrounding the Tate-LaBianca trials, which have been either attributed to the Family or suspected of having been carried out by its surviving members. Certainly, several of the Family members have at times bragged of up to thirty-five murders; it is impossible to either prove or disprove such statements, and the claim remains an open—if rather unsettling—possibility.

Bobby Beausoleil, convicted of the murder of musician Gary Hinman, remains incarcerated, most recently transferred to a penitentiary at Salem, Oregon. In prison, he has pursued his musical interests and developed a new prototype combination guitar/synthesizer. Bruce Davis, convicted in the murder of Donald Jerome Shea, converted to Christianity, and works in the prison ministry program at the California Men's Colony at San Luis Obispo, where he is incarcerated.

Steve Grogan, who had been found guilty in the murder of Donald Jerome Shea, is the only member of the Manson Family convicted of murder to be set free. In prison, Grogan maintained a good disciplinary record, married and fathered a child. In 1977, worried that he might never be released, Grogan contacted the authorities and offered to show them where he had buried Shea's body. Shea's remains were discovered intact: he had not been decapitated nor cut into pieces and buried in separate graves, as Manson Family lore had related.

Grogan's cooperation undoubtedly stood him in good measure with the Board of Prison Terms. His development and maturity were also noted during his regular parole hearings. In 1978, Dr. Melvin Macomber, the psychiatrist who examined him, declared: "For the last several years he has been quite confused, guilt ridden and fearful. He has shown considerable improvement at this time and there is no evidence of psycho-pathology which would indicate a potential for violence in the future. Grogan is not in need of psychotherapy. Violence potential appears to be below average. Prognosis for successful adjustment in the community appears to be very good."[1] Such evaluations worked in Grogan's favor, and he was eventually released on parole in the 1980s. He presently resides in California.

The lives, and attempts to gain their freedom through parole, of those who gave themselves willingly to the murderous abandon of the summer of 1969 continue. In 1978, all of the killers became eligible for parole. Even though the State of California has since voted the return of the death penalty, it cannot be applied on a retroactive basis. Thus, the Manson Family members and their leader were once again spared the verdicts of the courts.

Of those imprisoned, only Charles Manson appears unrepentant. "I did not break the law," he has repeatedly declared, "either God's law, or man's law."[2] Manson has had a relatively high-profile incarceration. He has been transferred from institution to institution due to disciplinary infractions and violations, including possession of weapons and illegal drugs. On 25 September, 1984, while incarcerated at the California Medical Facility at Vacaville, a fellow inmate sprayed him with paint thinner and set him afire; as a result, Manson suffered second and third degree burns on his face, hands and scalp.[3] He is currently housed in a special unit at the State Prison at Corcoran, California; among his notorious fellow inmates also kept under protective custody are Sirhan Sirhan and Juan Corona.

Even in prison, Manson has not shied away from the bizarre thirst for his attentions on the part of the media. He granted a five-part interview in 1975 to the NBC affiliate in Los Angeles, but, disliking the result, decided not to talk again. In 1981, he broke his self-imposed silence to appear on the NBC-TV talk show *Tomorrow* with host Tom Snyder. The interview was intensely controversial, not for the content, but because many were offended that television was now giving the convicted mass murderer a stage upon which to glory in his fame. He followed this with something of a media blitz, appearing, throughout the 1980s and 1990s, on NBC-TV's *Today Show*, on *Nightwatch* with Charlie Rose, ABC-TV's *Turning Point* with Diane Sawyer, and several specials hosted by Geraldo Rivera. Throughout, Manson appears in complete control, manipulative as always, alternately rambling incoherently and then making threats directly at the camera. As always, Manson is an effective actor, playing the part of madman which history has permanently assigned. "Manson," says Vincent Bugliosi, "has become adept at playing the lunatic. He isn't insane. He's a good actor. But he's evil. He managed to manipulate a group of misfits and nurture their own instincts for violence."[4]

Former Family member Bruce Davis concurs with Bugliosi's assessment: "I would describe Manson as an instrument of the evil supernatural. The crimes are just sort of the fruit of the tree. The crimes are just the parts you can see, and they're not the most— although they're the most tragic consequences interpersonally, they're not the most, what do you say, not the most threatening part of the situation. The most threatening part is what causes that destruction. And what we saw was the destruction, but that's not as important as what caused it."[5]

Manson remains a mass of contradictions, at times erratic and incoherent, at others, seemingly reasoned and logical. His most recent extended interview, conducted by Diane Sawyer for the ABC News magazine *Turning Point* in 1994, revealed a man who is keenly aware of playing the part expected of him, but perhaps growing a little weary of the charade. At one point during the broadcast, Patricia Krenwinkel declared that Manson knew exactly what he was doing with the media; watching her comment on a monitor, Manson smiled, looked Sawyer in the eye and said, "All the time."[6]

There were also sharp flashes of wit. "Is Charlie Manson crazy?" Sawyer asked him.

"Whatever that means," Manson answered. "Sure, he's crazy, he's mad as a hatter. What difference does it make? You know, a long time ago being crazy meant something, nowadays, everybody's crazy."[7]

Although he first went up before the parole board in 1978, Manson has consistently been denied release. He himself must know that it is a hopeless cause, and he appears to take the process as a simple joke. At one parole hearing, he declared he wanted to parole to Mars; at another, he sent the board members Monopoly money as a bribe. His position, when he chooses to state it, has always been clear. "I was never on the scene when anyone was killed," he declared at his 1992 parole hearing. "I think the law says you can only keep me seventeen years or eighteen years if I was never on the scene when anyone was killed. I was never on the crime scene of anything. The closest I came to the crime scene is I cut Hinman's ear off in a fight over some money."[8]

Only occasionally has he admitted to any responsibility for the crimes, and then, only in an indirect fashion. "I influenced a lot of people, unbeknownst to my own understanding of it," he has said. "I didn't understand the fears of the people outside. I didn't understand the insecurities of people outside. I didn't understand people outside. And a lot of things that I said and did affected a lot of people in a lot of different directions. It wasn't intentional and it definitely wasn't with malice or aforethought."[9] Almost no one, including Manson himself, can ever envision circumstances favorable to his release. In August, 1969, Manson was thirty-four years old; in prison, he has become a graying, slight, wrinkled inmate. Saved from death twice by the decisions of the California State Supreme Court when they pondered the issue of capital punishment, Charles Manson, mass murderer, symbol of evil for millions of people around the world, will undoubtedly end his days in an environment which he has frequently declared he finds hospitable: jail.

The Manson women—Van Houten, Krenwinkel and Atkins—all remain incarcerated at the California Institute for Woman at Corona. All are part of the general prison population, and, unlike Manson, interact with their fellow prisoners on a daily basis. All have expressed remorse for their crimes, and strongly lobbied to achieve parole.

If any of the former Manson Family members is released, it is most likely to be Leslie Van Houten. Having initially been convicted of the LaBianca murders in 1971 and sentenced to death, in 1976, a California Court of Appeals dismissed her conviction and ordered a new trial on the grounds that she received inadequate representation due to the disappearance of her lawyer Ronald Hughes. In March, 1977, she underwent a second trial, prosecuted by Deputy District Attorney Stephen Kay. The jury was hopelessly deadlocked, however, and a new trial was ordered. During the interval, Van Houten, with the support of friends and relatives, managed to raise her $200,000 bail and worked for a time as a legal secretary.

Her third trial began in March, 1978. While Van Houten had hoped for a verdict of manslaughter or second degree murder, Prosecutor Kay managed to convince this jury of her guilt, and, on 5 July, 1978, she was again convicted of two counts of first degree murder. Van Houten was devastated by the outcome. Yet, in spite of her frequent claims that she had only stabbed Rosemary LaBianca after she was dead, the jury believed that there was room for doubt. Her intent, whatever the status of Rosemary LaBianca, had been clear that night. She had helped hold the struggling woman down, so that Krenwinkel and Watson could stab her, and then herself joined in the frenzy, declaring later that she had enjoyed herself. Van Houten was not a passive observer at the LaBianca murders, but an active, and enthusiastic, participant.

In prison, Van Houten has taken full advantage of the opportunities provided for inmates, obtaining a BA degree in English literature, as well as editing the prison newspaper and working as a secretary. Subsequently, she has been turned down for parole on numerous occasions. Although several psychiatric evaluations determined that Van Houten posed no danger to society, Stephen Kay had his doubts. An episode in 1982 reinforced his belief. Van Houten had married while in prison; in 1982, her husband was arrested for writing bad checks, and was found to have a women's prison guard uniform at his house. The presence of the clothing suggested that he—with or without Van Houten's knowledge—was contemplating smuggling her out in the future. Van Houten divorced him, but Kay felt that the entire episode demonstrated her bad judgment, and continued to rally against her at parole hearings.

Van Houten has since allied herself with Susan Atkins, and the two have their own web-site, dedicated to promoting their eventual release. An organization, Friends of Leslie, works tirelessly on her behalf, to gain her freedom. Her most recent parole hearings have focused on Van Houten's psychological profile, which has alternated wildly. Severe depression, coupled with anorexia, has led to doubts concerning her ability to cope with the pressures of life beyond the institution. Nevertheless, at her parole hearing in May, 1998, Van Houten received only a one year denial—the minimum the Parole Board could impose.

Of all the former Manson Family members still incarcerated for the Tate-LaBianca crimes, perhaps the most accomplished, and the most changed, is Patricia Krenwinkel. In prison, she received her Bachelor of Sciences degree, and completed a course in vocational data processing. She has been an active participant in drug counseling programs, worked extensively as a volunteer and helped train female fire-fighters in the Los Angeles area. Unusually, throughout her years of her incarceration, Krenwinkel has never received a disciplinary write-up or infraction, and has been a model prisoner.[10]

Unlike Van Houten, Atkins and Watson, Krenwinkel has not claimed that any religious experience while in prison entitles her to freedom. Instead, she appears to have accepted her sentence, knowing that it is unlikely she will ever get out. At her 1993 Parole Hearing, she had no plans to present to the Board should she be released, saying simply that she herself recognized she would not be receiving a date.[11] She is now very apologetic about the criminal period of her life, and very anti-Manson Family.

Uniquely among the former Manson Family members, Krenwinkel genuinely seems to pose no threat to society. One prison psychiatrist defined her as "a person who responds rather conventionally to questions, who uses her intelligence to control her rebellious past, and who has achieved a good balance in her emotional functioning, neither given to depression nor being overly-active. She is able to lead a rather stable life and has developed appropriate feminine interests and guides her progress. Overall, no mental disorders expressed in this profile, and it has been stable over the years."[12]

Although her fellow Manson Family members continue to insist that they accept responsibility for "their part" in the crimes, only Krenwinkel has assumed complete blame, without excuse, for her actions. "It is apparent," wrote one prison interviewer, "that the understanding of her role in the Manson Family has helped inmate Krenwinkel to clearly see her dependency on this manipulator and her subservient role at the time. Her improved understanding and newly found assertiveness and activities have helped her to change her understanding of her responsibility of her shocking and horrendous criminal activity, especially as her victims are concerned." She is, according to reports, "Fully aware of her totally unwarranted and senseless crime. As a matter of fact, when describing her crime, she became emotionally involved in a manner which proves her remorse and understanding."[13] Psychologically, Krenwinkel has been found to have "no sign of mental disorder," and been deemed to be "functioning on a higher than average intellectual level," with an "emotionally well-balanced" personality. Her violence potential has been estimated to be "well-below average." Although examining psychiatrists told Krenwinkel in 1993 that "you are a violent criminal only by history, and you do not pose a threat at the present level of functioning in this setting, and it is predicted that you would not pose a threat in an uncontrolled setting if released into the community at this time," she has consistently been denied parole.[14]

The brutality of her crimes, her willing participation, and her ability to be easily-influenced remain obstacles which Parole Board members have found insurmountable to her imminent release. At her most recent parole hearing, on 19 March, 1997, she received the maximum five-year denial, the board citing the brutality of her crimes and her active participation on both nights of murder. "Every day I wake up," Krenwinkel has said, "and know that I'm a destroyer of the most precious thing, which is life, and living with that is the most difficult thing of all, and I do that, because that's what I deserve, to wake up every morning and know that."[15]

Both Charles "Tex" Watson and Susan Atkins have regularly appealed for release before parole boards. They have always been denied. Susan Atkins is now a middle-aged woman, her once long hair kept short and slightly curled, wrinkles beginning to show across her face. In 1974, Manson follower Bruce Davis, who, in

1973, became a born again Christian, began a lengthy correspondence with her. Atkins was receptive, and listened as other religious groups in her prison reached out to her. According to her own account, she became a born again Christian in September, 1974. Interviewed a year later, she broke down and cried, declaring that she now felt remorse for what she had done. She had acted, she said, under the powerful influences of both drugs and Manson. She even wrote a book, *Child of Satan, Child of God*, outlining her life with Manson, the crimes and her conversion.

According to Dr. Clara Livsey, who interviewed and examined many of Manson's female followers, Atkins "became a Born Again Christian in a grand manner. She is not one of thousands who quietly have converted and lead lives guided by the Bible's Christian principles. Instead she made it clear from the moment she suddenly embraced Christ that she regards herself as a leader, a person endowed with great spiritual qualities who is to preach the Word and minister to others. She does not hesitate to compare herself with great Biblical figures....There can be no doubt of Susan's aggrandized view of herself....One gets the clear impression that Susan does not worship God, but herself. She believes that today she is up front where she always wanted to be, where the action is, leading, and that is the reason, I would judge, why she feels at peace. Obviously she has decided that in her circumstances she can feel better and live better by relating to people who have a modicum of power and who admire and support her."[16]

In common with both Van Houten and Krenwinkel, Atkins while incarcerated, has taken college classes, obtaining an Associate of Arts degree. She has also completed courses in data processing, and to become a paralegal secretary. She has been married twice while incarcerated. Her first marriage, to Donald Lee Laisure, a man twice her age posing as a wealthy Texan, ended in divorce in 1982. In 1987, she married law student James Whitehouse, fifteen years her junior.

Unlike her fellow female Family members, however, Atkins has consistently received unfavorable psychiatric evaluations. Part of the problem is her selective memory and revisionist history of the crimes. While she gleefully admitted to anyone who would listen that she not only stabbed and chased Voyteck Frykowski but also helped kill Sharon—even going as far as to taste her blood—such admissions undoubtedly now harm her chances for a successful parole. In her book, she declared that she had killed no one, and even claimed not to have stabbed anyone except Voyteck, and then, just in the leg. Even this admission has subsequently been altered, to reflect her present position that she inflicted no stab wounds to any of the victims. In her 1981 parole hearing, she declared flatly she had lied at the time of the murders because she "felt guilty" at not having been more responsible.[17]

Her last parole hearing, in 1996, did not go well. Presiding Commissioner Carol Bentley began the meeting on an ominous note: "It struck me today, the number of murder victims that I had to write down. It was really kind of appalling to me. It sort of had a chill over me, because I do these all the time, and most usually we just have one victim, and here we have all these victims."[18]

Throughout the hearing, Atkins denied both her prison statements to Graham and Howard concerning her active participation in the deaths of Gary Hinman and the Cielo Drive victims; claimed she lied at both her Grand Jury testimony and during her murder trial testimony; and was only now telling the truth that she had stabbed no one nor helped kill them. The Parole Board members seemed hesitant to accept this explanation, especially in view of the multitude and enthusiastic abundance of Atkins' statements in the past to the contrary.[19]

By 1996, Atkins had several other problems which caused Board members concern. She had been found guilty of attempting to illegally use one of the institution's computers to compose a letter protesting legislation which would end inmates' conjugal rights, then lying about her violation. Members were also concerned that she had been dropped from her group psychotherapy class for lack of attendance. In both cases, Atkins attempted to blame her counselors and those at the institute.

This refusal to accept responsibility for her own actions, in addition to her selective memory where her crimes were concerned, led to unfavorable psychiatric reports. Dr. Robert B. McDaniel, Staff Psychiatrist, noted Atkins' "inclination to overcompensate," and "tendency to minimize" her participation in the crimes. The doctor further noted that Atkins "maintained what appeared to be an artificially cheerful demeanor."[20]

The psychiatric report noted both a "history of polysubstance abuse" and "anti-social personality disorder" present in Atkins. "While drug abuse and anti-social personality would set the stage for someone involved in criminal behavior," the psychiatrist wrote, "it does not explain, in my opinion, the extreme cruelty and viciousness involved in the crime." Summarizing McDaniel's report, Board Member Carol Cantu declared to Atkins: "When he questioned you about some of your feelings, he said that you tended to view this in other terms rather than her instant crime, and rather reluctant to describe it in any detail. 'The most she would describe was feeling that while she did not stab anyone, that she was guilty of not somehow halting the senseless slaughter that was to ensue.' And the doctor felt that upon review of the C-file [Atkins' incarceration history], that you were more involved than you're willing to discuss. He also felt that you, in some situations, some instances, you tended to minimize or completely avoid certain topics....And he feels that your tendency to minimize and avoid discussion of the crime and certain aspects of the crime is indicative of a pattern in which you rather skillfully and deftly deflect away from sensitive topics, that this would suggest that you're very adroit in conversation, diverting attention away from sensitive issues, that this would obviously reduce your level of discomfort, but may slow down your progress in psychotherapy. Psychiatric conclusions, he feels that the diagnosed psycho pathology, such as anti-social behavior, drug abuse, is related to your criminal behavior, that you have psychiatrically deteriorated slightly in the interval of three years ago. However, he does comment that you have matured considerably in the last twenty-five-years of incarceration. And in a less-controlled setting such as a return to the community, you can be considered at risk for deterioration for the following reasons. He believes that you continue to deny the seriousness of your crime, and that you do not deal with problems directly, but deflect them away during conversation."[21]

After the trials, when it became obvious that she faced the remainder of her life in prison, Atkins changed her stories, blaming all of her actions on Manson and on the drugs she took at the ranch. The simple fact is, even before she met Manson, Susan Atkins was a heavy drug user, with a criminal record. Whatever her protests, she possessed enough free will to flaunt her participation in the crimes while incarcerated in Sybil Brand Institute for Women, at a time when she was no longer under Manson's control, and continued to do so for several years thereafter. Numerous psychiatric reports have declared that she remains a probable danger to society, and that she demonstrates strong anti-social behavior.

Atkins' most recent version of events stands in dramatic opposition to both her previous accounts and those of the other participants in the crime. According to Atkins, as she and Watson stood in the living room with a terrified Sharon Tate, they began to argue whether to kill her or take her with them to have her baby. When Atkins protested against ending her life, Watson screamed, "Get the fuck out of the house!" and Atkins fled, standing alone on the front lawn as Watson himself stabbed the pregnant actress to death. Needless to say, this version of events is supported by no one but Atkins herself.[22]

As manipulative and selective as Atkins has been with her memory, it is nothing when compared with Charles "Tex" Watson, the man who admittedly stabbed Sharon to death. Watson never once expressed remorse for the crime, until it became convenient to do so under the guise of his own religious experience. Incarcerated at Folsom Prison after his trial, he began to work in the dispensary. In 1975, he declared that he underwent a religious experience and was born again. Conveniently, he managed to get his autobiography, *Will You Die for Me?*, into bookstores just before his first parole hearing in 1978.

Watson has continued his prison ministry in the various institutions in which he has been jailed. He participated in the prison chapel programs, trying to convert the criminal populations at Folsom and San Luis Obispo. Eventually, he received his own credentials as a minister. None of this has mattered to the parole boards. He has consistently sat before them and pleaded his case, declaring that, although he was guilty of the murders, he committed them only because of the influence of both drugs and of Manson. During one of his parole hearings, he admitted, "As far as me taking the lead role, I was the male at the crime, but at that time I did not consider myself a leader, I considered myself a follower of Charles Manson, carrying out his orders."[23]

Such an assertion stands in stark contrast to the evidence of Watson's crimes. His own narrative provides a stunning indictment of his culpability as leader. The pages of *Will You Die for Me?* reek of his responsibility on the night he killed Sharon: "I told the girls...," "I shot him...," "I told Linda...," "I crept to the front door...," "I kicked him in the head...," "I ordered Sadie...," "I stabbed him...."[24]

No one that night acted except on Watson's instructions. He cut the telephone lines; he killed Parent; he told Kasabian to search for an open window; he cut the screen to the dining room window, crawled inside and let the girls in; he ordered them to search the rest of the house; he killed Jay; he ordered Atkins to kill Voyteck; he killed both Frykowski and Abigail Folger; he stabbed Sharon Tate. Her personally killed both Leno and Rosemary LaBianca. Parole boards have always found the manner of the crimes, as well as Watson's eager participation in them, sufficient grounds for his continued incarceration. In addition, his denial of ultimate personal responsibility for his actions, as Susan Atkins has continued to do, does not bode well when examined by the board members. The fact that Watson, like Atkins, came into the Manson Family with a heavy previous involvement with drugs and a predisposition toward criminal acts, has mitigated against his pleas of innocence. Similarly, the fact that, after the murders, Watson left the Family on his own, without informing Manson, because he had simply had enough, speaks volumes about his ability to control his own actions at the time when the crimes were committed.

In 1990, a psychiatrist wrote that it had only been "during the last three years of one-on-one therapy that he begun to truly experience a sense of deep remorse, both for the crime victims and for the families of the crime victims." When a troubled parole board member asked Watson what, then, he had been feeling the previous eighteen years, he replied, "Well, its not that I haven't experienced that before, but there's been things happening in my life over the last few years that have really brought it home more so." He said that, since becoming a Christian in 1975, it had been "great to know that I have been forgiven by God for what I've done. But I think sometimes we can hide behind that, and the last three years I've had the opportunity to really see myself in a new light in the sense that I've opened myself up to really look at the crime through other people's eyes other than just my own."[25]

This devastating revelation made the board members uneasy. They kept prodding him for answers, asking why it had taken eighteen years for him to begin to feel real remorse. Clearly irritated, Watson replied that, "At the time of the crimes, the people we killed weren't human beings to us." "I'm sorry," one of the board members said finally, "but you talk as if you're from another planet."[26]

While he campaigns for release, Watson remains a dangerous man. Continued psychiatric reports have declared him a potential threat to society. A 1982 report referred to him as "a walking time

bomb," with an incredible degree of repressed hostility and a high
potential for violence.[27] Five years later, another psychiatric report
declared that he was "able to demonstrate no real responsibility for
the offenses and cannot comprehend at an effective level feelings of
remorse."[28] His 1990 report flatly asserted that he suffered from a
borderline personality disorder with an unpredictable level for
potential violence.[29] In 1993, rather than submit to questions from a
new hearing board concerning his financial dealings and fearing that
he would be relocated to another prison, Watson voluntarily waived
his right to parole, stipulating to his unsuitability.[30]

In prison, Watson has married, and, through conjugal visits,
fathered four children. His wife and children are financial depen-
dents of the State of California. Additionally, he founded a corporation, Abounding Love Ministries, or ALMS, through which he has
allegedly funneled much of the money he receives in donations
back to his wife. This led to a California State Fraud Investigator's
raid on the house where Watson's wife and children lived. The state
suspected that Kristen Watson had lied to authorities about her
income from ALMS, committed perjury and filed false applications
for financial aid in a deliberate attempted to defraud the Medi-Cal
fund from which she received regular payments each month.[31]

Watson has kept himself carefully insulated, refusing to do interviews and cooperating only with members of the Christian community who have embraced him. On his web site, he has recently
declared, "I've learned that it doesn't do any good to beat myself up
with guilt." On the question of forgiveness, his position is clear: "I've
been marked in the eyes of man as a murderer and God has protected me. But the mark has been removed in God's eye, and in the
eyes of all those who love Him."[32] With this deft move, Watson managed to shift the onus of forgiveness from himself to the grieving
families of the victims.

Rather than accept responsibility for his actions and the consequences, he has manipulated the issue of repentance to suit his own
ends. According to Watson, it is he who is enlightened, forgiven by
God; he prays that the families of those he killed can be similarly
imbued with the spirit of forgiveness. If they do not forgive him,
they have somehow fallen short of the beatific grace he himself
claims, and do not share in the Christian fullness he promotes.

"The Mansonites and their supporters," writes Dr. Clara Livsey,
"continue to try to convey the idea that a great injustice has been
inflicted on them, that they really have gotten an unfair deal from the

judicial system. Their idiom is cautious, but listening to them one gets the impression that they believe society is the loser because they are in prison instead of being free, leading normal and constructive lives...."[33] She points out the subtle attempt to re-direct the finger of guilt away from those responsible: "It has been said of the Mansonites who participated in the Tate-LaBianca murders that they have suffered enough, that they will bear a stigma for the rest of their lives. In other words they are thus presented as the victims of their own actions."[34]

Whether Watson or Atkins has converted to Christianity, whether Krenwinkel now realizes the errors of her past, whether Van Houten feels genuine remorse for her participation in the murder of Rosemary LaBianca, the needs of society—and the desire of society for retribution in the deaths of the innocent victims they killed—have not, according to Doris Tate, been met. The justice system exists to serve four distinct purposes: to remove from society those who pose a threat to the safety and well-being of others; to impose a deterrent factor on society which would mitigate against the commitment of any future crimes; to rehabilitate criminals if possible and address the reasons for their crimes; and to provide retribution on behalf of society against those who have transgressed the established laws. "I don't care what lawyers for Atkins or Watson argue," she said. "I don't believe or care that their clients no longer pose a threat to society. They still owe a debt to society, and that debt is retribution. That's all society has left to take from them. Society didn't take their lives, like they took my daughter's life, and for that, they should be grateful."[35]

Writing of Watson and Atkins, Dr. Clara Livsey declared: "The way in which these two prostitute religion is shocking, yet it has served them well in attaining a great deal of publicity and good connections. Each has written books that tell their own self-serving account of their lives and their criminal activities. The pair, who have no qualms in proclaiming that Jesus is their attorney, work assiduously towards being paroled not just—they claim—to enjoy a free life, but because humanity is awaiting their ministrations."[36]

Manson himself has been cynical of the jailhouse religious conversions of his former Family members. "If, in fact, they are as sincere about Christianity and as strong in religion as they were sold on drugs and deceit during the time our lives ran parallel," Manson wrote, "then God has got two very devoted disciples. But if, on the other hand, they are with their God as they were with me, they are still going to do just as they please."[37]

Chapter 36
I Will Fight as Long as I Am Alive.

AFTER SHARON'S FUNERAL, ROMAN POLANSKI REMAINED IN LOS Angeles, staying with friends as he dealt with the emotional ordeal of cleaning out 10050 Cielo Drive and dispersing her things. During the investigation into the crimes, he undertook his own search for those responsible for her murder. The announcement of the arrest of Manson and his Family members brought him no relief, no sense of satisfaction. Everything in Los Angeles—the circle of friends he kept, the city, the lifestyle—reminded him of his loss. Taking a few belongings with him, he returned to London, where he lived in the Eaton Place mews house he had shared with Sharon. "After Sharon's death," he said, "everything seemed so futile. Nothing made sense. Nothing. I had difficulty finding anything worthwhile."[1]

Roman's first film after Sharon's death was a new production of *Macbeth*. English writer Kenneth Tynan worked with Polanski on the screenplay. Tynan, who had known both Sharon and Roman during their earlier London residence, noted that his friend seemed distressed, emotionally drained. During the filming of the murder of Macduff's wife and children, Polanski supervised as make-up artists swabbed the young actor playing Macduff's son with blood. When Tynan asked if stab wounds would really result in so much blood, Polanski replied, "You didn't see my house in California last summer. I know about bleeding."[2] When it came time to smear blood across the four-year-old girl playing Macduff's daughter, Polanski asked casually, "What's your name?" "Sharon," she replied.[3]

Victor Lownes also had a hand in the film, getting Playboy Enterprises to provide financial backing for the project. It was a hard period for Polanski, and he threw himself blindly and passionately

289

into the film. Although the film, which opened in late 1971, was widely regarded as a critical success, the violence and blood contained in it sent reviewers running to their typewriters, to churn up armchair analysis of how deeply Sharon's murder had affected Polanski. Roman himself was indignant at the comparisons. "You have to show violence the way it is," he declared in an interview. "If you don't show it realistically, then that's immoral and harmful. If you don't upset people, then that's obscenity."[4]

Polanski followed *Macbeth* with several other critical successes, the most famous of which was his epic *Chinatown*, starring Faye Dunaway and his friend Jack Nicholson. It was at Nicholson's house, not far from his old residence at 10050 Cielo Drive, that, in March, 1977, Roman had sex with thirteen-year old Samantha Geimer, a would-be model and actress. He was arrested and pled guilty to sex with a minor on August 8, 1977, the eighth anniversary of Sharon's murder. Although Roman claimed that he had not known the girl was under-age, the judge ordered him to under-go psychiatric testing, and sentenced him to a period of time at the California Men's Prison at Chino. He was due to stand trial the coming winter, but slipped out of Los Angeles and out of the country before he could be apprehended. He fled to Paris, where he was born, and spent his time in the capitals of Europe, often creating more scandalous headlines, his romance with fifteen-year-old actress Nastassia Kinski generating a good deal of publicity for both of them.

During his European exile, Polanski directed his remarkable version of Thomas Hardy's *Tess of the d'Urbervilles*. Before she had sailed from England in July, 1969, Sharon had left her husband a copy of the book to read, saying she thought it would make a great film. Polanski had originally envisioned it as a vehicle for Sharon. In the end, the film starred Polanski's new girlfriend, Natassia Kinski. Released in 1980, it bore the poignantly simple opening dedication, "To Sharon."

Polanski remains in exile; charges are still pending against him in California, and it is unlikely that he will ever return to Los Angeles. He is thus unable to visit the grave of his wife or his unborn son. Occasionally, he telephoned Sharon's parents, with whom he remained in touch. Only rarely did they meet. "For a while, I couldn't bear to see him because in my state of denial I would always expect to see Sharon with him," Doris Tate admitted.[5] But these rare meetings formed Roman's only connection to that part of his life with Sharon.

In his autobiography, Polanski wrote: "There used to be a tremendous fire within me—an unquenchable confidence that I could master anything if I really set my mind to it. This confidence was badly undermined by the killings and their aftermath....I doubt if I shall ever again be able to live on a permanent basis with any woman, no matter how beautiful....My attempts to do so have always failed, not least because I start drawing comparisons to Sharon....I shall always remain faithful to her till the day I die."[6]

For Polanski, however, life carried on. After a succession of public affairs, he met Emmanuelle Seigner. Beautiful, with dark hair and classic features, Seigner—like Sharon—was an actress, the product of a distinguished theatrical family. The similarities between the two women were stunning: like Sharon, Seigner's abilities were widely ignored, her experience comprising roles which called more on her physical presence than her acting talents. As had Sharon, she found the Polish director fascinating. He was double her age when, on 8 August, 1989—the twentieth anniversary of the murder of his wife and unborn son—Roman married Seigner. Four years later, on Roman and Sharon's wedding anniversary—20 January, 1993—Seigner gave birth to Roman's first child, a daughter named Morgane. A son, Elvis, followed several years later, finally providing Polanski with the family which Sharon's death had denied him.

Ultimately, the final chapter in the story of Sharon's life and death rests with her mother Doris and sister Patti, and the legacy they embraced and championed. It was Doris Tate who, grieving over the loss of her daughter, channeled her pain into the work which she alone could perform for victims. Through the work of her mother and youngest sister, Sharon's tragic murder has finally taken on a sense of courageous and passionate purpose.

Following the delivery of the guilty verdicts in her murder trial, Sharon's family retreated into obscure silence. Doris returned from Houston to Palos Verdes with Deborah and Patricia, and the two girls re-enrolled in a local school. Paul Tate, having taken early retirement from the Army to help discover Sharon's killers, took a job as a private investigator. Doris opened a beauty salon called Tate's, naming the way she cut hair "the Sebring method."[7]

The sense of normalcy, however, was a horrible charade. According to Doris, she went from day to day, "just hanging in there and going on. I had to continue on for the other children."[8] As much as they tried to shield their daughters, however, neither Paul or Doris could hide the wound Sharon's death had caused in their lives. "The most painful thing for me was to watch my parents grieve, to watch their hurt and know their hurt," remembered Patti. "When my mom was alive, I couldn't help her or my father with their sadness. As a young child, I saw all that and realized that there was so much I couldn't do. You want so much to help, but how do you help someone who is grieving so?"[9]

In the Tate house, a large photograph of Sharon stared down from the living room wall; shelves and tables held other memories. But her name was rarely mentioned. "Talking about Sharon brought up so many memories, and it was almost impossible to separate the good from the bad," Doris recalled.[10] It was easier for Doris to deny Sharon's death than accept the devastating loss. "For three years," she explained, "I could not mention her name. I was so grief stricken, for ten years to be exact, that I couldn't even talk about this. I was in a pattern of denial. For three years, I could not even say that my daughter was dead."[11]

"I had a very hard time," Doris said. "At first, I couldn't even come back to the cemetery. It took me six months before I could visit Sharon's grave. I had to be ready to separate the body from the soul, and she's not there. I know where she is."[12] More than anything, it was the brutal and senseless manner of Sharon's death which overwhelmed her family. "I can't imagine a man holding a pregnant woman down and stabbing her to death," Doris said. "My mind will not allow me to imagine what she went through."[13]

"It is impossible for anyone who hasn't gone through it to understand the depth of the pain that one goes through when losing a child to murder," Doris explained. "It is very hard if you can't understand that emotion. Life changes forever. As a parent you never expect to outlive your own children."[14]

The trauma of Sharon's death was made even worse, though, by the constant swirl of publicity. Her murder was dredged up relentlessly by the media throughout the following decades; as the Supreme Court struck down the death penalty; as Lynette "Squeaky" Fromme tried to assassinate President Ford; as Vincent Bugliosi's book *Helter Skelter* was first published, then made into a mini-series for television; as Manson began to give interviews; as Leslie Van Houten was granted a new trial; as the murderers went up for parole for the first time; and as the anniversaries of the murders came and went. "It took me ten years to recoup," Doris said. "Some parents get over it in less time, but it took me ten years, because I kept denying that it had happened."[15]

"When I got to the point where I couldn't stand it," Doris remembered, "I flipped open the Bible. Through my religion I learned you go directly to your God. That's where the answers come from." She eventually turned to Proverbs 24:17-18: "Rejoice not when thine enemy falleth, and let not thine heart be glad when he stumbleth; Lest the Lord see it, and it displease Him, and He turn away His wrath from him." For Doris, the words literally saved her. "The scripture was the only thing that did pull me through. I knew it was someone else they were going to have to deal with. I just left my revenge with the Lord. He led the way. He took care of me."[16]

Increasingly, Doris turned to prayer for comfort. "I am very religious, a Catholic, and Christianity is a big part of my surviving," she declared.[17] Her deep faith gave her a sense of serenity, but it was not until 1982 that Doris was forced to publicly confront Sharon's death. Ironically, it was the potential release of prisoner Leslie Van Houten—one of the Manson Family members who had not participated in Sharon's murder—which drew her out of her shell.

By 1982, Leslie Van Houten had collected some 900 signatures on a petition asking for her release from prison. To many, it looked as if she might win an early parole. Stephen Kay, who had helped in Bugliosi's original prosecution of the defendants, was worried enough to recall a promise which Doris had made to him a decade earlier. Then, when the trials had come to an end, Sharon's mother had told Kay that if he ever feared that any of the killers would win release from prison and there was anything she could do to help, he should telephone her. With Leslie Van Houten actively petitioning the Board of Prison Terms, Kay rang the Tate house in Palos Verdes. "Leslie Van Houten has 900 signatures that they are going to present to the Board for her release," he explained. "I need your help."[18]

Kay's telephone call broke Doris's self-imposed distance from the tragedy. Although Van Houten had not been among her daughter's killers, she was still horrified that any of the murderous Manson Family might be free to walk the streets again. "If they can get 900 names, surely I can get enough people to agree with me they should not be released," she remembered.[19]

Ironically, in view of the deplorable sensationalism which had surrounded the murders and the trials, Doris went to the one source she knew would give her a voice. She contacted the tabloid *National Enquirer* and asked if they would help. "I told them that I would write a story for them if they agreed to publish it, and if they would run a coupon that people could clip and send to me opposing her parole."[20] The article, on the potential release of Van Houten, told of Doris Tate's efforts to spearhead a letter-writing campaign to deny parole for any of the Manson killers. It worked. Doris Tate soon had over 350,000 letters from people all over the world, all of them united in opposition to the release of any of the convicted killers who committed the crimes at either 10050 Cielo Drive or 3301 Waverly Drive. The petitions and letters went in dozens of boxes to the parole board pondering Van Houten's fate: it was enough to make them change their minds, and Van Houten was denied a parole date.[21]

The experience changed Doris Tate's life. Where previously she had relegated her daughter's death and the fate of her killers to the painful recesses of her mind, she now decided the time had come to confront the issue head on. A gentle, soft-spoken woman, Doris hardly seemed a likely candidate for a crusading champion of victims' rights. Yet, taking the painful experiences of her own tragedy, she managed to build a platform which would eventually attract the attentions of the world's media.

She immediately joined the Los Angeles Chapter of the organization Parents of Murdered Children, a support group for the families of the victims of violent crimes. "Once I was prepared to face Sharon's death," she explained, "then I was able to counsel other families." Although an undoubtedly painful experience, especially at the beginning, Doris was determined to make a difference in the lives of those who, like herself and her family, had suffered at the hands of violent crime, either directly or indirectly. "Why not turn something that was so horrible into something worthwhile for her memory?" she declared, summing up her growing motivation as an activist.[22]

A large part of Doris Tate's work was with victims' rights groups. She was an advisor and member of the Victim Offender Reconciliation Group; Parents of Murdered Children; and the group Justice for Homicide Victims, and founded COVER, the Coalition on Victims' Equal Rights. She also served on the California State Advisory Committee on Correctional Services, as a victims' representative to various parole boards and prison authorities.

"My target is the first time offender," she once explained. As a member of the Victim Offender Reconciliation Group, she made regular pilgrimages to various institutions, to meet with inmates and to share her story with them. There were also videotaped presentations from other victims' families, and comments from survivors of violent crime. At times her receptions were cool, and she was frequently seen as the enemy by many inmates—at least until she began to speak. One of Doris Tate's greatest assets was her ability to speak about Sharon's tragic death, and the emotional impact it had had on not only herself but on her family as well. Putting a human face on the victim was an essential part of this work. "If you can rehabilitate even one, or two or three of these people, you have saved some victim's life," she explained.[23]

Much of Doris Tate's work as a member of the California State Advisory Committee on Correctional Services was a determined effort to reform the prison system. She actively campaigned for a number of important changes, all of which she believed were necessary to bring the system in line with public expectations. This included inmates having to work for a minimum wage and learn productive skills during their period of incarceration. Under Doris Tate's proposals, prisoners would have paid taxes with the money they earned, paid room and board to the state, made restitution to victims, and been forced to save a substantial sum for their future use on the outside in the event of a parole.

She was intimately involved in the successful passage of California Proposition Number 8, the "Victim's Rights Bill." This measure, which went into effect in 1982, for the first time allowed victims to make impact statements at the sentencing of their attackers, of, in the case of murder, the families of the victims. The Bill also gave victims access to any pre-sentencing investigative criminal and psychiatric reports prior to sentencing, and outlawed the use of plea-bargaining in certain cases, mainly murder, armed robbery, rape or arson. Finally, and perhaps most importantly, it allowed victims or the families of victims to make impact statements at parole hearings, and to be granted prior access to any of the relevant criminal or psychiatric documents which the inmate might use at the hearing. It was a stunning victory for Doris, and propelled her further along in her quest to protect those victims of violent crime whom she regularly encountered.

Energized and convinced that she had the ability to make a difference, Doris ran for the California State Assembly in 1984 as a strong advocate for victims' rights. She lost, but this did not stall her efforts on behalf of victims' rights. Along with her friend Stephen Kay, she campaigned actively for the passage of California Proposition Number 89, which allowed the state's governor to over- turn parole decisions made by the Board of Prison Terms. When it passed, it was thanks in large part to their ceaseless activism.

Her work within the corrections system made Doris Tate a strong advocate not only of reform but of stricter sentencing and use of capital punishment. At the time of the Manson trial, when asked to comment on the death sentences handed down to her Sharon's murderers, she shyly answered that she believed it was wrong to take a life, be that the life of her innocent daughter or those who had mercilessly slaughtered her. Gradually, however, after spending years hearing the stories of other families who had suffered at the hands of those inmates who had killed and then been paroled to commit further crimes, she changed her views.

"We are depending on our legislators and assemblymen to make decent laws," she said in one interview, "but they are letting us down." When faced with the frequent objection that the death penalty is merely state-sponsored killing, she angrily declared, "Look, we are not murdering these people, they bring it on them- selves when they commit the crimes." Even so, she was not a blan- ket proponent of the death penalty. Only in the most heinous of crimes, like the murder of her daughter and six other innocent vic- tims, did she feel that its use was justified.[24]

Because her daughter's murder was, and remains to this day, a uniquely high-profile crime, Doris was determined to turn her own personal pain and loss into a public platform allowing her to not only fight for victims' rights but also against the faults she perceived in the corrections system. Speaking of the Manson case, she declared: "It won't go away, and that's the reason I feel I've got to do whatever I can do. That it won't go away is fine with me. It affords me an opportunity to do something in my daughter's name. If there's such a thing as destiny, then this is my plight."[25] She added: "I would like to see the whole system changed. My work can only be done through the Manson family."[26]

In this capacity, she was a frequent guest on numerous talk and interview shows dealing with crime and with victims' rights. Once she began this work, there was no shying away from the ensuing publicity it brought, and she realized that, if she were to do any good, it would have necessarily to come through a public discussion of her own personal tragedy. Naturally enough, a large part of her energies were directed at specifically opposing any attempt by those involved with her daughter's death.

She and her husband began attending the parole hearings of both Charles "Tex" Watson and Susan Atkins, the two Manson Family members who had actually stabbed Sharon, when the specifics of Proposition 8 were introduced into the California Penal System. The first face-to-face meeting she had with Watson, in 1985, was a distinctly uncomfortable experience. In a small room, Watson, accompanied by his attorney, sat at one end of a long table, with Doris at the other. She later recalled feeling almost possessed, saying, "I could have killed him."[27] Her husband, glancing over to Watson occasionally, told the parole board, "That man should never, never, never be turned out into society."[28] This first effort was successful, for Watson was denied parole, not for the first, and not for the last time.

At Susan Atkin's parole hearings, Doris Tate was confronted with a tearful, middle-aged woman who continually declared that she was a changed person, that she should be set free. Although the tears seem real enough, Doris declared, "I can't pay attention to that."[29] Instead, looking at one of her daughter's killers, she said bitterly, "You're an excellent actress. The greatest job since Sarah Bernhardt." To the parole board, Doris read a brief statement: "This woman is guilty of eight murders, which means that she cannot live in an unsuspecting society. I feel very sorry that these people chose this way of life. But, after eight convictions of murder, there's no turning back. And society has been kind to Ms. Atkins by overturning the death penalty, and that is more concern than she gave my daughter."[30]

Doris was so adamantly opposed to the release of any of the convicted Manson Family killers not only because they were responsible for her daughter's death but also because she saw it as a terribly dangerous precedent. Many of her arguments involved the issue of releasing serial killers upon society. Where, she would ask, would society then draw the line? If members of the Manson Family were released, then why not other serial killers? It was one of the most pertinent points in her case against release, and one of the most compelling as it did not rest simply with the vengeful mother of a murdered daughter but with a genuine concern about setting and enforcing limits on the corrections system itself. "What an embarrassment to the State of California to let these people out," she once said. "I will fight as long as I am alive to keep them in."[31]

Likewise, Doris Tate took a dim view of the religious conversions of both Atkins and Watson. Without questioning their sincerity, Doris was adamant that the matter of their faith had nothing whatsoever to do with the granting of parole. "They should be judged not by the faith they profess but by the crimes they committed," she said. "If religion opened the prison doors to everyone who declared themselves converted, most of the correctional institutions would be empty."[32]

In 1990, this view brought Doris into a painful conflict, ironically with another relative of a Manson Family victim: Suzanne LaBerge, Rosemary LaBianca's daughter. At the time of the original trials at the beginning of the 1970s, the death of her mother and stepfather so affected LaBerge that she claimed to suffer a nervous breakdown. In the years following the murders, she herself became a Christian. It was while watching a film about religion in prison that she first heard of Watson's declared conversion. She visited him in prison on several occasions before revealing her true identity. The pair quickly formed an alliance, dedicated to gaining Watson's release.

The issue came to a head at the last parole hearing for Watson which Doris attended. It took place in May, 1990, in a small room at the Correctional Institute at San Luis Obispo. "I dread going—and at the same time I wouldn't miss one," Doris told a reporter the day before the hearing. "I feel that Sharon has to be represented in that hearing room. If they're pleading for their lives, then I have to be there representing her—how she lost her life and how she pleaded for her life, and how her pleas were ignored....Watson seems to think that because of his faith he doesn't have to pay for the crimes that were committed."[33] She added: "He won't get out while I'm alive and breathing. I'll never let Tex live that down."[34]

When Doris Tate entered the parole board hearing room the next day, she found LaBerge waiting for her. She tried to convince Doris that Watson was a changed man who deserved to be let out, but Sharon's mother would have none of it. LaBerge was adamant, however, and was prepared to make an impact statement saying as much—ironically a statement made possible by the work which Doris had undertaken on behalf of victims' families.

During the hearing, Doris gazed at Watson, but he himself always refused to look at her. She found it troubling to sit through a re-hash of the crimes, only to hear Watson's consistent remarks that Manson was responsible for controlling the killers. On one occasion, she reminded Watson of his statement to Frykowski on entering the house at Cielo Drive, "I'm the Devil, and I'm here to do the Devil's business." "As far as I'm concerned, Mr. Watson," she said, "you're still in business."[35]

On May 4, 1990, Doris sat silent at one end of the board table as Watson, beside his attorney Allen Jay, sat to one side. She listened as the circumstances of the crimes were read, a list which included a stab-by-stab recitation of the wounds her daughter had received in death. At the conclusion of the boards' statement, the three-man board allowed Watson to make a statement.

"I take full resonsibility for doing this," he began slowly, in a slight southern accent. "It's very hard to sit here and listen to this....It really hurts....There's not much I can do except to go through the pain I go through day to day." When questioned about the role Manson had played in bringing about the crimes, Watson responded, "I don't place the total blame on him. I think I've said in the past that if there hadn't been a Charles Manson, there wouldn't have been a crime, so I guess that is blaming him....We were followers. Even though I've matured and grown over the years to develop into an individual who has leadership qualities I don't think I had leadership qualities then. We were very much deceived and at the same time very much manipulated by a man who was a con man."[36]

Stephen Kay, who was present in his role as one of the original assistant prosecutors, made a long statement pointing out the considerable reasons why Watson should be denied parole, and made it a special point to reiterate his leadership role at the Tate house that first night. He was followed by the two impact statements from the victims' families. The first to speak was Suzanne LaBerge. When she readied her notes, Doris Tate stood up and walked out of the room. She would return only after LaBerge had completed her pleas for the release of her daughter's killer.

When it came time for Doris to make her statement, she looked at Watson for a long time. "I might say I feel sorry for this man, that he chose this way of life, and once choosing, there's no turning back. You cannot, or society cannot trust you living next door to them. What mercy, Sir, did you show my daughter when she was begging for her life? What mercy did you show my daughter when she said give me two weeks to have my baby and then you can kill me, what mercy did you show her? In twenty-one years, I would liked to have asked this prisoner why? He did not know my daughter....How can an individual, without knowing, without any abrasive feelings, go in and slice up this woman, eight and a half months pregnant? How can you? What about my family? When will [Sharon] come up for parole? When will I come up for parole? Can you tell me that? Will these seven victims and possibly more walk out of their graves if you get paroled? You cannot be trusted."[37]

In the end, Watson was denied his parole, as he had been numerous times before. It was a small victory for Doris, but only one in a chain of triumphs in the name of all victims, not only her daughter. Her sense of justice and honor, her passion and vitality, and the terrible loss of her daughter and unborn grandson, all drove Doris Tate to confront the horror of Sharon's murder and to turn her pain into something productive. "You can't make sense out of the innocent slaughter of Sharon and the other victims," Doris once explained. "The most that I, or any other person touched by violence, can hope for is acceptance of the pain. You never forget it, not even with the passage of time. But, if, in my work, I can help transform Sharon's legacy from murder victim to a symbol for victims' rights, I will have accomplished what I set out to do."[38]

Chapter 37
I Promised My Mom Before She Died that I Would Continue On

ORIS TATE DIED ON 11 JULY, 1992, AFTER A LONG BATTLE against a brain tumor. She was sixty-seven years old. In the months before her death, her tireless work on behalf of victims' rights was recognized by President George Bush, who named Doris as one of his "thousand points of light." Her sense of purpose and her relentless pursuit of justice in the war she waged in her daughter's name for the rights of all victims did not die with her. As Sharon's memory passed to her mother and motivated her work for other victims, so did Doris's memory similarly inspire others.

It was Sharon's youngest sister Patti who took over where their mother had left. "I promised my mom before she died that I would continue on," she said. "This...started because it was her dream to pull together all the victims' groups to make a difference in government and so that we can all stand united."[1]

One of Patti's first tributes to her mother was the establishment of the Doris Tate Crime Victims' Bureau. A non-profit organization dedicated to monitoring criminal legislation and raising awareness of public safety issues, the Bureau opened its doors in West Sacramento, California in July, 1993, a year after Doris's death. In 1995, the Doris Tate Crime Victims Foundation was also established, providing further assistance to victims of violent crime and their families. Patti also took over her mother's difficult role as victim's next-of-kin representative at the parole hearings for members of the Manson Family. She explained that she felt she had a duty "to speak for my sister, to be the voice that they took away from her, to stand up for her rights, which she can no longer stand up for."[2]

Not surprisingly, Patti found the parole hearings an emotional ordeal. She had never before come face-to-face with those responsible for the death of her pregnant sister. In 1993, she attended her first parole hearing, for Patricia Krenwinkel. Krenwinkel appeared genuinely remorseful, often breaking into tears as she looked at Sharon's sister: "It's grotesque," she said, "it's absolutely horrible. It's very difficult for me to live with the fact that I could do anything so horrible and so horrendous because that is not who I am, that is not what I believe in. I have always felt that things should be treated with gentleness, tenderness, and love, because that's the most lacking thing that I have found in my life and in most people's lives. I never tried to create something that was ugly and that's what came out of me. So, I try everyday the best I can, to deal with that. Everyday of my life, I try to define myself that I have a little bit of self-worth because it is terribly difficult to deal with this....I cannot change it, no matter what I do, I cannot change one minute of my life, and as I've said before, I don't expect the Board to say that I can go home. I am paying for this as best as I can. I have—there is nothing more I can do outside of being dead to pay for this, and I know that's what you wish. But I cannot take my own life."[3]

> "It is very confusing [for] me," Patti said in response, "to sit here and listen to her say that she was not capable...of doing what she did, and then to sit and listen to a psychological report saying...that she'd be fine out. Well, she said herself that she didn't think it was in her then. I don't want any chances [taken]. I don't trust her, I don't trust any of these people. I don't want them out. I think, as her attorney said, that yes, her crimes are bad...[and] that...[she] should stay in prison for the rest of [her life], like my sister will stay in her grave for the rest of time [with] her baby, and Abigail Folger....I feel like...she has no memory of what happened that night, and what she did. And she didn't know them, I knew [them], I knew Gibby. Does she remember what she looked like, does she remember when she led my sister down the hallway what she looked like? She doesn't...remember what she did. And I want to put some faces and some feelings....I mean, I feel like she's just so blank....Gibby, you know, [had] beautiful black hair, did she ever bother to look at these people?...I've seen the pictures of the aftermath of what she did and what the rest of these prisoners did, to my sister, to Gibby, to Jay, to Voyteck, to the kid out in the car....And there's no face with this story....Well I remember my sister's face, and I remember her belly that stuck out to here. And I remember Gibby and Voyteck and Jay...they were wonderful people, and she didn't know my

sister....Tex, Atkins, Manson—none of these people knew my sister or any of the other victims...and nothing can be done about
it, absolutely nothing....My sister and Gibby and all of them paid
with their lives, and I think that she should pay with her life, in
prison.....I get countless letters...people are afraid of them, people will always be afraid of them, because they were easily led,
they were led by Charles Manson, and I don't want to take
chances that she's...going to get out there, I don't care if she's
sixty-eight or 102, I don't wanna take a chance at any of these
people getting out at any age and being led again like they were.
And I think that most people...aren't willing to take that chance
either....It's caused my family much, much, much pain. What she
did will affect [us] down through generations, and generations,
and generations. You know, it's a terrible thing to have to live
with, I realize that she has to live with it, too, but she seems so
blank about it....It's such a loss, such a loss to my family. My sister didn't deserve...when she led her down the hallway to her
death. Gibby didn't deserve it when they went [on] stabbing [her]
over and over and over again. What, she couldn't get enough? I
can't understand these people, I can't understand why we even
put them up for parole, I don't know why we sit here, but that's
her right, and this is my right to come...here and speak my mind,
and I am thankful for that."[4]

The hearings allowed Patti a voice, but also forced her to
endure often agonizing speeches made by the inmates as they
sought their freedom. In 1996, Patti sat silent as Susan Atkins
declared that she need not seek the forgiveness of the Tate family
because she had found God: "As a Christian, remorse can not work
without having somebody to go to repent. I have experienced
remorse. Remorse naturally causes repentance. I could ask repentance [sic] today for society, I could ask repentance today, or ask forgiveness from society and from the Parole Board and from Ms. Tate.
And to the best of anybody's ability, considering what I participated
in, none of you would be able to adequately forgive me with the
type of forgiveness that I have needed all my life, and I had to seek
a higher power....I can't come before my God, before the Parole
Board, before the people who love me and support me, before Ms.
Tate or anybody and say I did things that I didn't do, when the
things that I did were so horrible and beyond the human heart's ability to forgive me, but I have found that forgiveness. And God,
through His love, through the Word, through the reading of the

Word, through the 12-Step principles, through attending church and finding support from people who were willing to help me come to terms with what I've done, I have been able to forgive myself."[5]

Without offering an apology to Patti or to any of the victims' families, Atkins then adroitly went on to compare her plight to that of Moses and to other Biblical figures, who, despite their sins, had been forgiven by God. Her argument seemed fixated on her own troubles, her own struggles to come to terms with her deeds, and her subsequent peace of mind once she had decided her crimes were in the past.[6]

Considering Atkins' speech, Patti's response was restrained:

"The only thing I brought is the only thing I have left of my sister, [and that] is my memory and the pictures. This is it. This is all my family has because of this woman. She could have easily stopped them. She could have gone and gotten help....I don't care how many times I face these people. It's as hard and maybe even harder every time, and preparing [to come] today I thought, you know, 'I'm going to work real hard on being rational in a real irrational situation,' because...it's very difficult...to look at the person who's responsible for my sister's death, and know that this is the face, the last face, my sister saw before she died....I don't care how many years go by....Susan's bottom line is that she committed crimes because she was at the mercy of Manson's power over her and...was brainwashed....We have to remember that Manson didn't brainwash Susan or any of these other people as she'd like you to believe. Manson was simply the catalyst that allowed Susan to act upon what already naturally came to her....She sits here today telling you what a changed person she is, but when I hear her talk, I don't hear [the] words of someone who's rehabilitated. I hear the desperation of someone trying to get the heck out of here. She'll tell you anything you want to hear, just so she can be let go. She has changed her story so many times, it's hard to keep up....First she said she stabbed Sharon, then she said she didn't [at] different phases of her trial, and now I...ask which one is it, but it doesn't really matter. Did she go into my sister's with...rope so they couldn't escape? Yes. Did she dip a towel in my sister's wounds and print the word 'PIG' on the door? Yes, she did. One way or the other, my sister and the others died at [Susan's] hands....As sure as if she plunged the knife into their bodies...she is responsible for all those deaths....She doesn't...want to remember a lot of things. [I] tell you, there [are] things that I block out, too, that I really don't want to remember, like the days after my sister's death. I can't tell you what my family did on a daily basis. I have no recollection....I know you have to look at these [inmates] as what they are today, but...I don't understand how we can take people like them and ever...think, good God, even think of letting these types of people out of prison. I don't understand it. Seven, eight lives these people have taken that we know [of]...and to even think...I don't know, I can't rationalize it....I listened to [Susan's] hopes and...dreams, and she wants to go home. I would love my sister to come home, too, but that never, ever will [happen] because of [Susan's] decision. She had decisions. She [was capable of killing] before she ever even hooked up with Manson. There were many, many people at the commune...but there were only a few who went on this murderous rampage, and that was for one reason, because it ran in their blood, and each of them knew who had the capability of...killing....I think the greatest charity given to her is life in prison. It [is] exactly where she should be for the rest of her natural life....If she does good deeds and spreads the Word of God, that's great if she [does it] within these prison walls. She does not deserve to ever walk the free streets....She doesn't talk too much about the victims' lives she's taken. She doesn't pray too much. She prays in here for a lot of people...[but] she never prays for my family. She never prays for us, for what she's done to us."[7]

"It's hard, real hard," Patti later explained of the parole hearings, "because every emotion comes out of you. You're mad, sad—everything just comes out and you have to sit there and listen to how well they are doing, how they've gotten their college degrees, how they have received all kinds of help to make them better people. And I just want to vomit. People think that, 'Oh, they [can't] get out of jail,' when in fact they can get out of jail. That's why I tell people all the time that we have to know what is going on at the capital and what needs to be changed. We need to start paying attention to our elected officials and how they are voting. Are they working for us? Are they going to be tough on crime? I am so passionate about this because I feel that people [will] make a change [if] they...know that they can....We all have to be fighters."[8]

The parole hearings were just one of the ordeals which Patti was forced to confront. The twenty-fifth anniversary of Sharon's death, in 1994, heralded a new, inexplicable public fascination with the Manson Family, echoing, in Prosecutor Vincent Bugliosi's words, the "seemingly tireless resonance of the case."[9] The anniversary not only prompted media discussion of the crimes but an almost macabre celebration of Manson's rising folk-hero status.

"Manson," wrote one author, "is the only figure who can compete with Malcolm X for the kind of iconic power that attracts disenchanted, disenfranchised, and disaffected white kids."[10] Two decades after the Tate-LaBianca murders, this hypnotic reach extended not only to television documentaries and books but, ironically, to the very medium in which Manson himself had sought recognition: the music industry.

During the Tate-LaBianca trial, members of the Family arranged to have the recording sessions from the summer of 1968 released. The album, called *Lie*, featuring the same wild-eyed photograph of Charles Manson which had stared from the cover of the 19 December, 1969 issue of *Life Magazine*.

In 1982 came a second album, this one a bootleg illegally taped during Manson's incarceration called *Charlie Manson's Good Time Gospel Hour*, a third, *Charles Manson: Live at San Quentin* followed several years later. Stephen Kaplan of Performance Records, distributor of *Lie* in the 1980s, recalled: "Kids buy it thinking they're going to get devil-worship music. But when they get home and find they have an album of mediocre folk songs, a lot of them are disappointed."[11]

But the attention sparked interest among a new group of Manson admirers: recording artists. On their 1982 album *Born Innocent*, Redd Kross included a version of Manson's song "Cease to Exist," as well as a song called "Charlie" whose lyrics included the lines: "Flag on the couch/Lady on the floor/Baby in the gut/widdle biddy boy."[12] The 1988 album *Creator* by Evan Dando and the Lemmonheads included notes thanking "Susan, Lynette, Gypsy, Katie, Mary, Sandra, Leslie, Snake, Ouisch, Little Paul, and, of course, Charlie." The group Sonic Youth recorded a song, "Death Valley, 69" in tribute to the Manson Family, and, in 1990, a rock opera, *The Manson Family*, premiered at Lincoln Center in New York, which had commissioned the piece from composer John Moran.[13]

In the early 1990s, the music industry's fascination with Manson achieved a new prominence. In September of 1988, Rudolph Altobelli sold the estate at 10050 Cielo Drive where Sharon had been murdered for $1,999,000. Ironically, the agent assigned to the sale was twenty-four-year-old Adam Jakobson, son of Manson Family associate Gregg Jakobson.

After the murders, security around the estate had been reinforced. A new gate was placed across the driveway, video cameras set up, and the number of the property changed from 10050 to 10066 Cielo Drive in an attempt to throw curious tourists off-track. Following the twentieth anniversary of the murders in 1989, when television crews crowded the end of the cul-de-sac, the new owner erected a ten foot high batten-board fence and gate, cutting off all views of the property from the end of the roadway.

The house was often leased on a short-term basis. One of the tenants was Trent Reznor, lead singer for the industrial rock group Nine Inch Nails. Reznor later claimed that he had not known it was the Tate house until he moved in. "It's a coincidence," he explained. "When I found out what it was, it was even cooler. But it's a cool house anyway and on top of that has a very interesting story behind it. The whole thing about living here, I didn't even think of. I didn't go on a press campaign saying, 'I live in Sharon Tate's house, and I'm really spooky.'"[14]

Reznor turned the living room of the main house into a studio which he dubbed "Le Pig." Here, in the same room in which Sharon had been killed, he recorded songs for his album *The Downward Spiral*, including "Piggy" and "March of the Pigs." Brian Warner, the recording artist known as Marilyn Manson, also used "Le Pig" to work on his first album. "If you thought about what happened there," Warner said, "it was disturbing late at night, but it wasn't exactly a haunted house. No rattling chains or anything, but it did bring across some darkness on the record."[15]

At the time of the twenty-fifth anniversary of the crimes, a new furor erupted involving Manson's music and folk-hero status. Rock band Guns N' Roses, led by singer Axel Rose, released their album called *The Spaghetti Incident?* which included a cover of Manson's song, "Look at Your Game, Girl." During their tour in support of the album, Rose often sported shirts from Zooport Riot Gear of Newport Beach, California which featured Manson's face and slogans such as "Charlie Don't Surf," and "Support Family Values." Rose's promotion of the shirts made them popular items, and the Lemmons Brothers, who owned Zooport, reportedly sold over 50,000. Manson had himself agreed to the promotion: "I Charles Manson, grant permission for my likeness to be used on a T-shirt created by Dan Lemmons," read his hand-written contract. "I agree to accept the .10 cents/T-shirt royalty to be paid to me on a quarterly basis." At the bottom, Manson added: "I don't know about stuff like this, you take care of this."[16] The brothers, in turn, dispatched $600 in royalties to Manson in prison.[17]

Word of this financial windfall came as the public learned that Manson himself was set to earn $62,000 in royalties for every million copies sold of *The Spaghetti Incident?*[18] In 1971, Voyteck Frykowski's son Bartek had brought a civil suit against Manson, Watson, Atkins and Krenwinkel; he was awarded a $500,000 Federal Court judgment against the Manson Family, which, with interest, had grown to $1.5 million by 1994.

Bartek Frykowski was the only victims' relative to have renewed his civil judgment. He finished film school in Lodz, Poland, was living with his wife and two children when his lawyer in Los Angeles, Nathaniel Freidman, informed him of the Guns N' Roses controversy. Now, Freidman petitioned to have these proceeds diverted from Manson to help pay the award. "Manson ruined my life," Bartek said. "He has to pay for that."[19]

The Lemmons Brothers, who declared themselves to be fundamentalist Christians, refused. "Why should we give money to a drug dealer's son?" Dan Lemmons said. Instead, he announced that they would donate the money to the anti-abortion organization Operation Rescue.[20] Eventually, Bartek Frykowski, living in Germany, received a check for $72,000—money derived from the Guns N' Roses royalties.[21]

The media attention and controversy outraged Patti Tate. She instituted a boycott against Geffen Records, Guns N' Roses recording company, claiming that they were "putting Manson up on a pedestal for young people who don't know who he is to worship like an idol."[22]

Ed Rosenblatt, President of Geffen Records, responded to her public criticism by saying he "would have preferred that the song wasn't on the album, but given our belief in freedom of speech as well as the clear restraints of our legal agreements with the band, it is not our decision to make. That decision belongs solely to Guns N'Roses. We genuinely regret the distress the situation has caused."[23]

Patti eventually had a private meeting with Geffen executives in December, 1993. "Nothing came out of it," she said, "but it was necessary for me to sit down with them, face to face, and ask them, 'Do you realize what you are creating here?' This isn't about whether or not Manson is making money....This is about Manson still profiting by becoming a cult hero, an idol to a lot of young kids out there who will buy the album....I needed to touch them with my story, with my sister's story, with her memory."[24]

Epilogue

O N 26 SEPTEMBER, 1970, THE RAMBLING COLLECTION OF FALSE fronts, movie sets and outbuildings which comprised Spahn Ranch burned to the ground in a mysterious fire. By the following day, when the fires died down, all that remained was the property itself, a barren wasteland littered with the rusting bodies of automobiles stolen and then stripped by the Family. It was, in many ways, a fitting end to the grim place from which Manson had dispatched his legion of killers on their hellish missions of murder.

There are few reminders of those momentous events in the summer of 1969. In Death Valley, Barker Ranch remains much the same as it was when Manson and his Family were captured during the raid of October, 1969; a guestbook, left for the curious to sign, is filled with the thoughts of visitors. "It is always good to have places like this to remind us of what horror goes on in the world," wrote a visitor from Vancouver, Canada in the spring of 1999. "But we should use this piece of history to remind us of what has happened in the past so it doesn't happen again. It saddens me to read messages that give sympathy to Manson's life. If we sympathize with him, that only makes us just as bad. Let's stop the madness."[1] The famous Manson Family bus has disintegrated with the passage of time, the rusting skeleton of its frame lying in the barren desert the only evidence of its existence. The adjacent Myers Ranch, where the Family also stayed, recently burned to the ground, victim of suspected arson.

The house at 10050 Cielo Drive, after a number of temporary tenants, was finally torn down in 1993. The new owner, weary of the ever-present stream of curious tourists and macabre interest, had the house razed; in its place, he erected an enormous Mediterranean-style mansion, perched atop a wide crescent of concrete. It is the largest house in Benedict Canyon, visible for miles. The only reminder from Sharon's tenure is a lone telephone pole beyond the gates, the same pole which Charles Watson climbed that hot August night to cut the phone lines, ensuring that none of his victims could call out for help.

Across Los Angeles, only the LaBianca house remains much as it was the night of the murders. A number of changes through the years have transformed the once-sloped green lawn at the front of the house into an underground garage and series of terraces, but the residence itself has been left alone. Until recently, it was owned by a lady from the Philippines, who took great pride in the house's grim history.

Only fragments, too, remain of Manson's Family. Although hard-core members of the Family were locked away, for a time it continued to flourish, directed in exile by two of Manson's most vehement followers, Lynette "Squeaky" Fromme and Sandra Good, christened "Red" and "Blue," respectively, by Manson himself. Fromme, who had always seemed a more intelligent, gentle member of the Family, achieved her own notoriety on 5 September, 1975, when, dressed in a long red cape, she aimed a gun at President Gerald Ford during a visit to Sacramento.

Had she wished to do so, Fromme could most likely have assassinated the President; while her action was almost certainly no more than a publicity stunt to draw attention to Manson, she nevertheless received a life sentence without parole on 19 December, 1975.

Fromme disappeared from the headlines for many years, but, on 23 December, 1987, she managed to escape from the Federal Penitentary at Alderson, West Virginia, where she had been incarcerated. Hearing erroneous rumors that Manson was suffering from cancer, she wanted to be near him. Two days later, she was discovered hiding in the woods near the prison, and was transferred to a more secure facility in Kentucky.

Fromme was the subject of a recent biography by author Jess Bravin. In a letter to Judge Thomas MacBride, who had presided at her 1975 trial for attempting to assassinate President Gerald Ford, she wrote: "I did not contribute to this book; while I can't complain that Bravin was out to get me, some of those interviewed for the book gave distorted or fictitious stories."[2] "I've never published a book," Fromme added in a 1998 letter. "Thought the trees were worth more, but I've also long considered it."[3]

A week after Fromme's encounter with President Ford in 1975, Sandra Good released a list of government officials and business executives who she declared were enemies of the earth. If they continued to pollute the environment, she warned, they would die. For this thinly-veiled threat, she was put on trial, and found guilty of "conspiring to commit offenses against the United States by causing to be delivered by the Postal Service according to the directions thereon, letters addressed to persons, containing threats to injure the person, addressee, and others." Having served a ten year sentence, she was released in 1985.

Good remains Manson's most vocal proponent, residing in California and supervising, along with George Stimson (Sandra Good's boyfriend), Manson's official web site, ATWA, an acronym for Air, Trees, Water and Animals. As author Bill Nelson has pointed out, it is one of the great ironies that the same forces behind the promotion of Manson's ecological vision were the very people who left the areas round the Spahn, Barker and Myers Ranches littered with old car parts, beer bottles and debris from their tenure.[4]

The web site seems to focus on winning Manson's freedom, contending that he was denied legal proper representation. The thirtieth anniversary of the crimes, however, did not go unnoticed. "We are not going to participate in the media's 30th anniversary celebration of the murders," the site announced. The same article, presumably with the full approval of both Good and Manson, went on to declare "it is true that we do not have sympathy for the victims of these murders."[5] Such a stunning admission, however, is in character for Good. "It's like a soldier's reality," she has said of the murders. "If these people in Hollywood have to go, so be it. That made sense to me, and that made sense to all of us. In war, sometimes killing is needed."[6] She remains defiant, Manson's "Blue," unwavering in her devotion.

The reach of the Family continues to be felt. As recently as July, 1998, Inyo County District Attorney Phil McDowell, accompanied by author Bill Nelson and several officials, spent an afternoon at Barker Ranch in Death Valley, searching for bodies believed to be buried there. In 1969, Susan Atkins bragged that the Family had murdered several people at Barker Ranch and buried their remains there. One of those allegedly privy to the intimate details was Larry Melton, known in the Family as White Rabbit. McDowell offered Melton the following immunity agreement in exchange for information: "I, Larry Allen Melton, also known as White Rabbit, agree to fully cooperate with the Inyo County District Attorney's Office in the investigation of a homicide case involving the death of two adult males and one minor female occurring on or about October 6, 1969, at Barker Ranch in the Panamint Range in the County of Inyo, State of California."[7] The search party was unable to locate any bodies, however, and it remains but one of many open questions which surround the murderous activities of the Family.

Of the others involved in the Family, Barbara Hoyt, who was fed an LSD-laced hamburger during the Tate-LaBianca trials in an attempt to prevent her testimony, lived in Death Valley where she maintained friendships with Paul Watkins, Juan Flynn, Brook Poston, and Paul Crockett. She has since moved away from California and has a successful career. Most of the former members of the Manson Family are now widely scattered: Dianne Lake, Danny De Carlo and Kitty Lutesinger, Bobby Beausoleil's former girlfriend, all reside in California; Nancy Pitman relocated to the Pacific Northwest; Catherine Share lives in Texas; and Mary Brunner returned to her native Wisconsin.

Linda Kasabian disappeared into obscurity. She now lives under an assumed name near Tacoma, Washington, with her daughter Tanya. Bugliosi's star witness has not had an easy life. A car accident left her with chronic leg and back pain, and made viable employment difficult; she had no resources, no bank account and no marketable job skills. According to a report filed with Pierce County officials, Kasabian, in her own words, "survives however she can." The court eventually found her indigent.[8]

On 24 October, 1996, members of the Tacoma, Washington Police Department served a search warrant on the apartment owned by Kasabian's daughter Tanya, known to the authorities as "Lady Dangerous." Kasabian, as well as Tanya's two young children, were present when the police arrived. Their report stated: "In the master bedroom (defendant's bedroom) officers located a small baggie containing suspected rock cocaine and a large bundle of cash in a dresser drawer. On top of the dresser was a box of baggies. Also in the room officers located a .45 caliber semi-automatic handgun, ammunition, electronic scales, a plate with cocaine residue, and another bundle of cash. In a hall closest officers located an A-1 Army Rifle. In the children's closet officers found a loaded 30-30 Remington rifle. Officers also searched Kasabian's purse and located a small amount of suspected methamphetamine. In the defendant's vehicle officers located five bags of suspected rock cocaine (43 grams total) and a baggie of powder cocaine (30 grams). The suspected cocaine and methamphetamine field-tested positive."[9]

Tanya, found guilty of possession of controlled substances, was sentenced to a year in state prison. Kasabian, in possession of methamphetamine, was allowed to plea a reduction of her sentence and attended drug counseling classes rather than serve time. Neither the members of the Tacoma Police Department nor the Prosecuting Attorney for Pierce County had any idea that, nearly thirty years earlier, their suspect had, for a time, been one of the most notorious women in America.

For those incarcerated members of the Family, December, 1996 saw the end of conjugal visits, a measure which Doris Tate and Bill Nelson had long worked to pass. She was enraged that Charles Watson, the man who had slain her daughter and unborn grandson, had himself become the father of four children while in prison. "It's unbelievable," she said. "That man should never have been allowed to have any children. He gave up his right to have a family when he took Sharon's away from her. If they want to have sex in prison, fine—make them get vasectomies. No child should have to suffer through knowing that their father is in prison for murdering eight people."[10]

In subtle ways, the work which Doris undertook, and the appearances Patti continued to make at parole hearings, seem to have inspired and strengthened the determination of other victims' families. In 1994, Alice LaBianca, Leno LaBianca's first wife and mother to his three children, published a novel about their life together, *No More Tomorrows.* "We have nine grandchildren," she says, "and none of them knew their grandfather. I wrote the book for them. I wanted to concentrate on Leno as I knew him, and not on the murders."[11]

"For twenty-five years," Alice said in 1994, "we've been subjected to this, and we have nine grandchildren, and they're subjected to it. It's been a devastating thing, and it goes on, and on, and on. And it's as if Manson's some sort of celebrity himself, a god or something, that everyone is so thrilled with what he has to say."[12]

In 1998, Alice became the first member of the LaBianca Family to present a formal objection to the parole of Leslie Van Houten. She did so in the form of a letter, written on behalf of her entire family:

> Manson and his minions thrust our family name into public focus when they murdered Sharon Tate and her house guests one night, then they killed my former husband and his wife in the most brutal manner the next night. Their shocking criminal actions became known as the Tate-LaBianca murders. We lost out privacy and our obscurity.
>
> My Family never became vocal, we did not become activists, we relied on the justice system to seek and find the justice that was due us. We have never been asked by the District Attorney's Office to participate in opposing the release of any of the killers. After all, they all received the death penalty, and that was all our family could expect.
>
> But we can no longer remain silent. Let me preface my remarks with this statement.We do not desire to become activists. We do not desire to be bombarded by the media and have our privacy destroyed. Yet we must make a statement about the parole hearing for convicted murderer Leslie Van Houten....Sympathy for these killers, and especially this one, is misplaced. Sympathy, understanding and compassion, should be given to the victims of the murders, and not the killers. In all these years, not one of these killers have expressed remorse to our family, not even Leslie Van Houten, who says she did the least in the murders. If she is really ready for parole then amends to the family should have already been done....
>
> We emphatically oppose the release of any of the Manson menage....It's a sacrilege to Leno's memory that the family has to be confronted with the parole hearings for these individuals every few years. We are glad for her maturity and her model prisoner status, but that does not equate to freedom. We also want to say that Suzanne LaBerge, daughter of Rosemary, the murdered wife of Leno at the time, does not represent the LaBianca family. She certainly did not represent us at the May 4, 1990 parole hearing for Tex Watson, when she made that pathetic appeal for his release because she "forgave him." As Ms. Van Houten continues her incarceration, let her continue to remember that what she did that fateful night was forever. The Manson Family mark on this society is deep. As deep as the stab wounds to their helpless victims.[13]

Like the LaBiancas, the family of Steven Parent long remained silent. His sister Janet recalls the painful memories of the Tate-LaBianca trial, and the devastating aftermath which followed the verdicts. Once the trials were over, the police released the victims' personal property which had been held in evidence. The white, 1966 Ambassador in which Steve had been shot and killed by Watson, was duly returned to the Parents. "The police had taken the panels out of the car," Janet remembers, "and when we got it back, Steve's blood was still in the cracks, along the seat and under the console. They also brought back an envelope which had my brother's personal effects. His watch and his class ring were still covered with dried blood. There was no feeling about it at all. My brother was a nobody as far as everyone else was concerned, but he was a somebody to us."[14]

The subject of parole remains an understandably painful one with Janet Parent. She takes umbrage at the seemingly endless series of hearings given to Manson, Watson, Atkins, Krenwinkel and Van Houten. "I want to do what I can do to keep them in there," she says, "but I don't want to do anything that will endanger myself and my family. I just want somebody to make me understand how this can even be happening. I just can't rationalize any of it. These are people who we know have killed already. Why do we want to put them back out? I fear for my life, I fear for the lives of others. They're putting everyone in jeopardy. I know that somebody has got to help keep them in there, but at the same time, I'm upset, I'm afraid. I don't even know how to deal with it. They have to keep rehashing it, and giving these people the chance to get out. They shouldn't even be alive, they shouldn't be here. There's no way they can ever be rehabilitated. I just don't understand why people support them."[15]

On 7 July, 1999, media attention focused on the California Women's Correctional Facility at Corona, where Leslie Van Houten was scheduled to attend her thirteenth parole hearing. The year before, on receiving a one year denial from the Board of Prison Terms, she had smiled broadly at the commissioners. In 1999, there was much talk that the photogenic and well-spoken Van Houten might finally be given a release date.

Also present that day were three disparate players: Stephen Kay, Deputy District Attorney who had assisted Vincent Bugliosi at the original Tate-LaBianca trial and tried Van Houten in her two following trials; Angela Smaldino, niece of Leno LaBianca; and Bill Nelson, an independent producer, author of two books on the Manson Family, and owner of a web site dedicated to the history of the crimes.

It was obvious from Van Houten's initial appearance before the Board of Prison Terms that this day was to be somehow different. Kay noted: "She looked like she didn't sleep last night, she had big circles under her eyes, she was shaking and quivering."[16] Van Houten scarcely glanced at Smaldino and Kay as she took her seat. Van Houten began her parole hearing by raising an objection. She was incensed that Nelson, among others, was offering copies of her various parole hearings for sale. "I feel," she told the Board of Prison Terms, "that this has gotten a little out of hand, and I believe that there is really no reason for the camera to be in the board room, when it's being gotten to somehow and sold for profit. And I believe that the internet has become a place where there's a lot of exploiting of violence, and this man has a shopping list, and I am part of that shopping list, and if you allow the camera in here then I'm partaking in it, and I can't do that."[17]

After some discussion, however, the Board members refused to remove the camera. Visibly upset, Van Houten continued to voice objections. "I think there's a lot of things going on," she said, "that are not proper and correct. I feel like I'm part of a circus, to tell you the truth, and I need to get an attorney to look into why these decisions are being made the way they are, because I don't think it's right. I think someone's manipulating the system to make money, and I can't be part of that."

Van Houten turned to Angela Smaldino, Leno LaBianca's niece, who sat at the end of the table. "I deeply apologize to you," she began, "for all the pain I caused you," before Presiding Commissioner Carol Bentley interrupted, telling Van Houten not to speak directly to the family member. Van Houten, however, ignored the Commissioner and continued to speak over her objections, finally declaring, "I gotta go, I can't be part of this hearing. I don't know how this works, I don't know if I'm postponed, I just know that I can't sit here and do this knowing that someone's going to sell it."

On her feet now, Van Houten was on her way out of the hearing room when Bently stopped her, suggesting that the Board take a recess to discuss the matter. When the three member Board of Prison Terms returned, they told Van Houten that her parole hearing would be postponed until her objections could be examined.

"I'm going to look into hiring an attorney also," Van Houten added. "This has gotten too big for me...I um...I don't know...how many cameras are outside? How many news media are outside, how many agencies? Do you know? Do you know if Mr. Nelson is on the grounds?"[18]

Nelson was indeed on the grounds, there to obtain his video copy of the proceedings. He stood outside the facility, watching a live feed from the hearing room along with other media representatives. "I heard her mention my name, and I turned away from the monitor in disbelief and said, 'I've just become the story.'"[19]

As soon as the hearing was adjourned, the collected media swarmed round Nelson, shouting questions and demanding to know how much income he had derived from his web site sales. He patiently explained his permission to tape the proceedings, and that the majority of sales from his site were made to researchers and television producers. The press, however, was reluctant to let the story drop with this simple answer; he was described on the KNBC news broadcast that evening as "an obsessed man with a web site."[20]

Nelson, however, was something altogether more substantial. For several years, he had traveled with Doris Tate round America and to Europe as she spoke to various gatherings on victims' rights; had authored two insightful books on the crimes; cultivated friendships with former Family members; actively opposed parole for Watson, Atkins, Krenwinkel and Van Houten; and he maintained the world's largest web site on the case, www.mansonmurders.com, a forum which had brought him into contact with several of the victims' families.

"I started the site because I wanted to do something to support the victims and their families," he says.[21] Nelson, a genial former Secret Service officer and pastor, opposes the release of any of the Manson Family on principle, and has made no secret of the fact, speaking out on his web site against Van Houten's possible parole only a few days before the actual hearing. He had been instrumental in assisting Leno LaBianca's first wife Alice when she submitted a letter to the Board of Prison Terms in 1998 opposing Van Houten's possible parole, and also in the presence this day of Angele Smaldino at the hearing.

It is unclear whether it was Nelson's relentless campaign opposing her release; his legitimate sale of the parole hearings themselves; or, as Deputy District Attorney Stephen Kay suggested after the adjournment, the presence for the first time of a LaBianca relative,

Angela Smaldino, which so unnerved Van Houten. "I know Leslie pretty well," Kay said. "We sat next to each other in the original trial. I tried her on both of her re-trials, and I've been to all thirteen of her parole hearings....She usually is very well spoken, but she had trouble with her words today, and what this was all about was that for the first time in any parole hearing a relative of the LaBianacas showed up, and she was going to have to face Angela Smaldino, who was a niece of Leno LaBianca, and hear about the devastation that these murders caused the LaBianca family, and even worse than that for Leslie, the Board was going to hear about the devastation."[22]

Smaldino certainly believed that it was her presence which led to Van Houten's shaken appearance. She told Court TV correspondent Clara Tuma: "I wanted her to face what she did to the whole family. We know what she did to Leno and Rosemary. They died in fifteen minutes, but our family died slowly, over the last fifteen years."[23]

There was certainly an air of theatricality in Van Houten's performance at the hearing, as well as a hint of insincerity. As recently as April, 1999, Bill Nelson had tried to arrange a private meeting between Van Houten and members of the LaBianca family. At that time, Van Houten had declared that she had no interest in meeting with anyone.[24] Smaldino told Court TV's Clara Tuma that she thought it was "appalling that this day, in public, Leslie Van Houten would reach out" to her.[25]

For Nelson, it was simply more evidence that Van Houten was unsuitable for parole. "She blew it," he says frankly. "She had the opportunity to have a lawyer there, and passed it up. She's had cameras in the board room for years now—why didn't she object before this? She should have worried about her hearing, and not about what she thinks I am doing. I wish I had as much power as she seems to think I do with the Board. Instead of making her case, what did she do? When the stress became too much for her, she picked up her toys and left the sandbox. If she can't deal with the small amount of stress in a controlled environment like the Board of Prison Term's hearing room, how's she going to react when she has to face life outside the prison gates? I am a realist. Leslie Van Houten will get a parole date one day. But she proved that it is still too soon to trust her to control herself in society."[26]

"Many people I know in Los Angeles," wrote Joan Didion,

"believe that the Sixties ended abruptly on August 9, 1969, ended at the exact moment when word of the murders on Cielo Drive traveled like brushfire through the community, and in a sense this is true. The tension broke that day. The paranoia was fulfilled."[27]

Thirty years after her death, Sharon lives on, not only in the hearts and minds of her family and friends, but also on memorial pages scattered across the internet, operated by those too young or too removed to ever have known her in life. A "Sharon Tate Webring" links a collection of sites, run from locations as varied as the United Kingdom, California and Texas. Natalie Grumbles owns "Sharon Tate: The Angel," at http://flyto./sharontate. She, like most of the other webmasters, is fascinated by Sharon, enchanted by her beauty, entertained by her brief body of work, dreaming of what might have been. Grumbles' site offers a range of pages, including message boards, online classifieds, a filmography and a photo gallery. "I wanted it to be more fan friendly," she explains, "a place where Sharon's fans can pitch in. Hence, the newsletter, different committees, a 'Sharon United' Pen Pal service and Sharon wallpaper and e-mail." The interest has, Grumbles confirms, only increased since she began the site in July, 1997.[28]

Allison Lowe, who lives in Swansea, South Wales, operates a site called "Star 69," at www.geocities.com/Hollywood/Boulevard/7686. Lowe, who is twenty-seven, says: "I started the site in the hope of communicating with other like-minded people around the world, and I've been quite thrilled with the mostly positive feedback I've received. I had such a collection of Sharon memorabilia that it seemed such a waste to let it gather dust in my house, when it could be on the web, where others could see it and hopefully get some enjoyment out of it. I was also fed up with the emphasis on her death, and wanted to give her life and work a bit of support."[29]

Sharon Marie Tate Polanski continues to haunt the minds of the American public, an admittedly morbid fascination, but also a measure of her immense charm, beauty and sense of innocence which came to an abrupt end that hot summer night at Cielo Drive. No one knows what might have become of her career as an actress. The one area where she appeared to be heading, that of a comedic actress, might have proved a showcase worthy of her talents had she gained more experience and starred in further roles. Ultimately, and unfortunately, what Sharon so wanted in life she managed only to achieve in death: stardom.

Sharon's real legacy lies not in her movies or in her television work; not in the glowing memories of friends and colleagues whose recollections may be accused of having fallen to the inevitable trap of nostalgia; nor does it lie in the monstrous end which she suffered, and the ensuing trials and incarcerations of one of the most sinister groups ever to surface in the United States. Sharon Tate's legacy must be viewed as the one which her mother and sister Patti have so tirelessly endeavored to promote: the fight for victims' rights. The very fact that, today, victims or their families in California are able to sit before those convicted of a crime and have a voice in the sentencing at trials or at parole hearings, is largely due to the work of Doris Tate. Their years of devotion to Sharon's memory and dedication to victims' rights, ironically wrought from devastating tragedy, have helped transform Sharon from mere victim, restore a human face to one of the twentieth century's most infamous crimes, and finally sever the link between her name and that of Charles Manson.

"Sharon Tate," wrote Gerald Malanga (a writer-actor at Warhol's factory), "enjoyed her life to the utmost while it lasted and contributed to a high and joyous quality to the life of others. Death could not alter this fact; for however death may affect the future, it cannot touch the past....Sharon came into existence and has passed out of existence. Yet between that birth and death she lived her life, has made her actions count with a scope and meaning that the finality of death cannot defeat."[30]

Acknowledgments

A great number of colleagues, friends and researchers have helped craft this book, fill in gaps in information, share resources and help complete the picture of Sharon's life and death. I am especially grateful to those friends of Sharon who submitted to interviews, answered my queries, provided me with valuable information and assisted with this book. While some of those interviewed requested anonymity, and others—while allowing me to mention their contributions wished that specific information not be attributed—all deserve my sincere thanks.

I would like to particularly express my gratitude to Joyce Behncke, Pat Boone, Herb Browar, Vincent Bugliosi, Leslie Caron, Robert Dishaw, John Dobie, Ross Duden, Patty Faulkner, Philippe Forquet, William Garretson, Hal Gefsky, Kathryn Glennie, Natalie Grumbles, Barbara Hoyt, David Ingersoll, Stephen Kay, Aaron Kincaid, Jeff Kinoz, Alice LaBianca, Cheryl Lockerbie of the Doris Tate Crime Victims Bureau, Allison Lowe, Mike McGann, Will Melendez, Cynthia Melin, Mike Mindlin, Howard Miller, Janet Parent, Alan Patierno, Michelle Phillips, Sheila Boyle Plank, Art Schultz, Kay Smithson, Joe Spitz, Elizabeth Gedwed Stroup, Tracy Tait, Corey Urbach, Skip Ward, Brodie Williamson, Jim Wilson, Mick Woelk, Ib and Paula Zacko, and Brent Zachy for the support and contributions. I went straight from one book deadline to the next, and my friends have proved, as ever, understanding and patient. Sharlene Aadland, Daniel Briere, Liz and Andy Eaton, Marlene Eilers, Laura Enstone, Jake Gariepy, Nils Hanson, Barbara and Paul Harper, Gretchen Haskin, Kathy Hoefler, DeeAnn Hoff, Dianne Holme, Jeff Hooks, Angela Manning, Cecelia Manning, Mark Manning, Grant Michael Menzies, Denis Meslans, Russ Minugh, Steve O'Donnell, and Anne Shawyer have never let me down, even in the face of peculiarities imposed by my chosen career. And my parents, Roger and Helena King, have again given their invaluable support—emotional, practical and financial.

I would like to thank those who, against my deadline, have generously shared their own information on Sharon and alerted me to resources I might have missed: David Allen, Monty Hinson, Allison Keene, Stephanie Ogle of Cinema Books in Seattle, and Christopher Simmons. Ted Spittal has been instrumental in making the connections which allowed me to interview many of Sharon's former schoolmates from her time at Vincenza American High School.

As always, Susanne Meslans has been of immense help. Her valuable suggestions have always helped craft my books, and I thank her especially for her work on this book.

My friend Candace Metz-Longinette-Gahring sacrificed her own time and writing interests to pursue information on the Manson Family and their victims; discuss ideas; and, during an already hectic weekend, make time to read through the manuscript and offer important insight. Without Candace's insight, this book would be sadly lacking.

Manson author and researcher Bill Nelson literally opened doors which were long closed, putting me in touch with those involved with Sharon's life and with the case which followed her death. His ideas, inspiration and continued support of this project made my quest much easier. Having studied the Manson case for many years, I am firmly of the opinion that no one on earth knows more about this subject than does Bill. His razor-sharp mind and voluminous archives are treasure troves, and I thank him immensely for having so graciously assisted me in the face of his own concerns.

Penny Wilson literally put her busy life on hold to not only read the manuscript and make corrections, but also step in during an emergency and rescue the delivery of the book. Her contributions have been immense, especially under such pressure, and her enlightened comments on Sharon's life have added immeasurably to the finished product. She has proved to be a true friend and confidant. And Tom Wilson has generously assisted with the production of the finished manuscript never complaining when I frequently kept his wife on the telephone until four in the morning to argue content and direction. Both have my grateful thanks.

In 1991, former Manson Family prosecutor Vincent Bugliosi first put me in touch with Doris Tate. At that time, I suggested the idea

of a biography of Sharon. Although initially reluctant, Doris warmed
to the idea, and began sharing information about her daughter's life
with me through letters and telephone calls. A few months later,
Doris became ill. The last time I spoke with Doris, she was unwell,
and our conversation was brief. She apologized, saying that she no
longer had the strength to assist me with the project, but that she
hoped we could move forward with the idea in the future.
Unfortunately, her illness worsened, and she died before any
arrangements could be formalized. I only hope that her legacy of
advocacy on behalf of victims' rights, so admirably carried on by
Sharon's sister Patti, continues to effectively remind us all of the
beautiful daughter whom she never ceased to mourn.

Greg King
March, 2000

Source Notes

Chapter One

1. Brottman, 18.
2. Art Schultz to author.
3. Doris Tate to author.
4. Ibid.
5. Bob Lardine, "Reaching for Instant Stardom: Sharon Tate is on a Crash Program to get to the Top." In the *New York Sunday News*, 16 December, 1966.
6. Art Schultz to author.
7. Doris Tate to author.
8. Edwards, 67.
9. *Eye of the Devil* Pressbook, MGM-Filmways, Inc., 13.
10 Musel, 24.
11. Doris Tate to author.
12. Musel, 26.
13. Bowers, 27.
14. Lydia Lane, "Sharon Tate's Big Discovery." In the *Los Angeles Times*, 24 October, 1967.
15. Doris Tate to author.

Chapter Two

1. Art Schultz to author.
2. Ibid.
3. Will Melendez to author.
4. Art Schultz to author.
5. Will Melendez to author.
6. Howard Miller to author.
7. Bowers, 27.
8. Sheila Boyle Plank, on "The Last Days of Sharon Tate," *True Hollywood Stories*, E! Entertainment Channel, produced by Brent Zacky, 1999.
9. Elizabeth Gedwed Stroup to author.
10. Sheila Boyle Plank to author.
11. Sheila Boyle Plank, on "The Last Days of Sharon Tate," *True Hollywood Stories*, E! Entertainment Channel, produced by Brent Zacky, 1999.
12. Bowers, 27; details are also drawn from Sharon's 1961 Vincenza American High annual, *Nostra Italia*.

13. Art Schultz to author.
14. Will Melendez to author.
15. Lydia Lane, op. cit.
16. Bowers, 27.
17. Howard Miller to author.
18. Art Schultz to author.
19. Ibid.
20. Ibid.
21. Jim Wilson to author.
22. Art Schultz to author.
23. Polanski, 252.
24. Art Schultz to author.
25. Skip Ward to author.
26. Bob Lardine, op. cit.
27. Pat Boone to author.
28. Ibid.
29. Ibid.
30. Doris Tate, in *Sharon Tate the Victim, Charles Manson the Killer*, videotape produced by Bill Nelson, California Breeze, Costa Mesa, California, 1990.
31. Sheila Boyle Plank, on "The Last Days of Sharon Tate," *True Hollywood Stories*, E! Entertainment Channel, produced by Brent Zacky, 1999.
32. Art Schultz to author.
33. Ibid.
34. Crivello, 38.

Chapter Three

1. Stern, 7.
2. Musel, 24-6.
3. Skip Ward to author.
4. Ibid.
5. Ibid.
6. Bowers, 27.
7. Crivello, 38.
8. Hal Gefsky to author.
9. Hal Gefsky, quoted in *TV Radio Mirror*, November, 1969, 12.
10. Hal Gefsky to author.
11. Doris Tate, in *Sharon Tate the Victim, Charles Manson the Killer*, op. cit.
12. Sanders, 72.
13. Crivello, 38.

14. Bowers, 27.
15. Hal Gefsky to author.
16. Schessler, 11.
17. Hal Gefsky to author.
18. Crivello, 38.
19. Ibid, 38-9.
20. Musel, 24-6.
21. Bowers, 27.
22. Mike Mindlin to author.
23. Hal Gefsky to author.
24. Crivello, 38.
25. Hal Gefsky to author.
26. Ibid
27. Bowers, 27.
28. Herb Browar to author.
29. Bowers, 27
30. Lindsay, 45-6.
31. Musel, 24.
32. Lindsay, 45-6.
33. Polanski, 250.
34. Lindsay, 45.
35. Ibid, 100.
36. Bowers, 28.
37. Herb Browar to author.
38. Ibid.
39. Ibid.
40. Mike Mindlin to author.
41. Hal Gefsky to author.
42. Rollin, 55.
43. Musel, 26.
44. Cox, 150-151.
45. Bowers, 28.

Chapter Four
1. Philippe Forquet to author.
2. Hal Gefsky to author.
3. Philippe Forquet to author.
4. Ibid.
5. Ibid.
6. Holt, 318.
7. Philippe Forquet to author.
8. Young, 49.
9. Nalven, 286.
10. Ibid, 290.
11. Cox, 137.
12. Musel, 26.
13. *Eye of the Devil* Pressbook, MGM-Filmways, Inc.
14. Musel, 24.
15. Bowers, 28.
16. Rollin, 55.
17. Bowers, 28.

18. *Eye of the Devil* Pressbook, MGM-Filmways, Inc.
19. Mike Mindlin to author.
20. Herb Browar to author.
21. Cox, 137.
22. Ibid, 79-80.
23. Nancy Kulp to author.
24. Musel, 26.
25. Philippe Forquet to author.
26. Bowers, 28.
27. Philippe Forquet to author.
28. *Los Angeles Herald-Examiner*, 27 May, 1964.
29. Philippe Forquet to author.
30. Bugliosi, 26.
31. Philippe Forquet to author.
32. Bowers, 28.
33. Philippe Forquet to author.
34. Hal Gefsky to author.
35. Crivello, 40.
36. Lardine, op. cit.
37. Crivello, 41.
38. Bowers, 28.
39. Ibid, 27.

Chapter Five
1. Skip Ward to author.
2. Douglas, 325.
3. Michelle Phillips to author.
4. Douglas, 315.
5. Skip Ward to author.
6. Ib Zacko to author.
7. Edwards, 67.
8. Doris Tate to author.
9. Schessler, 47.
10. Jacobson, 11.
11. Aaron Kincaid to author.
12. Skip Ward to author.
13. Kleiner, 142.
14. Bailey, 102.
15. Roman Polanski, LAPD Polygraph Examination Transcript, 11 August, 1969.
16. Paula Zacho to author.
17. Skip Ward to author.
18. Toffel, 146-47.
19. Skip Ward to author.
20. Crivello, 41.
21. Hal Gefsky to author.
22. Ibid.
23. Heitland, 223.

Chapter Six

1. *All Eyes on Sharon Tate*, MGM-Filmways promotional featurette, 1967.
2. Mike Mindlin to author.
3. *All Eyes on Sharon Tate*, op. cit.
4. Musel, 26.
5. *All Eyes on Sharon Tate*, op. cit.
6. Braun, 201.
7. *All Eyes on Sharon Tate*, op. cit.
8. Ibid.
9. Ibid.
10. Sanders, 73.
11. *All Eyes on Sharon Tate*, op. cit.
12. Polanski, 251.
13. Bowers, 26.
14. Polanski, 212.
15. Victor Lownes to author.
16. Leslie Caron to author.
17. Victor Lownes to author.
18. Skip Ward to author.

Chapter Seven

1. Leaming, 16.
2. Polanski, 34.
3. Leaming, 30.
4. Roman Polanski, LAPD Polygraph Examination Transcript, 11 August, 1969.
5. Polanski, 143.
6. Thompson, 46.
7. Polanski, 142-43; Leaming, 30-1.
8. Leaming, 31.
9. Polanski, 159.
10. Leaming, 52-3.
11. Polanski, 191.
12. Ibid, 203.
13. Ibid, 203.
14. Kiernan, 180.
15. Polanski, 206-07.
16. Ibid, 208.
17. Ibid, 221.
18. Roman Polanski, LAPD Polygraph Examination Transcript, 11 August, 1969.
19. Tynan, 89.
20. Private Information.
21. Roman Polanski, LAPD Polygraph Examination Transcript, 11 August, 1969.
22. Leaming, 76.
23. Polanski, 250.

24. Ibid, 251.
25. Roman Polanski, LAPD Polygraph Examination Transcript, 11 August, 1969.
26. Bowers, 28.
27. Polanski, 252.
28. Roman Polanski, LAPD Polygraph Examination Transcript, 11 August, 1969.
29. Polanski, 252.
30. Ibid, 252.
31. Roman Polanski, LAPD Polygraph Examination Transcript, 11 August, 1969.
32. Bowers, 28.
33. Roman Polanski, LAPD Polygraph Examination Transcript, 11 August, 1969.
34. Polanski, 252-53.
35. Roman Polanski, LAPD Polygraph Examination Transcript, 11 August, 1969.
36. Polanski, 253.
37. Roman Polanski, LAPD Polygraph Examination Transcript, 11 August, 1969.
38. Polanski, 253.
39. Mike Mindlin to author.
40. Polanski, 253.

Chapter Eight

1. Polanski, 254.
2. Ibid, 254.
3. *The Fearless Vampire Killers*, Pressbook, Filmways, Inc.
4. Polanski, 256-57.
5. Mike Mindlin to author.
6. Polanski, 256.
7. Roman Polanski, LAPD Polygraph Examination Transcript, 11 August, 1969.

Chapter Nine

1. Polanski, 257.
2. Kiernan, 204.
3. Edwards, 67.
4. Du Bois, 110.
5. Bowers, 27.
6. Du Bois, 110.
7. Roman Polanski, LAPD Polygraph Examination Transcript, 11 August, 1969.

8. Polanski, 258.
9. Parker, 109.
10. Polanski, 214.
11. Bowers, 26.
12. Ibid, 29.
13. Steele, 64.
14. Polanski, 258.
15. Private Information.
16. Golden, 29.
17. Bowers, 26.
18. Lardine, op. cit.
19. Sanders, 76.
20. Crivello, 43.
21. Private Information.
22. Polanski, 258.
23. Roman Polanski, LAPD Polygraph Examination Transcript, 11 August, 1969.
24. Bugliosi, 81.

Chapter Ten
1. Bowers, 31.
2. *Don't Make Waves*, Pressbook, Filmways, Inc.-Cadre Films.
3. Curtis, 228.
4. Polanski, 260.
5. Ibid, 261.
6. Steele, 64.
7. Bowers, 31.
8. Leaming, 82.
9. Ibid, 84.
10. Flamini, 298.
11. Ibid, 146.
12. Ibid, 298.
13. Polanski, 266.
14. Castle, 194-95.
15. Polanski, 276.
16. Roman Polanski, LAPD Polygraph Examination Transcript, 11 August, 1969.
17. Polanski, 276-77.
18. Ibid, 268.
19. Leaming, 84-5.
20. Ibid, 85.
21. Hamilton, 92.
22. Ibid, 92.
23. Polanski, 271.
24. Ibid, 270-71.
25. Ibid, 274; Farrow, 123.
26. Farrow, 124.
27. Ibid, 157.
28. Hamilton, 92.

29. Ibid, 94.
30. Farrow, 120.

Chapter Eleven
1. Duke, 178.
2. Seaman, 286.
3. Duke, 178.
4. Golden, 30.
5. Susann, 54.
6. Edwards, 66.
7. Duke, 182-83; see also, Gerold Frank, 570-79.
8. Shelley, 69.
9. Duke, 179.
10. Duke, 180.
11. Ibid, 180-81.
12. Golden, 30.
13. Edwards, 66.
14. Ibid, 67.
15. Rollin, 55-7.
16. Duke, 185.
17. Polanski, 185.

Chapter Twelve
1. Playboy , March, 1967.
2. Private Information.
3. Mike Mindlin to author.
4. *Playboy*, March, 1967.
5. Edwards, 66.
6. Steele, 64.
7. Lardine, op. cit.
8. *All Eyes on Sharon Tate*, op. cit.
9. Wasserman, op. cit.
10. Steele, 64.
11. Edwards, 66.
12. *Don't Make Waves*, Pressbook, Filmways, Inc.
13. Ibid.
14. Golden, 29.
15. Polanski, 259-60.
16. Ibid, 275.
17. Reed, 7.
18. *Newsweek*, 27 November, 1967.
19. *Time*, 27 November, 1967.
20. *Variety*, 15 November, 1967.
21. *Eye of the Devil*, Pressbook, MGM-Filmways, Inc.
22. *The New York Times*, 27 November, 1967.
23. Duke, 186-87.
24. *Time*, 22 December, 1967.
25. Quoted, Crivello, 45.

26. The New York Times , 16 December, 1967.
27. Newsweek , 16 December, 1967.
28. Quoted, Crivello, 45.
29. Polanski, 289.

Chapter Thirteen
1. Lardine, op. cit.
2. Steele, 65.
3. Du Bois, 100.
4. Steele, 64-5.
5. Victor Lownes to author.
6. Polanski, 278.
7. Private Information.
8. Polanski, 284-85.
9. Biskind, 50.
10. Sanders, 79.
11. Polanski, 289.
12. Du Bois, 100.
13. Ibid, 100.
14. Bailey, 102.
15. Herb Browar to author.
16. Polanski, 286.
17. Ibid, 291-92.
18. Ibid, 288.

Chapter Fourteen
1. Lardine, op. cit.
2. Polanski, 292.
3. Maas, 57.
4. Biskind, 50.
5. Du Bois, 100.
6. Victor Lownes to author.
7. Polanski, 292-93.
8. Victor Lownes to author.
9. Young, Josa, 79.
10. Teague, 58.
11. Collins, 269.
12. Polanski, 293.
13. Teague, 58.
14. Crivello, 45.
15. Steele, 58.
16. Polanski, 293; Leaming, 92.
17. *The London Sunday Times*, 21 January, 1969.
18. "The Wedding That Barbara Parkins Can't Forget," in *Movieland and TV Time*, 81.
19. Leaming, 92.
20. *The London Sunday Times*, 21 January, 1969.
21. Steele, 59.

22. Polanski, 293-94.
23. Parker, 132.
24. Polanski, 297-98.

Chapter Fifteen
1. Evans, 139-40.
2. Parker, 110.
3. Kiernan, 208.
4. Victor Lownes to author.
5. Tynan, 94-5.
6. Kiernan, 212.
7. Maas, 57.
8. Kiernan, 211-12.
9. Bailey, 102.
10. Roman Polanski, LAPD Polygraph Examination Transcript, 11 August, 1969.
11. Private Information.
12. Patty Faulkner to author.
13. Skip Ward to author.
14. Private Information.
15. Skip Ward to author.
16. Michelle Phillips to author.
17. Ibid.
18. Ibid.
19. Phillips, Michelle, 148.
20. Ibid, 84.
21. Kiernan, 209.
22. Leslie Caron to author.
23. Leaming, 96.
24. Edwards, 67-8.
25. Leaming, 88.
26. Polanski, 290-91.

Chapter Sixteen
1. Polanski, 299.
2. Elaine Young, in "The Last Days of Sharon Tate," *True Hollywood Stories* on the E! Entertainment Channel, produced by Brent Zacky, 1999.
3. LAPD First Homicide Investigation Progress Report, DR 69-059 593, 8.
4. Phillips, Michelle, 118.
5. Paul, 46.
6. Hotchner, 231.
7. Bergen, 184.
8. Polanski, 299.
9. This description of the estate and residence at 10050 Cielo Drive is drawn from Bugliosi, 10-12; Sanders, 241-45; and from personal visits by the author.

10. Sanders, 139.
11. Polanski, 299.
12. Bugliosi, 229.

Chapter Seventeen
1. Herb Browar to author.
2. Hal Gefsky to author.
3. Quoted, Crivello, 46.
4. Crivello, 46.
5. Kiernan, 211.
6. Polanski, 298.
7. Bugliosi, 29.
8. Private Information.
9. Phillips, John, 290.
10. LAPD First Homicide Investigation Report, op. cit. , 8.
11. Phillips, John, 291.
12. Leaming, 100.
13. Biskind, 78.
14. Trial testimony of Shahrokh Hatami, 3 November, 1970.
15. Ibid.

Chapter Eighteen
1. Murphy, 33.
2. Manson, 29.
3. Ibid, 28-9.
4. Ibid, 30.
5. Ibid, 31.
6. Delores Longwell, in "Charles Manson: Journey into Evil," *Biography*, A & E Television Network, produced by Alan Goldberg, 1995.
7. Ibid.
8. Ibid, 34-5.
9. Charles Manson, in "Charles Manson: Journey into Evil," *Biography*, A & E Television Network, produced by Alan Goldberg, 1995.
10. Bugliosi, 137.
11. Robert Newell, "Dream Comes True for Lad: He's Going to Boy's Town," in the *Indiannapolis News*, 7 March, 1949.
12. Ibid, 138.
13. Ibid, 139.
14. Ibid, 140.
15. Ibid, 140.
16. Ibid, 141,
17. Sanders, 24.
18. Ibid, 23.

19. Ibid, 29.
20. Ibid, 29-30.
21. Bugliosi, 144.
22. Ibid, 144.
23. Ibid, 145.
24. Sanders, 31.
25. Bugliosi, 145-46.
26. Charles Manson, in "Charles Manson: Journey into Evil," *Biography*, on A & E Television Network, produced by Alan Goldberg, 1995.
27. Phil Kaufmann, in Charles Manson: The Man Who Killed the 60's , a Box Production for Channel Four, UK, produced by Peter Bate, 1994.
28. Bugliosi, 146.

Chapter Nineteen
1. Melton, White Rabbit .
2. Mary Brunner, in Manson , A Robert Hendrickson/Lawrence Merrick Film, 1972.
3. Sanders, 34.
4. Roger Smith, in "Charles Manson: Journey into Evil," *Biography*, on A & E Television Network, produced by Alan Goldberg, 1995.
5. Watkins, 10.
6. Raschke, 111.
7. Sanders, 114.
8. Ibid, 88-9; also, see Raschke, 113-14.
9. Bugliosi, 471. In the last decade, there has been an immense amount of speculation concerning Manson's contacts with various cult leaders. For a complete discussion, see Maury Terry, *The Ultimate Evil.* For a repudiation of Terry's speculation, see Lyons, 87-94.
10. Lyons, 89.
11. Sanders, 85.
12. Ibid, 148.
13. The Process Magazine, "Fear" Issue.
14. The Process Magazine, "Death" Issue.
15. Watson, 63.
16. Patricia Krenwinkel, in "Charles Manson: Journey into Evil," *Biography* on A & E Television Network, produced by Alan Goldberg, 1995.

17. Lynette Fromme, in "Charles Manson: Journey into Evil," *Biography*, on A & E Television Network, produced by Alan Goldberg, 1995.
18. Watson, 62.
19. Manson, 132.
20. Ibid, 122-23; Sanders, 46.
21. Manson, 122-23.
22. Capote, 212.
23. Gilmore, 37-8.
24. Ibid, 47.
25. Raschke, 100-01.
26. Ibid, 100-01.
27. Cited, Raschke, 111.
28. Sanders, 51-2.
29. Talese, "Charlie Manson's Home on the Range," in *Esquire*, March, 1970.

Chapter Twenty
1. Gaines, 190.
2. Bugliosi, 250.
3. Ibid, 251.
4. Ibid, 250.
5. Watkins, 84-5.
6. Bugliosi, 250.
7. Ibid, 251.
8. Life Term Parole Consideration Hearing, State of California, Community Release Board, Steve Grogan, CDC No. B-38773, Tuesday, August 22, 1978, Deul Vocational Institution, Tracy, CA., p. 34.
9. Life Term Parole Consideration Hearing, State of California, Board of Prison Terms, In the Matter of the Subsequent Life Parole Consideration Hearing of Steve Grogan, CDC No. B-28773, California Medical Facility, Vacaville, CA., Tuesday, October 20, 1981, p.33.
10. Life Term Parole Consideration Hearing, State of California, Community Release Board, Steve Grogan, CDC No. B-38773, Tuesday, August 22, 1978, Deul Vocational Institution, Tracy, CA., p.10.
11. Life Term Parole Consideration Hearing, State of California, Community Release Board, Steve Grogan, CDC No. B-38773, Tuesday, August 22, 1978, Deul Vocational

Institution, Tracy, CA., p.17.
12. Leslie Van Houten, "Charles Manson: Journey Into Evil," on *Biography*, A & E Television Network, produced by Alan Goldberg, 1995.
13. Watson, 40.
14. Psychiatric report by Vernon C. Bohr, M.D., on Charles Watson, 12 July, 1971, 3.
15. Watson, 49-51.
16. Ibid, 60.

Chapter Twenty One
1. Wilson, 182.
2. Schreck, 79.
3. Sanders, 98.
4. Watson, 80-1.
5. Ibid, 55.
6. Testimony of Terry Melcher before the Los Angeles County Grand Jury, 5 December, 1969, 134.
7. Phillips, John, 302.
8. Sanders, 98.
9. Watkins, 65.
10. Ibid, 73.
11. Lynette Fromme, "Charles Manson: Journey into Evil," on *Biography*, A & E Television Network, produced by Alan Goldberg, 1995.
12. Leslie Van Houten, "Charles Manson: Journey Into Evil," on *Biography*, A & E Television Network, produced by Alan Goldberg, 1995.
13. Subsequent Life Term Parole Consideration Hearing, State of California, Board of Prison Terms, In the Matter of Steve Grogan, CDC No. B-38773, California Medical Facility, Vacaville, CA., Tuesday, October 21, 1980, p. 30.
14. Watkins, 45.
15. Watson, 70.
16. Watkins, 35-6.
17. Life Term Parole Consideration Hearing, State of California, Community Release Board, In the Matter of the Subsequent Parole Consideration of Steven Grogan, CDC No. B-38773, Wednesday, October 17, 1979, Correctional

Medical Facility, Vacaville, CA., p. 21.
18. Watkins, 54.
19. Watson, 75.
20. Watkins, 73.
21. Sandra Good, in *Manson*, A Robert Hendrickson/Lawrence Merrick Film, 1972.
22. Rose and Smith, "The Group Marriage Commune: A Case Study," in *Journal of Psychedelic Drugs*, September, 1970.
23. Life Term Parole Consideration Hearing, State of California, Community Release Board, In the Matter of the Subsequent Parole Consideration of Steven Grogan, CDC No. B-38773, Wednesday, October 17, 1979, Correctional Medical Facility, Vacaville, CA., p. 22.
24. Livsey, 178.
25. Vincent Bugliosi to author.

Chapter Twenty Two
1. Watkins, 122.
2. Murphy, 16-19.
3. Watkins, 121-22.
4. Bugliosi, 239.
5. Watkins, 245.
6. Bugliosi, 245.
7. Watkins, 148.

Chapter Twenty Three
1. Bugliosi, 377.
2. Nelson, Behind , 20.
3. Trial testimony of Rudolph Altobelli, 3 November, 1970.
4. Watson, 77.
5. Gaines, 206.
6. Manson, 148.
7. Gilmore, 78.
8. Testimony of Terry Melcher before the Los Angeles County Grand Jury, 5 December, 1969, 140.
9. Sanders, 193-94.
10. Manson, 184-85.
11. Maas, 87.

Chapter Twenty Four
1. Watkins, 153-55.
2. Sanders, 195.
3. Bugliosi, 284.
4. Watkins, 165.

5. Trial testimony of Juan Flynn, 1 October, 1970.
6. Van Houten testimony, Subsequent Parole Consideration Hearing, State of California Board of Prison Terms, in the Matter of the Life Term Parole Consideration Hearing of Leslie Van Houten, CDC Inmate #W13378, 29 December, 1993.
7. Conway and Siegelman, 203.
8. Watson, 121.
9. Michelle Phillips to author.
10. Conway and Siegelman, 203.
11. Watson, 83-4; see Nelson, *Tex Watson*, for more complete information.
12. Watson, 123.
13. Sanders, 200-01.
14. Ibid, 206.
15. Nelson, Behind , 23.
16. Sanders, 215.
17. Ibid, 243.
18. Ibid, 243.
19. Atkins, 94-5.
20. Ibid, 95.
21. Ibid, 95-6.
22. Sanders, 248.
23. Atkins, 97.
24. Sanders, 248.
25. Atkins, 97.
26. Ibid, 98; Sanders, 249.
19. Gilmore, 101.

Chapter Twenty Five
1. Michelle Phillips to author.
2. Polanski, 299.
3. Michelle Phillips to author.
4. Kiernan, 214.
5. Polanski, 303.
6. Ibid, 302.
7. Roman Polanski, LAPD Polygraph Examination Transcript, 11 August, 1969.
8. Polanski, 302.
9. Ibid, 303.
10. Kiernan, 214.
11. Polanski, 303.
12. Ibid, 303-04.

Chapter Twenty Six
1. Thompson, 46B.
2. Ibid, 46.

3. Kosinski committed suicide in 1990.
4. Parker, 138.
5. Sanders, 135.
6. Leaming, 95.
7. Roman Polanski, LAPD Polygraph Examination Transcript, 11 August, 1969.
8. LAPD First Homicide Investigation Progress Report, DR 69-059 593, 27.
9. Roman Polanski, LAPD Polygraph Examination Transcript, 11 August, 1969.
10. Parker, 138.
11. Bugliosi, 31; Sanders, 135.
12. Bugliosi, 31.
13. Leaming, 96.
14. Michelle Phillips to author.
15. Leaming, 95; Sanders, 136.
16. Patty Faulkner to author.
17. LAPD First Homicide Investigation Progress Report, DR 69-059 593, 9-10.
18. Maas, 147.
19. LAPD First Homicide Investigation Progress Report, DR 69-059 593, 9.
20. William Garretson, LAPD Polygraph Examination Transcript, 11 August, 1969, tape 32116.
21. LAPD First Homicide Investigation Progress Report, DR 69-059 593, 10.
22. Leaming, 106.

Chapter Twenty Seven
1. Michelle Phillips to author.
2. Doris Tate, in *Sharon Tate the Victim, Charles Manson the Killer*, op. cit.
3. Kiernan, 215.
4. Michelle Phillips to author.
5. Phillips, John, 304.
6. Private Information.
7. Patty Faulkner to author.
8. Ibid.
9. Crivello, 48.
10. Ibid, 49.
11. William Garretson to author.
12. Patti Tate, on *Leeza*, hosted by Leeza Gibbons, produced by Jason Walker, 1994.
13. Patti Tate, in the *Los Angeles Times*, 10 January, 1994.
14. Sanders, 261.

15. Douglas, 315.
16. Sanders, 261.
17. *Hollywood Citizen News*, 30 August, 1969.
18. Phillips, John, 302.
19. LAPD Second Homicide Investigation Progress Report, DR 69-059 593, 4.
20. See Sanders, 262; Krassner, 198, for further discussion of the alleged incident.
21. Quoted, Sanders, 262.
22. Capote, 219.
23. Krassner, 197.
24. Hotchner, 236-37.
25. Michelle Phillips to author.
26. Mike McGann to author.
27. Sanders, 262.
28. LAPD First Homicide Investigation Progress Report, DR 69-059 593, 11.
29. Ib Zacko to author.
30. Crivello, 48.
31. Ibid, 53.

Chapter Twenty Eight
1. Bugliosi, 50.
2. LAPD First Homicide Investigation Progress Report, DR 69-059 593, 11.
3. Polanski, 305; Bugliosi, 50.
4. Trial testimony of Winifred Chapman, 24 July, 1970; also, testimony of Winifred Chapman before the Los Angeles County Grand Jury, 5 December, 1969, 121.
5. LAPD First Homicide Investigation Progress Report, DR 69-059 593, 12.
6. Parker, 150.
7. LAPD First Homicide Investigation Progress Report, DR 69-059 593, 12.
8. Ibid, 12.
9. Ibid, 27.
10. Bugliosi, 51.
11. LAPD First Homicide Investigation Progress Report, DR 69-059 593, 13.
12. Leaming, 102.
13. Bugliosi, 51.
14. LAPD First Homicide Investigation Progress Report, DR 69-059 593, 12.
15. Ibid, 13.
16. Bugliosi, 52.
17. Crivello, 48-9.
18. Leaming, 102; Seaman, 313.

19. LAPD Second Homicide Investigation Progress Report, DR 69-059 593, 4.
20. LAPD First Homicide Investigation Progress Report, DR 69-059 593, 13.
21. Sanders, 282.
22. William Garretson, LAPD Polygraph Examination Transcript, 11 August, 1969, tape 32116, 36.
23. Ibid, 17.
24. Janet Parent to Bill Nelson.
25. LAPD First Homicide Investigation Progress Report, DR 69-059 593, 16.
26. Janet Parent to Bill Nelson.
27. William Garretson to Bill Nelson.
28. Trial testimony of William Garretson, 24 July, 1970.
29. William Garretson, LAPD Polygraph Examination Transcript, 11 August, 1969, tape 32116, 28-32.
30. William Garretson to Bill Nelson.
31. Trial testimony of William Garretson, 24 July, 1970.

Chapter Twenty Nine
1. Manson, 198-99.
2. Trial testimony of Linda Kasabian, 28 July, 1970.
3. Testimony of Susan Atkins before the Los Angeles County Grand Jury, 5 December, 1969, 33.
4. Trial testimony of Charles Watson, 1 September, 1971.
5. Atkins, 103.
6. Watson, 137.
7. Atkins, 104.
8. Patricia Krenwinkel, "Charles Manson: Journey into Evil," on *Biography*, A & E Television Network, produced by Alan Goldberg, 1995.
9. Bravin, 100.
10. Watson, 136.
11. Trial testimony of Charles Watson, 1 September, 1971.
12. Watson, 136.
13. Watson, 137.
14. Cooper,10.
15. Watson, 138.
16. Trial testimony of Linda Kasabian, 28 July, 1970.

Chapter Thirty
1. Watson, 138.
2. Peter A. French, "On Blaming Psychopaths," in Cooper, 73.
3. Watson, 138.
4. Trial testimony of Linda Kasabian, 28 July, 1970.
5. Watson, 138-39.
6. Ibid, 139.
7. Atkins, 104.
8. LAPD First Homicide Investigation Progress Report, DR 69-059 593, 17.
9. Atkins, 105.
10. Testimony of Susan Atkins before the Los Angeles County Grand Jury, 5 December, 1969, 44.
11. Watson, 139.
12. LAPD First Homicide Investigation Progress Report, DR 69-059 593, 3.
13. Watson, 139.
14. LAPD First Homicide Investigation Progress Report, DR 69-059 593, 19.
15. Watson, 139.
16. Trial testimony of Linda Kasabian, 28 July, 1970.
17. Watson, 139.
18. Ibid, 139; trial testimony of Linda Kasabian, 28 July, 1970.
19. Watson, 140.
20. Trial testimony of Linda Kasabian, 28 July, 1970.
21. Bugliosi, 17.
22. Atkins, 105.
23. Testimony of Susan Atkins before the Los Angeles County Grand Jury, 5 December, 1969, 51.
24. Ibid, 51.
25. Atkins, 105.
26. Watson, 140.
27. Ibid, 140.
28. Bill Nelson to author.
29. Atkins, 105.
30. Watson, 140.
31. Atkins, 106.
32. Testimony of Susan Atkins before the Los Angeles County Grand Jury, 5 December, 1969, 52-4; Atkins, 106.
33. Testimony of Susan Atkins before the Los Angeles County Grand Jury, 5 December, 1969, 55.
34. Watson, 140-41.
35. Testimony of Susan Atkins before

the Los Angeles County Grand Jury,
5 December, 1969, 55.

36. Atkins, 106.
37. Ibid, 106.
38. Trial testimony of Ronnie Howard,
22 October, 1970.
39. Watson, 141.
40. Testimony of Susan Atkins before
the Los Angeles County Grand Jury,
5 December, 1969, 56.
41. Watson, 141.
42. Ibid, 141.
43. Atkins, 106.
44. Testimony of Susan Atkins before
the Los Angeles County Grand Jury,
5 December, 1969, 57.
45. Watson, 141.
46. Atkins, 106.
47. Testimony of Susan Atkins before
the Los Angeles County Grand Jury,
5 December, 1969, 57.
48. Watson, 141.
49. Ibid, 141.
50. Testimony of Susan Atkins before
the Los Angeles County Grand Jury,
5 December, 1969, 58; Atkins, 106.
51. Atkins, 107.
52. Watson, 141.
53. Bugliosi, 19.
54. Watson, 141.
55. Ibid, 141.
56. Atkins, 108.
57. Testimony of Susan Atkins before
the Los Angeles County Grand Jury,
5 December, 1969, 59.
58. LAPD First Homicide Investigation
Progress Report, DR 69-059 593, 16.
59. Watson, 141; testimony of Susan
Atkins before the Los Angeles
County Grand Jury, 5 December,
1969, 60.
60. Testimony of Susan Atkins before
the Los Angeles County Grand Jury,
5 December, 1969, 60; Atkins, 107.
61. Atkins, 107; Watson, 142.
62. Atkins, 107.
63. Watson, 142.
64. Atkins, 107.
65. Watson, 142.
66. Ibid, 142.
67. Ibid, 142.
68. Trial testimony of Linda Kasabian,

28 July, 1970.
69. Ibid.
70. Ibid.
71. Testimony of Susan Atkins before
the Los Angeles County Grand Jury,
5 December, 1969, 65.
72. Ibid, 66.
73. Atkins, 107.
74. Psychiatric report of Ira Frank,
M.D., on Charles Watson, dated 28
March, 1971, 3.
75. Ibid, 3.
76. LAPD First Homicide Investigation
Progress Report, DR 69-059 593, 19.
77. Watson, 142.
78. Testimony of Susan Atkins before
the Los Angeles County Grand Jury,
5 December, 1969, 67.
79. Patricia Krenwinkel testimony.
Subsequent Parole Consideration
Hearing, State of California Board of
Prison Terms, in the Matter of the
Life Term Parole Consideration
Hearing of Patricia Krenwinkel,
CDC Inmate #W-8314, 29
December, 1993.
80. Ibid.
81. Patricia Krenwinkel to Diane
Sawyer, on *Turning Point*, "The
Manson Women: Inside the
Murders." ABC-TV, Produced by
Denise Schreiner, 1994.
82. Watson, 142.
83. Patricia Krenwinkel testimony.
Subsequent Parole Consideration
Hearing, State of California Board of
Prison Terms, in the Matter of the
Life Term Parole Consideration
Hearing of Patricia Krenwinkel,
CDC Inmate #W-8314, 29
December, 1993.
84. Patricia Krenwinkel to Diane
Sawyer, on Turning Point , "The
Manson Women: Inside the
Murders." ABC-TV, Produced by
Denise Schreiner, 1994.
85. Patricia Krenwinkel testimony.
Subsequent Parole Consideration
Hearing, State of California Board of
Prison Terms, in the Matter of the
Life Term Parole Consideration
Hearing of Patricia Krenwinkel,

CDC Inmate #W-8314, 29 December, 1993.

86. Trial testimony of Virginia Graham, 22 October, 1970.
87. Trial testimony of Barbara Hoyt, 18 September, 1970.
88. Trial testimony of Susan Atkins, 15 February, 1971.
89. At her 1993 Parole Hearing, Krenwinkel claimed to have been at the guest house during Sharon's murder, and to have re-entered the living room only as Watson and Atkins were leaving. In this she is contradicted by both Watson and Atkins. Patricia Krenwinkel testimony. Subsequent Parole Consideration Hearing, State of California Board of Prison Terms, in the Matter of the Life Term Parole Consideration Hearing of Patricia Krenwinkel, CDC Inmate #W-8314, 29 December, 1993.
90. Watson, 143.
91. Testimony of Susan Atkins before the Los Angeles County Grand Jury, 5 December, 1969, 66.
92. There is some disagreement as to who exactly yelled this. Atkins says that it was Watson, 108; Watson claims that it was Krenwinkel, 143.
93. Patricia Krenwinkel, in Nelson, Behind , 185.
94. Watson, 164.
95. Ibid, 143.
96. Trial testimony of Susan Atkins, 15 February, 1971.
97. Trial testimony of Ronnie Howard, 22 October, 1970.
98. Watson, 143.
99. Trial testimony of Virginia Graham, 22 October, 1970.
100. Testimony of Susan Atkins before the Los Angeles County Grand Jury, 5 December, 1969, 69.
101. Ibid, 69.
102. Atkins, 109.
103. Trial testimony of Virginia Graham, 22 October, 1970.

Chapter Thirty One

1. Testimony of Susan Atkins before the Los Angeles County Grand Jury, 5 December, 1969, 71.
2. Trial testimony of Linda Kasabian, 28 July, 1970.
3. Watson, 144.
4. Psychiatric report of Ira Frank, M.D., on Charles watson, dated 28 march, 1971, 4.
5. Watson, 144; Patricia Krenwinkel testimony. Subsequent Parole Consideration Hearing, State of California Board of Prison Terms, in the Matter of the Life Term Parole Consideration Hearing of Patricia Krenwinkel, CDC Inmate #W-8314, 29 December, 1993.
6. Watson, 144.
7. Testimony of Susan Atkins before the Los Angeles County Grand Jury, 5 December, 1969, 78-9.
8. Atkins, 110.
9. Watson, 13.
10. Atkins, 110.
11. Patricia Krenwinkel testimony. Subsequent Parole Consideration Hearing, State of California Board of Prison Terms, in the Matter of the Life Term Parole Consideration Hearing of Patricia Krenwinkel, CDC Inmate #W-8314, 29 December, 1993.
12. Sanders, revised edition, 424; Manson, 207.
13. Information from Watson's web site, www.aboundinglove.org.
14. Sanders, 295.
15. LAPD First Homicide Investigation Progress Report, DR 69-059 593, 21.
16. Manson, 207. Contrary to this, Prosecutor Vincent Bugliosi does not believe that either Manson or any member of his Family returned to 10050 Cielo Drive following the murders. "Why would Manson, who had done everything possible to distance himself from the actual crime, return to the scene of a terrible slaughter?" he asks. "Shots and screams had been heard all over the canyon that night, and there is no reason to think that the killers, once they returned to Spahn Ranch,

wouldn't have expected that the crime scene had been discovered at once. Would Manson really have gone back to that house, without knowing if police and officials from the coroner's office would be present?" However, it should be pointed out that Manson, if he indeed returned to 10050 Cielo Drive, could have determined from Benedict Canyon if the crimes had been discovered. It is possible, therefore, that he cautiously approached the property, discovering from the lack of police lights and activity that the murders had not yet been reported. Vincent Bulgiosi to author.

17. LAPD First Homicide Investigation Progress Report, DR 69-059 593, 17.
18. Ibid, 14.
19. Ibid, 19.
20. Ibid, 15.
21. Testimony of Winifred Chapman before the Los Angeles County Grand Jury, 5 December, 1969, 119.
22. LAPD First Homicide Investigation Progress Report, DR 69-059 593, 15.
23. Bugliosi, 5-6.
24. Ibid, 6.
25. Ibid, 7.
26. LAPD First Homicide Investigation Progress Report, DR 69-059 593, 3.
27. Bugliosi, 7.
28. LAPD First Homicide Investigation Progress Report, DR 69-059 593, 4.
29. Ibid, 8.
30. Ibid, 5.
31. Ibid, 4.
32. Jerry de Rosa to Diane Sawyer, on *Turning Point*, "The Manson Women: Inside the Murders." ABC-TV, produced by Denise Schreiner, 1994.
33. LAPD First Homicide Investigation Progress Report, DR 69-059 593, 16.
34. William Garretson, LAPD Polygraph Examination Transcript, 11 August, 1969, tape 32116, 46.
35. Bugliosi, 11; Gilmore, 118.
36. LAPD First Homicide Investigation Progress Report, DR 69-059 593, 4-5.
37. Ibid, 6.
38. Bugliosi, 19.
39. Patti Tate, in the *Los Angeles Times*, 10 January, 1994.
40. Bugliosi, 11-12.
41. Ibid, 12.
42. Ibid, 13.
43. Ibid, 14.
44. Time , 15 August, 1969.
45. Ibid.
46. Doris Tate, in Sharon Tate the Victim, Charles Manson the Killer, op. cit.
47. Evans, 32.
48. Patti Tate to Diane Sawyer, on Turning Point , "The Manson Women: Inside the Murders." ABC-TV, produced by Denise Schreiner, 1994.
49. Patti Tate, in the *Los Angeles Times*, 10 January, 1994.
50. Lownes, 90.
51. Leaming, 102.
52. Polanski, 308.
53. Victor Lownes to author.
54. Ibid.
55. Polanski, 309.
56. Janet Parent to Bill Nelson.
57. Ibid.
58. Ibid.
59. Didion, 41-2.
60. Phillips, John, 301.
61. Michelle Phillips to author.
62. Phillips, John, 300-01.
63. Montgomery, 20.
64. Phillips, John, 301.
65. Montgomery, 20.
66. Ibid, 20.
67. Leslie Caron to author.
68. Thompson, 46B.
69. Noguchi, 132.
70. William Klaman, in *Esquire*, March, 1970.
71. Paul, 46.

Chapter Thirty Two

1. Sanders, 296.
2. Atkins, 110.
3. Trial testimony of Dianne Lake, quoted in Nelson, *Behind*, 149.
4. Patricia Krenwinkel testimony. Subsequent Parole Consideration Hearing, State of California Board of

Prison Terms, in the Matter of the Life Term Parole Consideration Hearing of Patricia Krenwinkel, CDC Inmate #W-8314, 29 December, 1993.

5. Leslie Van Houten testimony. Subsequent Parole Consideration Hearing, State of California Board of Prison Terms, in the Matter of the Life Term Parole Consideration Hearing of Leslie Van Houten, CDC Inmate #W-13378, 29 December, 1993.

6. Leslie Van Houten testimony. Subsequent Parole Consideration Hearing, State of California Board of Prison Terms, in the Matter of the Life Term Parole Consideration Hearing of Leslie Van Houten, CDC Inmate #W-13378, 29 December, 1993.

7. Trial testimony of Linda Kasabian, 29 July, 1970.

8. Patricia Krenwinkel, "Charles Manson: Journey into Evil," on Biography , A & E Television Network, produced by Alan Goldberg, 1995.

9. Trial testimony of Juan Flynn, 1 October, 1970.

10. Leslie Van Houten, "Charles Manson: Journey into Evil," on Biography , A & E Television Network, produced by Alan Goldberg, 1995.

11. Leslie Van Houten testimony. Subsequent Parole Consideration Hearing, State of California Board of Prison Terms, in the Matter of the Life Term Parole Consideration Hearing of Leslie Van Houten, CDC Inmate No. W-13378, 29 December, 1993.

12. Leslie Van Houten to Diane Sawyer, on Turning Point , "The Manson Women: Inside the Murders." ABC-TV, produced by Denise Schreiner, 1994.

13. Patricia Krenwinkel testimony. Subsequent Parole Consideration Hearing, State of California Board of Prison Terms, in the Matter of the Life Term Parole Consideration

Hearing of Patricia Krenwinkel, CDC Inmate #W-8314, 29 December, 1993.

14. Leslie Van Houten to Larry King, on Larry King Live , CNN Television Network, 9 August, 1994.

15. Nelson, *Behind*, 24. The apartment of Suzan LaBerge was located a half-city block down Greenwood from the apartment complex where Watson had lived. The area was notorious in 1969 for the free-flow of drugs, and a house on the corner between the two apartment complexes was known as a place where drugs were sold. It is highly unlikely that Watson, with his involvement with illegal drug activities, did not hold a similar position in the neighborhood.

16. Sanders, 52.

17. Alice LaBianca to author.

18. LaBianca, 402.

19. Nelson, *Behind*, 17.

20. Watson, 147.

21. Ibid.

22. Ibid, 148.

23. Leslie Van Houten to Larry King, on *Larry King Live*, CNN Television Network, 9 August, 1994.

24. Trial testimony of Linda Kasabian, 29 July, 1970.

25. Leslie Van Houten to Larry King, on *Larry King Live*, CNN Television Network, 9 August, 1994.

26. Leslie Van Houten to Diane Sawyer, on *Turning Point*, "The Manson Women: Inside the Murders." ABC-TV, produced by Denise Schreiner, 1994.

27. Watson, 148.

28. Ibid, 149.

29. Ibid.

30. Leslie Van Houten to Diane Sawyer, on *Turning Point*, "The Manson Women: Inside the Murders." ABC-TV, produced by Denise Schreiner, 1994.

31. Watson, 149.

32. Leslie Van Houten testimony. Subsequent Parole Consideration Hearing, State of California Board of

Prison Terms, in the Matter of the Life Term Parole Consideration Hearing of Leslie Van Houten, CDC Inmate #W-13378, 29 December, 1993.

33. Ibid.

34. Patricia Krenwinkel to Diane Sawyer, on *Turning Point,* "The Manson Women: Inside the Murders." ABC-TV, produced by Denise Schreiner, 1994.

35. Watson, 149.

36. Leslie Van Houten testimony. Subsequent Parole Consideration Hearing, State of California Board of Prison Terms, in the Matter of the Life Term Parole Consideration Hearing of Leslie Van Houten, CDC Inmate #W-13378, 29 December, 1993.

37. Watson, 150.

38. Bugliosi, 432-33.

39. Leslie Van Houten to Diane Sawyer, on *Turning Point,* "The Manson Women: Inside the Murders." ABC-TV, produced by Denise Schreiner, 1994.

40. Testimony of Susan Atkins before the Los Angeles County Grand Jury, 5 December, 1969, 103.

41. Trial testimony of Patricia Krenwinkel, 16 February, 1971.

42. Leslie Van Houten testimony. Subsequent Parole Consideration Hearing, State of California Board of Prison Terms, in the Matter of the Life Term Parole Consideration Hearing of Leslie Van Houten, CDC Inmate #W-13378, 29 December, 1993.

43. Alice LaBianca, on *Leeza,* hosted by Leeza Gibbons, produced by Jason Walker, 1994.

44. Alice LaBianca to author.

45. Bugliosi, 64.

Chapter Thirty Three

1. Autopsy Report of Sharon Marie Tate Polanski, Los Angeles County Office of the Chief Medical Examiner, File #69-8796, 10 August, 1969.

2. Noguchi, 137.

3. Ibid, 138.

4. Autopsy Report of Sharon Marie Tate Polanski, op. cit .

5. Noguchi, 129.

6. Victor Lownes to author.

7. Thompson, 46; Leaming, 107.

8. *Hollywood Citizen News,* 14 August, 1969.

9. Polanski, 309.

10. Collins, 268.

11. Doris Tate to Bill Nelson.

12. Michelle Phillips to author.

13. Crivello, 50.

14. Michelle Phillips to author.

15. Toffel, 223-24.

16. Doris Tate, in the *Los Angeles Times,* 9 July, 1982.

17. *Hollywood Citizen News,* 12 August, 1969.

18. Farrell, "In Hollywood, the Dead Keep Right on Dying."

19. Maas, 147-48.

20. *Newsweek,* 18 August, 1969.

21. Du Bois, 98.

22. *Newsweek,* 25 August, 1969.

23. Ibid, 18 August, 1969.

24. *Time,* 15 August, 1969.

25. Ibid, 22 August, 1969.

26. Thompson, 43.

27. Ibid, 46B.

28. Ibid, 44.

29. Montgomery, 73.

30. Truman Capote to Johnny Carson, on *The Tonight Show,* NBC-TV, 27 August, 1969.

31. Montgomery, 73.

32. Ibid, 74.

33. *Hollywood Citizen News,* 19 August, 1969.

34. Probate papers, in private collection, supplied to author by Bill Nelson.

35. Leaming, 113.

36. Probate papers, in private collection, supplied to author by Bill Nelson.

37. The *Los Angeles Times,* 10 September, 1969.

Chapter Thirty Four

1. William Garretson, LAPD Polygraph Examination Transcript, 11 August,

1969, tape 32116, 19-20.
2. Doris Tate to Bill Nelson.
3. LAPD First Homicide Investigation Progress Report, DR 69-059 593, 29.
4. Bugliosi, 54.
5. William Garretson, LAPD Polygraph Examination Transcript, 11 August, 1969, tape 32116, 22.
6. William Garretson, in Nelson, *Behind*, 361.
7. William Garretson, "The Last Days of Sharon Tate," *True Hollywood Stories*, on E! Entertainment Channel, produced by Brent Zacky, 1999.
8. Vincent Bugliosi to author.
9. Roman Polanski, LAPD Polygraph Examination Transcript, 11 August, 1969.
10. Bill Nelson to author.
11. Roman Polanski, LAPD Polygraph Examination Transcript, 11 August, 1969.
12. Ibid.
13. Ibid.
14. Du Bois, 102.
15. Biskind, 78.
16. Phillips, John, 305; Polanski, 318-19.
17. Bugliosi, 14-17.
18. Thompson, 46B.
19. Mike McGann to author.
20. Life Term Parole Consideration Hearing, State of California, Community Release Board, In the Matter of the Subsequent Parole Consideration of Steven Grogan, CDC No. B-38773, Wednesday, October 17, 1979, Correctional Medical Facility, Vacaville, CA., p. 18-19.
21. Barbara Hoyt to Bill Nelson.
22. Life Term Parole Consideration Hearing State of California, Community Release Board, Steve Grogan, CDC No. B-38773, Tuesday, August 22, 1978, Deul Vocational Institution, Tracy, CA., p. 25.
23. Barbara Hoyt, Statement of Witness, Interview, 18 November, 1970, in the presence of Paul Whiteley, p. 1-2.
24. Trial testimony of Juan Flynn, 1 October, 1970.

25. Dianne Lake to Bill Nelson.
26. Bugliosi, 76.
27. Mike McGann to author.

Chapter Thirty Five

1. Vincent Bugliosi to author.
2. Bishop, 45.
3. Charles Manson to Judge William Older, Trial Transcript, 16 June, 1970.
4. Bishop, 65.
5. Statement of Charles Manson, in the Los Angeles Times , 24 July, 1970.
6. Trial statement of Vincent Bugliosi, 24 July, 1970.
7. Ibid.
8. Felton, 28.
9. Sanders, revised edition, 410.
10. Janet Parent to Bill Nelson.
11. Ibid.
12. Ibid.
13. Livsey, 48-9.
14. Vincent Bugliosi to author.
15. Statements of Irving Kanarek and Vincent Bugliosi, Trial Transcript, 27 July, 1970.
16. Statement of Paul Fitzgerald, Trial Transcript, 27 July, 1970.
17. Trial testimony of Linda Kasabian, 28 July, 1970.
18. Zamora, 135.
19. Bishop, 8.
20. Statement of President Richard M. Nixon, in the *Los Angeles Times*, 4 August, 1970.
21. Bishop, 7-8.
22. Trial testimony of Charles Manson, 19 November, 1970. See Schreck, 37-65 for complete statement.
23. Trial transcript, 5 October, 1970.
24. Ibid, 17 November, 1970.
25. Trial statement of Vincent Bugliosi, 13-15 January, 1971.
26. Trial transcript, 25 January, 1971.
27. Ibid.
28. Doris Tate, in the *Los Angeles Times*, 9 July, 1982.
29. Doris Tate to author.
30. Trial transcript, 29 March, 1971.
31. Farrell, "The Manson Jury," 67.
32. Markman, 187-88.
33. Ibid, 188.

34. Psychiatric report of John M. Suarez, M.D., on Charles Watson, dated 28 May, 1971, 5.
35. Psychiatric report of Ira Frank, M.D., on Charles Watson, dated 28 March, 1971, 3.
36. Quoted, Markman, 189.
37. Psychiatric report of Vernon C. Bohr, M.D., on Charles Watson, dated 12 July, 1971, 5.
38. Markman, 189.
39. Psychiatric report of Keith S. Ditman, M.D., on Charles Watson, dated 19 September, 1971, 4.
40. Psychiatric report of Ira Frank, M.D., on Charles Watson, dated 28 March, 1971, 3.
41. Watson, 184.
42. Psychiatric report of Joel Fort, M.D., on Charles Watson, dated 8 July, 1971, 7.
43. Paul Tate, in *Newsweek*, 27 March, 1971.

Chapter Thirty Six
1. Report of Dr. Melvin Macomber, Life Term Parole Consideration Hearing State of California, Community Release Board, Steve Grogan, CDC No. B-38773, Tuesday, August 22, 1978, Deul Vocational Institution, Tracy, CA., p. 28.
2. Charles Manson, in *Charles Manson: The Man Who Killed the 60's*, a Box Production for Channel Four, UK, produced by Peter Bate, 1994.
3. Bugliosi, revised edition, 497.
4. Vincent Bugliosi to author.
5. Bruce Davis, on *Charles Manson: The Man Who Killed the 60's*, a Box Production for Channel Four, UK, produced by Peter Bate, 1994.
6. Charles Manson to Diane Sawyer, on *Turning Point*, "The Manson Women: Inside the Murders." ABC-TV, produced by Denise Schreiner, 1994.
7. Ibid.
8. Charles Manson testimony. Subsequent Parole Consideration Hearing, State of California Board of Prison Terms, in the Matter of the Life Term Parole Consideration Hearing of Charles Manson, CDC Inmate #B-33920, 21 April, 1992.
9. Ibid.
10. Bugliosi, revised edition, 506.
11. Subsequent Parole Consideration Hearing, State of California Board of Prison Terms, in the Matter of the Life Term Parole Consideration Hearing of Patricia Krenwinkel, CDC Inmate #W-8314, 29 December, 1993.
12. Ibid.
13. Ibid.
14. Ibid.
15. Patricia Krenwinkel to Diane Sawyer, on Turning Point , "The Manson Women: Inside the Murders." ABC-TV, produced by Denise Schreiner, 1994.
16. Livsey, 176-77.
17. Subsequent Parole Consideration Hearing, State of California Board of Prison Terms, in the Matter of the Life Term Parole Consideration Hearing of Susan Atkins, CDC Inmate #W-08304, 16 September, 1981.
18. Subsequent Parole Consideration Hearing, State of California Board of Prison Terms, in the Matter of the Life Term Parole Consideration Hearing of Susan Atkins, CDC Inmate #W-08304, 25 June, 1996.
19. Ibid.
20. Ibid.
21. Ibid.
22. Susan Atkins to Bill Nelson.
23. Subsequent Parole Consideration Hearing, State of California Board of Prison Terms, in the Matter of the Life Term Parole Consideration Hearing of Charles Watson, CDC Inmate #B-37999, 4 May, 1990.
24. Watson, 138-42.
25. Subsequent Parole Consideration Hearing, State of California Board of Prison Terms, in the Matter of the Life Term Parole Consideration Hearing of Charles Watson, CDC Inmate #B-37999, 4 May, 1990.
26. Ibid.

27. Subsequent Parole Consideration Hearing, State of California Board of Prison Terms, in the Matter of the Life Term Parole Consideration Hearing of Charles Watson, CDC Inmate #B-37999, 13 January, 1983.
28. Subsequent Parole Consideration Hearing, State of California Board of Prison Terms, in the Matter of the Life Term Parole Consideration Hearing of Charles Watson, CDC Inmate #B-37999, 2 April, 1987.
29. Subsequent Parole Consideration Hearing, State of California Board of Prison Terms, in the Matter of the Life Term Parole Consideration Hearing of Charles Watson, CDC Inmate #B-37999, 4 May, 1990.
30. Letter of stipulation, from Charles Watson to California Board of Prison Terms, dated 4 January, 1993.
31. See Nelson, *Behind*, for details.
32. Charles Watson interview, on web site www.aboundinglove.org.
33. Livsey, 74.
34. Ibid, 85.
35. Doris Tate to author.
36. Livsey, 74-5.
37. Manson, 176.

Chapter Thirty Seven
1. Weinraub, 36.
2. Tynan, 102.
3. Ibid, 104.
4. Weinraub, 36.
5. Doris Tate, in the *Ontario Daily Report*, 8 August, 1989.
6. Polanski, 324.
7. Holt, 319.
8. Doris Tate, in the *Los Angeles Times*, 9 July, 1982.
9. Patti Tate, in the *Los Angeles Times*, 10 January, 1994.
10. Doris Tate to author.
11. Doris Tate to Bill Nelson.
12. Ibid.
13. Doris Tate, in the *Los Angeles Times*, 9 July, 1982.
14. Doris Tate to author.
15. Doris Tate, in the *New York City Tribune*, 22 March, 1990.
16. Doris Tate, in the *Los Angeles Times*,

9 July, 1982.
17. Doris Tate to author.
18. Doris Tate to Bill Nelson.
19. Doris Tate, in the *Los Angeles Times*, 9 July, 1982.
20. Doris Tate to Bill Nelson.
21. Doris Tate, in the *New York City Tribune*, 22 March, 1990.
22. Ibid.
23. Ibid.
24. Ibid.
25. Doris Tate, in the *Ontario Daily Report*, 8 August, 1989.
26. Doris Tate, in the *Los Angeles Times*, 9 July, 1982.
27. Sanders, revised edition, 468.
28. Statement of Paul Tate. Subsequent Parole Consideration Hearing, State of California Board of Prison Terms, in the Matter of the Life Term Parole Consideration Hearing of Charles Watson, CDC Inmate #B-   . 37999, 13 January, 1985.
29. Doris Tate, in the *New York City Tribune*, 22 March, 1990.
30. Statement of Doris Tate. Subsequent Parole Consideration Hearing, State of California Board of Prison Terms, in the Matter of the Life Term Parole Consideration Hearing of Susan Atkins, CDC Inmate #W-08304, 16 December, 1988.
31. Doris Tate, in the *New York City Tribune*, 22 March, 1990.
32. Doris Tate to author.
33. Doris Tate, in the *San Luis Obispo Telegram*, 4 May, 1990.
34. Doris Tate, in the *New York City Tribune*, 22 March, 1990.
35. Doris Tate statement. Subsequent Parole Consideration Hearing, State of California Board of Prison Terms, in the Matter of the Life Term Parole Consideration Hearing of Charles Watson, CDC Inmate #B-37999, 2 April, 1987.
36. Subsequent Parole Consideration Hearing, State of California Board of Prison Terms, in the Matter of the Life Term Parole Consideration Hearing of Charles Watson, CDC Inmate #B-37999, 4 May, 1990.

37. Statement of Doris Tate. Subsequent Parole Consideration Hearing, State of California Board of Prison Terms, in the Matter of the Life Term Parole Consideration Hearing of Charles Watson, CDC Inmate #B-37999, 4 May, 1990.
38. Doris Tate to author.

Chapter Thirty Eight
1. Patti Tate, in the *Los Angeles Times*, 10 January, 1994.
2. Ibid.
3. Subsequent Parole Consideration Hearing, State of California Board of Prison Terms, in the Matter of the Life Term Parole Consideration Hearing of Patricia Krenwinkel, CDC Inmate #W-8314, 29 December, 1993.
4. Patti Tate statement. Subsequent Parole Consideration Hearing, State of California Board of Prison Terms, in the Matter of the Life Term Parole Consideration Hearing of Patricia Krenwinkel, CDC Inmate #W-8314, 29 December, 1993.
5. Subsequent Parole Consideration Hearing, State of California Board of Prison Terms, in the Matter of the Life Term Parole Consideration Hearing of Susan Atkins, CDC Inmate #W-08304, 25 June, 1996.
6. Ibid.
7. Statement of Patti Tate. Subsequent Parole Consideration Hearing, State of California Board of Prison Terms, in the Matter of the Life Term Parole Consideration Hearing of Susan Atkins, CDC Inmate #W-08304, 25 June, 1996.
8. Patti Tate, in the *Los Angeles Times*, 10 January, 1994.
9. Bugliosi, revised edition, 493.
10. Rubin, 64.
11. Ibid, 66.
12. Ibid.
13. Hoskyns, 182.
14. Hochman, 25.
15. Reighley, 39.
16. Royalty Agreement between Charles Manson and the Lemmons brothers,

in private collection of Bill Nelson.
17. Rubin, 152.
18. Ibid, 66.
19. "Bartek Frykowski: Seeking Dollars From a Killer Named Manson," in *People Magazine*, 3 April, 1995, Volume 43, No. 13, p. 43.
20. Rubin, 152.
21. Bugliosi, revised edition, 500.
22. Patti Tate, in the *Los Angeles Times*, 10 January, 1994.
23. Ibid
24. Ibid.

Epilogue
1. Guestbook at Barker Ranch. Information provided to author by Bill Nelson.
2. Letter to Judge Thomas MacBride, dated 12 July, 1997, from Lynette Fromme, in author's possession.
3. Undated letter from Lynette Fromme, in author's collection.
4. Nelson, *Behind*, 7.
5. "Manson's Supporters and the Media," on Access Manson web site, www.atwa.com.
6. Sandra Good, on *Charles Manson: The Man Who Killed the 60's*, a Box Production for Channel Four, UK, produced by Peter Bate, 1994.
7. Immunity Agreement for Larry Melton, dated 24 July, 1998, issued by Inyo County District Attorney Phil McDowell, in the possession of Bill Nelson.
8. State of Washington, Pierce County, Pre-Trial Services Information and Indigency Report, Case No. 97-1-00475-8.
9. Declaration for Determination of Probable Cause, State of Washington, County of Pierce, Case No. 97-1-00475-8, Office of Prosecuting Attorney, dated 5 February, 1997, signed by Douglas J Hill.
10. Doris Tate to author.
11. Alice LaBianca to author.
12. Alice LaBianca, on *Leeza*, hosted by Leeza Gibbons, produced by Jason Walker, 1994.

13. Letter of Alice LaBianca. Subsequent Parole Consideration Hearing, State of California Board of Prison Terms, in the Matter of the Life Term Parole Consideration Hearing of Leslie Van Houten, CDC Inmate No. W-13378, 28 May, 1998.
14. Janet Parent to Bill Nelson.
15. Ibid.
16. Stephen Kay, on Court TV, 7 July, 1999.
17. Leslie Van Houten. Subsequent Parole Consideration Hearing, State of California Board of Prison Terms, in the Matter of the Life Term Parole Consideration Hearing of Leslie Van Houten, CDC Inmate No. W-13378, 7 July, 1999.
18. Ibid.
19. Bill Nelson to author.
20. KNBC News, 7 July, 1999.
21. Bill Nelson to author.
22. Stephen Kay on Court TV, 7 July, 1999.
23. Statement of Angela Smaldino, read by Clara Tuma, on Court TV, 7 July, 1999.
24. Bill Nelson to author.
25. Statement of Angela Smaldino, read by Clara Tuma, on Court TV, 7 July, 1999.
26. Bill Nelson to author.
27. Didion, 47.
28. Natalie Grumbles to author.
29. Allison Lowe to author.
30. Gerald Malanga, "The Permanence of Sharon Tate," in *Interview*, Issue #1.

AUTHOR S NOTE

I have elected to use several crime scene photographs in this book. While these photographs are graphic and disturbing, they are not used for sensationalism. Rather, no matter how many words might be spilled in describing the brutality of the murder which took Sharon's life, it seems to me that there is no better, mute testimony as to why none of the Manson Family members still incarcerated should ever be released than the vivid depiction of their own acts.